PLACE

A Story of Modelmaking, Menageries and Paper Rounds

Terry Farrell: Life and Work: Early Years to 1981

LAURENCE KING

Published in 2004 by Laurence King Publishing Ltd
71 Great Russell Street
London WC1B 3BP
Tel: +44 20 7430 8850
Fax: +44 20 7430 8880
e-mail: enquiries@laurenceking.co.uk
www.laurenceking.co.uk

Copyright © 2004

This book was designed and produced by
Laurence King Publishing Ltd, London

A catalogue record for this book is available from the
British Library.

ISBN: 1 85669 332 5

Printed in Singapore

Edited by Henrietta Heald
Designed by Jason Godfrey

Acknowledgements

This is an altogether different book from the one I started writing almost three years ago. I had virtually finished a short autobiographical monograph and then decided to write instead at greater length about my early experience of 'place', and of how this particular awareness grew into my hobbies and then my educational choices and then into a career in architecture and urbanism.

These evolving pathways involved all those helping me in many changes of direction, as together we reworked and reworked the story and the material we unearthed. In my office Maggie Jones, my first secretary who remains with me decades later, typed all the various manuscripts since I write longhand and usually with a hasty illegibility that only she can decipher; Emma Davies also played a major part, having done all the picture research and initial layouts; Jane Tobin helped with various elements of the main text and the project pages, and David Abdo and Paolo Pirroni helped with graphics.

I am particularly grateful to Jason Godfrey (who designed the book), Henrietta Heald (copy editor) and Nico Jackson (who did the interviews and helped on various text evolutions); as independent designers/editors/writers, they seemed to me to go well beyond most sensible contractual notions as they committed themselves so creatively and enthusiastically to the project.

The work of an architect is not isolated like that of a poet or a painter, but involves many others, including staff, teachers and collaborators. At different times during this period I also depended a great deal on my personal family relationships and my professional partnerships. My very sincere thanks to all those involved, particularly to art teachers and my own teacher, Maurice McPartlan – I have no doubt at all that my life would have been quite different without him.

Terry Farrell

Contents

1

UP TO 1956: CHILDHOOD

Introduction and my first home: Manchester • Modelmaking and creating new worlds • Social places: heaven, hell and uniforms • Manchester: the larger urban world • **The move to Newcastle** • Menageries, habitats and paper rounds • Walking and running: campsites and fairs • Personal identity and group place • Art: painting, drawing, an inspirational teacher and discovering my career • The 'temporary' move to Blackpool

Introduction and my first home: Manchester

Created by the layered work of many hands over time, our cities and towns, villages and hamlets tell their own stories. So, in a way, individual walls and windows are like letters, houses words, streets sentences, neighbourhoods chapters and cities whole books, and each region or country is a complete library.

Understanding what makes a place today means knowing about the characters that built and once inhabited each particular piece of the earth's surface and the real-life plots associated with it. The conscious acts of place-making – call it urban design, town planning or simply development – and of building the inhabited visual objects that we recognize as architecture have preoccupied me all my life. Consciously or not, my fascination began as early as I can remember – so to recount my early years in terms of remembered places and buildings seemed a self-evident way to structure my own story.

But this structuring evokes the events and people within the buildings and places, and also causes me today to reflect on change and to compare places then and now. So there is something of a stream of consciousness about what I have written – it is not an autobiography, but it is generally chronological in pattern. It begins not just with place but with my childhood interests and hobbies which affected my sense of place and were always more important to me than formal schooling – drawing and painting, modelmaking, keeping pets, nature, walking, camping, paper rounds, running, fishing and travelling. It ends at the time I felt I had found my architectural place, when I was finally and fully independently on my own.

This is not a 'monograph' meant primarily as an architectural book for architects. In my mind, I felt I wanted to explain more widely what makes an architect, and particularly what made this one. I would hope that younger people contemplating art or architecture might find what I have recorded helpful or interesting – although I accept that this will read as something of an historical document to them, concerning events up to and beyond half a century ago. It might also be of use to teachers, including those who might otherwise advise the young – as they still do – that an architect is primarily the product of maths and physics, which is just not true. I have huge respect for

Desperate Dan, one of the cartoon characters who populated the *Dandy* and *Beano* comics of my childhood, published by the Dundee-based publishing company D.C. Thomson. Dan, Lord Snooty and so many others were created by Dudley D. Watkins.

After art school in Nottingham and Glasgow, Dudley D. Watkins joined D.C. Thomson in 1925, and stayed there for his entire career, becoming the most popular British comic artist of his time.

'Oor Wullie', along with the Broons, filled Watkins's weekly cartoon pages in the *Sunday Post* – a Glasgow newspaper that was available in the North of England along with Christmas annuals.

Three views of Sale in the mid 20th century: Northenden Road in 1940 (top); the town hall in 1948 (centre); and Cross Street in 1951. I particularly like the untrafficked view of Northenden Road, with its wide pavements, shop awnings and trees; it was the stereotype of the new suburb.

A sketch of our area of Sale

1 Our home,
  17 Langdale Road
2 Langdale Road
3 Corner shops
4 Crashed German plane
5 Main road
6 To Altrincham and
  school
7 Woods
8 To town centre
9 The Doyles' house
10 Rodney Glover's house
11 Doctor's surgery
12 Stop for school bus
13 Shops
14 More shops
15 St Hugh's Catholic
  church
16 The canal
17 Detailed sketch of
  the ground floor and
  garden of our home

teachers the world over, particularly art teachers, whose sphere of influence is truly life-enhancing and indeed life-forming – and I would like to dedicate this book to art teachers and to my own teacher, Maurice McPartlan.

Modelmaking and creating new worlds

My birthplace – Sale, part of outer Manchester – was, and still is, no more than a typically English suburb-cum-small-town, yet I dwelled on and absorbed every part of it. I was born just before the Second World War and remember bombs dropping and a plane that crashed in a front garden in the next street demolishing the front wall and its little wrought-iron gate. In our own street, so untypically for the English, a giant street party was held for all of the local children on VE Day in 1945. At one end of that street was the little bow-windowed newsagent's shop where for us children the only reading that was available was American Marvel comics, until the great day when *Dandy* and *Beano* were published again, with Dudley D. Watkins's characterful renderings of Desperate Dan and Lord Snooty. It was in the same quiet, untrafficked street that I learned to ride a bike at the age of six, with my dad running behind holding the saddle. The need for a bike and the emptiness of the street were both features of the unplanned, formless character of the suburb.

I often sat at a table in the front garden of our house, 17 Langdale Road, making buildings from pre-printed paper-cutout books that my mother had bought me. I eventually assembled a small town of houses, castles and forts, all connected and glued with marked tabs. This method of making three-dimensional objects from drawings was a childhood version of creating built environments from architects' drawings. Assemblages from kits-of-parts passionately absorbed me, as did fret-work – cutting intricate shapes with a fine-tensioned saw blade. With this tool I made 'useful' things – letter racks, waste bins, toast racks, fire screens – from cheap materials, with competent and decorative results. The sheet materials were merely one step forward from paper cutouts, and the objects I made had similar two-dimensional components layered, lapped and joined together. It was all done very simply and cheaply – we were living in a postwar era of shortages and rationing, whose products were later dubbed 'utility style'.

The particular magic in modelmaking, as in all miniatures, is that the scale reduction allows the modelmaker to see how all the parts fit together to make the whole. Small worlds evoke a thrilling illusory power as we touch, feel and manually revolve those representational objects to comprehend from a giant's simplifying perspective the seemingly myriad complexities that went into making them. There is something akin to role swapping, too, in that the adult's world is brought within a child's range, so that the child is empowered to handle, with his imagination engaged, the larger world around him. I have kept many of the architectural models from my career and – as at Sir John Soane's house in London's Lincoln's Inn – the Lilliputian representations of buildings are today juxtaposed in my studio living space with models of ships and aeroplanes.

My father introduced me to larger constructional ambitions. With my uncle Jim, my mother's elder brother, I 'helped' to dig an enormous hole in the back garden, which was then lined with railway sleepers and turfed over to make an air-raid shelter. I remember sitting there many a time late at night during the war, under the back garden with my parents and brothers, listening to sirens and bombs and thinking how cosy and exciting it was. Immediately after the war I helped dad to dismantle the shelter and reassemble the sleepers to make an open-topped 'jeep'. We went together to a nearby car-breaker's yard to buy a steering wheel; it was fixed onto the frame, which instantly became a full-size play vehicle in which my brothers and I spent many happy hours and days.

Dad built makeshift tents in the garden for us to play in, but the big step forward was a rambling toy fort with turrets and crenellations made from packing cases. He coated the walls in glue, sprinkled sawdust over them and painted over this with representations of stones, ivy and camouflage. From bits of nothing he made entire new worlds that expanded and enriched our lives. We moved home six times during my childhood, and each time we arrived somewhere new my dad went about fitting shelves, wallpapering and generally making the place unique and personal, created by us for us – or so it seemed. None of this was spectacular innovation – it's what parents do all the time for their children – but, for me, the possibility of making worlds was born and grew, and lasted throughout my life.

Top: Even the humble suburban street can become a festival place. Shown here is a VE Day children's party held in Langdale Road, Sale. My brother Tony peeps out on the far left and one of the Doyle brothers is on the far right. Our house was just like those in the background: newly built in fields and costing my parents £340 in 1936.

Centre pictures: Instant placemaking by my father in our garden: a sheet hung over a clothes line becomes a house or a school classroom. When these pictures were taken I was almost five, and had not yet started school – but my brother had, and returned home to give us lessons.

Bottom: My parents sold their Manchester house in 1946 and moved to Newcastle to rent a more modest one. With the sale money my father bought a Ford 8 car (CN 8421). The mobility our family gained made a very big impact on us all – weekend trips around Northumberland, camping all over England and frequent return visits to Manchester. This picture of the family was taken outside my grandparents' house in Levenshulme, in Manchester, probably around 1950.

The Alhambra citadel and palace in Granada, southern Spain. Built by the Moorish kings in the 13th and 14th centuries, it was a form of paradise – a heaven on earth. For Catholics, too, heaven and hell were real places.

I have always seen the act of creativity as being rooted in transformation – all seemingly fixed states are transitional conditions that we nudge, push, massage and lead into new states. I saw that forest trees had become railway sleepers for trains to run on, which were reassembled to become a bomb-proof underground shelter, and then reassembled again to make a four-seater make-believe jeep. And so it was with the larger environment – for example, open fields were transformed into streets, among them the very building that was our family's first home. Likewise, one day I would see larger and larger transformations, entire parts of cities would evolve. One such example was the 6th Duke of Bedford's garden-produce market, which had grown into the Covent Garden market; then, after the market moved out, the area endured a period of dereliction, but somehow transformed itself all over again into a thriving international tourist place with street performers, shops and restaurants, and new arcaded entrances and frontages to the Royal Opera House.

Social places: heaven, hell and uniforms

By the time my family moved to Newcastle when I was eight years old, I had experienced and absorbed a full range of what urban living was about. During Saturday morning children's hour at the Odeon cinema, I had been terrified by the roaring of the huge MGM lion, and had enjoyed the astounding *Wizard of Oz*, where place, characters, fantasy, palaces, gardens and terrifying forests were created by art and imagination. Well, that was as powerful as any experience – although sung Latin Mass at St Hugh's Catholic church, with its men in long robes and the whole ritual of standing, sitting, praying and chanting, took some beating for orchestrated fantasy land. Then there was St Vincent's Roman Catholic school, Altrincham, with its outside toilets, where cardboard milk-bottle tops were the favoured wartime toys; public transport on buses to school (when the fare was a penny farthing); and places of assembly like St Hugh's, where I was made aware that I sinned and needed to confess my sins, and that at communion I ate part of what was actually the body of Jesus Christ.

It was no doubt at that time that I first began to perceive the idea of place in a religious sense. Catholics make a real issue of heaven and hell. There is a gripping part of James Joyce's *A Portrait of the Artist as a Young Man* in which a priest evokes a terrifying picture of hell to young boys. I had exactly the same experience as those boys.

When Catholic children reach puberty – at about the same time as they realize that there are more sins in life than they had ever thought possible – they are lectured on the relationship between different levels of sin and how this relates to purgatory and hell. Purgatory and hell – and that other state, heaven – are always described as if they were actual places.

When I visited the Alhambra in Granada many years later, I saw it as a sublime example of how all religions have differing ideas about this place called heaven. In the Spanish interpretation of the Islamic ideal, heaven is a transferred version of oasis. The Moors travelled along the north coast of Africa, moving through the desert, finding the occasional oasis, until they crossed over the sea to Spain. When they arrived at Granada, they went up into the mountains, where they sensed in the air the cooling impact of the Atlantic's plentiful moisture, which supported the rivers and trees and greenery. In their vision of heaven, water is plentiful, and so the town planning of the Alhambra is based on water, with fountains, cooling and storage systems, ponds and lakes.

During the middle years of the 20th century the modern architect's concept of heaven was 'light and air', and the aim of the modernists was to clear out the slums of Victorian England and replace 'hell' with the promise of 'heaven'. The idea of heaven shows itself in all utopian urban plans such as Ebenezer Howard's garden cities: there has always been an idea of paradise in urban design and town planning. When considering the influence of Catholicism on my own work, I have wondered if there were some motivation in the idea of human errors and sins being reflected in damaged cities and ruined places which can be redeemed through good work and transformed to be closer to the heavenly ideal, the good place. For Catholics, the unavoidability of 'original sin' meant life was never the ideal but a continual adaptation of our inherited life context.

School had its own rituals, assemblies and rules, and its own building organization of playground, classrooms, teachers' rooms – and, of course, there was school uniform. Uniform is an interesting aspect of placemaking. It is often said that clothes and architecture are related, and I have described the Consulate headquarters building in Hong Kong, which I designed in the 1990s, as tailored like a British person in a tropical Savile Row suit, and our colourful Henley Regatta building as a version of the peacocked males in bright club and school blazers and ties.

I became aware of the relationship between clothes and place at the age of 11, when I and one of my three brothers went to grammar school, where we could be identified by our caps, jackets and badges. Another brother went to a tough Newcastle Catholic secondary school, St Aloysius, and the fourth was sent away to train as a Christian Brother. The wearing of our various uniforms marked each of us out as different and was a kind of early social placemaking, separating us as discrete individuals in one family. Home from school and away from our uniforms, we would be united once more — all four boys around the same dining table. Uniform and dress signal physical location, and in Britain it is voice, too — if you have a regional accent, you are placed by other people both geographically in terms of birthplace and socially in terms of class.

Later on, clothes became an issue for me at Newcastle University, where the duffle coat was a self-imposed uniform. During my time there, there were only 2,500 students and they liked to stand out in the streets, so what they did was to wear duffle coats, imitating Second World War naval officers — as a student, you were officer class. You were, in fact, seen as 'posh', a wonderful British social-class indicator that had its root in geographical orientation — and how it affected your place on a boat. When sailing back and forth from Britain to what was then its Indian empire, the posh people were those whose cabins were 'port out and starboard home', thereby avoiding the most oppressive effects of the sun on both stages of the journey. My schoolmates left school with their ties and blazers, came to university and started wearing duffle coats. I — who had hated school uniform — had a big debate with myself: should I conform and join another club? (Eventually I compromised and bought an understated hoodless duffle coat that was different from everyone else's. It seemed such self-conscious agony at the time — teenagers probably do struggle more than any other age group with individuality versus peer conformity.)

I was told that the architect Jim Stirling fixed his clothing in the years 1959 and 1960. He decided that the clothes he wore had a bearing on his image as an architect. The legend goes that he never changed his look from desert boots, dark-blue shirts and grey trousers. He didn't sidestep fashion; he locked himself into a fashion era. The late Cedric Price was never seen without a striped shirt with a separate white collar and black tie; Richard Rogers's partner, Mike Davies, always dresses entirely in red, including his shoes (and his car is always red, internally and externally). Some architects have changed their attire over the years but fixed their architectural dress, having decided to be a permanent modernist, classicist or postmodernist, for example. In the case of Stirling, while he fixed his clothes he continually changed his architectural appearance.

The façade of a building is a piece of clothing ('fabric' engineers deal with the building's 'skin'). Throughout history people have taken down the façades of historic buildings and rebuilt them by, say, putting a Gothic front on a Georgian house or vice versa. John Nash reversed the process by designing the façade of Regent Street first, so that anyone could buy a ready-made building façade and then afterwards do what they liked with the inside — but they had to retain his façade design. The same classical 'façadism' applied in James Craig's New Town in Edinburgh and John Dobson's Grey Street in Newcastle. English Heritage and the modernists have been arguing for some 30 years over the question of whether it is legitimate to put a modern building behind an old façade. I think it can be perfectly legitimate since a façade represents a separate layer of social connection and communication. Additionally, each 'dress' I saw fitted a particular stage: school uniforms in the school, vestments in church, football and other 'kits' in sport, and duffle coats at university. The buildings, streets, town squares and playing fields were great indoor and outdoor stages, invented by us to act out our various roles — clothes and architecture were interconnected by activity as well as by metaphor.

Manchester: the larger urban world

The suburb of Sale represented the embryo, the DNA, of urban life as I would experience it in every urban situation from then on. It was permanently embedded in me wherever I was in the world. Sale gave me the very idea of place and of the containers we call buildings and rooms — perhaps safe (home) or perhaps mildly claustrophobic (church) or perhaps threatening (classroom). Going to Bellevue Zoo, trips to visit aunts and uncles, bus journeys to central Manchester to shop at huge stores, and my dad going to Manchester United matches up the road at Old Trafford and afterwards

Grey Street, one of the fine streets in the centre of Newcastle, was laid out by the developer Thomas Grainger and his architect John Dobson. The façades were designed independently of the interiors. In 1997 we created new interiors behind the façades shown here. Clothes and façades are all part of social expression.

(always in vain) checking the football pools on the dining-room table at home. Canals, back gardens as playgrounds, tarmac and pavements, boundaries and territories, all began in Sale. Outside there were bus conductors, teachers, priests, Germans who bombed us, grandparents who visited us and neighbours who lived in near-identical houses – all in the world beyond the front gate, behind which each family unit was wrapped in its own semi-detached house and garden. This was the world of the suburb, invented by us in England. After a thousand years of peace on this island, non-urban open land was always safely habitable, and – unlike European walled cities – the boundaries and edges of urban life could readily spread out with population expansion, eventually to create a new zone at the start of the 20th century that was not town, not country, but the so-called 'best of both worlds' – the suburb.

It was at about the age of five years old that I first became aware that the amorphous shapeless suburb was sub to an urb, and that half an hour's bus ride away at grandma's and granddad's was a densely built giant of a place called Manchester. When we left Manchester for Newcastle, I was too young to have formed an idea of Manchester's shape or form – unlike Newcastle, it has no strong topography or major river feature. Manchester was all man-made; for good or ill, God seemed to have had no hand in it. And indeed, in respect of conscious planning and design, nor did the mind and imagination of man have much to do with Manchester's creation. It was the result of chaotic opportunism on a grand urban scale.

Manchester was truly a place of work, a monocultural creation of the Industrial Revolution where the specialized workplace was invented. It was one of the forerunners of the central business district (CBD) found in North American cities, which dies at night when people leave for dormitory towns. The Industrial Revolution began in Manchester (and Birmingham, Stoke and Glasgow), and not only was this a new kind of 'place', it also housed revolutionary new building types. The mill, the factory and – it astonishes me still to think of it – the world's first railway station, at Liverpool Road. Now every city in the world has a railway station. And the first ever was off Deansgate in Manchester.

Manchester today seems a city with a great man-made continuum – a place of work and business, where people migrate to get a better chance. Newcastle, I realized

Opposite page:
Top right: Smithfield Market during the late 19th century: Paddy Maguire's place of work in Manchester.

Centre: Patrick (Paddy) Maguire, my great-grandfather on my mother's side.

Far right: Amusement park at Bellevue Zoo, Manchester – a favourite place for our family to visit.

Top, left and right: Hulme Street, Little Ireland, in 1912. With Macintosh Mills (above, in 1857), the area still survives, a remnant of 19th-century industrial Manchester.

Above centre: A Little Ireland terrace in 1958.

Above: Bridgewater Canal in the 1950s; alongside it runs the Altrincham railway line. When I lived in Sale I was unaware of rivers – canals were the only waterways I knew (compare Wigan Pier drawings, p.17).

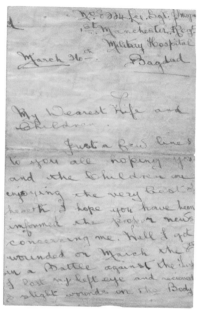

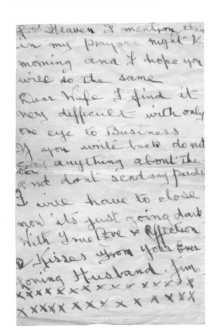

Top left, above and right: The London hospital staff who cared for my grandfather after his return from Baghdad. He is sitting near the front with a patch over his eye. Beneath the photograph is the letter received from my grandfather in Baghdad three months after a Requiem Mass had been held to mark his death. Back home in Manchester, he outlived almost everyone who had been at the Mass.

later, was different. In its centre, it was a county town, country meets town, with wide streets, parades and fine terraces. Industry had grown elsewhere, in outlying towns and pit villages. But Manchester was the workplace itself. From the time of my great-grandfather, Patrick Maguire, up to the present, Manchester has kept renewing and reinventing itself along with its inhabitants. It is like the railway sleepers that became an underground home then a jeep. Driven by resourcefulness, energy and desperate circumstances, Manchester is an ever-moving, ever-changing metropolis.

One of seven brothers, 'Paddy' Maguire left Ireland during the famines of the 1870s and 1880s to find food and a home for his pregnant young wife. From Dublin, Paddy travelled through Liverpool, left his wife with friends in Manchester and went to look for work.

When he returned several days later, his wife was dead – malnutrition and childbirth, the doctor said – and my grandfather Jim had been born. After that, Paddy worked for the rest of his life at Smithfield Market in Manchester. His son, Jim, grew up in Gorton and joined the Manchester Infantry. He fought in the Boer War, later drove a Manchester tram, then returned to the army to fight in the First World War on the Western Front and in Mesopotamia. He returned badly injured from the siege of Kut, to spend the remainder of his working life as night caretaker in an office block off Deansgate called Gaddam House.

My grandfather Jim kept everything of importance to him: letters, medals, articles, clocks and postcards from the Western Front. For him – a rural, orphaned, uprooted individual – continuity of place and time was of great value. I particularly treasure a picture of him taken outside his parents' home in Glennamaddy, County Galway. In the spirit of my grandfather, I recently collected all his material together into a scrapbook for my children, and next to this photo my caption reads:

'Glennamaddy, Southern Ireland (County Galway), was the Maguire family home. This picture was taken, I believe, in the mid-1960s by my father and shows granddad Maguire and his daughter, my mother Molly, standing in front of what was then remaining of the home. The story my mother told me was that, due to the famine, six brothers left the farm in 1879. All six went to Liverpool first, where five then sailed on to new lives in Canada and Australia. The sixth, my great grandfather Patrick, had a wife who was almost at full-term pregnancy and was, therefore, not accepted on the boat. So "Paddy" took his wife to stay with friends in Manchester and went off to look for a job. He returned a few days later to find his wife had died giving birth to granddad and, as I mentioned earlier, Molly always said that the official cause of death was malnutrition. So the return visit of granddad and mother to the house must have been one of mixed feelings, with a sadness for the hardship and suffering that must have been experienced by those that lived in this little stone building.'

My family's hands are among the millions that made Manchester, whose stories seem dug into the history of the 19th-century industrial city. Little Ireland and the rubber factories around the Macintosh Mill were, by today's standards, horrific urban workplaces where daily survival was the routine that energized the very fabric of Manchester. And yet the powerful warehouses, high railway viaducts such as Castlefields, canals, and the great Victorian landmarks of commerce (by architects from Charles Barry to Edwin Lutyens) and civic pride (Alfred Waterhouse's town hall, the John Rylands Library) are being renewed, reinvented,

Left, above: Grandfather Jim and my mother revisiting the Maguire home in Galway in the mid-1960s.

Left, below: Both sets of grandparents c. 1933 – maternal at the front and paternal at the back.

Salford Quays, part of Manchester Dock, 1949.

Manchester's Liverpool Road station was the first railway station in the world. This print dates from c. 1830.

My father Tom, a racing cyclist, with a friend at the Bellevue racetrack.

Top, left and right: Two views of the mining village of Bedlington in Northumberland. On the left is a photograph I took in the 1960s; on the right is my painting of the village, executed when I was in my teens.

Above, left and right: These representations of a fantasy Wigan Pier were among the many paintings I did as a teenager of the industrial north of England.

reinterpreted today, as Manchester becomes an expanding star in the current era of urban renaissance.

Today's young people relate less to a pretty historic market city like York or a college city like Oxford than to the virile and robust realism of more recent times that Manchester embodies. It is a place where people got a chance to change their lives and make an impact. The film *Blade Runner*, if made 100 years earlier, could have been based on Manchester, yet the 19th-century architecture surpasses anything in London at that time. In a way, the same applies to Newcastle, in that most of the great masterpieces of architecture were in the north and not in London, and even Karl Friedrich Schinkel on his visit from Berlin in the early 1820s recorded his great admiration for the mills and factories of northern England. But to me as a young boy visiting relatives – aunts, uncles, cousins and both sets of grandparents – all around Manchester, none of this coalesced into a sense of place. I saw the city as confusing, shapeless and sometimes oppressive. Today there are pop stars and senior educationalists, London developers, streetwise students and well-off city workers investing their time, money and energy in Manchester – people who are not exploited or merely surviving, but who are joyfully saying to themselves that they are in the city from choice, because it is the best place to be, and they want to spend their lives there. What a change! It probably could not have happened without the painful period of chaos that undermined our sense of what a place is or should be.

It is a lesson for the town planner that good placemaking can be founded on intense, mistake-ridden risk-taking – every bit as readily as on self-consciously manufactured visions of what a place should be. So what does that say about the public realm, the domain of the collective? How do the vitality and originality of place equate with a plan, a vision? Compare Disneyland or Milton Keynes with Manchester's rawness and realness. In the best cities, a balance has been achieved between planning and individualistic anarchy.

The process of creating a silk purse from a sow's ear intrigues me. In the 1980s I was called 'Dr Farrell' when I argued that the damage caused in the 1960s and 1970s to cities like Manchester by motorways and comprehensive redevelopment could be 'healed' by making new places from the ruins. I am drawn to the 'before' and 'after' views with which the landscape architect Humphry

Repton illustrated his *Red Book*, and I think the best of British landscape design is about conversion. I have always liked the fact that the 18th-century landscape gardener Lancelot Brown was known as 'Capability'; but I never knew why they called him Capability, assuming it meant he was very capable. When I recently read his biography, I found out that it was because he was good at looking at the landscape equivalent of a sow's ear and finding great capabilities there. This approach helped me to look at towns in a different way.

Le Corbusier once wrote an essay called 'The eyes that do not see'. The notion embodied in its title reminds me of how we can condition our eyes so that, while we see the damage and deprivation in our cities, we cannot imagine how they can be transformed; this creates a kind of collective myopia – a lack of faith in the possibilities – the 'capabilities' – of a place. But cities like Manchester are now, at the beginning of the 21st century, reinventing themselves in an age of true urban renaissance, not only by recognizing the value of continuity with the past but also by adding new layers of creative placemaking to what has been left. The devastation caused in Manchester by the 1996 IRA bomb provided the impetus for the city's revitalization. From a limited area of bombed buildings and ruined lives, at last Manchester's people have recognized the 'capabilities' of their city and begun to address 100 years of decline and decay.

The move to Newcastle

Menageries, habitats and paper rounds

Newcastle was completely different from those Lancashire towns that grew and merged into each other across and through the Pennine hills and valleys. Newcastle was a unique, self-contained, somewhat isolated city with a language and culture all its own. When my parents moved there in 1946, it was with the purpose of self-improvement.

By today's standards my parents had not had much education. When they met, my mother was a secretary in a laundry and my father was a postman. He had taken the job because it allowed him to ride a bike – one of his passions was racing at Bellevue velodrome. The end of the Second World War created new opportunities. My dad was rapidly promoted to sorting-office clerk, then to clerical officer, then he got a job in Newcastle at the Ministry of Pensions and National Insurance – part of the

St Charles, my primary school in Gosforth (top), and Kirkley Close on the Grange Estate. Both these photographs were taken in 1998.

One of my favourite childhood places: Seaton Sluice on the coast of Northumberland, where I fished and camped out on the dunes.

My family's first house on the Grange Estate, in Kirkley Close. Built in 1946 in steel frame and clad in asbestos, it was entirely prefabricated by workshops that had manufactured wartime aeroplanes.

newly created welfare state, located in a vast prefabricated 'office city' in Longbenton just outside Newcastle. There was huge change ahead. In spite of winning the war, Winston Churchill and his posh officer class were out and, in what was Britain's most radical political upheaval of the 20th century, a new socialist world was promised.

Our new life in Newcastle seemed to be a world of temporary prefabs – not only my father's offices but also the housing estate where we lived, which was home to a mixture of 'slum clearance' families, local miners and relocated 'professional' families who had arrived to help run the welfare state. There was grand-scale placemaking at work here that I only vaguely grasped at the time. People believed that the new Labour government could put right the unfairness of the Depression.

North-east England – scene of the start of the Jarrow march, one of the most memorable images associated with the mass unemployment of the 1930s – was to receive major investment in large, newly relocated government departments, as well as new large-scale public housing, both of which we experienced first-hand. Over the next eight years, farmland north of the suburb of Gosforth was built on to become the Grange Estate of 2,000 rented council properties. We lived in the first street to be completed – a row of steel-framed, asbestos-panel-clad, two-storey terraced houses designed and built by former aircraft-industry workers to meet the postwar housing shortage.

The location of the Grange Estate, while somewhat bleak, was right on the edge of open countryside and I immediately took to the fields, rivers and woods, enjoying a freedom to roam that Sale had never given me. I began catching fish and, with my father's help, created a menagerie for the wide range of pets that shared our home – rabbits, guinea pigs, mice, tortoises, terrapins and tropical fish. I made boxes and runs, and bought heaters and filters for the fish. Meanwhile, I began reading books on wildlife habitats.

Over time, every part of our house was invaded by the animal world, including mice in a 'town' made of intersecting large boxes and cages. My mother, to my deep regret at the time, drew the line at rats and snakes – and

she once had to come to school to drag me home when all the mice escaped into the washroom and stopped her from going in there (it was a Monday – wash day).

The tropical fish were, for me, particularly compelling, each tank full of such a variety of fish and all so beautiful. Beauty was a strong factor in my tropical-fish obsession. My collection included luminous neon tetras, speckled gouramis, darting zebra fish and slow-moving angel fish that resembled striped vertical saucers. I visited and grew friendly with other fish fanatics around Newcastle. Some of the adults among them had obsessively and passionately expanded their hobby by building whole outbuildings dedicated to tanks, where they spent much of their lives creating worlds within worlds, each tank a manufactured stage-set of colour and life.

Some years later, in the early 1960s, while I was learning enthusiastically about ecology from Ian McHarg at the University of Pennsylvania, Rachel Carson's *Silent Spring* was published. *Silent Spring* seemed to me an apt title not only for her book but also for my own experience of environmental pollution.

I had spent many childhood days wading in a small stream, the Ouse Burn, a mile or two from our house. The burn is a tributary of the Tyne that, further down-stream, runs through a romantic wild ravine in central Newcastle called Jesmond Dene, entering the Tyne at the edge of the East Quayside. The stretch of the Ouse Burn I knew was a world crammed full of sticklebacks, weeds, insects – every jam jar of water collected was full to the brim with life. But when I went back there in my twenties a factory estate had been built upstream and the water was a lifeless sewer of white industrial waste.

As I grew older and explored more widely, I found in coastal and highland Northumbria layered worlds of many habitats. On the rocky coastlines there were gull colonies like vertical cities, with rows of nesting apart-ment blocks, and at the base of these when the tide was out were stranded natural aquariums in the form of rock pools, where crabs, shrimps and odd sea bugs darted about under stones and weeds.

At Seaton Sluice and Holy Island the sand dunes were home to rabbits, lizards and ground-nesting birds; the terrain was one of extraordinarily soft and fine wind-shifting sand bound by clumps and clumps of spiky, long, thin, extra-tough marram grass. Up higher in the Cheviots, beyond Wooler, there always seemed to be the sound of wood pigeons, crows and cruising birds of prey, and great multitudes of sheep, and rabbits that lived in and burrowed through the ground, building their own architecture of underground villages and towns. I realized that each habitat was a world, like my hutches and aquariums, my model forts and towns: every inch of them through and through had their own nature and character.

Habitats, or worlds within worlds, have continued to absorb me, and today I am busy with three public aquariums and a masterplan for London Zoo. Like humans, animals have their own sense of home and territory, and the dynamic relationship between human and animal is a truly fascinating one. From existing within a world dominated by nature, humans' growth and success has put our species in control of all nature's habitats and its destiny. Nature now survives on a knife-edge between our ability to wreck further what we have already damaged and our desire to recreate or regenerate natural habitats, through our applied intelligence and increasing understanding of life and its balance.

The intensity of my interest lay not only in the organization and harmony of a habitat but also in its beauty. Later in life, I lived for a long while next to a rookery, where night after night I liked to sit watching the flocking birds fly into their nests, silhouetted in the half-light at day's end; in a fierce wind, their interlocking, floating, weaving, darting flight paths and mastery of the swift air currents as they positioned themselves to land were visually exhilarating. After

landing they would squawk and talk to each other in their high-rise tree houses, reminding me of a lively Mediterranean village square or happy holidaying families on Blackpool's crowded beaches.

From the age of about 10 to 17, I delivered newspapers for Harry Eblett's on the Gosforth North Road. This earned me the money to pay for my various hobbies, particularly the tanks and equipment for the tropical fish. As my ambitions in this direction increased, along with the need to fund camping and other trips, I did more paper rounds, so that by the time I was 16 I was often doing one morning and two evening rounds a day – and learning about social differences. None of the council estate houses had private front gardens and all the doors were green. Flats had letters and numbers, so I would deliver to 17a or 6g, for example. On the next rung up the social ladder were tree-lined, older (pre-estate) streets where privately owned houses had enclosed front gardens with garden gates, 'beware of the dog' signs and side doors for tradesmen, and where house numbers were often less favoured than names such as 'Sunnyhills' and 'Heatherlands'. At the top of the social scale was 'The Grove' in central Gosforth, which, in common with nearby streets, had driveways, brick-built garages, front lawns and house names also starting with 'The': 'The Elms', 'The Beeches', and so on. Each group read different newspapers. The tabloids, women's weeklies and comics went to the first group; *Radio Times*, *News Chronicle* and *Guardian* to the second; and *The Times* and *Daily Telegraph* to the third. Had I thought about it, I could have written an excellent report on the social profiles of different classes and their reading habits just from the observations of a paper boy. Here was a community where placemaking expressed in so many different ways its members' aspirations and sense of belonging. Just as animal and aquatic species – gulls, rabbits and fish – have their habitats, so do human groups each have their own territory within their different houses, streets and neighbourhoods.

Left: Visiting Newcastle in 1998, I returned to Eblett's the newsagent, where I worked in the 1950s. Harry Eblett was still running the shop but retired soon afterwards.

Walking and running: campsites and fairs

From the time I arrived in Newcastle until I began grammar school at 11, I continued modelmaking and making things. My creative work in later life had its roots not in formal school lessons but primarily in what I did outside school. In the same way, school sport based on intensely competitive team games did not appeal to me. I preferred more solitary or self-contained

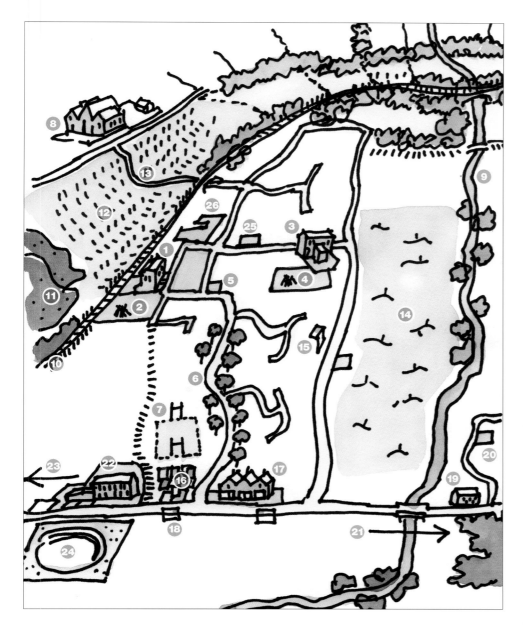

A sketch of the Grange Estate

1. Our first home on the estate, 7 Kirkley Close
2. Play area with bonfire
3. Our second home on the estate, 3 Lesbury Chase
4. Small field with bonfire
5. The O'Briens' house
6. Park Avenue
7. The rugby ground
8. Cox Lodge Catholic primary school
9. The Ouse Burn
10. Railway to Hazelrigg colliery
11. Pit heaps, Gosforth colliery
12. Farmers' fields with wheat or potatoes
13. Footpath to school
14. Golf course
15. School bus stop
16. Allotments
17. Shops, including Eblett's newsagent
18. Bus stop
19. Pub
20. Peter Smith's house
21. To Morpeth
22. Territorial Army base
23. To Gosforth and Newcastle
24. Dog-racing stadium
25. Hugo's house
26. Pat's house

activities such as swimming, walking, cycling and particularly running – all of which I have continued through life. The one area where my interest grew and grew was getting out into the Cheviot Hills and walking and camping. From an early age, we children would go off on bikes on our own during school holidays. These trips opened a new door. Hillwalking was my father's great love at this time, and I often joined him to walk along Hadrian's Wall. The hills and moors were subtle shades of brown, yellow and purple, with bracken, gorse and heather. I have always been attracted to unconventional use of colour – perhaps because the light of the north doesn't fit the Mediterranean classic art stereotypes. Antonio Gaudí once expressed the view that his contemporary, and no doubt 'rival', Charles Rennie Mackintosh could never create beauty in his architecture because the Glasgow light was so dull – you needed Mediterranean sunshine to succeed. Much as I admired Gaudí, I thought this was a narrow viewpoint limited by his own geographical prejudice.

My father introduced me to walking maps, which show every path and track, every contour and physical feature of the land. Maps as representations have always intrigued me, particularly those of wildernesses dominated by a multitude of natural features, which are both hard to depict and challenge the connection between a perceived 'place' and its position in relation to the wider natural world.

Exploring the landscape was not simply an aesthetic pleasure. It also involved the joys of moving and walking, with the extraordinary rewards of changing scenery as the movement of the body lifted and lowered horizons, changed vistas and connected to it in a tactile way with feet and hands on water, stones, grass and mud. Later, while at grammar school, I went to the Lake District and stayed at the Achille Ratti walkers' cottage near Grasmere. There I discovered in local shops Alfred Wainwright's wonderful handwritten and hand-illustrated books about the area, where simple but beautiful sketches and plans orientated and explained the world of the Lake District. I use descriptive details in the books today to convince urban dwellers of the similar joys to be had from walking in our towns and cities.

Walking is the most rewarding form of transport, yet in so many cities it is the most neglected. I believe that moving through the landscape of a city is, or can be, as pleasurable as moving through the rural landscape.

Colin Rowe's *Collage City* (1978) makes a connection between Humphry Repton and his one-time partner John Nash: Nash created new urban plans by adapting the man-made terrain of existing buildings and streets – just as Repton did with the existing English countryside. Not for them the tabula rasa of French rural and urban plans with their grand axes, which totally remade land and buildings, usually deliberately eliminating all existing features.

My father took my elder brother, Tony, and me on several camping expeditions in the Cheviots, where we established our miniature settlement in glorious isolation, among pine woods and rocky valleys, living a brilliant, self-contained life. We walked and we cooked – and in this way my father made simple patterns for the days' events that gave me a great sense of purposeful, planned independence.

Later, more ambitiously, in 1951 Tony and I went with dad on a long camping trip around England, culminating at a huge campsite at Crystal Palace in London, where we stayed while we visited the Festival of Britain. I clearly remember all those temporary cities laid out at Crystal Palace, and on the South Bank around the Festival Hall and in Battersea Park, where there was a tree walk and the Guinness clock. I had no mental map of London – it seemed to be a huge collection of different places – but the festival was a world created for a moment in time. With its Skylon and Dome of Discovery, the festival helped me to see the force of design and introduced me to Joseph Paxton's original Crystal Palace, a surviving remnant of which had been erected on the South Bank (its third home).

My interest in campsites and temporary homes was given a dramatic scale shift when – on one of the most memorable days of my childhood – I was taken to a self-contained temporary city erected for the annual Hoppings fair. Recognizing my love of running, my father had entered me for one of the children's races in the 1947 June Race Week, which coincided with the Hoppings. Newcastle has a great tradition of running – Brendan Foster in the 1970s, Steve Cram in the 1980s – and, like the Great North Run, the Race Week brought everyone together at one moment in time. The Hoppings was held on a huge piece of cattle-occupied moorland, the 'town moor', which came right up to the edge of Newcastle city itself (a connection later largely severed by 1960s motorways).

On the day that I was due to take part in the races, my family dutifully turned up to watch, but, as good fortune would have it, we arrived too late for me to run. (I never actually liked racing – I just liked to run, and run long distances, enjoying the kind of kinaesthetic high that comes from seeing places on foot at speed.) My parents had two more events planned for us children that day: a visit to the fair – they gave us a shilling each to spend – and a viewing of Walt Disney's *Bambi* at the Globe cinema back in Gosforth.

The Hoppings, the largest fair in Europe at the time, would probably have contravened all manner of modern laws, from health and safety to child labour and trade descriptions. While the rides themselves were simple and tame and much less interesting than they are today, the fair was nevertheless full of startling oddities: two-headed dogs, Siamese twin piglets in bottles and bearded ladies, as well as boxing matches, strongmen and acrobats. I was gripped by this temporary city – a miracle of instant placemaking populated by gypsies, fairground people with tethered horses, pet dogs and children, and entire families all engaged in a life together. Perhaps it was the influence of the travelling Celts and tinkers of Ireland among my ancestors, but I was much impressed that this was a city made by the hands of the very people I could see around me. It was magical with its painted colours, vibrant patterns, sounds of metallic organs, steam engines that worked the roundabouts, and hustling buskers who sucked you into their tents to see the 'fantastic' marvels inside.

I soon lost my parents and walked on and on. After a few hours I realized I had to make a plan, so I kept enough money to buy a ticket for the cinema in Gosforth, 3 miles away. I half expected to meet the rest of my family in the cinema queue. Little did I know that they were at the police station reporting me missing – fearing that, by now, I might be halfway to the Continent in the back of a gypsy caravan. But I went in to see *Bambi* and for the second time that day was overwhelmed by a visual fantasy world – this one created by draughtsmanship, colour images and animation. I had loved reading American comics during the war and

Opposite: A photograph of the Cheviots appears top right, with drawings of the Lake District by A.W. Wainwright, published in his *Pictorial Guide to the Lakeland Fells* (1962), at bottom right. All the remaining images of the Northumberland land-scape I painted between the ages of 11 and 16.

'Before' and 'after' view of a Repton landscape from his *Red Book*, which showed designs based on the 'transformation' of one condition to another by watercoloured cut-out overlays.

Bambi and other Disney films opened up a new world. For me, Dudley D. Watkins's cartoon strips were just a step towards the Disney artists' brilliant animations.

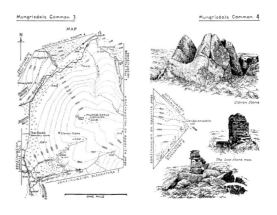

Bambi seemed to take their frame-by-frame visual story-telling a momentous step further. It was without doubt one of the most wondrous moments of my childhood when I sat there in the dark on my own watching this extraordinary creative explosion.

The great beauty of the early Disney films sprang from the fact that the Depression had so reduced labour costs that Disney's Hollywood academy could afford to employ armies of skilled, gifted, dedicated and innovative artists to handcraft feature animations. From a time of hardship came this creative outburst but later, in 'better' times, the drawings became simplified and overstylized because of high labour costs (although the age of computers has given us back this graphic fluency at low cost). Needless to say, my day of delight and discovery ended with a bump when I got home to a family not the least bit interested in my marvellous experiences.

Given my northern postwar upbringing on a newly built council estate, the world of Walt Disney at that time offered a cultural liberation quite distinct from that provided by stilted black-and-white movies, particularly the British-made ones, where actors spoke in middle-class accents just like radio newsreaders. Disney kindled my interest in popular culture, as well as showing me that the real ability of the artist is not merely to paint or sculpt objects for art galleries but also to create entirely new, accessible worlds from the imagination.

Years later, when I first went through the portals of Disneyland Los Angeles with my children, I was struck by the words of welcome: 'Here you leave the real world behind.' Disneyland represented a link, a transformation from the celluloid film world to the fantasy of the funfair, yet on a scale that – in respect of its industry, business organization and ambition – the world had never seen before. In retrospect, Disneyland makes the family tents and caravans of traditional fairs like the Hoppings seem like quaintly modest, haphazard survivors of a much earlier age.

Personal identity and group place

During my childhood I found it difficult to balance the creative stimulus of solitude with group friendships and sibling 'congestion'. I was the second of four boys. There were only three years between the three elder boys, and I did not have a bed of my own until I was 14.

Then, at 15, when my elder brother left home, I even had a room of my own. Daytime solitude, though, I found with great ease – going off to Blyth port on my bike to fish all day on my own, or walking over to the Ouse Burn on long summer evenings when the sun didn't set in that northern latitude until 11 p.m.

Since one of my passions was running, I have often reflected on this most lonely and insular of physical activities. I have vivid memories of the 1947 New Year's Day half-marathon from Morpeth to Newcastle. Standing outside Eblett's the newsagent, on the Great North Road, I watched the runners pass, which took nearly an hour from first to last. It was the personal challenge I understood.

When watching marathons today, I identify strongly with runners who, however low down the finishing order, determinedly press their own stopwatches as they cross the finishing line. All the individuals involved are on their own private mission to test what their bodies and minds can do under intense challenge and pressure, and to compare their times with past achievements and present expectations.

I felt less comfortable with family-based or organized group activities. I have always reacted against 'club' culture and regimentation. Ultimately, I turned against my family's adherence to the Catholic Church, but at an early age I also found myself unable to identify with organizations such as the Boy Scouts. Tying knots over and over again for no particular purpose, being marched about like a little army – I disliked it all.

On scout or school camping expeditions I felt there was a nightmare of unfeeling leadership, and on one scout trip near Wooler I left the Cheviot Hills midweek to return home – much to the disappointment of my mother, who had been enjoying some peace without the boys. During a storm in the night our tent had ripped open, so my fellow tent-dwellers and I had to move out and share with other boys. When the scout master said in the morning that our tent would have to be thrown away – and we would have to spend another week and a half sharing an overcrowded tent – I had both reason and incentive to take my leave. I asked if I could have the damaged tent material and got the bus home, taking the tent remains home to display to my mother, who, urged on by me, patched it up with an old raincoat cut into strips. I bought sticks and ropes, and in a day or two

Memories of the Festival of Britain, 1951, are recalled by an aerial view (right) and two paintings I did on a trip to London seven years after the festival (below, left and right). At the foot of the page are memorabilia including a photograph of my brother and me at the Festival.

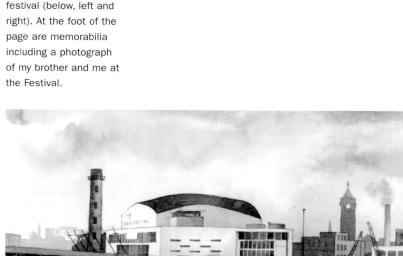

I had erected my own tent in the garden. I was in the camping business now on an independent basis. From the age of 12, I began organizing my own camping trips to the beach by the sand dunes at Seaton Sluice, and in my teens during each school summer holiday I organized groups of four or five boys to tour by bike or foot around Scotland, and later all over England. Planning, organizing and leading was my way of responding to group activity, and I remember an earlier event which probably started this pattern.

When we first moved to Newcastle and found ourselves in a more open community of children on the Grange Estate, my elder brother, Tony, who until then I had followed everywhere, excluded me from the group who were building the annual Guy Fawkes bonfire. From leading me and his younger brothers, he had become part of an older group of boys whom he then followed. It was a moment of challenge for me, involving the transfer of group and leadership roles. I gathered together all the other younger boys who had been excluded, including my two younger brothers, and we went off to build our own bonfire. I was only nine years old, but I was driven to build the biggest and greatest bonfire, and we worked all through the late summer and on through September and October. We succeeded, surpassing the older boys, and I repeated this ritual in later years, even after everyone else had lost interest. For me, it was a real commitment, an annual event or ritual that allowed me to prove that I could be effective and bring others along with me. I suppose, looking back, it was an early rehearsal for the kind of project-driven team leadership that designing buildings and planning cities would require later in life.

For years after, Guy Fawkes was the great celebratory day of my year – more important than Christmas, Easter or birthdays. It is typically British that we have no meaningful national day like Thanksgiving or Independence Day as they have in the USA, or Bastille Day in France. After all, who was Guy Fawkes but a minor historical figure and a Catholic – and here I was celebrating fires and explosions with the greatest enthusiasm. In terms of national symbolism, it meant absolutely nothing to us all.

I never enjoyed the anonymity of structured team play. In football I sometimes played goalkeeper but often opted out altogether and was left to my own devices. Together, the rejects – or 'scraps', as we were called –

Left, top: Race Week at the Hoppings fair, held annually on Newcastle's town moor in the 1950s. This was one of the biggest temporary fairs in the world and took place on an extensive stretch of moorland right next to Newcastle city centre, visible in the distance.

Left, centre and bottom: Two works by the local architectural genuis John Dobson: Newcastle railway station and St Thomas's church in the city's Haymarket.

and I invented our own games, went for runs or held our own version of the Olympic Games. I saw that these childhood Olympic Games gave a chance to fat boys and weedy boys and tiny boys and non-team boys to find something they each could do. It always seemed more fun – but somewhere in this are the roots of my attraction to outsiders, nonconformists and underdogs, and of my interest in politics (particularly local politics), protest groups, community involvement, advocacy and explanation. I grew up exploring the edges and opposites, combining creative leadership with listening and following, invariably turning against predictability and questioning conformist presumptions and seeing creative challenge in perceived difficulties.

My memories of our home on the Grange Estate are that it was anonymous and impersonal – a mono-cultural, mass-produced place. On reflection, perhaps it was partly the effects of time itself that I missed. For me, a true home needs to have layered onto it the marks of generations who have lived in and loved the place – to create the sense that we all built it, not the council or a planner or an architect. British new towns such as Milton Keynes are today being reappraised, with the intention of transforming them into higher density places with more diverse architecture and less reliance on cars. This highlights a lifelong dilemma of architects. We all want to live in mature places but must earn our keep by creating the new, the immature. London architects and planners live in old villages such as Hampstead and Highgate, often in Georgian houses. Paris, San Francisco and Venice may be the preferred dwelling places of the designer community, but what we create is more likely to be in Milton Keynes or Hong Kong.

The Prince of Wales said in his Hampton Court speech in 1984 that there is a double standard among many architects. Perhaps it is fairer to say that there is an inevitable paradox – what we like and believe in cannot be created solely by us; it needs occupation and loving residents over time to make a 'place'. I have often, in later life, gone back to see what has happened to the buildings I built. Some have been transformed by love or neglect; others have evolved or been adapted. Later in the book are photos of several projects as they were when built and as they are now, 20 or 30 years later.

After four years, my parents moved to the other side of the council estate, from Kirkley Close to Lesbury Chase. Both roads had been named, aspirationally, after picturesque rural places in Northumberland. Names of council-estate roads and other placemaking names are revealing. Many a grotesque, damp, spirit-collapsing place in the UK is called 'Mozart House' or 'Shakespeare Avenue', but a name cannot make a place, certainly not by association.

Looking back, our family moved from one incarnation of British 20th-century public housing (the techno-machine age of the Bauhaus and Gropius) to the other (the tradition of John Ruskin, William Morris, Ebenezer Howard at Letchworth, and Edwin Lutyens and others at Hampstead Garden Suburb). The house at Kirkley Close was assembled from a factory-made kit-of-parts, like a plane or car. Its prefab components included asbestos cement cladding that gave the building a corrugated, whitish look. Internally it was very well planned and functional. It was built by people who belonged to the 'designing from the inside out' school of thought.

These houses were brilliant examples of product design but they didn't feel permanent or solid, and within the estate the street had a certain stigma – the houses were seen as being cheap and insubstantial. Fifteen years later they were reclad with brickwork on the outside to give them a new coat of respectability that fitted in better with the neighbours, but inside all the intelligent, well-detailed intentions remained.

The house in Lesbury Chase was styled in the glorified British vernacular – Letchworth traditional, you could call it – copied both municipally and by speculative 'ribbon bypass' developers, and creatively and caringly reinvented in more recent times by architects such as Edward Cullinan, Richard MacCormac and Darbourne & Dark. Our terraced house was not self-consciously designed as a product because it was designed by the 'outside in' school. It was cosy and reassuring in softer brick with a clay-tiled roof. Although it was a bit gloomy, with cottage-sized windows, the concern was less about how it was made than with how it looked and its placemaking in terms of status, familiarity and harmony with similar terraced houses up and down the street.

I later learned that 'style groups' such as techno modern and vernacular traditional belonged to the architect–designer's own search for group place and personal creative identity. At that stage of my life, on the Grange Estate, I was merely an unwitting 'consumer'. The need to create often manifests itself as a push for exaggerated

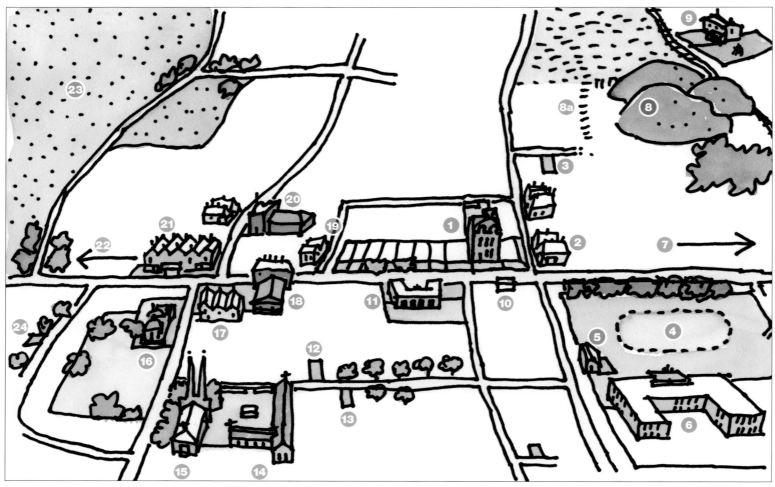

individuality and difference, but the occupants of houses have their own priorities and identity issues that are invariably far removed from those of the planners, developers and designers whose 'world' they occupy.

Art: painting, drawing, an inspirational teacher and discovering my career

St Cuthbert's grammar school – which involved a long journey into Newcastle – seemed remote and tough (I didn't go to the local school in Gosforth because we were Catholics). I recently learned from a contemporary that other schools nicknamed St Cuthbert's 'Belsen' at that time because the discipline was so strong. Long after I had left St Cuthbert's I revisited the school and for the first time in several decades I stood in the playground. The essential physical components were virtually unchanged: the place had all the typological features essential to the notion of school as place. The rectangular tarmacked playground (looking much smaller than I remembered it) sat between the open playing fields on one side and the main building on the other. The main building was essentially a central school assembly hall flanked by rows of classrooms, just like my

A sketch of central Gosforth

1   Our last home in Gosforth, 73 Lansdowne Terrace
2   Corner shops
3   Michael Key's house
4   Running track for Gosforth Harriers
5   Changing rooms
6   Gosforth grammar school (Church of England)
7   To Morpeth
8   Gosforth colliery and pit heaps
8a Footpath to Grange Estate
9   Our earlier home at 7 Kirkley Close
10 Bus stop
11 Gosforth library
12 The Sharratts' house
13 Francis Moran's house
14 St Charles's Catholic primary school
15 St Charles's Catholic church

16 The Memorial Clinic
17 Shopping parade
18 Odeon cinema
19 Corner shops
20 Globe cinema
21 Shops
22 To Newcastle
23 Newcastle town moor
24 The Grove (where Harry Faulkner-Brown later lived)

Maurice McPartlan, my art teacher, shown in wartime military uniform and as a student at the Slade art school.

future professor Louis Kahn's school, which I saw at Rochester, New York, in 1964 – a master space and servant spaces, Kahn would have called it. Then there were two ancillary groups – the house where the headmaster and the priests lived, with its chapel, and a sports hall which doubled as an area for school dinners. But the essence of the school wasn't buildings or even classrooms; it was its three bigger, unifying voids or spaces: 'the public realm'. It had a series of places that formed a transitional sequence from a high and airy communal hall to a roofless, semi-enclosed courtyard or playground to parklands beyond. Such simple building blocks – the essence of all great houses – remain with us all our lives in all our built places.

I underachieved academically and did not readily get involved in school life, but one teacher, Maurice McPartlan, changed this pattern. At the end of the first year, McPartlan held up in front of the class a landscape I had unselfconsciously painted on a Cheviot trip and gave me the only 'A' grade. He told me afterwards that he considered I had special artistic abilities. After that, trees, hills and rivers became my world of visual study. I had something I could do – this was a hobby and schoolwork too, and it was all linked to nature and habitat, walking and solitude. In this way, miraculous connections opened up and different elements of my life began to converge and coalesce.

My decision to become an architect was cemented by the winning of a drawing prize when I was 16 and had just finished my O levels, but I can trace it back to the very first year at St Cuthbert's and Maurice McPartlan. McPartlan was a man's man, a decorated war hero and an artist frustrated because the war had interrupted his study at the Slade art school in London, where he had won a scholarship. By the time the war was over, he had a young family and was forced to earn a living as a teacher. Maurice McPartlan became my guide, my mentor and eventually a substitute father figure. My own father, a sensitive and quiet man, seemed mild beside McPartlan, a man of military achievement and authority who made a life in art appear a solid option, and emulating him a desirable and masculine pursuit.

McPartlan was the one person who backed me and inspired me and gave my life its direction. Initially he directed me towards painting, particularly landscapes and trees. Unfortunately, they did not teach biology at St Cuthbert's, and I really did not enjoy my time there – until I reached sixth form, that is. Geometry, geography and art were my only strong subjects, and when I chose my O levels in the fifth form my teachers and parents were united in their belief that I was not sixth-form material, and that a university education would be academically too demanding for me.

One day when I was 14, my mother noticed a house I was drawing – the house I could see out of the living-room window – and said, 'Why don't you become an architect?' I suppose she thought it would be more of a career than art and I connected this thought with the repeated complaint of my hero, Mr McPartlan, that he was a reluctant teacher who had found it was not possible to survive by painting alone. Whenever I had struggled to decide on a career, my parents had pushed me towards joining the civil service like the rest of the family – an idea that was unacceptable to me. I didn't want a job that was separate from my interests, passions and hobbies. So, in the fifth form I transformed my academic record just in time for my O levels, and I got into the sixth form, which was an intellectual revelation. I loved history, had an excellent English teacher and could spend much more time on my art classes.

In the summer of 1954, before I started in the sixth form, Maurice McPartlan did two things that confirmed my vocation. He arranged for me to work for Ted Gunning, a local architect with a small office, and he entered me for an architectural drawing competition for schools organized by the Northern Architectural Association (the local branch of the Royal Institute of British Architects). Gunning's office was in the beautiful early 19th-century Eldon Square in the centre of Newcastle. I enjoyed the work in an atmosphere that combined practicality, design and artistry.

From there, I began to explore and understand the city, spending lunch hours and time after work walking the streets, looking for a subject for the competition. I found my subject for the drawing in a beautiful little oval church, All Saints, halfway down to the Quayside. It had been designed by a local architect, David Stephenson, in 1786. I drew it during the summer, interiors and exteriors. After we returned to school it was announced that I had won first prize, and my efforts were displayed outside the art room in the school hall for three weeks. For the first time in my school life, I was seen as someone who had achieved something. The experience transformed me: it reinforced my choice of study and career, and I entered the sixth form full of confidence and optimism.

The poet John Keats was a central part of my A-level English course. (I remember I particularly liked his observation that 'The excellence of all art lies in its intensity'.) I read a biography of Keats and was impressed by the distances he walked as part of daily life. I liked the idea of navigating the city on foot before the advent of public transport. Keats's father died by falling off a horse as he was going down Highgate Hill, but at that time it was more common for people to walk. Keats regularly

Left: Newcastle quayside, *c*. 1950s.

Below: Plans for the city centre in the 1950s. These extraordinary drawings show the extent of suggested demolitions and new road insertions that would have wiped out most of Grainger Town with its many listed buildings.

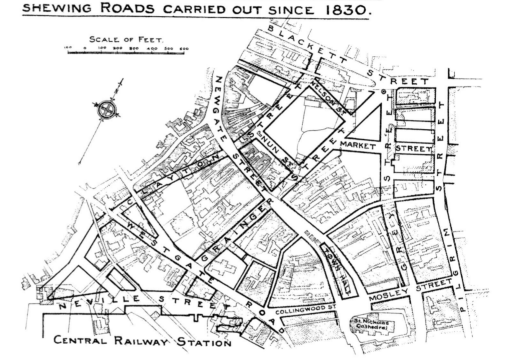

PLAN OF CENTRE OF NEWCASTLE-upon-TYNE SHEWING ROADS CARRIED OUT SINCE 1830.

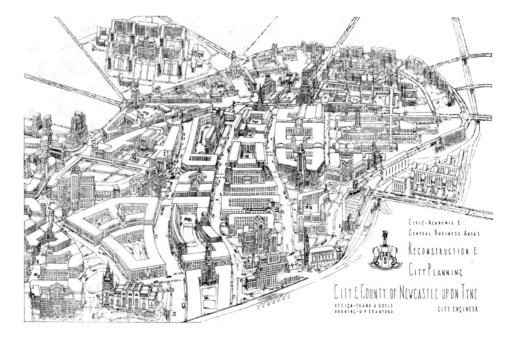

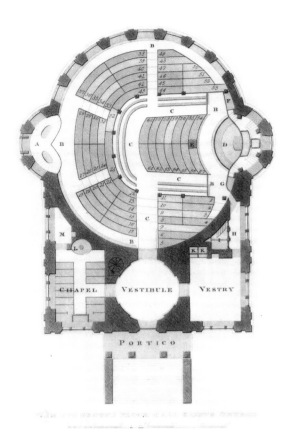

Above: The drawing for which I won the RIBA architectural award at the age of 16 (left) was of All Saints church (centre), designed in 1786 by David Stevenson; the church is shown in plan (right).

walked from his home in south London, where Guy's Hospital now stands, to his brother's house in Hampstead – a distance of about 6 miles. Walking in London is made particularly interesting by the series of 'urban villages' that make up the city. It is rewarding to walk through places characterized by a continuously even distribution of population, passing from village centre to village centre in a series of links, rather than the concentrated central business districts (CBDs) of America.

Newcastle has real shape and form, a clear visual plan. It is, and always has been, surprisingly more magical than most northern English cities. Even in 1842, the traveller William Howitt wrote, 'You walk into what has long been termed the coal hole of the north and find yourself at once in a city of palaces, a fairyland of newness, brightness and modern elegance.'

Newcastle itself is not an industrial town but a large regional market town. By the early 19th century Britain's largest internal market, in Grainger Town (1835), stood across the street from the world's first department store, Bainbridge's. Newcastle was the second biggest shopping city after London, and it was truly urban in that it was a walled town that had defended a natural

border during Roman and then Norman times, and later during the wars with Scotland. The topography of Newcastle is the key to its character. From the flat plain of the town moor, Grey Street sweeps down wonderfully to the Tyne, linking the low-level Quayside to the plateau above. The 19th- and 20th-century road and rail bridges sail across the river, linking the two banks so that the plain of the plateau is maintained high above the ground. The great feet of these bridges striding over the medieval Quayside alleyways below contribute to some of the most dramatic urban scenery anywhere.

Settlement began along the river banks at the bottom of the steep river gorge, and this is still the most interesting area of the city – at least, what is left of it – with steep narrow footways and steps cut between medieval houses. Robert Stephenson's wonderful bridge of 1849 was the first to connect the high land on either side of the river, effectively bypassing the old city below, leaving it to years of decay. On the new plateau a great classical stone city emerged, driven in large part by Thomas Grainger and his architect, John Dobson. Manchester's most distinguished architectural son is Alfred Waterhouse, Leeds's is Cuthbert Broderick, and Newcastle's is Dobson. Grainger Town,

Grey Street and the city's fine railway station make Newcastle a complete surprise to visitors from the south who think of it as a stereotypical black-sooted industrial town. The only bad parts are the 1960s office blocks and urban motorways; the rest of the city is characterized by sublime urban planning.

During the summer that I worked in Ted Gunning's office in Eldon Square I walked and walked, registering for the first time that the landscape of a fine city is as varied, stimulating and visually rewarding as anything the countryside can offer. I was not only making the link between art and architecture but also experiencing a more complex mental convergence between my love of landscape and a growing admiration and respect for the man-made world of the city. I was seeing as I walked that the landscape of a great city is a very beautiful thing – and, more than this, that it is an invented world, an act of transformation that is as artistic a creation as any painting, sculpture or great movie.

The 'temporary' move to Blackpool

Life was not all plain sailing since there was an unexpected change in my parents' plans. They had always wanted to go back to Lancashire and, with retirement approaching, imagined themselves before long at home without children. My father accepted a civil service job in war pensions in Blackpool, and six months before my A levels, in November 1955, we moved to Blackpool. Looking back, the move was academically destabilizing for me, but I got through my A levels at St Joseph's College and was offered a place at Newcastle University School of Architecture. As it turned out, it was I who went back 'home' and my parents who moved away, and throughout my college life their new home was to intrigue me: Blackpool and Lytham St Anne's seemed, and were, very different from Newcastle.

In identity and marketing terms, Blackpool could be called a 'one liner'. It had existed solely and simply as a summer holiday resort, and had been deliberately planned monoculturally to cater for a population that doubled or trebled during a fixed period each year. Yet it was fascinating. Its linear form was based on the sea's edge, the beach and the long promenade. The Victorian cast-iron seating, shelters and piers were really beautiful – and the town's marvellous popular architecture included the Blackpool Tower, its ballroom, the Winter Gardens, and Joseph Emberton's modernist Casino at the Pleasure Beach. Years later,

in October 1983, when contributing a column for the *RIBA Journal*, I revisited Blackpool and wrote:

'Over the August Bank Holiday weekend, I visited my mother who retired to live near Blackpool some time ago. I have spent several summer holidays as a student working as barman and waiter on the piers and promenade, and I am always impressed at the scale of the influx of visitors . . . . The impressive and extensive illuminations had just begun, proving that even the most unpromising environment can be completely redesigned at night-time by artificial lighting; I have always thought that in our northern latitude new buildings should be designed for night-time as much as day time . . . .

'At the Pleasure Beach the ingenious close packing of the endless events onto the tight 40-acre site is quite extraordinary and adds to one's pleasure as at virtually any point things are whizzing over, under and around one in a kind of three-dimensional moving maze. The experiences are so architectural – the kinetic architecture in the drawings of Saint Elia and the Italian futurists and Mendelsohn capture some of the space and movement thrills that the populace get from a fun fair.'

19 Ashley Road, the family home at St Anne's on the Lancashire coast. My mother stands in the doorway.

Blackpool Tower was the basis for both a history study I did at the end of the sixth form and my final design thesis. And Lytham, a lovely planned small town, was the subject of a town-planning study I completed at university. Those places on the Fylde coast of Lancashire extended and enriched my experience of urban architecture and planning.

Designing for pleasure, leisure and fun, and handling the edge – the coastline with its changing weather and light, the linear water's edge with its delightful tramway and winter illuminations – all added to the repertoire of possibilities for other towns, other places I would come across in the future.

Right: The Moorish Pavilion Theatre on St Anne's pier in 1903 (top); St Anne's Square in 1963 (centre); and the windmill and lifeboat house on 'the Green' at Lytham in 1903 (bottom). These elements of pier, square and green each give strong visual and spatial identity to Lytham St Anne's as a place.

1956–62: COLLEGE

Undergraduate in Newcastle • Away from home but returning home • Travelling and learning • Discovering Buckminster Fuller, my design thesis and the dilemma of personal 'style' • Developing my interest in urban planning • **One year's office experience** • The move to London • Working in London: the LCC • Working in London: Stillman and Eastwick-Field

Undergraduate in Newcastle

Away from home but returning home

From 1956 to 1961, I studied architecture at the University of Newcastle (which at that time was King's College, part of Durham University). My parents had less than a year earlier moved to Blackpool, but I returned to my home town of Newcastle, living there away from my family. There was no break at the end of the third year as there is today; the course was simply five years straight through with a single degree examination at the end. After that, all that was needed to get the RIBA professional qualification was to complete one year's practical experience and pass an external RIBA exam.

The institutionalized life of a hall of residence did not appeal to me, so I sought a measure of independence. My first idea was to buy a caravan and live on a mobile home park in north Gosforth, several miles from the centre of Newcastle. I was entitled to a state student grant of £150 for living expenses, which — if I earned enough money during the 20 weeks' annual vacation to cover my costs — left £5 a week to live on during the 30 weeks of study. As I received the whole £150 in advance, I calculated that if I bought a caravan on hire purchase it would be the same as renting a room, and at the end of the five years I would have an asset — the caravan!

I eventually abandoned the idea since the mobile home site was too bleak and I didn't fancy the travel into Newcastle, but it did awaken in me an interest in temporary and 'miniaturized' houses — tightly designed living spaces, with every part folding away, doubling up and creating small worlds in themselves, reminding me of the campsites of my childhood. During my time as a student and in my early years of practice, my interest continued in this alternative home type — factory-made in one piece and according to totally separate rules from those governing the building of a conventional house.

The rules we follow can seem so proper and clear until we encounter another complete picture of the world with its own distinct rules, invariably invented to re-inforce a self-contained insular view that has lent itself to becoming institutionalized. My Catholic upbringing, I began to realize, was one example of this conditioned

mindset. Doubts about the rigid and stifling rules imposed by the Catholic Church and various Catholic schools had I attended took root at university, when I moved out of an all-Catholic environment and met people from other religions with very different interpretations of life. Something about having been claustrophobically immersed in an institutionalized world made me realize that all society's attempts to give structure and order to the architecture of our collective arrangements often end up being thwarted. Minimum health and safety standards might be thought to be universal for all human habitats, since the core entity, the human being, is constant, but the world of mobile homes permit size and general volumetric and safety standards that are astonishingly different from those allowed by the building by-laws applying to permanent housing in bricks and mortar. Houseboats, caravans, ocean liners and sleeper trains each have standards applying to bedrooms, bathrooms, staircases and lighting that are set out and separately governed by different bodies acting with sublime indifference to each other.

At an early age I concluded that there was nothing sacrosanct about rules – a view reinforced over the years by observing the sweeping changes and variations made to town planning laws and requirements, and the radical alterations (sometimes for the better and sometimes not) to environmental regulations. Building health and safety standards are now so excessively restrictive that often more attention is paid to the legal consequences of any breach than to the original intention of keeping people safe. As with religion, transgressions of the rules, error and sin itself can become for the 'officials' more engrossing than the original higher-minded intentions. And, of course, the ultimate irony is that the Catholic Church confronted diminishing church attendance by relaxing its more difficult rules and eliminating the Latin language to popularize itself – the stiff, inhibiting rules that governed so much of my childhood were not that meaningful after all.

At the same time as I was looking for a caravan, I was designing my first building – an unforgettable experience for any student of architecture. We had been asked to design a weekend house or hut in a remote place where there were only indigenous ready-to-hand materials, no tools and only two lengths and sizes of timber. The 'house' had to be in the northern tradition – like the stone 'but and ben' (a primitive Scottish holiday hut) that Dudley D. Watkins, the *Beano* and *Dandy* cartoonist, drew in his

'Oor Wullie' and 'The Broons' comic strips (in the Glasgow *Sunday Post*, which was available in Newcastle), or like the wooden chalet in Cheshire that my grandparents built themselves from components. I wanted to make my design as 'realistic' as possible, and to make the construction simple and direct in labour and construction terms, with standardized repetitive components.

I was reminded of the fundamental primitive appeal of this project in 1997, when I came across an exhibit in a Connecticut museum that told the story of European immigrants who moved the short distance from New York over the Appalachian mountains to the source of the Ohio river, which flowed from there through virtually the whole USA, joining the Mississippi–Missouri complex and eventually the Caribbean Sea. They built standardized component rafts to a predetermined pattern that, on arrival at their final destination (usually along the Ohio), could be reassembled – like children's transformer toys – into homes: all the elements of riverworthy vessels became by clever design the permanent walls and roofs of buildings. What an adventure and what a piece of design! Complete family units – mobile homes on water, along with pets, farm animals and financial savings – sailed for months on those rafts to find a new life, avoiding rapids and marauding Indians. In retrospect, they made us European students in Newcastle designing weekend houses seem a long way from being 'realistic' – a long way from real need, real life and really ingenious temporary-home design.

After arriving at Newcastle, I lived with a Polish family who came to Britain as wartime refugees from Crakow. The house was in Sandyford Road and my first-floor bedsit faced Jesmond cemetery with its fine John Dobson gatehouses. The English 19th-century terraced house was universally a carefully planned, well-built affair – although I subsequently found that London developers did not build anything like as well as those in the north. The Sandyford Road houses, like many in Jesmond, Heaton and Gosforth, were of fine quality brick with stone detailing and slate roofs. Not for them the bodged construction hidden behind layers of forgiving stucco that made a London house; yet, as in London, they had a 19th-century plan form found throughout a large part of the British Isles. The finest room was invariably the grand front room on the first floor, and that is where I lived for four years, with a gas ring and a small sink, sharing the bathroom on the half-landing with Bart and Louise Lachecki and their children.

The first project in my
second year at university,
1957, was to design a
shop to sell Swedish
plates, knives and forks
and other manufactured
goods. It was a useful
lesson in how to respond
to Scandinavian taste. All
the illustrations shown
here are in watercolour,
using techniques I had
learned from painting
landscapes at school.

The growth of Newcastle University (highlighted in yellow). The illustrations are dated (from top): *c*. 1878 – the founding of Armstrong College; 1913 – the construction of the School of Architecture and the School of Art; 1938 – as it was when I was there, after the addition of the union building; 2003 – the university as it is today, vastly expanded and, together with Northumbria University, Newcastle's largest employer. These drawings are from our 2003 masterplan report.

The room cost £1 per week and was only ten minutes' walk from the Haymarket and the King's College campus. This set up a tightly knit small world for me, with no commuting. I would walk down Sandyford Road, past the Catholic chaplaincy – where we all, Catholic and non-Catholic, played table tennis for hours – across the road next to Dobson's great church of St Thomas at Barras Bridge, up King's Walk, past the Union building, through the arches and into the quadrangle where the School of Architecture stood: all more or less as it is today, nearly 50 years later. The Victorian 'Gothic' character of the buildings deliberately and knowingly recalled the external dress of a medieval Oxbridge college. The best bit of the entire stone-and-brick and ensemble is the much more recent quadrangle designed by J.S. Allen in 1947–49.

Now I am masterplanning this very campus for the university, with ambitions to open it up to the city. It has grown from 3,200 students when I was there in the late 1950s to 16,000 today and, together with the University of Northumbria on the other side of the Haymarket, is by far the biggest employer in Newcastle. Being a student then was for the minority, and education was seen as a non-productive occupation for privileged youth; now, education is probably the world's largest industry.

Allen's stunning simple quadrangle was (and still is) the *genus loci* of the university. With an arched gateway at each end, it is enclosed by the School of Architecture, the Armstrong Engineering Building and the Art School where Richard Hamilton, Victor Pasmore and Kenneth Rowntree, among others, taught during my university days. Beyond the eastern end is the Union building, where I ate, met girls, and went to jazz dances on Friday and Saturday nights; at the western end is the giant Royal Victoria Infirmary (where I went for physiotherapy after I broke my leg in second year). It was those medical and engineering departments that formed the 19th-century college that by the late 20th century became a major university building.

The campus has a great contribution to make to the city, primarily because of its central location and the compact quality of the buildings and quadrangle at its heart. Good traditional urban planning and straightforward architecture offers a much more valuable resource than that offered by the self-conscious 'statement' university architecture of the postwar British modernists and the greenfield universities. In the 1950s and 1960s, there was a lot of new architecture at universities, much of it challengingly avant-garde – often involving untried and untested construction techniques that sometimes failed – or self-consciously 'radical' in appearance, offering too much design and too little humanity, particularly when compared with contemporary Scandinavian educational architecture. For us students, the new architecture, although innovatory and exciting, was invariably characterized by stand-alone objects plonked in the centre of sites with little or no regard to the spaces around – as urban design, they usually failed.

During my first year at Newcastle I bought a motorbike – a 350cc 1946 BSA – for £18, on a three-year hire-purchase agreement. I reckoned it would pay for itself by saving the expense of long-distance coach fares to and from Blackpool at vacation times. I always went home for the long summers because Blackpool in the holiday season was just the place for good student jobs – I worked as a barman on the piers, in the tower ballroom and in the holiday camps (wonderful seasonal cities in miniature with their dormitory cabins converted from wartime army camps). But towards the end of the second year, when I was on my way back from Blackpool at Easter, a lorry driver crossed my path without looking and I ended up in Durham County hospital with a badly broken leg and a written-off motorbike. I spent four weeks lying in hospital looking over rooftops at one of Britain's finest urban views – Durham cathedral and castle set within a tight bend of the River Wear.

With the help of my father and local solicitors in Lytham St Anne's, I extracted the 'enormous' sum of £175 compensation from the lorry haulage company. This enabled me to put down a deposit on a small stone terraced house, two up and two down, in the village of Ryton in County Durham. Since I was under 21 and not old enough to have a mortgage, my father, a bit reluctantly, signed a guarantee. The loan was repaid by letting rooms to other students. I was now in the property business and had real independence. As my father had done so often in my childhood, I 'did up' the house in Ryton. I bought it for £950 and sold it two years later, when I had graduated, for £1,200 – a heady entrepreneurial undertaking that I repeated several times to make ends meet as my career and family grew.

Ryton was set either side of the Gateshead–Hexham road on the south bank of the River Tyne – matching a group of villages on the north bank linking Newcastle and Hexham. Like so many rural places in north-east England, it was essentially an agricultural settlement that had become an industrial and coal-mining community yet remained surrounded by beautiful countryside. The tiny terraced houses, the village and others like it were the inspiration for my very first urban design project, which I undertook in the fourth year (see pages 174–75).

Travelling and learning

My first trip to a foreign place was to Paris in 1957, at the end of my first year at Newcastle. My grandfather had fought in France in the First World War and received the Distinguished Conduct Medal for bravery in the trenches. My own parents had at that time never been abroad (except to Ireland). I remember challenging my French teacher over my poor grasp of the basics of the French language in first form at grammar school – as an 11-year-old, I thought even London was a foreign country and, as I said then, why learn French when I was never likely to travel to such a far-off place? Personal constructs of 'foreignness' and distance change with age, and so at 19 I went by train and boat to Paris.

The evidently superior urban 'lifestyle' of the French (with outdoor cafés, glamorous, creative shop-window displays and active street life) was, I assumed at the time, based on the fact that they were better off and living in a warmer climate than Britain's. It was some years before I realized that neither was the case; the contrast was due to cultural differences affecting how the respective countries developed urban placemaking. The French were and are more committed to urban life, and more care, energy and particularly money went into making sure that urban living was rewarding in every sense – it was a priority they have always had. Also, Paris, I later realized, is not significantly warmer than London. Its apparent warmth is more to do with a nation whose boundaries (and culture) reach down south to include those who live in a Mediterranean climate. Paris is a northern city in a southern-climate-orientated nation. London is the reverse – a southern city in a northern-climate-orientated nation. Perception, prevailing attitude and culture account for so much when explaining differences between places. In Paris, thanks to Baron Haussmann and others, the wide streets and very wide pavements, and the high-density living above and around, all make possible a very active outdoor urban life. Only by travelling and comparing do we begin to understand better the familiar 'home' places we have always known and taken for granted.

Our little house in Ryton, Co. Durham, where I lived during my fourth and fifth years at Newcastle. The lower picture is a view of the house in its terrace, Tweedies Villas, which I used in a fourth-year project as an urban-design precedent.

Observations on the use of colour in Scandinavian architecture – a part of my travel scholarship studies in 1959.

Personal photos, 1959

Top and centre: Courtyard housing by Scandinavian architect Jørn Utzon, who was an important influence on my work — on housing – particularly courtyard housing, which has led to many subsequent schemes right up to 2003.

Above: Rosemarie and I in 1959, shortly before we set off for a trip round northern Europe in our BMW Izetta bubble car.

Travel became an increasingly intense need during my first years at university, probably because much of my inspiration came not from the School of Architecture or the teachers but from the library, which revealed to me what was being built in the wider world, particularly in Scandinavia and the USA. I spent a large amount of time in the library looking at architectural magazines and books, the work of Le Corbusier, Frank Lloyd Wright, Charles and Ray Eames, and so many others.

As a child, I had been fascinated by collectors' books and museums such as the Hancock Museum in Newcastle, an extraordinary collection of stuffed birds. I liked the completeness involved in a collection, and at architecture school I was attracted by the Victorian collector's mentality that Banister Fletcher typified in *A History of Architecture by the Comparative Method for Students, Craftsmen and Amateurs* (1896) – a great book for all periods and styles of architecture. Another book I really enjoyed was *The Grammar of Ornament* (1856) by Owen Jones, a collection of historical drawings of decoration through the ages.

Collecting, juxtaposing and comparing is linked to travel and an open curiosity about all things; once collected, the sifting and comparing establishes patterns and relationships among diverse and hitherto strange and disconnected man-made objects. Thematic observation and collecting is a vital tool for the urbanist. Elements of buildings and parts of cities benefit from comparison. My own collections began in boyhood with fish, trees and birds, then my curiosity moved on to student travel experiences involving subjects ranging from chairs to barns, from squares in American cities to pedestrian movement. It continues in my later professional career as a basis for understanding how different cities look at common problems such as traffic congestion, conservation and pollution, and how some building types, from libraries to airports to shopping centres, are becoming universally adapted to regional locations. The books of Banister Fletcher and Owen Jones – the underlying comparative methodology reflecting the growing global awareness of the Victorians – were for me a personal inspiration for a working method that was intuitive and visual: a kind of artistic equivalent of today's opinion polls and social surveys.

From the belvedere viewpoint of the library on the top floor of Newcastle's architecture school, I began my virtual travels to the buildings of Erik Gunnar Asplund

This page and opposite: My first use of photography to record travel experiences, these pictures show a range of traditional and modern buildings that I saw in Denmark, Sweden and Norway during my trip of 1959 with Rosemarie.

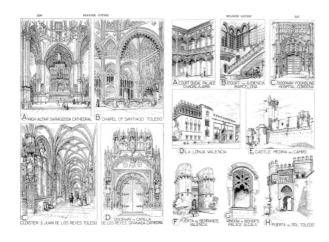

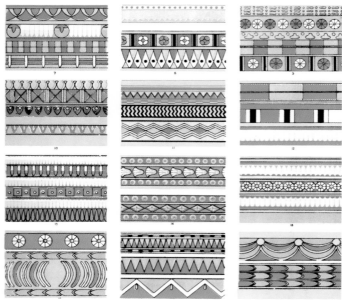

Above left and top left: Displays at the Hancock Museum in Newcastle were based on the collection of a well-known local taxidermist; they were established from material that was returned to the city after the Great Exhibition of 1851.

Above right and top right: Banister Fletcher's *A History of Architecture by the Comparative Method* (top) and Owen Jones's *The Grammar of Ornament* were two books that began my interest in thematic collecting and study.

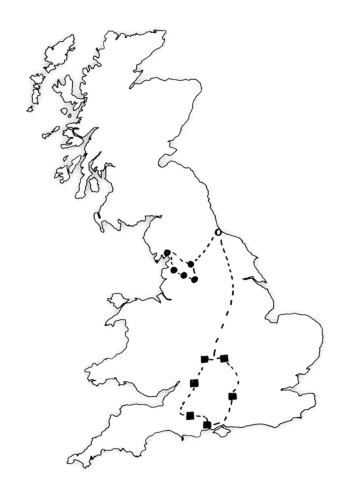

Right: In 1958 I toured northern England to study chairs and two years later toured south-west England to study barns. My routes are shown on the map.

Above and top: Two of the chairs I studied during my tour of 1958.

Below: Five of the great houses in which I found the chairs. They are (from left to right): Browsholme Hall, Holker Hall, Lytham Hall, Hall i' th' Wood and Samlesbury Hall.

in Sweden, Arne Jacobsen in Denmark, Craig Ellwood in California, and Frank Lloyd Wright in Chicago and Arizona. I also learned in parallel how the grand tour had inspired the British 200 years ago, and how in the early years of the 19th century Charles Monck had returned from his honeymoon in Greece to build one of the world's great neoclassical houses, Belsay Hall in Northumberland. What Monck brought back from his honeymoon spread and spread to become an entire urban ensemble when John Dobson, who had worked on Monck's home as a young man, went on, with his new employer Thomas Grainger, to develop Newcastle into a glorious reinterpreted classical city.

Actual travel needs two things: the desire and the means. The library created the first and travel scholarships did a lot to provide the second. I and my wife-to-be, Rosemarie – a wonderful partner in this and so much else – began our travels in a BMW Isetta bubble car partly financed by Rosemarie's mother. We travelled together around the north of England (studying chairs), the south of England (barns) and northern Europe (colour in architecture), all thanks to end-of-year student prizes and scholarships that I had targeted and won. (I felt some companionship in this drive when, some years later, I discovered that the great Sir John Soane had financed his grand tour of Italy 1778/80 from Royal Academy travelling scholarships.)

Touring Scandinavia in the bubble car and camping out each night gave me the opportunity to see not only great buildings by Asplund and Jacobsen but also more great cities – Copenhagen, Oslo and Stockholm. In Denmark and Norway we visited invented towns reassembled from historic traditional buildings – as the Americans had done at Williamsburg and Clough Williams-Ellis at Portmeirion in Wales. I saw these as collectors' towns, like pages from Banister Fletcher but built out in three-dimensional reality. Visiting the new towns around Stockholm, I drew and I painted buildings and districts. The pine trees and fjords offered a landscape that softened the modernist architecture and tempered its newness – whole new towns were more convincing as instant places than anything we were building in the UK. I saw how well modern architecture worked in this context. There was a lightness, freshness and optimistic humanism particularly in colour and construction techniques (which I also represented in some detail in my drawings) that English schemes, obsessed by the expressive use of coarsegrained in situ and precast concrete, did not remotely achieve. The late 1950s and early 1960s was the era of 'kitchen sink' drama in theatres and cinemas, brutalist architecture and 'warts and all' painters like John Bratby.

A decade or more of British public housing, shopping schemes and universities would have to be endured before the lightness and humanity so optimistically expressed at the Festival of Britain was rediscovered (firstly, I believe, by high-tech architects). A whole generation of brutalists and precast-concrete mass-housing specialists stood between the Skylon and Dome of Discovery and the work of Foster, Rogers and Farrell/Grimshaw. The Scandinavian architecture I saw was carefully considered and socially responsible without being bombastically exaggerated in style, and without the kind of anxious attention-seeking 'artistry' or earnest, joyless paternalism that characterized British architecture in the early years of the welfare state. That tour of Scandinavia sustained my belief in modern architecture for many years to come.

Part of what I love about travelling is the feeling of being a curious nomad. I like to use the word 'nomad' as a metaphor for life: we all travel through the ages in which we live, from childhood to old age. Throughout history, people have travelled for inspiration that they can transfer to their own time and place: Mesopotamia came to Egypt, the Egyptians influenced the Minoans, the Minoans influenced the Greeks. The British brought back Rome from the Grand Tour, and Frank Lloyd Wright was influenced by travels to Japan. To travel means to transfer knowledge from place to place.

Places are universal phenomena, yet fixed, so you have to move – you actually have to get up and go there – to see them. Travel has become, with education, a colossal world industry. The greatest places attract the most people, and it is always the buildings and streets – the 'free' sights – that people bring back from their travels in their minds and hearts. Apart from learning the architectural lessons from ancient Greece and Rome, gradually we have discovered the less tangible everyday pleasures of life, like eating foods from different countries, and over the years urban districts in Britain have established within them coffee shops modelled on those in the New World, bistros derived from bohemian Paris, and Greek and Spanish restaurants from package holidays. There are in fact entire districts that various immigrant nationalities have made their own in their adopted home cities. In the late 1960s, the Farrell/Grimshaw office in London was in the middle of London's version of 'Greece', represented by the restaurants in Windmill Street and Charlotte Street. The kebabs, ouzo and baklava, the Greek tailors and tradesmen created an

unofficial bit of elsewhere to remind us of the essential foreignness of London the immigrant city. And this kind of colonization of a district has happened in reverse in places like Greece and southern Spain, where masses of holidaymaking Britons have created streets full of 'Great Britain'. There, Englishness is mimicked to the point of parody, with Tudoresque pubs and restaurants where you can find 'English breakfasts served all day'.

One of the preoccupations of this book is the relationship between the nomad, travelling and the fixed place – how, when we travel, through history and different countries, we take particular times and places and bring them to the here and now. One of the purposes of travel is to bring something back, whether souvenirs, photographs or just memories, so that our sense of our own place evolves and changes.

Discovering Buckminster Fuller, my design thesis and the dilemma of personal 'style'

From the beginning, I pondered and agonized about the virtues of developing a personal style as against responding to context and what other people wanted. Potentially, there were genuine conflicts arising from these contradictory goals – for example, would the building or creation be 'mine' or 'theirs'? If I were to respond responsibly, would personal style have to come second? Could I apply my personal aesthetic values in every circumstance, and still celebrate and incorporate different approaches that could be a joy for everyone, including the designer? What I learned from my days in the library, looking at the increasingly extensive publication of works by all the great architects, increased the dilemma. The regional insularity that had helped John Dobson and even Frank Lloyd Wright was no longer available to my generation, for whom increasing knowledge and awareness made for an ever more difficult platform from which to develop and exercise choice.

As I experimented with furniture, interiors, architecture and urban design, and then read and travelled, I moved away from the standard educational approach prevalent in architecture at the time whereby pre-selected systematized shapes, colours and forms were brought to each project. Architecture schools, I observed, invariably rewarded students who were consistent at the same time as learning to be selectively different by developing a recognizable 'brand'. In recent times, much has been made of the benefits of branding in larger and larger marketplaces, where being noticed means exaggerating

These drawings of a home for a musician in Highgate, north London, were part of a third-year project at Newcastle in 1958. It had similarities with the Swedish shop (see page 38) but the influence of Craig Ellwood, Charles Eames and Mies van der Rohe was more obvious. Special features included a lightweight steel frame and the use of fabric with tension wires for diagonal support.

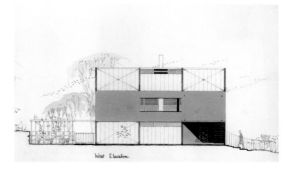

West Elevation.

South Elevation.

the differences between you and your competitors – even if this means a degree of self-caricature or even manufactured character invention.

I enjoyed the work of architects and artists whose personal style was more fluid, sensitive and flexible. I began deliberately to experiment with designing in the manner of one architect then in the manner of another, to see how the various styles felt and whether any suited me. My choices were, on reflection, removed from the European French/German mainstream: Scandinavian architects such as Jørn Utzon and Arne Jacobsen, and West Coast Americans such as Craig Ellwood and Richard Neutra. American Midwesterners particularly appealed to me; their robust individualism helped to develop idiosyncratic, indigenous regional characters such as Herb Green and Bruce Goff, but also giants of individuality and independence such as Buckminster Fuller and Frank Lloyd Wright.

Having spent some years in the late 1960s and 1970s teaching at the Architectural Association (AA), I noticed how much more conventionally 'successful' those students were who never changed and whose work had been deliberately branded from their early years. To some extent, Newcastle's comparative isolation had spared me from that pressure, and I played with and adopted different influences. Above all, I absorbed the work of Frank Lloyd Wright. It varied hugely during his career – from 1890s Chicago Arts and Crafts, to 1920s art deco in Los Angeles and Buffalo, to 1930s 'streamline' modern in the Johnson Wax Factory in Racine, Wisconsin, to almost 1950s Disneyesque at Main County, San Francisco.

One of the dilemmas of our times centres on style. Assiduously following one style is so easy, and the result is readily communicable but can also be superficial. But Frank Lloyd Wright absorbed style, made it his own,

Three great houses of Northumberland that I visited during my architectural course: Lord Armstrong's Cragside (below left), designed by Richard Norman Shaw, was the first house in the world to be lit by hydroelectricity; Seaton Delaval Hall (below) was the work of John Vanbrugh; Belsay Hall (bottom) was created by amateur scholar Charles Monck, assisted by the architect John Dobson.

Harry Faulkner-Brown, my final-year tutor at Newcastle, photographed shortly after his return from Canada (1959/60).

A still from Charles Eames's influential film of 1977, *The Powers of Ten*, which dramatizes scale differences and their interrelationships. In all town-planning projects I like to see the very big and very small picture – using, as Eames did, the telescope and microscope alternately.

played with it and thereby rose above it. The appearance of an object is a dress code, a club membership, an abstract sense of place which says, 'I belong here in a group that sees things in a particular way.' Place, I realized more and more, was not just a physical thing; it was cultural and stylistic, and the independent-minded Wright saw this – indeed, saw through it – and used it.

In contrast with the practice at many other schools of architecture, little of our design work at Newcastle was presented verbally. As a result, the drawings we submitted were everything. I experimented widely with different presentation and rendering techniques, trying watercolour and poster colour, line drawings, white-on-black reversals, and so on. I also became fascinated by architectural models. I used them particularly to study and explain three-dimensional structures.

In retrospect, art and the visual side of design were everything to me then. But a radical sea change occurred in my final year, when scientific methodology took over with the advent of a new head of school, Jack Napper. In the 1960s most schools adopted the so-called scientific route. Later, when teaching at the Bartlett School of Architecture in London between 1969 and 1971, I often said that this trend would have prevented me from becoming an architect since I would not even have had the qualifications for entry to the Bartlett, which included A-level maths and physics. I had been no good at maths, and I recall how my school friend Bill Stonor generously put aside time to coach me in structural calculations; without him, I would not have got beyond fourth year at architectural school. However, as I gradually discovered D'Arcy Thompson and Buckminster Fuller, I began to realize that there were patterns connecting shape, geometry and numbers – making an architecture of numbers. After this leap of insight (long after I had given up maths at school), I went forward with much more enthusiasm and confidence. It was the enforced mechanical teaching of the subject and its abstraction that had discouraged and diverted me from maths. I would still say today to any parent, teacher or student that the only subject that should be mandatory for entry to architecture school is art – and that skill in maths is no more useful than skill in any other subject.

I had always been interested in all things American, and when my fourth-year tutor, Harry Booton, saw me reading about Frei Otto in the library, he suggested that I look into the work of Buckminster Fuller, the American

designer best known for his development of the geodesic dome. I showed the books and my drawings to Harry Faulkner-Brown, my final-year tutor, who had recently returned from Canada. He encouraged me to design a dome, and apply my interest in Fuller to my design thesis. Years later, in 1968, when Buckminster Fuller came to London, I met him and drove him around London to various schools and exhibitions. I remember in particular driving him from his hotel and back in my old Sunbeam Rapier to the 1968 'sit-in' by the rebellious students at Hornsey School of Art, where Fuller spoke for over three hours. Along with Louis Kahn, he was the most inspirational of architectural teachers. What I learned from books on Bucky Fuller in 1960–61 was, I believe, well ahead of what preoccupied other British students and British architects generally at that time, even those who became leaders of what was known across the world as British 'high-tech'. The models I built for my student thesis were a deliberate attempt to explore Fuller's inventive engineering ideas in architectural form.

At Newcastle I worked more or less independently of the tutors until the final year with Harry Faulkner-Brown. He was a strong leader and a good teacher with an impressive war record – not unlike my art teacher at school, Maurice McPartlan. He had a broad viewpoint and a can-do attitude and personality. Although many of the tutors at Newcastle were practising as well as teaching, they weren't building much more than house extensions. But on Harry's return from working for several years in Canada, he set up an architectural office and was soon doing well. He would talk animatedly about North America and Canada and what he had done there. It was another world compared with that of the local architects I had met at Newcastle, who wore corduroy trousers and bow ties, and lived the lives of gentleman teachers without a great deal of fire in them.

When Harry knew I was interested in Buckminster Fuller he asked me which books I had read and suggested others, and he introduced me to practising engineers who could help me with the reality of my thesis. He was a great facilitator, as a really good teacher should be. Keen to broaden the perspective of his fifth-year students, Harry took us to London for a week. He showed us Millbank Tower, then under construction, and organized a visit to the Higgs & Hill builders' yard so we could see how contractors worked. We also saw the newly completed Barbican and Sanderson's headquarters on Berners Street, now a fine Philippe Starck hotel. I particularly remember that, on our last night in London, we went for a drink in a pub somewhere near Charlotte Street and then went to the nearby Architectural Association building and pissed on the door – a kind of marking of territory by us Newcastle students. I could never have guessed then that five years later I would be teaching there and the AA would have become my adopted educational home.

Over the years my fascination with scale difference was influenced by both Buckminster Fuller and later on by Charles Eames's film *The Powers of Ten* (1977), which presented a world view characterized by extremes of scale. I love ranging from the very largest outer-space scale to the micro scale, and in every planning project I always try to see the very big picture and the very small picture, using the telescope and the microscope alternately. Buckminster Fuller took city planning into a realm of scale that was quite distinct from anything mankind had ever envisaged: Le Corbusier might have conceived of the Ville Radieuse, but Fuller put a dome over the whole of New York! Fuller also made propositions on the micro scale, demonstrating, for example, that one could wash thoroughly all over in a quarter-pint of water providing it was propelled forcefully and in very fine, minute spray particles – making the bathtub, conventional shower and even the bathroom redundant.

It was Bucky's work that influenced my final-year design thesis on the Climatron, a high-tech, dome-covered holiday island connected by a pier to the base of Blackpool Tower. I wanted to reclarify the tower's urban and iconic importance by creating a public open square around its base, and I was intent on resolving the problem of building congestion that obscured the foot of the tower. I devised a railway that took visitors between the tower's legs and along the pier out to sea to the Climatron island. All the activities that had traditionally taken place in the complex of buildings that had hidden the lower part of the tower were moved to the holiday island, and the complex was cleared. To me, this was first and foremost a town-planning and conservation project in which architecture followed afterwards.

Blackpool was, of course, a highly seasonal holiday resort. The 'front' with its piers, Golden Mile and Pleasure Beach was used in summer only. It was aspirationally based on a Mediterranean-climate town plan –

taking a holiday in Blackpool transported you, it was hoped, to some happier, sunnier land. Yet the notion of outdoors and beaches was often a fantasy, since visitors were threatened by westerly winds and rain, and from that threat grew up the great Victorian indoor palaces where everyone retreated – the Winter Gardens (several acres of glass-roofed arcades) and the tower (with its collection of zoos, aquariums and ballrooms).

The Climatron, a building out at sea but connected by a pier to the foot of Blackpool Tower, was the subject of my university thesis in 1960–61.

The tower defines Blackpool as a place. Municipal leaders whose business is to promote and market their town or city have invariably recognized the importance of having a clear, physical visible icon. The Tyne Bridge in Newcastle, Sydney Opera House, the Eiffel Tower in Paris, and in recent times the Guggenheim museum in Bilbao, all serve this purpose: they are the singular faces of their cities. The Blackpool Tower, opened in 1894, brought together two new 19th-century technological phenomena: steel construction and electrical power in the form of lifts. The advent of mass holiday-taking in northern Britain (born of a workplace revolution that standardized the holiday break in a week called 'Wakes Week') – gave more and more people the chance to be enthralled by the technological achievements of their age. Such a sense of wonder is a long-established part of the British character – perhaps because the sheer chaos and social misery of inventing the Industrial Revolution polarized perceptions. Everyday life seemed, even until very recently, incapable of much change in qualitative terms, so symbolic techno-supremacy gestures restored a sense of direction and purpose. The Eiffel Tower and the Pompidou Centre were more than 100 years apart in construction, but the two have the same roots in that they celebrate techno novelty, a fascination with steel and electricity, and the modern wonders of moving people mechanically by means of lifts and escalators.

One thing that links Lytham, Blackpool and the Tyne Quayside is that they are all great edges. To me, there is a special beauty about edges, such as those found at a river bank, and I am fascinated by the energy derived from artificially contrived ones – created by wide boulevards, for example, or where a park meets urban sprawl. New York's Central Park is extraordinary for its edges: it's as if a piece of the urban structure had been removed en bloc, revealing inner organs that would never normally be seen. We don't see the city's street blocks unless we come to one of its edges. We don't know what is in the centre of the grain

The Crystal Palace was a lasting inspiration to me during my time as an architectural student. It was at a second-hand bookshop in Blackpool in my first year that my admiration for one of the greatest of innovatory buildings began.

This fourth-year project, undertaken in 1959, involved the design for a 15-storey block of flats. I particularly enjoyed playing with the three-dimensional interlocking of the living spaces. As usual I was experimenting again with graphic and presentational techniques.

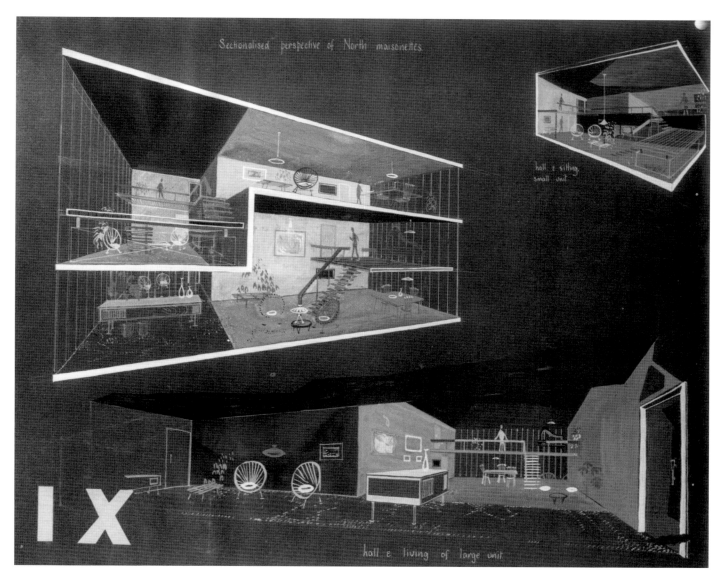

Sectionalised perspective of North maisonettes

hall & sitting, small unit

IX

hall & living of large unit

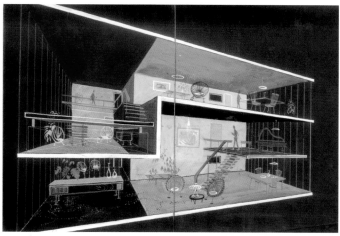

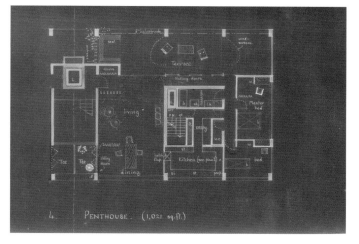

4. PENTHOUSE. (1,021 sq.ft.)

until we can stand back from it. A seaside promenade is all about the edge, and Blackpool is the stereotypical linear town: stretching along the coast for several miles, its promenade is the *genus loci* of the town.

Islands − another important element of my Climatron thesis − also have a powerful appeal, a romantic one, particularly because they touch something fundamental in us all; we can immediately 'belong'. There is no ambiguity of place on an island − which is also a limitation, of course. Great sprawling cities provide the chance encounters that stimulate change and cultural growth, while islands isolate. On several camping holidays at Lindisfarne off the Northumberland coast, I discovered the island's deep sense of place, inseparable from its unique history. Lindisfarne, also known as Holy Island, was where the light still burned in the Dark Ages, where learning continued and glorious illuminated manuscripts were created, which would eventually serve as a means to pass on the ancient world to southern Britain and the rest of Europe. Lindisfarne is remote, bleak and beautiful, with coarse grass and sand dunes. Inaccessible at high tide, it has a wonderful castle imaginatively adapted into a private house by Edwin Lutyens in the 20th century. Lindisfarne and Mont-St-Michel in Brittany are both sea-land phenomena with linear tidal-path links that dramatically exaggerate their isolation.

So my final-year thesis combined these elements: the long edge of Blackpool's promenade, the town's iconic focal point of the Tower, and a new offshore island with a pier connection that intersected with and interrupted the linearity of the town's plan. The Climatron was also a formal sculptural contrast to the tower − a smooth and rounded dome facing an energetic vertical point.

Five years of study at the School of Architecture culminated in presentations and interviews. In its scale and ambition, the final project was the crowning achievement of the journey from weekend hut to complex buildings and town planning − a journey of gradual learning and attainment. We all left feeling masters of the larger complexities of architecture − and most of us then faced a scale reversal, becoming juniors who did small-scale work and helped with details. School was, and still can be, an illusory experience for architectural students. We had gone through the full range of motions in a kind of long-drawn-out rehearsal for designing a building, but none of us had ever dealt seriously with the real thing.

Blackpool interiors: the Empress Ballroom at the Winter Gardens (top); the aquarium at the foot of the tower (above); and my proposal for a new aquarium within the Climatron (right).

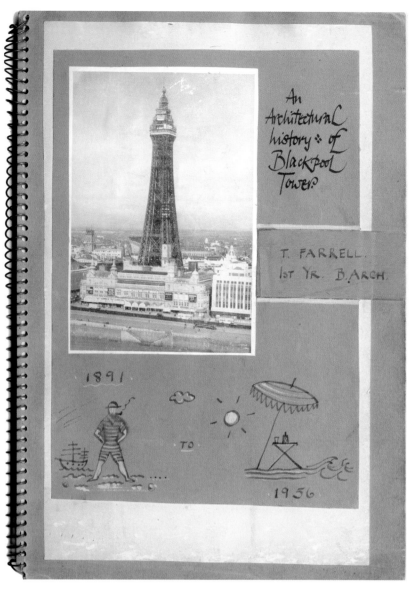

An Architectural history of Blackpool Tower

T. FARRELL. 1st Yr. B.ARCH.

1891 TO 1956

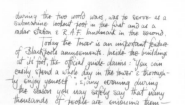

during the two world wars, was to serve as a submarine lookout post in the first and as a radar station & R.A.F. landmark in the second.

Today the Tower is an important feature of Blackpool's amusements. Inside the buildings at it's foot, the official guide claims: "You can easily spend a whole day in the tower & thoroughly enjoy yourself ; & any evening during the season you may safely say that many thousands of people are enjoying themselves between these walls."

It is one of the main centres of attraction of Blackpool today & most people make a point of ascending the tower during their holiday. The lift often travels over sixty miles a day, carrying 14,000 people in twelve hours. At the 380 foot level there are shops for souvenir hunters & a post office where mail is post marked "Tower Top."

Perhaps this is the reason for Blackpool Tower's drawbacks: it was built to as an advertisement, it's purpose is to give people a "thrill" of being higher than any other building in England, beauty of design was a minor consideration.

3. The Structure of the Tower.

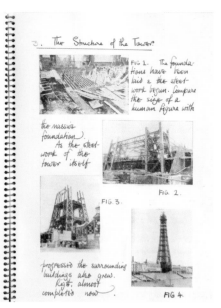

FIG 1. The foundations have been laid & the steel work begun. Compare the size of a human figure with the massive foundation.

As the steel work of the tower itself progressed the surrounding buildings also grew. Right, almost completed now.

FIG. 2.

FIG. 3.

FIG 4.

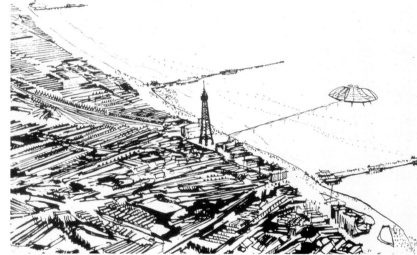

I began and ended my five-year course with the same building. The first two illustrations (above left and top right) show my first-year history study of the Blackpool Tower. The drawing from my final-year design thesis (above), shows how I proposed removing the buildings around the base of the tower and adding a new public piazza; the replacement accommodation in a Climatron island would be reached by a railway running within a new pier.

Left: Blackpool in 1946, seen from the air.

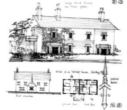

Drawings from a final-
year written dissertation
on Lytham St Anne's,
my first investigational
analysis of town planning.

Killingworth New Town: the award-winning head office of Northern Gas, just outside Newcastle, was designed by Ryder and Yates while I was at Newcastle and built after I had left. They were the only radical modernist architects in the North East at that time and were every bit as much our local heroes then as John Dobson was in his time.

Historical Killingworth: Stephenson's *Rocket* and the cottage where he lived. George Stephenson was the resident mining engineer at Killingworth in the early 19th century; his experiments with the invention of railway lines and sleepers were uncovered during the building of Killingworth New Town.

Developing my interest in urban planning

While my own experience of architectural mentors was positive and plentiful, from the beginning of my studies at Newcastle I felt ambivalent about the role of the contemporary architect–planner, particularly in England. I enjoyed much of the revolutionary, anti-conformist modernism that was prevalent in contemporary architecture, but unfortunately, in England, Le Corbusier's town-planning followers were more than followers of style. They introduced radical ideas of social engineering to the postwar welfare-state spirit and began decades of mistakes and destruction.

Immediately after the end of the war and the election of the Labour government, planners advocated wholesale demolition to put an end to slums at a stroke and to create land for new housing. Whole areas of towns and cities were proposed for clearance, seemingly without much reference to the people who lived there or the quality of the buildings that would vanish. In the 1950s, another battalion of zealots arrived on the scene, whose ardent enthusiasm for the motor car led to traffic planners cutting swathes through cities for new ring roads and motorways. Both these town-planning thrusts were inspired partly by the philosophical idealism of Le Corbusier's *Plan Voisin* – which cleared the historical centre of Paris for new tower blocks and roads – and partly by an exaggeration of the causes of the housing shortage and traffic congestion.

After my first three years at Newcastle, my interest in urban design and planning grew in response to the larger-scale projects set at the school. I began to explore alternatives to the prevailing mood of desperation and demolition – and, having seen what was happening in Scandinavian housing, to look for an urbanism that was modern but closer to tradition.

In the fourth year, when I had moved out of Newcastle to live in the village of Ryton, we were given a project to design a new village. I chose to explore marrying precast-concrete technology with traditional terraced housing and traditional village layouts. For me, this project combined the universal and the familiar, and involved working from the outside in as well as the inside out. Experience of living on the Grange Estate had convinced me that large-scale experimental new planning could cause dislocation, disorientation and lack of continuity, and I felt strongly that placemaking on a large scale had to be grounded in the familiar.

For my final-year written dissertation, I decided to study the small Lancashire town of Lytham, where my parents then lived – a town deliberately planned and managed for over a hundred years. The simple principles of Lytham's plan have always been something of a touchstone for me. The main street – the microclimatic heart of the town – is one block inland from the sea's edge, as is the case with Lord Street in Southport, whose lights can be seen across the Ribble estuary from Lytham. (I have read that Lord Street inspired Haussmann, who once visited Southport, to go back and build wide, handsome streets in Paris.) Years later, when working on areas bordering the Thames in central London, I revisited this lesson in planning for the microclimate, with the Strand to the north and Belvedere Road to the south, both one urban block back from the exposed weather conditions of the river.

After graduating, and not long before leaving Newcastle for my year's practical experience in London, I went to see Roy Gazzard, the architectural head of Killingworth New Town, just outside Newcastle. I was astonished to find that he had ingeniously created an instant place by building a lake as the focus of the new town. At a stroke, his entrepreneurial vision had done with landscape what architecture and buildings would have struggled for a long time to do on their own. Gazzard also showed me the remains of 19th-century railway experiments at Killingworth – probably conducted by George Stephenson – that had been dug up during construction of the new town. Early in the 19th century, Stephenson had been the resident engineer at High Pit, Killingworth, and the new town was built on reclaimed colliery land.

It was dramatically clear that rail transport was being 'invented' in Newcastle in Stephenson's time. The experiments set out to determine whether the rails should rest on timber sleepers and, if so, at what intervals and with what fixings. What we now take for granted as a railway track was the result of trial and error in the fields of Killingworth. The size of the gap between the rails is based on the width of pit ponies in harness, and this determined the width of the eventual railway carriages and steam engine. The Newcastle pit pony lives on worldwide, as I saw decades later in Sweden, when in the town of Vasteras (after winning a competition to design their railway station) I was presented with a section of the first railway line laid in that country in the 1860s, which had been made in England. The

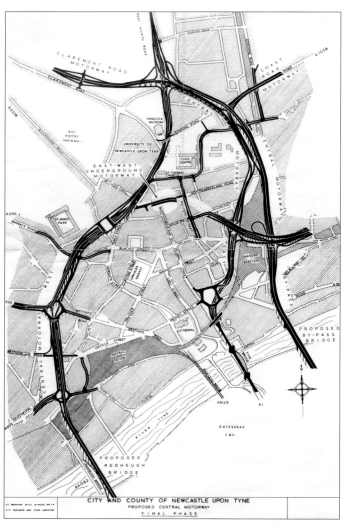

CITY AND COUNTY OF NEWCASTLE UPON TYNE
PROPOSED CENTRAL MOTORWAY
FINAL PHASE

profile and track width were by then standard throughout most of the world. A revolution in town planning and urban life was invented in fields outside Newcastle.

The modern metropolis relies enormously on the application of technological ideas invented and tested in Britain. Electric light and power have transformed the efficiency, size and capacity of the world's cities. It was the 19th-century Newcastle industrialist Lord Armstrong whose experiments with water power in the 1880s turned Cragside, his beautiful Northumberland home by Richard Norman Shaw, into the world's first electrically lit house. The light bulb – the hackneyed symbol of a flash of insight and new ideas – was invented here in Newcastle upon Tyne. Blackpool with its trams and street lights, London with its underground railway, and many other British cities pioneered a new kind of urban place where electricity changed how people lived.

Forward-looking northern urbanism gave rise to concentrations of similar specialized places of work, such as the potteries in Stoke-on-Trent, the steelworks in Sheffield, and the docks and mines in Newcastle. This development has left a lasting physical presence in the form of new urban quarters containing well-constructed dock buildings, warehouses and canals so full of history and individual character that they, like so much of 19th-century industrial Britain, have unique placemaking value. In Manchester's 'Little Ireland' area, Quaker cotton mills were located next to gasworks, the by-products of which led to the manufacture of the world's first waterproof product, the macintosh raincoat. Today, I am replanning this area, reusing the mills for studios and housing, rebuilding river walls, and celebrating the conjunction with railway arches and high chimneys.

Transport remains one of the integral elements of the urban experience, but over the past 40 years transport systems in Britain have been treated as separate from the cities themselves. When I arrived in Newcastle in 1946, the city's transport system was based on trams. There were tramlines in the street, cables in the air and an efficient infrastructure in place. Then, in the 1950s, the traffic engineers decided to modernize the city by replacing the trams with trolley buses, which were like trams with their overhead cables but had rubber tyres. Six or seven years later, they modernized again: trolley buses were ousted in favour of motorized buses. By the 1960s, motorways were being built in Newcastle for a car-dominated transport era, decimating parts of the

Left: One of the approach roads to Newcastle, just north of the Tyne Bridge, before the 1960s 'improvements' (top) and after (centre), showing the destruction and chaos resulting from the roundabout alterations. The map at the foot of the page shows one of the many extraordinary proposals for new road-building schemes that came out in the 1950s and 1960s.

A Newcastle tram in the mid 1940s. The trams gave way to trolley buses, then to diesel buses, and eventually to the metro. Trams are now returning to the city.

city. In the 1970s and early 1980s, it became clear that motorways had not solved the transport problems, so the traffic engineers resolved to install a metro system. (There had been suburban train lines when we arrived in 1946, but these must have been pulled up in the 1950s.) They reinstated the old railway lines and built tunnels to connect them with the town centre. By the 1990s, the city was again focusing on pedestrianization. And now it is looking at guided buses and trams again.

I regard this as an example of 'continuously reinventing the wheels' and believe that many cities in Britain have made little real progress in spite of much chopping and changing of urban-transport priorities, considerable investment of time and money, and often great disruption. So much waste – and so much of it resulting from political short-termism. Contrast what happened in Newcastle with European cities like Prague, which went into economic decline after the Second World War but kept its trams going, and consequently still has a highly efficient tram system. In Britain, we have come back to trams: Manchester and Sheffield are very proud of their new tram systems. Blackpool is the only British town to have kept its trams throughout, and they are so good that they are being exported. When I went to San Francisco in 2002, I saw a wonderful cream-and-green streamlined 'art deco' tram that looked just like a Blackpool one – and, indeed, I found out that this is what it was. Like the $1 trams in Hong Kong, it was a reject tram from Britain.

Immediately after I had left Newcastle for London, the area around the city's All Saints church (the subject of my school drawing, see page 31), now separated from the rest of the town by a motorway, became the victim of an appalling piece of 1960s road planning. A huge roundabout and three new office buildings were plonked there and, because the church was 'All Saints', one building was called Cuthbert, another Bede and another Aidan. The three great saints of north-east England must have been squirming in their celestial residences in response to the precast-concrete office buildings that had been named after them. I am now, 40 years later, replanning the area, which is intended to form part of a new pedestrian route linked to Gateshead's Millennium Bridge that rediscovers the connectivity of that part of the city. I had always loved Newcastle as a walking city, but under Wilf Burns and others in the 1960s whole areas of the city became virtually inaccessible to walkers.

In the 1960s, instead of Britain's 19th-century past being valued, much money was spent trying to eliminate it. In subsequent decades much of my urban-design expertise was gained from rectifying the damage done in Britain in the 1960s, when the money pumped into the system was used not only to destroy but also to corrupt. Newcastle became a symbol of the malaise, with its Pilgrim Street roundabout and inner motorway, which devastated half the town and destroyed historic buildings such as John Dobson's world-class Royal Arcade. Some of the men responsible for the desecration were eventually gaoled for corruption, most notably T. Dan Smith, the city leader, who was sentenced in 1971 to six years.

The Newcastle of my childhood had rows and rows of brick terraced housing with solid slate roofs. Often, instead of following the contours, these streeets ran straight down the steep banks of the river to the quays and docks on which the residents depended for their livelihoods. The houses were tightly packed and quite dramatic in their impact. Their designation as slums led to enormous clearances in places like Scotswood and Byker. The fact that they were often replaced by higher rise, more socially alienating buildings represented a sad loss to the urban character of Tyneside,

Misguided development in the 1960s damaged parts of Newcastle. The quiet tree-lined road along which I travelled by bus to school became a motorway with underpass right in the middle of the city (top); the area just north of the Tyne Bridge (see page 80, top picture) became a roundabout overlooked by ugly offices (centre); and row upon row of residential tower blocks were built in the hinterland of Newcastle, from Byker to Scotswood (bottom), replacing well-built terraces containing whole communities of people. All this was part of the chief planner Wilf Burns's vision to create 'the Brasilia of the North'.

but additionally the long period of demolition and rebuilding created a twilight world of no-place – one aspect of which was dramatically highlighted by the sad life of Mary Bell, the child murderer, which was encapsulated in press pictures of Scotswood at the time that showed children playing amid the rubble and wide-open urban desert where little terraced houses had once stood. There are many areas of London such as Shepherd's Bush, Fulham and Battersea, with streets and streets of terraces basically no bigger and no better than those demolished in Newcastle, but they have been loved and cared for, and make good (if expensive) middle-class homes. What a confusion of town planning and social principles when the dwellings of decent workers (or artisans, as southern estate agents term them) can be ruthlessly demolished in deprived areas, and restored and valued in rich areas. Between 1940 and 1980, oversimplified, political 'quick win' gestures got rid of vast numbers of good housing stock for no good reason – and with devastating results.

Urban planning, civic leadership and modern architecture lost respect to such an extent in northern England that those cities where there had been a great deal of postwar development spent decades in decline – making their current renaissance all the more spectacular. In contrast, London and historic towns such as York, Bath and Edinburgh were not allowed to fail. Although a huge amount of urban rebuilding took place in Britain in the 1960s and 1970s, London escaped much of it. The national politicians responsible for many aspects of the provincial schemes lived in conserved areas of London such as Hampstead; there they helped to stop the 'inner London box' motorway of the 1960s, and successfully campaigned against 1970s traffic-planning threats such as the Highgate–Archway road-widening scheme. Since these politicians voted for destructive road schemes elsewhere in the country, the result was a widening of the north–south divide as the centres of cities such as Liverpool, Newcastle, Sheffield, Glasgow and Manchester began to fail. New towns were built on the edges of failed cities to get people out of the 'problem' cities themselves, depopulating the centres and accelerating their downhill spiral. By a twist of fate, I spent the next few decades in London, where little of the urban fabric changed at all – whereas the north of England, where I had spent my entire life until arriving in London, saw many of its great cities pulled apart and some of them changed beyond any hope of restoration to the robust urban places they were in 1945.

Mont-St-Michel, on the coast of Brittany (left), and Lindisfarne (or Holy Island) on the coast of Northumberland (below left) were inspirations for the Climatron. Both islands are linked to the mainland by causeways.

One year's office experience

The move to London

In 1961, I made the deliberate and unhesitating decision to move to London, where I intended to get the one year's practical experience of working in an architect's office that I needed before I could apply to be a fully qualified architect. The southward drift was an inevitable consequence of my education, which had raised my expectations as well as my skill levels. Coming to London at the end of my studies offered opportunities for cultural events, lectures and talks, as well as chance encounters with possible future friends and working partners. As part of a sixth-form project on 'the city', my daughter Milly recently created a tower of multiple pinball tables in which the many rolling silver balls made lit-up connections. Her proposition was that 'chance' – the rolling balls – was the key to the city, a

The damage done to Newcastle in the 1960s and 1970s is captured in this recent history of the city by Robert Colls and Bill Lancaster. It includes this 1960s comment by T. Dan Smith: 'One result of slum clearance is that a considerable movement of people takes place over long distances ... the task is to break up such groupings even though the people seem to be satisfied with their miserable environment and seem to enjoy an extrovert life in their own locality.'

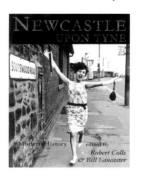

The documentary drama *Cathy Come Home* drew attention to the housing problems of London in the 1950s and 1960s, and led to the founding of the charity Shelter.

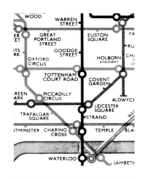

Harry Beck of London Transport and the map of the London Underground that he devised in 1933. It became a classic of 20th-century design, and for many people is their only 'mental map' of London.

place where you maximized your chances in life through the unplanned events that were intensified in large, mixed populations. Although London in 1961 was a place of great opportunity, the streets were not quite paved with gold. Yet they were larger, busier and more vibrant than anything I had known before because London is the immigrant city par excellence – built for trade and commerce, with an insatiable appetite to absorb newcomers and their energies.

I spent six weeks looking for somewhere to live. With the proceeds from the sale of my little house in Ryton, at first I aimed to buy a house with my fellow Newcastle student Peter Smith, who was going on to study at the Courtauld. London, I soon found, was suffering from an intense housing shortage. Peter and I could afford a house together for about £2,000, which meant we had to accept what was called a sitting or protected tenancy as part of the purchase. We often saw whole families living in desperate poverty and squalor in one or two rooms. I was astonished by the sight of the crammed-in humanity living in the multi-occupancy houses we inspected on the fringes of Kentish Town and Camden Town. London, evidently a place of wealth and power, had at its wide edges a third world of *barrios* within and behind genteel façades. At that time, the fate of the poverty-stricken at the foot of the housing ladder led to national scandals centred on exploitative London landlords such as Peter Rachman and television exposés such as the docu-drama *Cathy Come Home* (1966), about the desperate plight of a single homeless mother (which led to the establishment of Shelter, the charity for homeless people).

Since the beginning of the 20th century, London had had a serious shortage of subsidized public housing for rent (what is now called 'affordable' housing), and many ingenious legal and town-planning measures were dreamed up over the years to get the private or public sector to build housing for all. The story of the capital's provision of housing in the last 50 years is one of numerous ill-thought-out schemes that have never added up to a resolute urban programme to house communities properly or adequately.

But then London always has been, and still is, without a plan. It is a fast-trading, flexible place run not by civic leaders but by central government politicians, many of whom have second homes elsewhere and who see London as the goose that lays the golden eggs for the

benefit of all the nation's cities. I have always believed that the prospect of a well-planned, well-organized, well-run and self-run London is seen by our political leaders as a threat to national political control.

I have engaged with housing in London over a long period of time, admiring the ingenuity of developers and architects, private owners and housing associations who divide terraced housing of all periods into flats, convert offices into lofts, build roof extensions and redevelop corner plots, odd sites, backlands, brownfield lands, even power stations and churches, into very liveable dwellings – all without a grand plan or a rousing ideology. But, while our London homes continue to increase in value (my little semi-detached house in Maida Vale steadily out-earned me year by year, silently appreciating while I went out to work each day), my classmates who stayed in Newcastle on smaller incomes bought large houses with acres of garden, often out in the Cheviots. They had ample disposable income for two cars and overseas holidays – and a mere 20-minute journey to work each day from sheep-filled fields to their Jesmond offices. They seemed to be home each day an hour or two before their London counterparts finally passed through their front doors after surviving another cramped journey by bus, tube or train.

Deliberately and opportunistically unplanned, London might well have been without a mental map to aid orientation and familiarity. Yet it has a brilliant graphic: the tube map of 1933 by Harry Beck of London Transport. Although we Londoners may travel in appallingly maintained, claustrophobic, ill-lit underground tunnels, we have the exhilarating advantage of access to the city's best (and only) clear piece of wayfinding. Above ground the location of each tube station captures and reinforces the only real plan of London that makes sense: an almost random accumulation of focused village centres that have congealed to make a metropolis that has never gone through the intervening phase of being a 'city' in the continental European sense.

A city it is not, and London happily confuses us by claiming to contain within it, in addition to its boroughs and villages, two small cities: Westminster and the City. Yet the tube map holds it all together for newcomers, visitors, the young and old and less well off. As soon as we resort to the rubber-tyred transport of cars, buses or taxis, orientation and placemaking crumble into a maze of one-way streets, strange Victorian-based bus routes and a road system that appears to have been, as one 1960s American guidebook put it, 'laid out by a herd of wandering cows'.

Transport systems reflect a singular interpretation of place based on each system's self-interested view of itself. For example, many people in Britain today define where they live in relation to the nearest motorway junction: 'I live near exit 18 on the M6.' It used to be railway stations or bus stops, but now we look to junction numbers. I encountered the most extreme example of this mentality while a student in the USA, when I was attempting to drive around Philadelphia by car. I got hopelessly lost because there was nothing to indicate where particular places actually were. The self-serving system contained signs that merely directed the hapless driver to other highways, like 'Highway 160 south', 'New Jersey turnpike east', 'Freeway 262 leading to highway 1'. The world of the spaghetti-junction road system meant nothing to me. I had to know how the system worked before I could understand how to use it, and I was asking the wrong questions. Transport systems appear to have been conceived as an end in themselves for the entertainment of those employed in their design and management: a bus stop is where buses stop, not where the passenger begins a journey; a railway station is where the trains are stationed, rather than being a passenger take-off and arrival point.

Ever since arriving in London 40 years ago, I have walked and walked and enjoyed the old villages and royal parks, and studied the more regularly planned parts that appear in disconnected patches to help make sense of it all. I have come to see it as a special challenge to help divine and clarify the understanding of the innate order of inner London. Gradually the climate, intellectually and democratically, has been changing, and the 'pedestrian public realm' and the 'shared mental map' are high on the agenda of many of London's current civic leaders.

When I was working at the London County Council (LCC), I travelled to work on the Circle underground line, a cut-and-cover, early steam-engine railway system characterized by fresh-air vents, as at Baker Street, and open-air stations such as Earls Court, Edgware Road and South Kensington. I boarded the tube at Sloane Square station, where I would experience the extreme shallowness of the cut-and-cover element, because the River Westbourne flowed above my head in a huge, clearly visible metal tank. Created by

digging up streets and putting the 'lid' back on after the railway had been placed below, the Circle line is easy to relate to the shape and form of most of London because, of necessity, it follows roads. Its northern section goes along the Marylebone Road and Euston Road and its southern section comes back along the north bank of the Thames. Travellers simply walk down short flights of steps to the cut-and-cover Circle line stations; there are no deep, long escalators.

We use the word 'tube' incorrectly when we describe the Circle line because, in contrast to the genuine tube lines, it does not consist of deep, bored tunnels, whose route bears no relation to what happens above ground. These later 'tube lines' came about because it was easy to drill deep down through London clay soil – and cheaper to drill underneath the city, since it avoided issues of acquiring property ownership. The deep-lying tunnels that characterize the tube meant that ventilation could have been a problem, but the engineers realized that, if they made the tube train a tight enough fit in the tunnels, the train would push a plug of air ahead of it, resulting in a self-ventilating system with the occasional vertical chimney. The deep tube lines often connected with, and were built under, the earlier, shallow Circle line, sometimes resulting in stations with an astonishingly three-dimensional complexity, where long passageways connect the deep escalator system with the shallow stair system.

During the last 30 years, I have wrestled with replanning complex underground stations such as Hammersmith, South Kensington, Bank, London Bridge, King's Cross and others including, of course, Charing Cross, where Terry Farrell & Partners' new building stands on a main-line station above two cut-and-cover lines and three deep tube lines. Whenever the replanning of one of London's nodal villages is attempted there are these underground arteries and their above-ground concentrations of entrances and exits to contend with. Although the clarity of Harry Beck's map evaporates above ground, for many people the underground railway system, with all its limitations, is their most significant and structured experience of London.

While working at the LCC I lived in a second-floor flat in Tite Street, Chelsea, just off the Thames embankment, next to a house where Oscar Wilde once lived. It was only a short stride down the street to the north bank of the river, from where I could look across to Battersea

Opposite: The Blackwall ventilation buildings (top) was my project at the LCC. Other buildings later sprang up around them, including the Millennium Dome on the south side.

Above and top: Aerial views of Tite Street, Chelsea, where I lived while working at the LCC.

Views of the Thames: a section of the privatized and neglected north bank (top); the ice fair, in earlier times (centre); illustration from *Tideless Thames in Future London* (bottom).

Park, which brought back vivid and happy memories of the funfair at the 1951 Festival of Britain. So my work in the very grand County Hall building by Ralph Knott and my home in Tite Street were on the river, and for that period of my life the Thames and its banks and bridges were my spectacular but sometimes soulless habitat.

During my time at Tite Street I became familiar with the character of the Thames itself. The river is wide and quite fearsome in that twice a day vast volumes of water race inland and back in great unnatural surging sweeps. The Thames is swirling, speeding and muddy, like a continuously emptying dirty bath that refills just as quickly, covering and re-covering tidemarks and boulder- and refuse-filled mud banks; at high tide it can, alarmingly, fill right up to the brim of the flood walls.

With its width and long low bridges, the Thames was windy and exposed for many months of the year, or gloomily eerie when the fog closed in – the 1959 Clean Air Act had not yet had its full effect. The banks themselves featured mostly hostile roads (where traffic sped faster than on any normal London street), office car parks and industrial sites such as Battersea, Bankside and Lots Road power stations. The only river park was Battersea on the south bank, and the only river walk was along a limited section of the park established by the 1951 Exhibition; the north bank was, and is, mostly flood walls and wide, fast-trafficked roads.

Years later, I took part in various campaigns to 'rediscover' the river, including the 1991 Royal Fine Arts study, which considered a scheme for a non-tidal Thames that was not eventually exhibited. I had enjoyed a fascinating book on the subject called *Tideless Thames in Future London* (1944) by J.H.O. Bunge. Bunge demonstrated that the 17th- and 18th-century ice fairs and the Canaletto painting of Venetian-like ferrymen on the Thames relied for the still, pond-like nature of the river at that time on the weir effect of the close-centred supports of old London Bridge, which tempered the effect of the tides. There is much to be said for a friendly non-tidal river in preference to an angry tidal sea that charges in and out as a consequence of human intervention. Those who romantically say that this contest with nature and the elements is something to be enjoyed forget that it was the artificial channelling of the banks that changed the very wide (over 1 mile in some sections), soft river basin that the Romans forded 2,000 years ago into what is now a giant man-made sewered culvert. The small tributaries such as the Fleet, Westbourne and Tyburn, and the great Thames itself, are all in meanly emasculated, unnatural forms.

A more frank and deliberate expression of the man-made, such as a non-tidal London focus, would be no less natural and probably a better way to bring the city together. Water transport of all kinds would work as it did 350 years ago, when Christopher Wren was rowed in a small boat each day from his house on the south bank to St Paul's construction site opposite. It is evident from many drawings of London from the 15th to 18th centuries that the river was the *genus loci*, just as it is today in Paris or Prague; the Thames then was the great public space and main thoroughfare. Today, with global warming and the rising North Sea, we will one day need to reinvent the Thames again, either by building more extreme tidal dams and flood walls, or by allowing it to return to a more natural form with wide flood plains and marshlands.

When I arrived in London in 1961, the realization that the river had some post-industrial urban quality to offer the city was only beginning to take hold. The transformation of the entire stretch of river from the estuary (now optimistically termed the 'Thames Gateway') to the 'Tides-end Town' of Teddington is today doing more to drive the unified replanning of London than any other feature of this great city.

Working in London: the LCC

My first contact with the realities of an architect's office after graduating from Newcastle was at the London County Council in 1961, during the first six months of my year's practical experience. Initially I had had interviews with leading architects in the capital – Lyons Israel & Ellis, Denys Lasdun, and Jim Stirling and Jim Gowan. At the time, both Denys Lasdun and Stirling & Gowan occupied beautiful houses in Regent's Park. Stirling & Gowan had no work at the time, but were happy to chat for what seemed like hours. Lasdun offered me a position, but in the end I chose a job with the LCC at County Hall.

At that time, in the spirit of Edwin Lutyens's office off Portland Place, private-sector architects tended to be based in what had been private houses. These included Stillman and Eastwick-Field's Georgian house in John Street, Jim Stirling's beautiful Nash house in Regent's Park, Denys Lasdun's studio in Peto Place and

Opposite: Aerial photos from exactly the same viewpoint – an extraordinary change in fewer than 40 years! West India Docks, 1962 (left) and Canary Wharf 2000 (right).

Left: Parts of London that I got to know in the early 1960s included the area of Lincoln's Inn Fields (top), where I worked for Stillman and Eastwick-Field; the Thames near Charing Cross, with the LCC building, where I also worked, on the far right (centre); and the Hayward Gallery on the south bank (bottom), designed by the LCC while I was there in 1961 and subsequently built during the 1960s.

many indications that the people within the great group of buildings comprising County Hall were not fully in control.

The LCC taught me valuable lessons about how a public body works and about the need for leadership and sound office management. What belongs to everyone belongs to no one was a fact of life that I'd recognized as a child on a council estate, and I felt that it applied to the LCC architecturally. Nobody took overall responsibility for very much, and as a result there were a few maverick entrepreneurs who were able to take advantage of the leadership void and set about designing and building their own projects. Some innovative and some rogue projects got through the system and were built – which gave certain individuals notoriety and often brought trouble on everyone else – but there was little that the general mass of employees, or the LCC, could do about it without fundamentally changing the structure of the organization. I was struck by the risks architects took. People were experimenting with system housing and prefabrication – and with people's lives and their futures – without thorough testing of their ideas.

It seemed that no one was really in charge. In contrast with the larger offices of today, such as Foster and Partners or Skidmore, Owings & Merrill, which are well-oiled, well-managed machines accustomed to a high volume of work and a diverse range of clients, during the 1960s it was beyond the capabilities of the largest public office in the UK to control many hundreds of designers working on an enormous diversity of projects. Those were the days of the all-powerful welfare state, when socialist local councils shared a belief that everything should, and could, be done by the public rather than by the private sector. The LCC of the 1960s had its own in-house engineers, quantity surveyors and consultants, but its leaders and managers were, in my youthful opinion, out of their depth. Their widely ambitious and ideologically driven aims were not matched by an organization that could deliver. But, in the LCC's defence, during its early heyday in the 1930s, 1940s and 1950s, under leaders such as Herbert Morrison, who planned the 1951 Festival of Britain, it had been a very successful organization, characterized by memorable Lutyensesque housing estates and fire stations, which were enough to

Colin Buchanan's fine Victorian house in Exhibition Road, South Kensington. These private practitioners were at the other end of the spectrum from a public body such as the LCC and its big town hall, which would accommodate a whole architects' department. It seemed to me that the choice between working for the public or the private sector included the choice of the type of building you worked in, since each sector had a quite different perspective on what constituted a workplace.

I had been married to Rosemarie for six months by the summer of 1961, and she was on her way to London to join me, so there was pressure on me to find a job and a home for us both. Perhaps I chose the LCC because, in my temporary insecurity, I was instinctively drawn to my family's safe civil service roots. But I soon found it was not for me. I began to resent the office atmosphere and the formalities about who had which desk and which piece of carpet under their desk to signify their position in the bureaucratic hierarchy. Attaching great value to territory and personal domain can lead to uplifting places and great architecture – but, in communities where bureaucratic tribalism has destroyed positive working relationships, it can result in an obsessive concern with trivialities. The LCC had had a great impact on London (particularly in the form of fine purpose-built flats and estates between the wars) but the city's own growth and eventual overblown loss of direction led to the abolition of its governmental body (the Greater London Council, or GLC) by central government in the mid 1980s. During my time at the LCC I saw

ground, while I was given a job of my own: the Blackwall Tunnel buildings, which engaged me with the Thames, a new river crossing and the renewal of east London.

When I first took the tube out to Blackwall, I had no idea where I was going. I wandered round this desolate no-man's-land and tried to imagine that some day there would be new tunnels and roads there. This was before the building nearby of Ernö Goldfinger's Balfron Tower flats (1965–67), Peter and Alison Smithsons' Robin Hood Gardens (1968–72) and, much later, Cesar Pelli's Canary Wharf Tower (1988–91) and Richard Rogers's Reuters building (1989) and Millennium Dome (1999). My remit included the linings to the tunnels, and this involved studying how best to use colour within and without, and the choice of tunnel-cladding materials. But the task of designing the ventilation, or fan buildings, and a supervisor's office at the point where the old and new tunnels met gave me a chance to create real new buildings and do it virtually on my own. The fan buildings as they evolved were fairly innovative. It turned out that there were engineers at the LCC who were interested in spray concrete and facilitating the realization of free-form shapes, and I took full advantage of their knowledge and enthusiasm – I had become a one-man entrepreneur hidden or lost within the system. Blackwall felt like the middle of nowhere in 1961, in time as well as place. Still suffering the aftermath of the decline of empire and the heavy bombing of the London docks during the Second World War, it was in a kind of limbo, a silent no-place awaiting its fate. In the subsequent 40 years it has seen prodigious new development, epitomized by Richard Rogers's Millennium Dome, built around Blackwall Tunnel's southern ventilation building. In 2001, both ventilation buildings were listed of Grade II historical interest.

I often use in lectures a photograph taken by Peter Cook to show that the prevailing tendency in nearly 50 years of British architecture is expressed at Blackwall by buildings designed in an industrial machine aesthetic, such as those by Rogers, Smithson and Goldfinger (to the extent that they look as if they don't contain people), while the only building in the photo that is truly industrial and contains only machines – the northern fan building – has a playful human character. I really enjoy the irony of this image.

Nick Grimshaw and I spent long lunch hours walking around the neighbourhood of the County Hall building on the south bank of the Thames. It is a coincidence

show that architecture could be anonymous, economic and collaborative yet at the same time highly artistic and of real value to society.

For the first few days at the LCC, the architect at the neighbouring desk said not a word to me, nor I to him. Eventually I mentioned my dissatisfaction with the organization of the office, and he expressed his sympathy and suggested we talk over lunch. That marked the beginning of my close friendship and eventual partnership with Nicholas Grimshaw. Together we formed a maverick but pretty insignificant unit within the vast bureaucratic set-up of this local-government organization. Nick was working on the Crystal Palace recreation that much of our independent working lives since have centred on the area. I went on to masterplan the South Bank complex and Hungerford Bridge and to build the new Charing Cross station and its environs, while Nick masterplanned Waterloo station and built the international train terminal.

From the third-floor window of the LCC architects' department, Nick and I saw Howard Robertson's rather weightily conservative Shell Centre begin construction. Much later came the National Theatre, but the South Bank Centre was being designed at the same time as I was working on the Blackwall Tunnel. Since the LCC was short of staff, I was pulled off the ventilation buildings to work upstairs on the South Bank Centre for a full day before being sent back to my original drawing table. I remember with some amusement being asked to join a team drawing attractive girls in frocks walking in front of the concrete complex, and to show it covered in ivy, to make it look more popular and acceptable for the laypeople on the planning committee – something akin to what many architects have been trying to do to the actual buildings in the 40 years since their completion.

The building of Blackwall Tunnel in 1968.

Walking along the south bank of the Thames in the early 1960s was a depressing experience. I had seen the wonderful structures put up for the Festival of Britain, but the Tory government of 1951 had destroyed most of the fine buildings to erase any memory of what were seen as Labour government successes: the Dome of Discovery, the Skylon and everything else disappeared. The area was run down and felt remote from both south and north London. Today, by contrast, the new South Bank walkway is one of the best bits of London's public realm and is a focus for all the areas around. What a reversal! It is the culmination of a turbulent history, starting from the war and industrial decline, followed by the heights of the Festival of Britain and the lows of the South Bank and Shell centres, with their alienating, introverted campuses and intimidating upper-level walkways. Now there are two new mainline stations either side of the river, at Waterloo and Charing Cross, and the London Eye evoking the spirit of 1951; the upper walkways have begun to be demolished, and a wonderful new riverside walkway runs from Lambeth Bridge to well beyond Tower Bridge with the Design Museum, Butler's Wharf, the new Tate Modern, Globe Theatre, Oxo Tower and the Greater London Authority (GLA) headquarters along it. In the true tradition of British urban-planning

successes, the south bank is a triumph of unplanned yet expensive and time-consuming trial and error – and of accretive, pragmatic but bitty public-realm planning (more often than not motivated by getting rid of mistakes) – over buildings, architecture and even the actual use of buildings. County Hall, the former headquarters of the Greater London Council, is now a hotel with leisure use, and its reincarnation in the headquarters of London's new government, the GLA, is a fine river addition, regenerating the London Bridge station area. It is as though the first headquarters of London's government in County Hall was merely a temporary but very wasteful stepping stone in urban regeneration and political structuring – a pioneering institution that vanished, just as most of the elements of the Festival of Britain had vanished.

Working in London: Stillman and Eastwick-Field

After six months I left the LCC to join the private-sector office of Stillman and Eastwick-Field, which occupied a pair of Georgian houses off John Street in Gray's Inn. The practice was well known for its rigorous approach to system building, specializing in precast-concrete schools and housing. There was certainly a lot of work in the office, and within four or five weeks I had recommended that they ask Nick Grimshaw to join the staff. He had also wanted to leave the LCC, and on the basis of my reports was enthusiastic about joining Stillman and Eastwick-Field, which he did in the spring of 1962.

At Lincoln's Inn, Coram's Fields and Lamb's Conduit Street I experienced another London village. The Georgian streets were still intact there and helped me to experience the astonishing otherworldliness of the lawyers' privileged domain, where boys educated first at public schools and then Oxbridge spent a life in law and never resided or worked in any environment other than one with medieval-style cloisters and rooms off open staircases, all set within railed enclosures with lawns, trees and gravelled paths (and to reinforce their tribalism and insular detachment they dressed in court, as they still do, in a kind of medieval garb topped with wigs).

I now commuted by bus, getting to know a transport system that, like the lawyers, existed in its own world. The ghost of George Shillibeer, who originated the London bus system in 1829, still seemed to be ordering the obscure but deeply embedded routing systems that went from outer to inner to outer London bus depots, on journeys that seemed designed more for the bus-route managers and operators than for the passengers. Bus travellers often feel out of touch with London in orientation terms. They are sitting on part of a linear route – like being somewhere on a piece of string – where the ends are unknown places, but the middle has the essential two connecting bus stops. But the compensation is being able to see streets, buildings, people and daylight. It is an extraordinary irony that you can either travel around London by bus above ground in daylight and see the sights without grasping the disorientating shape, form and direction of the metropolis and the whole odd transport pathway you are on – or, thanks to the brilliant tube map, you can travel blindly below ground in the dark, and in your head know the whole map of London based on its underground system.

While still at Stillman and Eastwick Field I had applied for, and won, a Harkness Fellowship, so I was obliged to give notice. But before leaving I worked on staff housing for a Northampton hospital. On my student travels I had been particularly inspired by the courtyard housing of the Swedish architect Jørn Utzon – courtyards and enclosures of outdoor spaces that intensified the indoor–outdoor relationship in the home. Somehow a courtyard reads as a captured room, albeit outdoors, and the spatial continuum between outdoor private and indoor private enriches the home much more than an open garden does. In Utzon's houses, the mono-pitched roofs and the geometric pattern of low walls give bulk and distant views from upper rooms, so the home is not restricted to walled enclosures. At Northampton I designed similar linked units, playing with repetition to create variety within a limited spatial and geometric pattern.

Since its external walls are shared with neighbouring houses, courtyard housing is introspective. Grouped together, the houses generate an urban fabric with a clear separation of public and private open space. The relationship of rooms to the courtyard and of the housing to its neighbours express man's various roles as family member, neighbour and citizen.

The organization of the courtyard house is the opposite of that of the conventional suburban detached house, which looks outward over its surrounding space rather than inward into the space it surrounds. The detached house needs views out, while the courtyard house can be a microcosm of the whole world

of nature. The one represents humankind as the dominant force over nature, while the other suggests man capturing and preserving nature.

I did not see the Northampton houses being built because I was in the USA at the time, where I met Serge Chermayeff and colleagues at Yale, who were also fascinated by courtyard houses. Their more linear house type helped me develop tight low-rise housing in London in the form of a rooftop courtyard house at the Colonnades in Bayswater (1972–76, see pages 221–23) and, much later, a scheme at Swiss Cottage that again carpeted a flat roof over a much bigger-span building. The Colonnades houses are above shops and offices, and those at Swiss Cottage are above a sports complex. Even more recently, Terry Farrell & Partners designed a group of courtyard houses at Petersham, Surrey. Extending the interest further, this building type was the basis for entire villages we studied in the Thames Gateway.

I recall hiring a sporty Wolsey 1.5 with Nick Grimshaw and two other staff and racing up the recently completed M1 to the site in Northampton, seeing if I could reach 100 miles an hour. The UK's first motorway was such a novelty that – compared with the rest of the road system, where for so long the only decent roads were those laid by the Romans! – it seemed like a Grand Prix racing circuit. Given modern congestion, speed restrictions and familiarity with motorways, it is hard to imagine an hour on the M1 as the liberating experience of speed and freedom of movement that it then was.

Stillman and Eastwick-Field was a reasonably disciplined practice but working there was a hand-to-mouth existence, as was typical of many private firms. If a competition came into the office we dropped everything at a moment's notice. There was no room for bureaucracy. Space shortage meant that I had to work in a corner of John Eastwick-Field's own private office, with another young architect in the opposite corner of the Georgian room. It was a world apart from the LCC obsession with desks and workspaces as tribal status symbols. Client meetings were held in our presence, and the vitality and enthusiasm rubbed off on me, as did an appreciation of how such an office operates at the sharp end. Interestingly, although it was a private-sector office, almost every job we undertook was for the public sector – state schools, council houses and so on. It confirmed once and for all that the belief of my parents and family, and of many of my architectural friends, was wrong: the undiluted public sector did not work, and the private sector was more vital, creative and effective, particularly if combined with the public good.

At that time, many of the private offices were trying to imitate the larger multi-disciplinary practices. I went for an interview to the Building Design Partnership which, under Grenfell Baines, was experimenting – as many others were – with bigness, multi-disciplinary working, staff partnerships and shared ownership. All members of staff were to be shareholders, and would be offered a share of profits based on projections from the previous year. They offered me something like one and seven-elevenths. I disrespectfully thought it would never work, but I was impressed at the steps they were taking to invent the modern private-sector practice. These were

pretty heady days and I was learning from all sources about management and leadership. I had had first-hand experience of public and private offices, and had used my year well, I thought, to understand the basic organizational elements of a modern architectural practice.

Nick and I stayed in touch after I left Stillman and Eastwick-Field, and he visited me in America while he was on a travelling scholarship with two other AA students. We were on the same wavelength. He was fascinated by the development of my career and by the work of Fuller, which I had introduced him to, and I was grateful for his friendship in London. Unlike me, he was a middle-class southerner, someone from what was then perceived as the officer class, and I felt reassured by his self-confidence and familiarity with professional life.

Revisit photos, 2003
The houses for nursing staff at a Northampton hospital were inspired by Jørn Utzon's courtyard housing. The project was begun in 1961, while I was working at Stillman and Eastwick-Field, and completed in 1965, when I was in America.

3

1962–65: AMERICA

Graduate School, USA • Arriving in the USA: the *Queen Mary* and city grids • The University of Pennsylvania: Davidoff and Kahn; planning and designing • The grand US tour: houses, city squares and national parks • **Global tourist and back to London** • The grand tour: Tokyo, Hong Kong and Delhi • Back in England: time to settle down • London: a permanent home: Kensington and Colin Buchanan

Graduate School, USA

Arriving in the USA: the *Queen Mary* and city grids

Throughout my time at architecture school, America had interested me more than anywhere else, and in 1962 I applied for and was awarded a Harkness Fellowship to go there. I walked up from my flat in Chelsea one day in May 1962, went through Hyde Park and crossed Park Lane to meet the interviewing group of university vice-chancellors, leading academics, writers and top businessmen on the Harkness interview panel in their Georgian house in Mayfair – an intimidating but ultimately successful encounter.

It seems hard to believe today, but I did not know anyone who had actually been to America – people I knew just didn't go there! The long boat journey was an impediment; jet travel was in its infancy and far from being the low-cost mass transport it has become today. The only people, it seemed, who could give me useful advice and help me progress towards the fulfilment of my ambition were at the Saarinen American embassy in

Grosvenor Square. The embassy put me in touch with the architect Jane Drew, and it was she who recommended that I should apply to go to Pennsylvania because Louis Kahn was teaching there.

The Harkness organization arranged for me to travel to the USA on the *Queen Mary*, which was more of a floating village or small town than a boat with its population of over 3,000 inhabitants – passengers and crew. It was an entire floating world of compressed life. We hit a severe storm but I loved it, and I walked and walked the corridors and decks, which were like swaying and rocking urban streets with shops, cinemas, swimming pools, dance halls, bars and restaurants. Five days later, I saw New York sailing towards me, and I experienced the extraordinarily elegant and dramatic sense of arrival that comes with slowly gliding waterborne transport. I went back to see the *Queen Mary* in 2002 in Los Angeles with my 18-year-old daughter Milly. Exactly 40 years on, I found a still stylish world – an island like the static one in my Blackpool thesis (see pages 176–85), but capable of moving across oceans at speed. It reminded me that in the early 1960s I had been very interested in the

Arriving in New York by boat – an extraordinarily elegant and dramatic way to arrive.

Below left: Cross-section of the *Queen Mary*, on which I travelled to New York: a floating city with its streets, public places and residential areas.

Bottom left: Hans Hollein's collage of an aircraft carrier in a landscape: a juxtaposition that jolts our perception of scale, context and place.

Bottom centre: 1960s proposal for a floating city by the metabolist Kenzo Tange.

Bottom right: Conceptual floating city by the School of Engineering, University of Tokyo.

I began to take
photographs as soon
as I arrived in New York:
the Guggenheim Museum
(top, left and right);
and Wall Street offices
(above, centre and right).

floating towns, cities on the water, that were being invented by the Japanese metabolists as a fantasy response to overcrowding in Japanese cities.

The *Queen Mary*, or any ocean liner, is a megascaled mono-functional container, and as such is a specialized, temporarily used but fixed-format place like, say, an opera house or a sports stadium. But its overriding purpose as a means of transport, and all the features that go with being a 'vehicle', must coexist with its function as a large-scale human habitat, a place that can accommodate the normal range of natural, accretive activities of any

hotel, village or town. The combination of these two things fascinated me. First, there was the container itself – its unique boat shape and specialized functioning of engine and boiler rooms, captain's bridge, waterproofing and seaworthy devices such as lifeboats. Second, there were ordinary human activities interlaid within the ship's 'public realm' of gangways and decks, the 'public gathering spaces' of sports, ballrooms and dining areas and the 'residential areas' of stacked cabins with portholes for windows. All of this, unlike a naturally grown urban habitat, is designed and built in the specialized construction workplace of a shipyard and then fixed in time, as all specialized containers are by their nature. The result was that the *Queen Mary* embodied a 1930s view of life, which included berths divided into 'first', 'cabin' and 'tourist' classes. Unlike in a bus or train, these compartments were built-in, with separate dining rooms, bars and shops so that the various social classes could be kept apart for many days – creating a kind of floating apartheid, albeit a benign and voluntary one based on the price you could pay. As a museum piece now in Los Angeles, the *Queen Mary* (like the uncovered Pompeii) conveys as much about society and its values at a point in time as it does about a form of transport.

A few years later, at the Archigram Folkestone Festival of 1966, I saw Hans Hollein's collage of an aircraft carrier on a hillside – a juxtaposition that jolted our perception of containers and place, and asked how much town planning is, or will be, simply a question of scale as buildings get larger and larger. Buckminster Fuller's

dome over New York and Frank Lloyd Wright's 'Mile High' skyscraper were the most powerful relevant images of gigantism and habitat containers at that time.

The Statue of Liberty, the skyscrapers, ferries and wide rivers of New York were a huge scale shift from anything I had seen in Europe. The city was exhilarating and intimidating in its power and success. The sense of entering another world is something I still experience in the first few hours after first arriving in a great world city. Hong Kong has a similar effect on me, as do Kyoto and Venice. Until then, I had been affected by the sense of a place as being genuinely totally different from every other place only a couple of times in my life. The first was as a boy on a school trip to Edinburgh, on a misty damp winter's day, when the silhouettes of the Old Town's towers and steeples in the half-light, the steps and levels and narrow streets produced in me an overwhelming realization

New York's majestic Pennsylvania station – a glorious marble hall, like an opera house foyer; so different from an English rail traveller's experience.

Below, this page and opposite: I made these drawings of New York from the window of a friend's apartment in 1962.

Nick Grimshaw with me and my daughter Bernie (born in 1963) on a trip to New York. Nick and I were already good friends long before we set up in practice and he stayed with us during an AA trip to the USA.

of the complete sense of oneness of the city's history and culture. The second was on my first journey abroad, to Paris in 1957, where I was as much affected by the city's street life, its pavements and shops, and the well-dressed, well-off people, as I was by its boulevards and ornate architecture.

This uniqueness of urban place is a quality achieved only by many creative hands working in mysteriously guided collective 'writing' over many generations, including through turbulent and changing times – unlike, say, the creative process of the artist, who can invent difference and novelty alone in a studio with little time or materials. We all know that the world is full of towns and suburbs that resemble each other, repetitive 'anywhere' towns dominated by roads and motor cars. Then there are towns and cities with, say, one-off distinctive landmarks that locate them permanently in our minds. But there is another order of achievement involving many lives over many decades and

centuries – places that are so astonishingly original and special that they take the very word 'place' to another level of meaning and of urban quality and uniqueness. New York, I realized on my first day there, was one of these places.

I spent a week inside Manhattan's skyscraper forest (like redwoods man-made in brick and stone). I saw Joan Baez and Bob Dylan perform in small side-street venues and, full of respect and admiration, I visited my first Frank Lloyd Wright building (the Guggenheim). Of the many layers of New York I discovered during my two years in the USA, the one that most strongly endures is of the capital city of art deco (a style then, and even now, dismissed as unserious in the UK). New York's great era was the 1920s and 1930s; I absorbed the most sublime architectural details and interiors from that time, such as those at the Rockefeller Center, No. 1 Wall Street and the Chrysler Building, which carried the whole 'deco' spirit so committedly from the top of the tower right down to

its lobbies, elevator-car interiors and smallest details. Art deco is not a direct cousin of modernism; it is, like surrealism and postmodernism, more of an antidote or even an alter ego to modernism's frequent over-steering into elitist and earnest self-righteousness (and, in this sense, the antidote has a very 'serious' role indeed). The essence of art deco is that it was spontaneously born, had mass support from top to bottom of society, and was probably, thanks to movies and widely circulated popular magazines, the first truly global artistic style. Although some of the great names of architecture, such as Frank Lloyd Wright, played elegant games with the style – namely, his zigzag Mayan-influenced Hollyhock House, and his Johnson Wax streamline moderne – most great art deco buildings are recognized for themselves alone, usually with anonymous or unfamiliar authors (who ever registers the architect of the Chrysler Building?).

I made my way to Philadelphia by Amtrak. The railway stations in New York and Philadelphia were both of a building type I had not seen before. Europeans, particularly the British, have vast, steely, single-volume industrial sheds – great for the trains, but not quite so good for people, I felt, who are left to mill around at the feet of the rolling stock. (Nicholas Grimshaw's new Eurostar station at Waterloo is based on this arrangement, proudly defended as being in the Victorian tradition.) The Americans, in the land of people as consumers, were among the first to reverse this layout. Passengers gather in glorious marbled halls that resemble opera house foyers and the trains are accessed by well-organized stairways to the level immediately below the passengers' feet. Appropriately, the transport machines occupy the secondary, merely functional space. Departure and arrival points of trains are arranged to suit passengers' convenience, and the entire choreography of movement is more like today's sophisticated air travel than the jumbled, intermixed movements in Britain's Victorian sheds.

New York's great gridiron layout had been adapted for Philadelphia by the city's founder, William Penn. It was such a new experience for me as a European: cities deliberately planned on a large scale in relatively recent times. This was a young country, I soon realized, where town planning had been and was still a serious necessity. I really like the gridiron plan. Each 'line' has its own

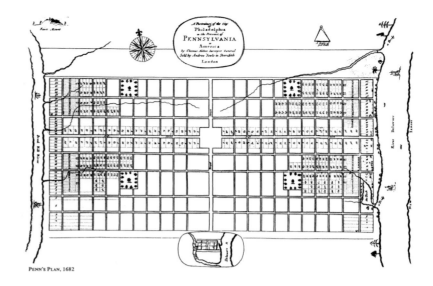

PENN'S PLAN, 1682

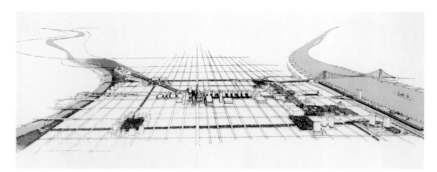

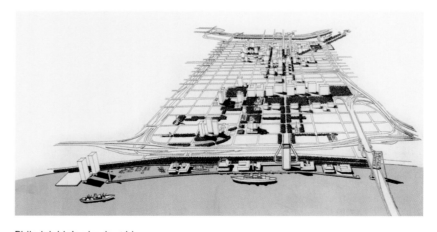

Philadelphia's simple grid layout represented the very best of 'mental maps'. Here it is shown in an early map of the city (top) and in drawings from the city-planning document (above) drawn up by Ed Bacon and his team in the 1960s.

Personal photos,1962

Until going to America I had assiduously recorded my 'grand tours' in sketches and water-colours. However, I arrived in the USA fully equipped, with a Leica and Canon and several interchangeable lenses to set about recording the next two years of travel and exploration. I began with New York, then Philadelphia and moved on to the Western states, and eventually to Japan and India. Above is a police station from the early 1960s by Geedes, Becker & Quail. On the right is the Art Museum (top), Louis Kahn's Medical Research Building at Pennsylvania University (centre); and a row of houses in West Philadelphia (bottom).

place, and the variations on a regular geometric theme really do work (as so evocatively captured in Piet Mondrian's painting *Broadway Boogie Woogie*). Some years later, I learned from Fred Koetter (the co-author with Colin Rowe of the 1978 cult book *Collage City*) how the US city grid originated in a land agents' method of plot disposal – which possibly helps to explain why I, a lover of city walking, had arrived full of prejudice, expecting the grid to have been designed solely to benefit commercial interests. For the pedestrian, everything would seem to point to repetition and dullness.

Instead, having arrived in Philadelphia in a humid early autumn, I walked and walked the gridded streets, and loved it. London's streets – those 'rivers and streams' of road movement – had been replaced in my urban consciousness by Philadelphia's grand 'canals' with

between the central point and the river, are four squares. Off to one side is a great diagonal route leading to a grandiose classical art gallery in the distance, and, on the Delaware side, the landscaped Independence Mall links two of the squares. All the streets running in one direction were given well-ordered numbers, and those running at right angles were given names, mostly names of trees – Pine, Maple, Chestnut, and so on: such simple moves, yet capable of adding much variety and complexity to the realization of an urban vision.

Town planning does rely, has to rely, for management, orientation and comprehension of its layout upon simple and effective moves. During the following two years of travelling in the USA I learned about the delightful variations that were possible within gridded layouts – such as the plan imposed on hilly San Francisco. (Jasper

Above: In 2002 I visited the grave in Bodega Bay, California, of Jasper O'Farrell, who twisted the city grid of San Francisco to fit the landscape.

long vistas, total clarity of orientation, and a city map that had its own simple genius. To make a big city from scratch involves establishing a mental map for all the inhabitants to share. (I have spent much masterplanning time in London trying to 'rationalize' street shapes, to find an order that bus routes and pedestrian paths can cling to through the wandering, shapeless maze – to give some collectively understood framework.) William Penn placed the centre of his town at a point exactly equidistant between two great rivers, the Schuylkill and the Delaware. Two wide streets, Market and Main, converge there, and at this central point the city hall was built with William Penn's statue high on a spire, from where he could permanently and proudly survey and inspect his creation. Within the overall city grid, halfway

O'Farrell, the local town planner who later twisted the San Francisco city grid to fit the peninsula on which the city stands, was probably a long-distant relative of mine who escaped from Ireland's famines.) The grid was set out logically at right angles to the shoreline, but where the landform shifts the grid would have driven straight into the sea. O'Farrell's design connects two different grids – old and new – and contains within it some of the most interesting street patterns of San Francisco, creating a vital urban dynamic. In a similar way, New York's Broadway cuts across the regular city grid and consequently becomes the city's most interesting street. A former Indian trail, Broadway is the only irregular street in Manhattan, and each accidental connection to the grid is an event – and each event, like Times Square, is a

Personal photos, 1962
Above: Philadelphia's Beth Shalom Synagogue by Frank Lloyd Wright.

Above left: Philadelphia house by Louis Kahn.

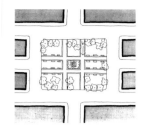

Counter-rhythmic squares in Savannah, Georgia, formed part of my urban squares study.

Personal photos, 1962
Among Louis Kahn's great works are the First Unitarian Church of Rochester, New York (below), and Esherick House at Chestnut Hill, Philadephia (below right).

unique place within the city plan. To my surprise and delight, the most enchanting invention of all was the southern town of Savannah, Georgia, where there are counter-rhythmic squares built right across the regular grid intersections. The cities of America have proved wonderfully instructive – not just on my first visits as a graduate student, but throughout my life. Their newness and speed of realization seem to intensify and compress our awareness of modern urban-planning issues, and their continued vitality and growth still transform visits by the urban planner into voyages of discovery.

The University of Pennsylvania: Davidoff and Kahn; planning and designing

The day after arriving at the University of Pennsylvania, I enrolled on a double master's course in civic design, which combined architecture and city planning –

itself, and I knew that I would really enjoy mixing with so many other students from different disciplines, where our collective world view was inevitably wider and non-specialized. So I embarked on a course in which urban planning with its messy edges overlapped the neat, ring-fenced world of my professional architectural training.

At Penn I had powerful teachers in a great institution of international standing and I was surrounded by some exceptional students. It was not just an architecture school but also a graduate school of fine arts, with mixed disciplines, including town planning, landscape architecture, architecture, sculpture and fine arts. At the time, the urban-design lecture courses were probably the best in the world, in that they brought together so many good people. However, I did not encounter much

reflecting my belief that art and design should engage inclusively and holistically with life. At Newcastle I had been motivated to explore variations in scale and had engaged with the possibilities of moving, travelling, and particularly walking, that the large scale offers. I also loved worlds within worlds and human habitats, and the idea of seeing my work inhabited and used was deeply fulfilling. It had never been my ambition to be in control to the extent that everything would be mine and 'perfect'. Rather, I liked awkward edges and unplanned deviations. I liked other people's involvement, and I particularly liked adapting and converting what was already there – doing more with less, not as a purist aesthetic but primarily as a social, economic and practical philosophy. As I saw it, pure design excluded much of life

good urban 'designing' as such in the studio classes at the school, since the syllabus awkwardly combined a camp of planners and a camp of designers – and there was little connection between the students or even the teachers in the two camps. The designer/planner divide – as I have seen repeatedly throughout my working life – reduces the potential of collective and creative city-making by distancing from each other the two professions that are most actively involved in the process. At Penn, however good the teachers were, it was generally left to the students themselves to synthesize these divisions.

The two cultures, of designers and planners, sat either side of us urban designers. The former believed that all urban problems could be solved with more architecture,

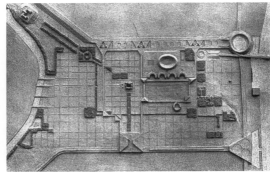

Above left and above:
Louis Kahn with a studio
class at Penn University,
during my time there, and
two of the clay models.

more intuitive, magical 'solutioneering'. The latter considered that three-dimensional design would somehow logically and almost mechanically materialize from proper analysis and understanding. Each camp relied on quite different skills, and during my entire career as an architect/urbanist, I have always found it hard to bridge between the camps. Urban planning is seen through two different pairs of spectacles, each of which reveals a different world, a different urban place. The really innovative pioneers, I felt, would be the bridge-builders who could bring Le Corbusier and Louis Kahn into the same territory as Jane Jacobs. Although I was not aware of it at that time, Robert Venturi's book *Complexity and Contradiction in Architecture* was then in genesis, while he was teaching at Penn; it is still, even today, the most powerful, elegant and eloquent manifesto for a middle way, a human, balanced and integrated view.

The divide did not matter very much to me then because the individual departments and their lecture and studio courses were so good. Architecture comprised design studies with Louis Kahn and lectures by the likes of Robert Venturi and Romualdo Giurgola. Very close at hand, on and around the university campus itself, were

modern masterpieces such as Kahn's Medical Research Building (1957–64), a students' dormitory by Eero Saarinen, the 19th-century Arts Library (a wonderful Arts and Crafts building by Frank Furness), Geedes Becker & Quail's police station, and Frank Lloyd Wright's Beth Shalom Synagogue. The Ivy League campus seemed to have as many traditional, leafy, brick-built quadrangles as any European university town, and the old arts building was a delightful and spacious Victorian construction. I was surrounded by architectural quality, but the real focus was Kahn's class.

Kahn was probably the best architectural teacher I have ever encountered. At Penn my interest in the use of architectural modelmaking took a new direction as a result of his teaching methods. He was a genuine educator who nurtured his students and was seriously intent on trying to understand them and bring them out. He taught three afternoons a week for four hours at a time. He would do no preparatory paperwork. Somebody else would choose the projects and write the briefs – he would simply turn up and look and talk. He would instruct us all to work in an identical way with clay models and line drawings, and he would then be able to compare students'

The beautiful Arts and
Crafts library at Penn
University by Frank
Furness.

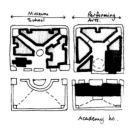

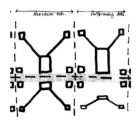

Above: My drawings for a project in Kahn's class involving the replanning of areas of Philadelphia.

Below: A visit with a fellow design student to Robert Venturi's first completed building, a house for his mother. Bob is in the porch and Denise is on the left.

work objectively, sometimes picking on the work of only two students in a whole afternoon and ignoring the work of rest of the class – a method I hadn't seen before and haven't seen since in an architectural school. He would merely place a student's model in front of him and talk about it, extrapolating generic lessons. He believed that everyone in the class could learn from only a couple of examples if there were a consistent and coherent teaching approach. The models we made had to be beautifully crafted and speak for themselves. By and large, Kahn did not encourage verbal presentation; his argument was that, when a building was finished, the architect would not be there to explain it – so he would stand in silence, sometimes for ages, looking at and studying the student's models or drawings in silence. He would then open up and then he would teach.

Kahn's work may have been highly architectural – it was what other architects thought architecture should be – but there was a powerful human side to him, too. Despite his tough philosophical abstractness, there was great discipline in his approach because his fundamentalism made him rigorously committed to seeking out the true nature of things. At its best, this method of teaching was profoundly moving, but I was worried about the guru status of the man and the excessively devoted students who cloned his work. I was not one to adhere to anything that had an element of institutionalized religion about it, but I learned much from him. Most influential of all was his question 'What does your building (or plan, or city) want to be?' I have often reflected that architects and urban designers have not only conventional clients to deal with but also their buildings' context and use – the places, our towns and cities, are our ultimate clients. Place leads. Place absorbs our results and, if successful, the new place adds and changes all life within it for the better.

Kahn was tolerant of alternative ways of doing things and approved of my resistance to a straitjacketed approach, but there was a tension between us,

and I think he recognized that I was never going to be one of his disciples. My models were too impatiently made and not executed with the perfect precision shown by some of his other students. I saw his classes as a passing experiment for me, not a long-term commitment, and I found his method too time-consuming and laborious. But the lessons I learned from making models with Kahn I have carried with me throughout my working life. In city planning he produced some fascinating conceptual drawings that abstracted the movement of cars in a rather poetic way, with a desire to dig under the surface and grasp the fundamental nature of urban traffic movement. Taking inspiration from his drawings and those of Saul Steinberg and the paintings of Paul Klee, I doodled and sketched my thoughts about pedestrian crossings, about where the people were in the sky, on the roads, even when enclosed in a vehicle. My thematically obsessive doodling (or 'Terrytoons', as my classmates called them) continued during my two years at Penn, visually analysing ideas about perception of urban life and what it meant to me personally (see pages 196–97).

With Louis Kahn, I was experiencing for the first time what it meant to be close to a guru, with its attendant hero-worship. He spoke of what a building itself 'wanted to be', and seemed to have a similarly open and tolerant manner towards his students, but he had created around him a world of blindly committed followers who drew, designed and thought as he did; all many of them 'wanted to be' was the master himself or a clone of him. I was fascinated by the idea of an architect as a religious leader-figure whose life and ideas were so persuasive and all-embracing that it had become for some a way of life, a total immersion in his world – for them, HE was the place.

Among the other teachers, Paul Davidoff was a brilliant and inspirational leader who taught planning theory in a way that utterly contrasted with Kahn's studio. Davidoff's 'choice' theories centred on the re-inclusion of disempowered people in the process of city-hall decision-making. It was a revelation to me that city planning and local grass-roots politics could be seen as interdependent. John F. Kennedy was president at the time, and in Davidoff's class were lawyers and sociologists who were very active in the civil rights movement and in liberal politics. One of Vice President Hubert Humphrey's campaign team was married to a fellow student – and I found myself becoming politicized, albeit modestly, for the first time in my life. In Britain, I had found the Labour versus Tory debates at best petty, partisan and fairly meaningless, and at worst a way of distracting people from real issues. But I had similarly found the communist versus capitalist posturing of my Newcastle student days far too ideologically abstract to be meaningful to real-life issues. At Penn, I became aware that good schools, good housing, ghettoization and even bus routes were town-planning issues – and bad urban management and bad decisions about the physical arrangements of a place went hand in hand with disadvantage and poverty. In Britain, 'top down' was the essence of city-making, and I remembered that most people who lived on our Newcastle council estate were at the bottom looking up and that they felt helpless to do much about it.

David Crane, a visiting lecturer, and David Wallace, our civic-design professor, introduced me to what might today be called mixed-economy or public/private town planning. Crane's 'capital web' theory relied on public investment initiatives to generate private investment. In Britain at the time there was no acknowledgement that the private sector might have a role in town planning. All UK planning involved public funds, large-scale public ownership and control of land. When it came to new towns, greenfield universities and transport infrastructure, an autocratic paternalism held sway. But at Penn,

Wallace, a planning practitioner, was in a private practice partnership with Ian McHarg, whose impassioned campaign for an ecological approach to the environment was ahead of its time. I particularly enjoyed a project that involved measuring, in a mere few weeks, the entire ecological balance – climate, inputs and outputs of air, water, and just about anything else – in the Philadelphia metropolis. No doubt it was scientifically pretty unsophisticated, even quite inadequate, but educationally it hit the mark for us all, particularly since the teacher himself encounterd reality in the world beyond academia, in broadcasting, advocacy and in the planning of real towns and cities. The quality of the teachers and teaching was captured very well for me in a booklet I recently found on a symposium held in 1963, which lists impressive contributors including: Edmund Bacon, David Crane, August Heckscher, Lewis Mumford, Robert Venturi and Ian McHarg.

A good friend and tutor was Denise Scott Brown, and through her I met Robert Venturi, her future husband. She was outwardly intense but surprisingly humorous, as well as being a committed and serious teacher. From her time in London, Denise was used to British irreverence – I think she saw me as someone who was getting more out of being in America than simply the courses and teaching, which was probably true. I remember her comment that she could always tell the difference between British students who had returned home from the USA and those who had stayed: 'The ones that go back home have spent their time immersed in American life, speaking mid-Atlantic, wearing trainers and

The drawings on this page formed part of my work during the summer of 1964 for the city-planning department at Camden, New Jersey. Camden is a small town across the water from Philadelphia, relating to the city in the same way that Gateshead does to Newcastle. My concern was to bring coherence and clarity to the town, creating a basis for a future 'mental map'.

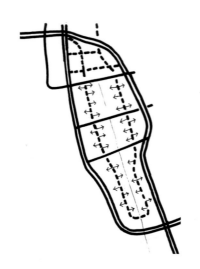
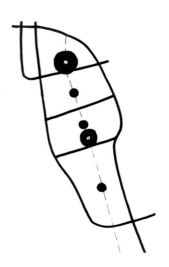

All the sketches and
plans on this page relate
to a study project I did
in the Kahn studio for
an arts complex in Fort
Worth, Texas.

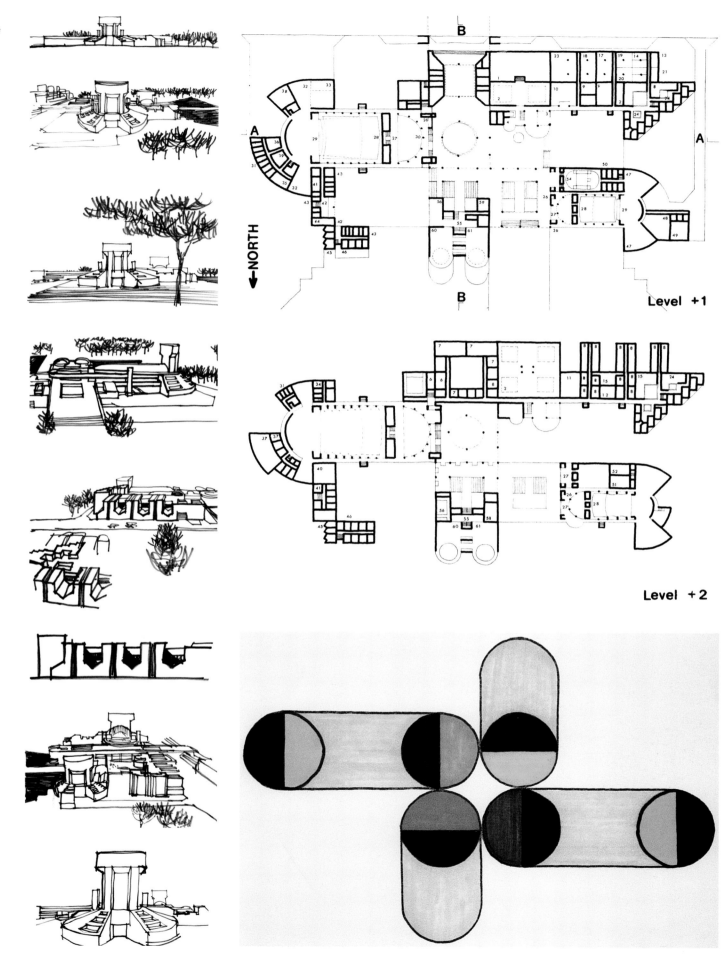

NORTH

B

A   A

B

Level +1

Level +2

Bermuda shorts, going to baseball matches and driving Chevrolets; the ones that stay exaggerate their Englishness, their accents become more like stage English, their clothes more traditional, and they capitalize on their situation by making a career from the American interest in things British.'

Pennsylvania was at the forefront of urban regeneration, and its renaissance was spearheaded by the city's energetic chief planner, Ed Bacon, who taught classes and gave crits to the urban designers. Under Bacon's plans, IM Pei built a new residential quarter in the city centre that was beautifully considered and detailed and, most importantly, part of a deliberate piece of urban renewal in a historic quarter. It seemed ironic that the Americans, with their relatively short history, were leading Britain in city placemaking through historical continuity. In Britain, conservation movements were seen as the enemy rather than as a critical component of planning, placemaking and architectural creativity. It was no doubt my experience in Philadelphia that led me in the early 1980s to be one of the few British architects who resolutely built new buildings at the same time as being very active in SAVE Britain's Heritage campaigns to preserve the country's architectural heritage, and in committee work at English Heritage, our national government body for conservation of the environment.

The early 1960s was an exciting, formative time in America. At Penn, teachers such as Paul Davidoff were campaigning for civil rights; Ian McHarg was campaigning for ecology and the environment; and Robert Venturi's *Complexity and Contradiction in Architecture* was in gestation. Rachel Carson's *Silent Spring* had been published in 1962, a year after Jane Jacobs's *Death and Life of Great American Cities*. Modernism – based as it was on a blind belief in the modern world – was questioned in America long before it was in Europe. This was a genuinely progressive culture compared with Britain, where the style of progress often seemed to matter more than the content, thereby successfully defying real change.

It gradually dawned on me that Britain was not a democracy in the same way that the USA was, and I became very critical of the British political system. Living in Philadelphia, birthplace of the Declaration of Independence and the new nation, I could not help but

be aware that the structure and form of the government of the USA was created there. The division of powers, the constitution and its public accessibility and transparency, the organization of elected houses, all had an order and logic, a kind of 'architecture' that I could readily comprehend.

It was a fact not lost on me that among the great men who debated and drew up this new order – Benjamin Franklin, George Washington, John Adams – was a fine architect, Thomas Jefferson (later third president of the USA). In the city plans they made for Philadelphia and Washington there was physical urban placemaking, architectural edifices with explicit symbolism that harmonized with the political structures they created. The fine written words and the places reinforced with clarity what they collectively had made for the government of the nation. I looked back at Britain and regarded its lack of a constitution as a means of dividing and confusing society. The workings of government were at best opaque and at worst the result of deliberate secrecy, which meant that none of us knew how to take control of our own lives. I looked back at the town planning and architecture of a city where all the great avenues led to a monarch's home, Buckingham Palace – yet the power was not there, but hidden in a Georgian terraced house in the tiny side street of Downing Street. The unplanned confusion of London's palaces, government buildings and Houses of Parliament gives visual expression to the maze-like structure of our political world. Jefferson and his contemporaries played the role of placemakers at the highest level, helping to plan a nation and its cities and buildings on the grandest of scales and with great effectiveness.

The relationship between individual states, the buildings for senators and congressmen in Washington, and the fixed terms and fixed geographical requirements for candidates is part of the American conception of place – place on this scale was clearly seen as requiring a mental map that everyone could grasp. In Britain, the confusion about the role of our government buildings in London's plan form, changing political boundaries, and particularly the peripatetic life of candidates who can be shunted around the country to 'safe seats', all add up to a disconnected and disorientating collective sense of what the UK really is in democratic terms.

Above, this page and opposite: Drawings by Colin Buchanan for his highly influential urban-planning study 'Traffic in Towns'. I have included them here to compare the high quality of the urban design drawings of Buchanan and Bacon.

My home in Philadelphia, at 4426 Osage Avenue, consisted of a tiny one-bedroomed flat at the rear of the house, which I and my wife, Rosemarie, shared with our baby daughter, Bernie.

Below, left and right: Drawings of proposed revisions to the layout of Philadelphia by the city's chief planner, Ed Bacon. Contemporaneous with Colin Buchanan's traffic-planning study, Bacon's plans emphasized not the traffic but the linked open spaces and the pedestrian public realm.

I remember trying to explain to my Democratic Party friends in the 1960s why in Britain, home of the 'mother of parliaments', we had the sudden resignation of Harold Macmillan as prime minister in mid-term, when there had been no consultation with either the electorate or most of his party or the House of Commons – and how a new prime minister, Alec Douglas-Home, an aristocratic member of the House of Lords, had taken office without having stood for any kind of election in his life. I also explained that this unelected prime minister, although having a modest terraced house as his official office and residence, had far more actual power over his government than an elected US president would have had. Later, there was something else to explain: how Douglas-Home had decided to offer some semblance of proper democratic process by becoming 'elected', and that he had done so in a risk-free, manipulative manner by arranging to stand for the next vacant 'safe seat'.

On the urban-design course at Penn there was an emphasis on teamwork – an important preparation for later life and the management of complex urban projects. There were also more female students than I had been used to. At Newcastle there had been only one woman on our entire course; at Penn there were many. Until then, I had concentrated on developing an artistic side to my work, but at Penn I gained intellectual confidence through friendships, coursework, reading, team debates and intense lecture courses.

As far as I was concerned, not only the spirit but also the language of postmodernism took root in Philadelphia in the 1960s. In 1963 there was a major exhibition of US pop art at the Philadelphia University art gallery. The emphasis on accessible content, communication and language over pure form made a big impact on me; posters, packaging design and beautiful images from comic books

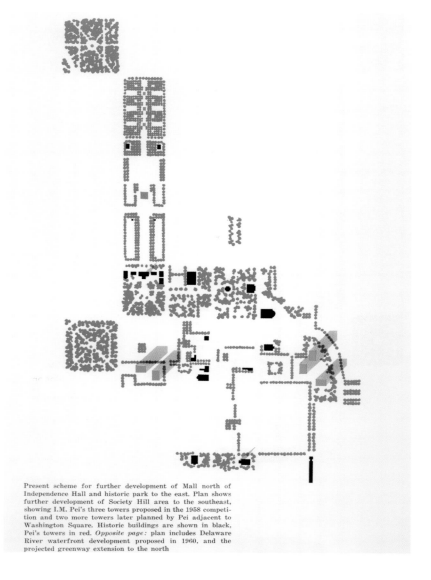

Present scheme for further development of Mall north of Independence Hall and historic park to the east. Plan shows further development of Society Hill area to the southeast, showing I.M. Pei's three towers proposed in the 1958 competition and two more towers later planned by Pei adjacent to Washington Square. Historic buildings are shown in black, Pei's towers in red. *Opposite page:* plan includes Delaware River waterfront development proposed in 1960, and the projected greenway extension to the north

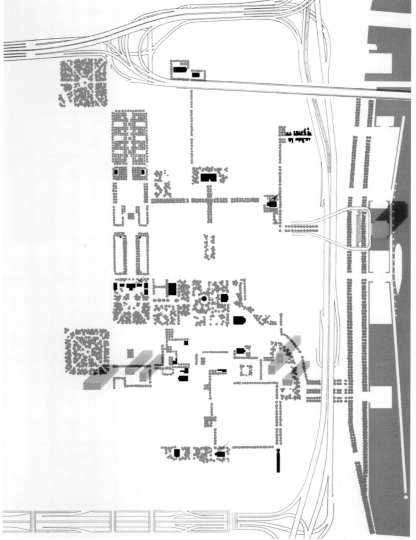

had been the everyday art world of my childhood. I also revelled in being near the centre of the modern art world – New York having largely taken over this role from Paris in the second half of the 20th century. I went to galleries there (it was only a short train ride from Philadelphia) to exhibitions of modern artists such as Andy Warhol, Roy Lichtenstein, Claes Oldenberg and Jackson Pollock with an enthusiasm I had never found before.

Apart from the influence of painting, my exposure to ecological concerns made me realize that there was another, postmodern way to look at life – an alternative to the utopia of ideological social engineering and the mechanistic pseudo-scientific view of international architecture. I began to see a world where design was closer to the humanism of Frank Lloyd Wright and Bob Venturi, where everyday life was the primary component, and to understand the concerns of ecologists and sociologists such as McHarg and Davidoff. This not only consolidated my childhood interests in habitats and landscape, but also gave new meaning to the two books that had particularly influenced me as an undergraduate at Newcastle, Joseph Paxton's *Construction of Crystal Palace* and D'Arcy Thompson's *On Growth and Form* (1917). The former was about a technological innovation that grew from enclosing and nurturing nature's abundance in glasshouses. The latter drew on inherent structures in nature that gave inspirational clues to the efforts of designers to understand the origins of their form-making.

As various influences converged and coalesced, my passions were moving forward apace. As I expanded my horizons, many more things connected with one another and made sense. The culmination of this period was an intensely personal thematic exploration of organic shapes and forms – many of them collages, repeated and reshaped from coloured pages of books and magazines. I called them my 'organics', and I still have some of them today (see pages 197–98). They were a kind of release, a therapy – eye and hand together synthesizing some of the multitude of ideas that I was now taking in.

The grand US tour: houses, city squares and national parks

An especially generous feature of the Harkness Fellowship was that, in the middle year, to enable fellows from outside the USA to see as much of the country as possible, we were each given a car and a travel allowance. For nearly four months in mid 1963, I visited over two-thirds of the states in my Chevrolet Bel Air with Rosemarie and our new baby, Bernie, who was only six weeks old when we set off. We drove up to 350 miles a day and stayed at motels, looking out each night for neon signs that flashed the lowest rates. It was essential for us to find a motel with a pool, but not at all essential to have a fall-out shelter – shelters were common then, in the wake of the Cuban missile crisis, which had occurred a few months earlier. In England there is 'countryside'; in the USA there is 'land' – an enormous amount of it – bordered not by seas but by vast oceans. We visited as many of the great national parks as we could, including the Grand Canyon, Yosemite and the California redwood forests, and we travelled for days through prairies, the Rockies, deserts such as Death Valley and up the Pacific coast to Vancouver, Canada.

Since arriving in the USA, I had seen how Le Corbusier and Alvar Aalto at Harvard, and Mies van der Rohe in Baltimore and in the Seagram Tower in New York, had imported sophisticated urban European projects. During my travels I saw more work by European architects such as Richard Neutra and Walter Gropius. I saw that at the Illinois Institute of Technology (IIT) Mies had gone one step beyond Louis Kahn's dominance of his students through educational ideas, teaching and student relationships. The master himself had designed and constructed a complete physical and educational campus-world and, enveloped within this Mies-made world, he was the chosen leader and principal teacher in architecture.

As usual, I had set myself study tasks on my travels to help me better understand the places I visited and so that I would have comparative observations to bring

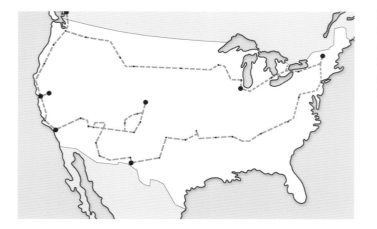

Personal photos, 1962–4
Opposite: Apart from the fascination of the built environment, America showed me landscapes totally different from anything I had experienced in England. To me this was a new scale of landscape altogether: the Grand Canyon (top), Mount Rushmore (centre) and Cypress Gardens, Florida (bottom).

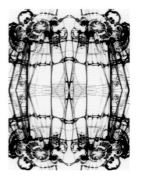

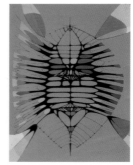

Above: Two of the many 'organic' drawings I did to provide relief from all the reading and writing I had to do for my course. My classmates called them 'Terrytoons'.

Left: Map of my first tour of the USA during the summer of 1963. We later made a second tour of the southern states, including Florida.

back for long-term reference. The first task was to record urban public squares based on a college project and the second was to visit as many of Frank Lloyd Wright's buildings as I could. As I travelled, I began to understand how the extent and variety of the land had helped to liberate indigenous American architects, and in what way they differed from Europeans. Response to context meant that nature, land and architecture were integrated as one. In the Midwest I met, and was warmly welcomed by, Bruce Goff, who was living at the top of Frank Lloyd Wright's Bartlesville Tower, Herb Green in his prairie house (just finished), and Paolo Soleri and his students building their new city called Arcosanti in the Arizona desert. Similar generous hospitality was exhibited by Wright's clients and building owners, and in just over three months I was able to enter many of his private houses, schools and churches (in those days, before security became paramount, I was simply able to ring on the door of Wright's houses and introduce myself in my best English accent).

In all things, context was Wright's starting point; his two Taliesin houses – Taliesin West in Arizona and Taliesin East in Wisconsin – were lessons in contrasting and lyrical responses to specific landscapes, local climate and building materials. Fallingwater with its rocks and waterfall, Marin County public offices with its California car-based culture, urban projects such as New York's Guggenheim, the San Francisco shop and the sublime suburban houses in Oak Park – all were non-universal and site-specific, growing out of land and location. The other aspect of Frank Lloyd Wright's long career that was so different from the contemporary European 'international style' (with its roots in the rejection of place context and time context) was how time context in terms of cultural eras affected Wright. His more classical Chicago work with Louis Sullivan was followed by Arts and Crafts at Unity Temple; he played with art deco at the Hollyhock House in the 1920s, European modernism at Fallingwater in the 1930s, streamline moderne at Johnson Wax, and even Disney populism at Marin County in the 1950s. 'Consistency,' wrote Oscar Wilde, 'is the last resort of the unimaginative' – on this basis, he would have no doubt have rated Wright very highly. Today, global obsession with 'branding' finds architects attaching themselves to a language and style, often for a lifetime.

Personal photos, 1963
This page: Among the buildings by Frank Lloyd Wright that I visited and photographed were the houses at Oak Park, Illinois (top right and left, centre left), the Robie House in Chicago (above) and the Johnson Wax Factory at Racine, Wisconsin (above right).

Opposite: More photos of Wright buildings: Taliesin West in Arizona (above left), Taliesin East in Wisconsin (top right), Fallingwater in Pennsylvania (below left) and the Hollyhock House in Los Angeles (centre and bottom right).

Personal photos, 1963
These photographs were taken while on a visit to Paolo Soleri in Arizona, where he and his students were building their new desert city of Arcosanti, and below, interior of the Marin County local authority offices in California.

A true artist such as Frank Lloyd Wright would travel and experiment; his attitude of mind and his attitude to work made him a kind of artistic nomad, a balanced intellectual contrast to his profound respect for physical place and identity.

However, it worried me that Frank Lloyd Wright at the two Taliesins had taken to even greater extremes the requirement that his followers immerse themselves in his world – like Louis Kahn and Mies van der Rohe, he was the group's teacher, guru and father figure; like Mies at IIT, the immersion extended to inhabiting his own buildings, landscaped environment and interiors, but additionally Wright had organized around him a closed residential community that lived, ate, slept and socialized all inside the architect–master's world. None of this appealed to me at all. I had been somewhat dominated in childhood by an all-pervasive religion with a one-world view, an intolerant mono-vision that seemed full of man-made fantasy and make-believe with rules that allowed for no counterview. How could it be right for an architect to do the same? An architect should surely be an enabler for others, and his art should be an inspirational response to life, not a closed self-serving social system.

It troubled me (and still does) that to be good and to excel seemed often to require a wholesale rejection of the real and complex world, and its substitution by a kind of utopian totalitarianism in which personal self-obsession and blanket domination of the people closest to us are essential requirements for our art to prevail. What kind of price should one pay for new architectural and urban ideas to be developed and applied? There was a kind of madness in Frank Lloyd Wright's life, just as I saw a kind of madness in Le Corbusier's vision for a new Paris – with its great historic centre replaced by highly repetitive work, all safely in the hands of the master himself, stretching in every direction and of such grandiosity that it would, if built, surely be the work of town planning gone mad.

Putting lifestyle and town planning to one side, Frank Lloyd Wright's Johnson Wax Factory and headquarters (like his demolished Larkin Building in Buffalo, New York) is a majestic example of the modern phenomenon of the 'workplace' – a place quite different from other places of assembly such as libraries, sports arenas and shopping centres. From the factories, warehouses and mills of Manchester, Derby and Newcastle to the office blocks and high-tech factories of today, the workplace is usually characterized by specialized production activities involving employers and managers on one hand and workers who freely attend in return for wages or salary on the other. Johnson Wax offered a more fulfilling work environment than had been known before, providing a vivid, imaginative iconic architectural imagery both internally and externally that gave the factory a real face and real identity. The coagulated, soft, waxlike stalactites in the interior are an extraordinary invention, and the overriding paternalistic presence of the owner and his designer extends to all the specially designed interiors, furniture and lighting. I later saw at the General Motors campus by Skidmore Owings & Merrill (a kind of complete 'work-town') and the Rockefeller Center, New York (a work-town in a work city), grand planning and elevated urban design for the workplace. It was another and a much better world, I thought, than the black mills and (literally) life-destroying coal mines that still existed in northern England and elsewhere, and the soul-destroying bureaucratic office complexes like the one I personally experienced at the London County Council.

Above, left and right:
Almost four decades
separate these two
photographs of Seattle,
taken from virtually the
same point in 1963 and
2002. On my first visit
to America I was struck
by the urban chaos and
vitality that permeated
this fast-growing country.

Below, left and right:
I photographed a view
of San Francisco from
Telegraph Hill during my
travels in America in
1963 (below left).
A photograph of the city in
2002 (below right) shows
how much it has changed.

Personal photos, 1963
This page and opposite: Most of these pictures of grain silos were taken in the American Midwest. They form part of an extensive collection of photographs of bridges, industrial complexes and silos taken during my travels across the USA.

If American architecture was different, so was American engineering. Not only were the cars differently conceived (generous mobile family living rooms on wheels, compared with the European tradition of cars based on high-performance macho technology), so were the huge but clumsy refrigerators and washing machines. In everything from barns to bridges, an unsophisticated directness, an unselfconscious pragmatism, created structures of a scale and grittiness that was quite new to me. I took many photographs during my tour of America, stopping frequently at the kerbside to catch, collect and record large-scale engineering objects that emerged above wide rivers and in the middle of great plains.

A trip to El Paso in Texas focused my interest in water conservation. My wife Rosemarie, a war 'orphan' – her father's ship went down within days of war being declared – had been sent food parcels during the war by two elderly American ladies. We went to El Paso to meet the women and they drove us to a high point where we could see below us the river that divides El Paso from Mexico. Across the river, hard to distinguish from the surrounding desert, was the grey and dusty Mexican town of Juarez. El Paso, in contrast, was totally green. A Third World country met a developed country either side of a river in what is basically one conurbation. One was a desert town and the other an oasis with hundreds of blue swimming pools. The sisters told me that El Paso, in the desert miles from natural water, reputedly has the largest number of swimming-pool drownings in America per head of population.

The fact that so many people were drowning in a desert brought home to me that I was looking at a new kind of highly artificial urban settlement. Towns used to be established from functional necessity on hills that were easy to defend, near ports or, say, coal and iron deposits. New towns in America's west were not locationally fixed in that work, building materials and water in vast quantities could be brought to them. The guaranteed sunshine of the desert became the point of attraction for a new kind of artificial verdant garden city. But as I looked at the contrast between Juarez and El Paso, I thought of McHarg and Rachel Carson

Personal photos, 1963
Below, left and right: Herb Green, a student of Frank Lloyd Wright, built this house in Arizona entirely from everyday materials. My Chevrolet Bel Air is parked in front; it carried me to over 40 states in 18 months.

Bottom row: Photos of the Watts Towers in Los Angeles, built by Simon Rodia over 33 years, from 1921 to 1955. The tallest of the nine towers is nearly 30 metres (100 feet) high and contains the longest slender column of reinforced concrete in the world.

and the exorbitant energy price that was being paid to support this seeming utopia. The nearby Wright houses and gardens, and the solid urban qualities of Juarez's Spanish colonial squares with their arcaded cloisters and fine churches, all seemed to me to have a better foundation for sustainable habitation.

In the main, London, Paris, Rome and other mature European cities have hardly changed for 100 years or more, but most US cities are in their infancy, still emerging, still building and discovering their identity. Los Angeles, in particular, has long fascinated British artists, writers and architects such as David Hockney and Reyner Banham, whose observations on his adopted home in the 1960s and 1970s did much to help a whole generation realize that there was a new kind of urban order under development in this city of car mobility and Hollywood. The sheer scale of this motorized city, and the definition of place within very widespread grid blocks with occasional centres, has made Los Angeles unique. Other emerging West Coast cities I admire are San Francisco, Portland and Seattle. One reason for my admiration is that city governance, for all its uniquely American problems, is real governance by elected leaders who have real powers and responsibilities.

In Britain, by contrast, local government cannot greatly affect education and health, or even housing, because powers are deliberately diffused and usually traceable back to central government. It is as though nothing much has changed since William the Conqueror landed and he and his successors governed colonial-style from London, building castles and fortresses all over the country to control the local populace. In our now democratic UK, a dependency has grown up, an expectation that it is the job of 'others' to manage and lead, which induces the British to accept that their towns and cities cannot be made better by their own efforts. Yes, bad political leadership and industrial decline knocked the stuffing out of northern British cities after the Second World War – but only a profound passivity in collective civic affairs and city management can explain why, in 1984, our central government could eliminate altogether the city government at County Hall in London, leaving the capital fragmented into 33 boroughs for a decade and a half. In Paris there would have been riots; in the USA such an event would plainly be inconceivable since cities are self-governing entities. In 1984 London was governmentally lobotomized and the people accepted it. In the 40 years since I left the USA, American cities have continued to run themselves – some badly, most very well, and some, such as Portland, Oregon, exceptionally well.

As the second year of my graduate course drew to a close, I faced the prospect of returning to England and bringing an end to my travels and studies. I was inspired by the idea of the nomad and how it related to modern design, particularly in Japanese architecture and design. At that time, I enjoyed experimenting with portable, lightweight and fold-up design, so I had furnished my apartment at 4426 Osage Avenue, West Philadelphia, with collapsible butterfly chairs, folding tables and inflatable seats. Everything was chosen on the basis that it could be transported back to England – a calculated design response to this nomadic period of my life. When my two years at Philadelphia were over, I rented a U-haul furniture-removal van, took all my portable furniture to the Cunard warehouse in New York, put it into a crate and shipped my personal world back to England to await my arrival.

Global tourist and back to London

The grand tour: Tokyo, Hong Kong and Delhi

One more journey was on the agenda: returning home the long way and seeing the rest of the world – an enterprise that would be funded by travel scholarships. I applied for and received two RIBA bursaries: the Hunt bursary and the Rose Shipman studentship. The architect Fumihiko Maki, who was then teaching at Harvard and was a frequent visitor to Penn, introduced me to various people in Tokyo as well as recommending a place to stay. Rosemarie and 15-month-old Bernie accompanied me on the adventure.

As soon as I arrived in Tokyo I went to see Frank Lloyd Wright's Imperial Hotel – just in time, as it happened, since the hotel was demolished shortly afterwards. Like all Wright's work, this masterpiece was singularly inspired by its time and place. With some reworking of his earlier tributes to Japanese culture, the Imperial was a strange period piece with an almost art deco feel that now seems more than a generation away from Wright's later work in the 1930s at Fallingwater and Johnson's Wax – a kind of an 'end of an era' project, yet every bit of it beautifully and passionately thought through.

Frank Lloyd Wright's connection with ecology, landscape and specificity of place was like that of few great architects on the international stage – in that respect, his work was the opposite of an 'international style'. I think many architectural historians mislead when they include Wright as a great 'modernist' because there were clearly many aspects of his work that were not modernist – particularly his commitment to place. His house in Arizona, for example, is quite different from his house in Wisconsin, while both have a singular contextual intensity in the use of indigenous materials, site layout, response to climate and natural landscaping. The fact that the Arizona landscape had to be handled in a completely different way from a more northern location was an aspect of design that very much concerned Wright, and which he passed on to students such as Paolo Soleri, Herb Green and Bruce Goff. Wright's design for the Imperial Hotel combined the personal (that is, his own hand), the global (art deco) and the local (it had a distinctively Japanese quality in its detailing and roofs, as well as in its earthquake-proof design).

My travel scholarship was to study public housing in Japan and, guided by the Japan Housing Corporation, I certainly saw a lot of it. In contrast to the rather elaborate, somewhat cottage-industry, mass-produced housing prevalent in the UK, the Japanese were building mass housing quickly, cheaply and on a very large scale. I was driven to far-distant satellite towns and suburbs to gaze on the most mechanistic, repetitive housing I had ever seen. The Eastern sensibilities, often reflecting an inversion of Western values, were a shock – and that sense of difference was reawakened in the 1990s, when over a period ten years I travelled to China, Japan, Korea and Hong Kong every four to six weeks. We urban Europeans are drawn to a middle scale with all its aspirations of 'society' and the 'civic', but I rarely found much interest in this approach on my trips to the East – it was as if the individual and the mass were the only two

realities the Chinese, Japanese and Koreans could deal with, acknowledging nothing in between.

The great temples and palaces of Kyoto and Tokyo were accretive, assembled from beautiful, detailed but repetitive small components. Traditional Eastern architecture is usually based on one small building module that is added to incrementally. Again, it seemed as if the medium scale had been left out, and the large scale was merely a very large accumulation, a multitude of the small. Graduated scale changes that we take for granted in the West are less familiar in the East. The great palace of Versailles is not made up of lots of individual house elements – but the imperial palace of Beijing in the Forbidden City is. The mass housing in Tokyo had miniaturized, introverted and often lovingly planned apartments, but the units were then dropped into a vast ocean of regimented blocks – which seemed to me more like a well-drilled naval fleet on display than a place to live.

The real fascination of Tokyo was the tiny streets with their tiny restaurants and houses – the miniature brought into the public domain. There was repetition in the grids and tatami-mat modules, but with endless variations of wall and roof, and elaborate gardens out front no bigger than doormats. At the detailed scale there was perfect order and harmony, but at the civic placemaking scale there seemed to be either blind conformity in the regimented housing blocks or total urban anarchy – exhibited everywhere in central Tokyo in chaotic telephone and electricity cables and poles, unkempt lanes and streets, and buildings developed apparently at random with no controls at all.

We were in Japan a few weeks before the start of the 1964 Tokyo Olympics, at a time when the work of Kenzo Tange was pre-eminent in architecture. I had equipped myself with a new camera as soon as I arrived in Tokyo, and I took colour photographs that were published on my return in the first colour edition of the *RIBA Journal*. Fumihiko Maki drove me in his old Mercedes to see the Tange buildings – confident, heroic, even monumental buildings, displaying a kind of modernism we in Britain didn't, couldn't, do. In contrast to the country's urban planning endeavours, Japan's emergence on the world's stage was being cele-

Above: The Imperial Hotel in Tokyo by Frank Lloyd Wright.

The Japanese architect Fumihiko Maki, who was teaching at Harvard when I was at Penn University. He made several visits to Penn and helped me to organize my trip to Japan.

Personal photos, 1964
Opposite, above: Among the Olympic buildings I visited in Tokyo was Kenzo Tange's swimming pool; a similar photo that I took appeared on the cover of the *RIBA Journal* in 1964, after my return to Britain.

Opposite, below: Some of Tokyo's powerful, traditional roofscapes.

brated by its elitist leading architects with considerable panache and conviction – they had a familiar and confident grasp of the grand scale.

I had not been prepared – perhaps could not ever have been fully prepared – for the impact Kyoto made on me. After returning there in the 1990s I looked again at my photos of the city taken years earlier, and I realized I had been fortunate to have seen it at a time when many traditional elements completely dominated the clothes, shops and vehicles of daily street life. The grid and its geometrical regularities underlie all formal structures in Kyoto, with an embroidered detail so rich that it never becomes tiring. These free-form incidents interlayered within the gridded order are so visually exuberant and stylishly confident in shape and colour combinations that their focus is truly exhilarating – from clothing to landscaping, from rockeries to bronze-fixing on timber elements. Unlike the modern metropolitan disorder of Tokyo, the scale relationships of Kyoto are so well nurtured that there is a powerful sense of everything in its rightful place – and it is easy to take it in, from the giant roof shapes down to the minutely scaled clasps and joints of the walls, floors and columns, with candles and lettering, porcelain bowls, chopsticks and wall hangings all neatly aligned. It takes time – centuries of balancing, measuring and harmonizing elements – to achieve such complete urban placemaking. And Tokyo shows how fragile this traditional balance really is, once modern urbanity takes over.

We flew from Osaka to Hong Kong in a small propeller plane through the lightning flashes of a typhoon storm, and I made the first of what would eventually prove to be dozens of landings at Hong Kong's Kai Tak airport. A Newcastle classmate, Cecil Chao, met us at the airport, and we spent two weeks in Hong Kong trying to make connections between this gutsy colonial port and buoyant trading and financial centre and the sensitivities of Kyoto. I had no sense at that time that I was looking at an embryonic 'world city' whose gross national product would eventually overtake that of entire nations; in the following 40 years Hong Kong surged and surged, grew upwards to the mountains and outwards into the harbour. Its indigenous energy ensured that it became a place for wealthy Chinese well before the colonial British formally left in 1997.

I travelled up to the border with China on a tourist bus and gazed across the paddy fields to the distant small agricultural town of Shenzen with its modest population of 60,000 or 70,000 people; Shenzen is now a city of 4.5 million – four times the size of Birmingham and twice the size of Philadelphia. I didn't know it then, but I was looking at what would become the scene of the greatest urban growth that the world has ever seen. Thinking about Shenzen as it was then is like remembering an earlier visit to a place where a giant volcano has subsequently erupted and changed the landscape for ever.

I gradually realized that, strangely, the *genus loci* of Hong Kong is a void – the harbour itself. A city such as Edinburgh has a castle as its solid physical centre. The Eiffel Tower in Paris and the cathedral in Lincoln are similarly solid, object-positive points of reference. Sometimes a city's greatest landmark links objects across a void, such as the low bridge in Prague and the high bridge in Newcastle. I did not realize it during my first visit or on many later trips, but Hong Kong harbour is the port, and the ships load and offload there. The busy criss-crossing of ships and boats is an ever-absorbing sight. The diversity of shipping in Hong Kong harbour reminded me of a coral reef habitat with its abundance of sea life of every shape and colour, which thrives there in such extraordinary variety simply because the rich ecological environment enables it to do so.

Such was the reliance on boats and the vitality of the city's economy that Hong Kong harbour was a boatbuilder's paradise. In this rich habitat there was a craft for everything – double-ended green ferryboats, red-sailed junks, dredgers, lighters, fishing boats, leisure boats, tankers, cargo boats and houseboats. I marvelled at such ingenuity, imaginative range and entrepreneurial application. There was energy in abundance: it was like an enormous overstocked fish tank. An extraordinary contrast within this diversity was the cruise ships that would occasionally berth in the harbour at Ocean Terminal; I found it astonishing that one man steered the whole of a liner the size of the *Queen Mary*; I saw it as a great scale shift, a whole town steered by a single human being, which had come to rest temporarily in this great harbour city like a visiting municipality.

PUBLIC HOUSING IN JAPAN

17 Akabanedai: The ordered spacious rational layout of projects such as this contrast sharply with the traditional urban situation. Pavements, drained streets, adequate street lighting, tree planting, room for parking – western civilisation has arrived!

52 'Unohara': This is not really a 'marine' civilization – it is superimposed upon the sea and is land-like in all its aspects.

Above: Types of public housing in Japan, from the report I submitted to RIBA on my return. In autumn 1964 I spent six weeks investigating Japanese housing with the help of the Japan Housing Corporation.

Above: Paddy fields on the edge of Shenzen, China, now a city of 4.5 million; I took the photograph from the Chinese border in Hong Kong.

Personal photos, 1964–99

Above: identical views from the Peak Tower, Hong Kong – in 1964 (above) and in 1999 (below).

Personal photos

Below: Photographs I took of Aberdeen fishing harbour, Hong Kong, in 1964 (left and centre) and in 2000 (right) as it looks today, a mini-city.

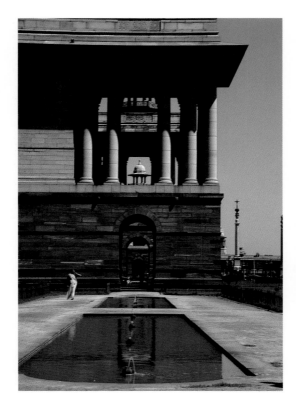
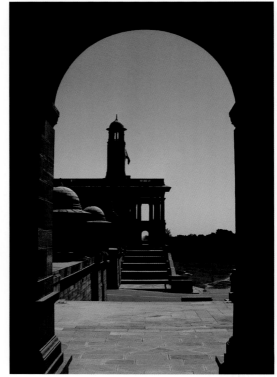

Personal photos, 1964

Top row: Government buildings in New Delhi, designed by Lutyens.

Above, left and right: Le Corbusier's city of Chandigarh, which I found deeply distressing.

Opposite, top left: Lutyens's government buildings in New Delhi, 1964.

Opposite, top right: Dawn in New Delhi, 1964, with the government buildings in the distance.

Opposite, centre and bottom rows: Jantar Mantar astronomical centre in Jaipur.

The last city we visited was Delhi, primarily because I wanted to travel from there by car to see Le Corbusier's city of Chandigarh. I didn't simply dislike Chandigarh – I was deeply distressed by what I saw, a place full of alien objects dropped from an artist's drawing board onto a struggling, poverty-stricken people. I have a belief, a hope, that one day these interventions will be assimilated, subsumed as cities are under new layers of growth

where they can take a subsidiary role as extraordinary, unique pieces of sculpture created by a brilliant man within the larger place. But in October 1964 there was an overwhelming ugliness that expressed more about the displaced arrogance of the European colonist than it did about the artist–architect. What a contrast with Lutyens's work in Delhi! In spite of its claims, modernist architecture has no preordained role to be democratic

and humanitarian; Chandigarh showed that it can be as overbearingly monumental as any traditional architecture, while Lutyens's more traditional work in Delhi was enacting a soon-to-be-defunct imperialist role with great finesse and beauty. I was not prepared for my reaction to Lutyens – coming as I did from an undergraduate environment in which we had all sought to escape the traditionalism of our first professor, W.B. Edwards, who had trained with Lutyens and enthusiastically promoted Lutyens's work to his students.

There was one edifice that I was delighted to find – a little building at the Red Fort. While at Penn I had done an imaginary drawing of a Paul Klee-like dream place – and there it was in reality, but with a red sandstone enclosing wall set within a small village of white marble domes. My Penn doodle drawing was a fantasy place – an ideal of the man-made place, an island of beautiful, crafted objects set apart and enclosed in a kind of artificial dream-like oasis. Such beauty I now found in reality, yet in a sea of poverty, need and neglect!

I went to see the astonishing Jantar Mantar astronomical centre at Jaipur, and left India more agitated about life and its fragility than before. Asia generally seemed to have traditional values of great force but I felt a helpless pessimism about India. How could an architect or town planner in India make any difference when faced with such waves of human suffering, where the evident gap between some of the best achievements of mankind and daily reality was so great?

Back in England: time to settle down

After landing at Heathrow we flew to Newcastle, where I took stock of what had happened there in the three years since my departure. Already Newcastle was being subjected to extensive so-called 'improvements' in the city centre. My former classmates were all very busy and there seemed to be plenty of work, but Rosemarie and I decided to return to London. I had been interviewed by Colin Buchanan and accepted a job in his office, formed from the team that had written the recent seminal report 'Traffic in Towns'.

Before taking up my new job, I went to stay with my parents in Lytham St Anne's for a few weeks. I was once again captivated by the very Englishness of the place. This

was partly regional, with Lancashire food such as 'fly pie', Eccles cakes, potato cakes, Bakewell tarts and, of course, fish and chips with mushy peas – all so very different from American food. Non-regional, more general differences included enclosed, personalized front gardens, controlled advertising and the general neatness of the streets. Whenever I return from abroad, it strikes me that British people seem to want little more from town planning than this small-scaled neatness and tidiness. I saw bungalows galore – the epitome of English taste in house styles, particularly for retirement and holiday homes. When I was building my first large-scale public housing scheme in Warrington, Lancashire, ten years later, I returned to and experimented with the bungalow as a dwelling type (see pages 226–28). It seems to be what so many British people say they want, and in retirement at Lytham St Anne's many were able to build their dream house-type.

We can be extremely judgmental in matters of 'taste'. Something that may seem to be wrong in terms of architectural taste may in the total scheme of things be quite right for its context. Conversely, an object in 'good' taste can be quite wrong for, and damage, its context. When I revisited Los Angeles in 2002 and saw Richard Meier's new Getty museum elevated on the suburban hillside, I was in two minds about the building. Artistically, as one might expect from such an accomplished architect, it is refined and well detailed – a fully committed design. But I also found the overall experience triumphalist, even Disneyesque, with its train ride and works of art presented overthematically – an insensitive visual manifestation of monetary conquest that overemphasized the power of the collector. To my mind, having views of hedonistic Los Angeles and subtropical beaches juxtaposed with ancient illuminated Christian manuscripts from Lindisfarne in the Dark Ages bordered on bad taste. I studied exhibited photographs of the original Getty collection being assembled: lorry-loads of objects arriving from Greece and Rome to be displayed in the museum like spoils of war. As a contrast, I went to look at the new sports arena, the Staples Centre by RTKL, in downtown Los Angeles. Architecturally the arena is not of the highest rank – in fact, it is very ordinary – but in terms of city planning and organization it is a fascinating urban enterprise that restores activity to a downtown area and that, together with the new concert hall, cathedral and art museum, is reconnecting the disaggregated fabric of the

Personal photos, 1964
Above: Street scenes I photographed in India. Below and bottom: The little white mosque I found inside the Red Fort in Delhi, and the sketch I did long before I went to India, representing a fantasy of an ideal building, based on drawings by Paul Klee and Saul Steinberg.

city centre. But, however good the masterplan, can ordinary architecture contribute collectively to top-rank urban design – and, conversely, can great architecture be reduced by inferior town planning to something substandard in value? The only answer is that we should demand the best of both new architecture and urban design.

Lytham St Anne's and its wonderful ordinariness helped to further my belief in the vitality and originality of a pluralistic view of taste. The square in St Anne's is formally planned and laid out from the little railway station (where I used to imagine Trevor Howard in *Brief Encounter*) to the elaborate Victorian pier in the distance that stretches out over miles of sand. The tide seems always to be out – so far out that it is usually out of sight. I have often thought that 'St Anne's on Sea' should really be 'St Anne's on Sand'. There is something endearingly forlorn about a highly decorative, busy pier reaching out to the sea when, for much of the time, the sea is nowhere in sight.

My parents' house was built of Accrington brick, a hard, dark red, no-nonsense northern engineering brick that would probably withstand nuclear attack. They had moved to Lytham primarily because my mother's father, Jim, had returned there ten years earlier. Then his son (also Jim) and daughter-in-law had followed, as had my mother's youngest sister, Kathleen, and her husband – so virtually the whole family recongregated in middle age and retirement, and spent their remaining years on each others' doorsteps in the town where they had all spent family holidays away from their homes in central Manchester. Many seaside resort towns that began as youthful family places gradually become old people's places as pensioners seek out the locations where they were once happiest. It is a transference that supports the very existence of predominantly retirement towns such as Bournemouth and Hove in the south and Lytham St Anne's and Southport in the north, and is becoming an ever-bigger industry worldwide, with ageing populations (and wealth) drawn to purpose-designed retirement towns such as Seaside and Disney's Harmony, both in the US holiday state of Florida. There is a strong link between particular times in our lives and particular places at which events were played out, and the same place is interpreted differently in childhood, in old age and in memories.

During those three weeks in Lytham I spent a lot of time at my grandfather's house listening to him talk. He had visited me in Philadelphia in 1963 and, even though he was 80 at the time, he had proved an energetic tourist, taking Greyhound buses from my apartment in Philadelphia south to Washington and north to Niagara Falls. Along with my art teacher Maurice McPartlan, my grandfather was an heroic male figure of my childhood. His own childhood had been dramatic. After the death of his mother shortly after his birth he was brought up by neighbours; he joined the Manchester Regiment, serving as a Boer War soldier, and moved on to become a warden at the Bombay garrison prison. Afterwards he became a tram driver in Manchester, where he was also a union representative, and in the First World War he went to the Western Front, where he volunteered to crawl out into no-man's-land and rescue two wounded officers, for which he was awarded the Distinguished Conduct Medal for 'gallantry'.

The story that particularly interested me was when he was sent to Basra port and marched up through Mesopotamia to the island of Kut to relieve General Townsend and his army, who were under siege. (The West's recent and continuing military campaigns in this area have roots in much earlier times; it seems ironic that this region, site of the first formal human settlements, is apparently destined to be always caught up in cycles of war and destruction.) Granddad was shot in the head, bayoneted twice and left for dead, but got up in the night – only to be captured by Turks and taken to a Baghdad gaol. Some months later he wrote from there to his family, who had received official letters informing them of his death; a full Requiem Mass had already been said for him. My grandfather gave me letters he had kept from that time, including the first one he had written from a Baghdad hospital with his left hand after being paralysed down his right-hand side. On this and later visits he talked about his life, including his exploits in the Second World War, when he was an office caretaker and night warden in Manchester in the early 1940s. My own father, Tom, was also an air warden, at Salford Docks, and the two of them, several miles apart, would spend their solitary nights looking out at the night sky for enemy planes and bombs, trying to save burning buildings and performing their civilian home guard duties to defend their home and their city. In the first half of the 20th century in Europe, these two father-and-son generations experienced two separate eras of destruction exactly one generation apart, often dividing and destroying the whole male family line.

I began at this time to think about the cycles of destruction in city-making, and how destruction and the reactions to it reveal so much about a society's cultural and urban values. I believe it was Guernica in Spain that experienced, during the Spanish Civil War, the world's first aerial bombing of non-combatant civilians in a town, but from time immemorial victors have been deliberate destroyers. Genghis Khan obliterated the physical evidence of other cultures on a huge scale – the nomadic warriors erased all the land-based agricultural and urban settlements they conquered, including many of those that had been the first to establish themselves in the Middle East from their Mesopotamian origins.

Buildings and cities have regularly become the symbolic objects of an aggressor's destructiveness. The survival of St Paul's cathedral in the air raids of the Second World War was London's icon of resistance. But how do we square Britain's passionate and caring wartime commitment to protect valued urban fabric with the fact that, some five years later, the Tory government hastily demolished the wonderful buildings of the Festival of Britain, erasing all their Labour predecessors' highly popular successes? Was it merely a kind of revenge on the people who had voted Churchill out at the end of the war? The demolition of the twin towers of the World Trade Center in New York in 2001 by fanatical terrorists was another, more recent act that was highly symbolic for the aggressor, and so became highly symbolic for the victims of aggression. The towers' destruction and the debate about their replacement was a repeat of history's many cycles of ritual destruction and renewal. Looking back, perhaps there was in the 1960s a very real climate of concern about Armageddon. I had been in New York during the tensest moments of the Cuban missile crisis of 1963, when the world was on the brink of destroying all civilizations through nuclear war. The threat has not gone away over the past 40 years, but in 1963 we realized for the first time that we had the technology to destroy in a matter of minutes not just our 'enemies' but also ourselves, as well as nearly everything else on the planet.

After the Second World War the Poles totally rebuilt and restored Warsaw, as the Germans did with most of their cities. However, in Britain, the war and the election of the first enduring Labour government immediately afterwards were seen as catalysts for profound urban change, which went hand in hand with the revolutionary social changes of the welfare state the Labour government then set about creating. As the Prince of Wales infamously remarked in his 1984 speech at Hampton Court: 'Planners and developers have destroyed more of the City of London than the Luftwaffe ever did.' Conservation or radical change, evolution or revolution – each country makes its choice, and each makes different choices at different times. War-torn mainland Europe became tired of revolution just as Britain embarked on a revolutionary period of radical social and urban engineering.

Political and social continuity has been a characteristic of life in Britain for 1,000 years, so ready acceptance of outward physical change is at first sight a contradictory feature of the British people. But the brave new postwar worlds for working-class people were designed for the most part by architects living elsewhere, in genteel Georgian towns such as Bath or in London residential areas such as Kensington and Richmond – so for those architects and many other professionals nothing much visibly changed. Razing the past became commonplace only in northern towns and non-historic urban areas.

I can understand why my father and grandfather both voted socialist in 1945. But why, having won the war, and defended their buildings and towns, did the British collectively go along with demolition on a scale that no other European country did? Was there something here that Genghis Khan would have recognized? Perhaps not, given that the choice about which parts of the old order to eliminate was so deliberate. It was northern places that went, not Harrow and Eton schools, nor the clubs of St James's, nor the grand palaces on the Mall. There was a bizarre double standard afoot: if the masses want socialism, give them new slab blocks to live in; we, the leaders (on left and right) are fond of our Oxbridges, Inns of Court and fine London houses, so we will keep them, thank you very much. Professional classes everywhere played a double game, epitomized by aristocratic champions of

Below: Radical extensive demolition of existing buildings was the order of the day in postwar city city centres. The 1945 Abercrombie plan for Manchester envisaged 'replacing most of the out-of-date city centre with the new buildings phased in over a period of time'.

socialism such as Anthony Blunt and his Cambridge friends who were eventually exposed as major Soviet spies, and middle-class architects living one kind of life but promoting another. The reassurance of a permanent sense of place was available only to the well-off. This void, this empathy gap, was at the root of the badly designed, poorly built structures and the destructive urban planning of the era. The tide of reaction turned very slowly indeed, probably beginning with the collapse of the Ronan Point tower block in 1968.

Contemporary photographs of Paternoster Square in London after the Blitz of 1940 and films of the devastation in Docklands and the East End show the kind of destruction that my father and grandfather nightly saw in Manchester in the early 1940s. The normal measurement of war's devastation is the number of lives lost – and yes, this is a critical measurement that results in monuments commemorating those who died, permanent physical substitutes for lost lives. Among the most moving places on earth are the memorial fields to be found in the former battlefields and graveyards of Europe. These are truly places of the dead – like villages or towns – monuments and memorials, where the living come to walk the grass avenues and gravelled paths and streets between the well-ordered ranks of tombstones. But I personally feel grief when looking at old postwar photos – grief for places, buildings, cities and towns, and for the loving work of forefathers, bricklayers, plasterers, artists and craftsmen; for the hours of labour by those from whom we came, who in building their cities and buildings were thinking of their children's and grandchildren's generations. I believe their lives and therefore ours are made less worthwhile, less meaningful, if the continuity and natural accretive evolution of place and its identity is held cheaply. Wars destroy places and therefore collective memory and cultural identity, and, for me, an overriding opposition to war is based as much on places lost as lives lost.

Destruction and demolition were very much in the postwar air of the 1940s, 1950s and 1960s, as though the radical changes of war and its aftermath created a climate of irreverence for all that had once been valued. The horrific pictures of destruction after air raids were seen all over Britain, yet some of the proposed postwar demolitions would in many cases have been even more

drastic in their effect on our historic fabric. John Nash, the great urbanist, seemed a particular target for 'bombing' by clean-sweep modernizers. Plans were drawn up to replace Carlton House Terrace, the great sweep along the Mall and the Regent's Park terraces with slab blocks and towers along the lines of some of Le Corbusier's prewar diagrams for Paris, which ironically escaped both his and Hitler's demolition work. Even the Foreign Office and other Whitehall buildings were tabled for possible demolition because they represented an old order in the minds of the modernizers. What an extraordinary set of proposals these were. The buildings are now listed of Grade I historical value, and Parliament Square in Westminster is part of a World Heritage Site. There was definitely a madness in the air at that time – if the enemy had failed to destroy our cities, we would do the job ourselves.

For me, the finest example of the reverse nature of humankind, where the labours and creativity of earlier societies has been more than conserved – elevated respectfully and lovingly integrated into new work – is in one of the most moving and beautiful buildings in the world, the Mezquita great mosque at Cordoba in Spain. This huge mosque was built in several stages from the classical remains of the Roman city that had been in this area of the town. Neighbourhoods around the mosque were then colonized by Jews – a wonderful, densely compacted urban quarter full of Middle Eastern-style, tall courtyard town houses. Finally, a Christian cathedral was carved into the centre of the mosque, woven into the early work of Romans and Muslims, making the building a triumph of the common culture of urban humanity. What a beautiful way of making towns and architecture; what a precedent for the benefits of tolerance and harmony over destruction and revolution. If any one of the stages had completely obliterated its predecessor, our total artistic experience of the place would have been poorer. Obsessions with purity, consistency – and utopian visions of 'now' as the only perfect time – limit the imagination and lead to less convincing and less enduring designs.

I saw that there was a cycle of change in the north that I could not relate to, and so for the second time I chose to leave the north and go to London. The appearance of beautiful central Newcastle was being radically altered

For me the Mezquita great mosque in Cordoba, southern Spain, represents the most sublime integration of many different, often opposing, cultures in one unified collage, celebrating the underlying humanity of great architecture.

by motorways and demolitions, but, underneath much of the unsatisfactory development, social and economic values were the same. London was the reverse: nothing was physically changing, but there was a revolution afoot led by young people of my age.

London: a permanent home: Kensington and Colin Buchanan

For the second time, Rosemarie and I arrived in London to look for a home, this time with a small child – Bernie was by then 18 months old. We found a flat in Kensington Church Street, from where I could walk across Hyde Park to my new job in Exhibition Road. I began to appreciate again the liveable nature of 'village' London. Earlier I had lived in 'village Chelsea' on the river and travelled to 'village Westminster' to work. I now lived and worked in 'village Kensington'.

As I now walked to work, my experience of London was very different from that of the public transport commuter, who relied on systems designed more than 100 years ago to carry the masses with little thought given to comfort. Walking is not exactly an obsession of mine, but I would confidently say that the ability to live in a place that is easily and enjoyably walkable makes for one of life's great riches. I lived in Kensington for a year, near shops, park and palace, galleries and cinemas – all one needed in all seasons and all weathers. Each day, on my way to work, I walked past the astonishing Albert Memorial (which had been held up at Newcastle School of Architecture as the worst piece of design from the worst era of British architecture – that is, the Victorian age). I would pass the Royal College of Art (RCA) and recall its associations with Prince Albert. (The art college was established at the time of the Great Exhibition, which led to the creation of Exhibition Road and the founding of the Victoria & Albert Museum, whose collection was based on artefacts from the Great Exhibition.) Every day I would walk past the doors of the RCA, where there was inside an enormous surge of artistic achievement; students and teachers included artists such as David Hockney, Peter Blake and Patrick Caulfield. Meanwhile, Nick Grimshaw (who was in his final year at the Architectural Association) and I would meet near the RCA at lunchtimes at a café in Hyde Park, built on the very site of the former Crystal Palace, and gradually talk ourselves into setting up in practice together.

On my walks past Kensington Palace and down Exhibition Road I gained a sense, for the first time, of ceremonial London. Kennedy's funeral in 1963 and the parade through Washington – with the tradition of the boots of the fallen warrior being reversed on a riderless horse – had already made a great impression on me. Likewise, Winston Churchill's funeral in 1965 (his last home was just off Kensington Gardens) was a very moving event that opened my eyes to the possibilities a city offered for ceremonial procession. More recently, this same part of London saw the funeral of the Princess of Wales, the Queen's Golden Jubilee celebrations and the Queen Mother's lying in state at Westminster Hall, for which people queued for hours along the river bank. The first time I ever saw a state event was when King George VI visited Newcastle in 1951. Our whole school was given the day off, and all the city's schoolchildren stood on the Great North Road and watched the royals go by. I love the way that such events and annual parades enlarge and heighten the theatrical drama of the public realm. Philadelphia has the great Mummers' Parade and New York its ticker-tape parades. In Paris there were some wonderful scenes along the Champs Elysées when France won the World Cup in 1998. London has the Notting Hill Carnival – in an 'unheroic' public realm, with its networked maze of small streets and lanes. In contrast, the London Marathon is on a grand metropolitan scale that takes over widely spread parts of London, from Greenwich to Docklands and Tower Bridge to the West End, Parliament and Buckingham Palace. I have become fascinated by the way everyday public spaces are used for great events, such as the demonstrations in Trafalgar Square; and the way protesters are herded by the police to Hyde Park – the very part of Hyde Park, next to Park Lane, where traditionally soldiers trained for wars. The battle of Waterloo was rehearsed there, behind the Duke of Wellington's Apsley House at Hyde Park Corner.

A photo I took of the funeral of President John F. Kennedy in Washington in 1963.

I worked at 47 Exhibition Road for the great planner Colin Buchanan. Buchanan and his senior staff were all teachers and researchers at nearby Imperial College. The rhythm of office life – serious working sessions

Shown below are aerial views of two of Bath's great glories, the Royal Crescent and the Circus. The drawings are ones I did independently while working at Buchanan's office in Bath, where I was trying to define levels of conservation priorities.

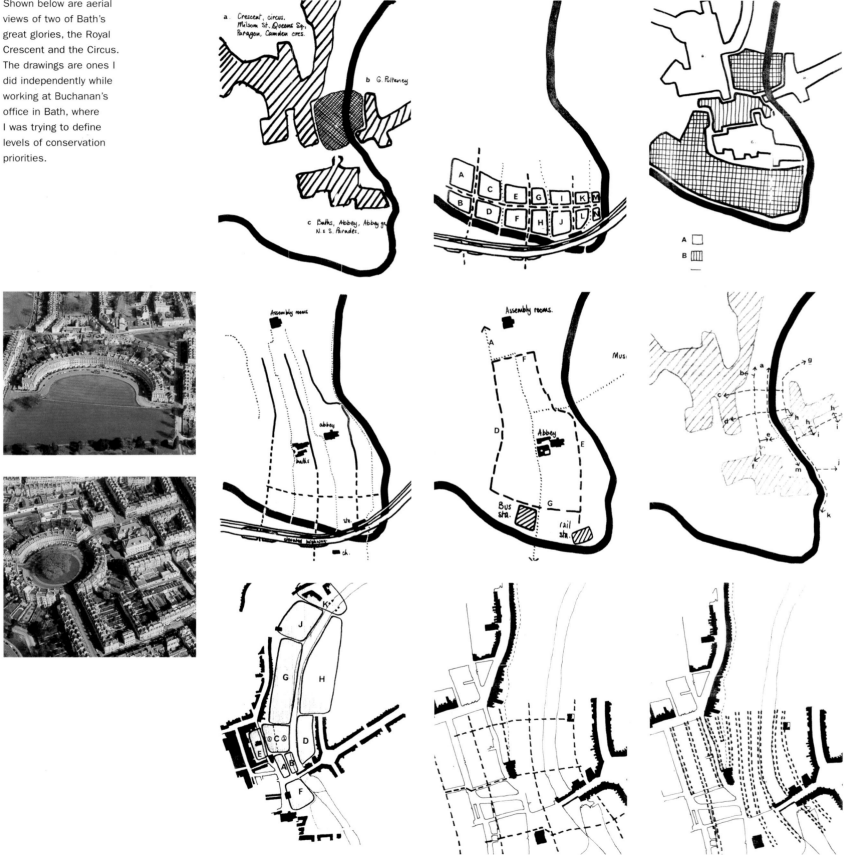

a. Crescent, circus.
Milsom St., Queens Sq.,
Paragon, Camden cres.

b G. Pulteney

c Baths, Abbey, Abbey gr.
N. & S. Parades.

A ☐
B ▥

Assembly rooms.

abbey

baths

sta.

elevated highway

ch.

Assembly rooms.

Mus

A

F

D

Abbey

E

Bus
sta.

G

rail
sta.

b a g

c

d h h h i

e i

f m j

k

K

J

G H

E C D

A B

F

combined with teaching – recalled my days at Penn. In my mind, there seemed to be a link between Colin Buchanan and Philadelphia's chief planner, Ed Bacon, since they both combined education and practice. But Bacon started from place, whilst Buchanan – like those involved in revolutionary UK mass housing, or Le Corbusier's planning ideas – began with an issue. Buchanan's working method was to state a problem and present closed-logic options to solve it. Everyone in welfare-state Britain was doing it at the time: architects, planners and politicians solved crime, homelessness and traffic by applying generic answers to perceived generic problems, yet applied them wholesale in specific neighbourhoods, towns and cities. Abstract traffic theories resulted in tight ring roads that nearly destroyed wonderful towns that I grew to know well, such as Chester and Huntington.

Buchanan himself was a thoughtful and intelligent man, part civil servant, part academic, part private-sector planning consultant, but rightly remembered as an advocate and investigator – and as Britain's pre-eminent thinker at that time on the relationship between place and the new personal mobility offered by the motor car. He sought an answer to the question: 'How can the predicted traffic growth be best assimilated and designed into our great towns and cities?' To me, the question was posed in the wrong way. It should have been: 'What is so essential to the character, nature and quality of our places that these characteristics survive despite technological and democratic changes in people movement?' From Buchanan's 'Traffic in Towns' study came a well-presented, well-argued book of the same name.

Some of my current project preoccupations are linked with my work for Buchanan in the 1960s. What had been a 'Buchanan offices' local tube station, South Kensington, now features as the central part of Terry Farrell & Partners' masterplan for the area – and the traffic engineers are Buchanan's firm. We are looking at pedestrianizing parts of South Kensington – an idea that would never have been seriously considered in the 1960s. Then, we would have asked: 'What is the least change for the most car gain?' Forty years later, we are working with the help of Buchanan's office to conserve South Kensington by enlarging pavements and improving pedestrian connections, including the foot tunnel

linking the tube station to the museums. Pedestrians and public transport are our starting points, and we are examining how far we can go in restricting the freedom of the car to achieve our aims. It is a completely different urban-planning culture from that of the 1960s. I have also been looking at Buchanan's proposals for Tottenham Court Road as part of TFP's rethinking of the Marylebone and Euston roads.

While at Buchanan's I was given my own project within a larger team working on an ambitious study for Bath, which addressed the likely impact on one of Britain's premier historic cities of a predicted increase in car movement. Not surprisingly, it turned out that wider issues of conservation, local democracy, funding and the limitations of planning controls would need to be resolved in parallel, and so without major work on these fronts the study turned out to be somewhat academic and self-serving. In 2002, I visited Bath during an extremely busy pre-Christmas shopping day. The traffic was unpleasantly congested and intrusive, the car parks were full, and the pedestrian streets were heaving with people. But in the evening the streets quietened down and Bath reasserted itself as an acceptably liveable place – a lesson, perhaps, in the benefits of non-planning. With the introduction of 'park and ride', micro-management of streets, modest pedestrianization and the effect of congestion itself being a natural deterrent to cars, the draconian measures tabled in 1965 proved unnecessary. Future traffic management innovations – combined, possibly, with changes in society's attitude to shopping, shorter working hours, the advent of cleaner, smaller, quieter vehicles and better public transport – should allow historic Bath to emerge as an intact, harmonious place, a working, living city in spite of, as well as because of, its world heritage status. As it turned out, the ambitious road plans for greater car ownership as addressed in my Buchanan office days will not be needed, and Bath has been and will be better off left as it is.

Some time before the age of 'conservation areas', I became interested in the idea of groups of informal buildings and whole streetscapes that did not have the status of formal set-pieces such as crescents and circuses, and where buildings may not individually have been of the highest standard but drew their importance collectively from being a fine group. How could one protect their more elusive qualities? In Buchanan's office I made my own analysis of areas and street blocks and their relative values, and tried to analyse the characteristics that made the places unique.

The true originality of Bath lies not only in its fine Georgian architecture as such, but in how the layout of these buildings exploits the contours and gradients of the city's site. The 18th- and 19th-century demand for fine-house building to be widened to include a mass market (albeit a middle-class one) made it possible to build layer upon layer of serpentine stone terraces up the valley slopes, reinforcing the place's unique geography. Like New York and Venice, Bath has an intense, all-built-at-once, time-capsuled personality – its flair, architectural quality and urban integrity will always endure.

Bath is a compelling example of the differences that can exist between the fronts and backs of buildings. The fronts create the spaces (the crescents and circuses) and the backs are left to let hang – never in any other town have I seen such a contrast between the two. It seems to me that the backs of the terraces make the fronts look like public fancy dress. The sublimely controlled classical fronts define geometrically pure spaces and face parkland, while the private backs form a random picturesque composition and face fields or the backs of other terraces. The result is two kinds of space: the back gardens have all the idiosyncrasies and personalization of allotments, while the front gardens are solely concerned with their part in the public realm. The backs of Bath's houses are extraordinarily complex and quite beautiful in their own right. Jim Stirling once mischievously said that he often preferred the backs of buildings to the fronts, and it is possible in Bath to be sympathetic to this viewpoint. Later in my career, at Oakwood, TVam and elsewhere, I deliberately designed buildings with fronts and backs. But modern architecture has not given much recognition to fronts and backs since it has dealt with buildings as objects standing alone in the round.

My own project was to see if a linear car park could be integrated into a riverbank slope below Walcot Street. It was the kind of three-dimensional urban design project that particularly intrigued me, demanding ingenuity with levels, car access and air rights above the new car park. But I always felt it was something of a paper project and,

like the studies in 'Traffic in Towns', it was one of a series of test cases that at best illuminated the generic problems of English towns and cities, and at worst became lost in the many difficulties of modern town planning.

Architects' disillusionment with planning led to a polarization between those who felt the only answer was total demolition and comprehensive redevelopment, and those who wanted to retain all historic built fabric regardless of social, economic and technological changes. These opposing factions were frequently perceived as modernists versus traditionalists – an over-simplification that acquired momentum in the 1970s and continued into the 1980s. Planners, architects and politicians paraded dangers and problems like the impact of car ownership in the manner of witch doctors whose bloodletting and other remedies often endanger patients' lives. Come to think of it, witch doctors might have done less damage to our towns and cities than many of the city fathers, whose 'cures' were often worse than the perceived illnesses, and whose grasp of the future proved no more soundly based than fortune-telling by crystal balls. In spite of this ignorance, inner-urban road-building in Britain blindly took place with a zealous confidence on a grand scale.

I worked at Colin Buchanan's office for seven months – the only 'employment' I have had since qualifying as an architect. Since leaving Buchanan's I have only ever worked for myself – indeed, within three months of starting there I had already decided to embark on an independent path with Nick Grimshaw. But a positive memory of my time with Buchanan's has remained with me. I was among a committed, intelligent and thoughtful group of people, and the projects we undertook tried hard, if unfashionably and thanklessly, to address many contemporary urban problems.

The next step was to set up my own architectural practice. I had to face the reality of dealing directly with clients, fees, premises and, above all, the daily business of designing, making and building. For a while, urban planning, placemaking, the feelings and needs of the often invisible multitude of hands creating our cities, all faded from my daily life. I had two children, so there were now two 'families' – a domestic one and an office one – to occupy all of my available time and more!

Colin Buchanan, as he appeared on the cover of *I Told You So*, a book which focuses on his lifelong preoccupation with the influence of the motor car on our cities, a subject also examined in *Mixed Blessing*. His seminal work on planning was 'Traffic in Towns'.

4

1965–81: PRACTICE

Farrell/Grimshaw Partnership: early years • Islington: setting up practice • Windmill Street and Fitzrovia: the world of the Architectural Association • Bayswater: the students' hostel and other conversions • Park Road: a new home, a first new building • **FGP: an established practice** • The Colonnades: architecture meets urban design • Survival by design: one office, two diverging viewpoints • The new paradigm: mass housing without modernism • Maida Vale: a new home, a new family, a new view of life • **Ending FGP and starting TFP** • Rethinking the industrial shed: taking high-tech out to play • Temporary buildings and garden centres • Learning from Chigwell and bungalows • The house as a small city; transitions of scale • End piece

Farrell/Grimshaw Partnership: early years

Islington: setting up practice

The years 1965 and 1966 were an adventurous and exciting time, but marked by change, upheaval and problems. With virtually no experience, Nick Grimshaw and I had thrown ourselves in at the deep end of building construction and practice, and we soon discovered that partnership was a very adult world, requiring for its success a mature and committed attitude. At its best, a partnership is liberating and supportive and opens up greater opportunities. I felt in childhood it had served me well to develop a sense of myself and my own independence by always mentally separating myself from my three brothers and, later, from my class colleagues and rivals at architecture school. But in my twenties working and personal relationships grew and evolved, which changed everything, and by my 27th birthday I had a married partnership with Rosemarie and had become a professional architectural partner with my good and close friend Nick Grimshaw.

Nick was in his last year at the Architectural Association (AA), and although I had accepted the position of unit master for the year from Roy Landau, third-year master at the AA, I also had to manage the day-to-day running of the new practice. I had not been particularly attracted by the prospect of teaching, but it had seemed a practical solution to covering some of our costs, and the AA offered the opportunity to meet stimulating and inspiring staff and students from all over the world.

I had felt very much on the back foot when I first returned to London from the USA, with the realization that many newly qualified architects were getting better jobs than I was being offered because of the number and quality of the contacts they had cultivated, or because they had been getting two years' experience while I continued my education. Being good wasn't enough. But at last things took a turn for the better. Through Nick's uncle, I rented a large but derelict house in Islington, north London, on condition that I did it up. When the work was complete we had a house with three rooms to let, as well as enough room for

Left, top: The house in Alwyne Villas, Canonbury, north London, where we set up office and home.

Left, second from top: An aerial view of Canonbury and Highbury in the borough of Islington, with Highbury Fields top left.

Left, second from bottom: A three-dimensional map of Mayfair's Grosvenor estate by Stephen Conlin, which clarifies the layout of the estate.

Bottom: A map of the London aristocratic estates. Planned and laid out with care, they benefit from continuing stewardship, reinforcing a patchwork of place identity within London's disorganized mass.

my family and a basement office for Farrell/Grimshaw Architects. This single entrepreneurial arrangement provided free accommodation for my family and cheap rent for our practice, and the three architectural students who rented the rooms soon became useful part-time employees. I remember the delight of sitting on a hill in Hampstead after earlier walking out of the Kensington High Street branch of the National Westminster bank, where I had successfully arranged an overdraft for £675 to convert the house, and with a mixture of relief and surprise repeating over and over again, 'The world works – it actually works!'

Our house was in Canonbury, an estated part of Islington owned by the Earl of Northampton, making it part of a long tradition of British land ownership often traceable back to the Norman invasion of 1066 and based on the subsequent division of Norman lands, whose aristocratic and benignly autocratic control has evolved so slowly over a period of 1,000 years that its feudal roots still show. This book was partly written at a cottage I rented on the great estate of Badminton in Gloucestershire, where the Duke of Beaufort 'reigns' – his presence as a land monarch is manifest in everything around, from great parklands with high deer-proof fencing and impeccable drystone walls to villages full of neat estate workers' houses and cottages. The estate reflects the positive contribution made by stewardship, which enabled the preservation of a total sense of place, wherever it was, in the country or in the town.

In the modern urban world we rarely manage well the estate of the public domain. Roads, for example, are the victims of a free-for-all between the police, traffic engineers, telephone and communication engineers and others, who regularly and discordantly rip up streets and pavements and have the power to decide which territory can be occupied by pedestrians or cars, in an anarchy of signs and street furniture. From my experience of studying Lytham, I learned that it takes generations of continuously intense interest and care to make the public domain a good place to be. The New World also taught me about custodianship. When I went to Philadelphia, I saw that the Quaker city fathers had ensured that their big city plan was implemented properly over a long period of time. Some of the British land-holding princes were also instrumental in developing good urban areas. The 4th Earl of Bedford had laid out much of Bloomsbury in the 17th century and, in particular, the Covent Garden piazza, which has again become an important element of London's urban heart, as well as containing Inigo Jones's fine church of St Paul's and the Royal Opera House. Like the Duke of Bedford, the Earl of Northampton at Canonbury applied himself to great London improvements, including his 'new river', a man-made but natural-looking landscaped waterway that fed reservoirs close to Sadler's Wells, supplying fresh water to the City of London. Canonbury was totally different from my previous homes in Chelsea and Kensington High Street, but it had a settled liveability that came from good terraces and villas that had been managed well over time. Later on, when I acted for Grosvenor Estates and got to know Mayfair, I developed a respect for the careful custodianship of land, streets as well as buildings, demonstrated by the urban landed estates. And later, when we had offices off Marylebone High Street, my admiration extended to include big managed London estates such as Portman, Cavendish and Harley.

And so, Rosemarie and I had a home for several years on the Northampton estate, and there Nick and I set up our first office, in one of Canonbury's generous Victorian semi-detached villas, with the New River running along the end of the garden. At the top of the street lived the architect Basil Spence (who, in the true spirit of the times, proposed knocking down the whole conservation area and rebuilding to his own grand designs), and various well-off city financiers, but at the other end, and in the area generally, was a very mixed society indeed, with multiple occupancy homes and council estates right next door to houses owned by professional people who had just moved into the area. In contrast with American cites, the mixture of income and social groups in London is often closer, more overlapping and less static. The location of each of these groups has changed considerably over time. The Victorians identified socio-economic placemaking in the Booth maps over 150 years ago – a brave and revealing documentation of the social housing range and its extremes in Victorian London. Throughout the 20th century the social groupings and their locations ebbed and flowed – Islington, although I didn't know it then, was at the beginning of an era of what soon became known across London as 'gentrification', as poorer people moved out further north and east, and professional city workers, gradually recognizing the qualities of the tree-lined terraced streets so close to their workplace, moved in. I enjoyed my time in Islington, I went with friends to jazz at Cross Street and saw Chris Barber and Humphrey Lyttleton, and played football and picnicked on Highbury Fields. In our office we assembled furniture, equipment and part-time secretarial help. We acquired telephones, diaries, bank balances and rudimentary cash books (Nick's responsibility). Gradually we set up shop, working for ourselves in the two-roomed basement.

Windmill Street and Fitzrovia: the world of the Architectural Association

In the summer of 1966, we moved our office out of the Canonbury house. By then Rosemarie and I had had our second daughter, Jo, and we needed the extra room. Farrell/Grimshaw rented an office for £500 a year in Windmill Street, off Charlotte Street, north of Soho. We sublet half of it to Archigram, the architectural group formed in 1961 by Peter Cook, Michael Webb and David Green, and later joined by Ron Herron, Dennis Crompton and Warren Chalk, whom I had met in passing on my one day working for the London County Council on the South Bank project. By happy chance, 37 years later I was on the RIBA awards committee that nominated Archigram for the Royal Gold Medal.

Archigram, our tenants for about a year, seemed to me to be the 1960s architectural equivalent of a pop group such as the Beatles – chaotic, highly innovative and creative. Sometimes all of them would be there; sometimes their office would be deserted. But always they attracted architectural tourists and students from around the globe. International fans would mistakenly knock on our door, asking in broken English, 'Archigram, yes?' – to which we got used to replying, 'Archigram, no!' Our move from suburban Canonbury had, it seemed to me then, located us right in the centre of the global architectural scene.

Windmill Street in 1966 was an area of restaurants, the rag trade and a growing contingent of media companies. It was close to the Bartlett School of Architecture at University College London; the Architectural

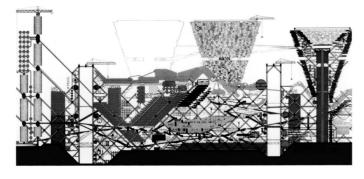

Right, top: Image of 'Plug-in City: Maximum Pressure Zone' (1964) by Peter Cook of Archigram.

Right, dome pictures, from top: Design for a dome over New York by Buckminster Fuller; a sectionalized inflatable dome created by my AA architectural students in the back garden of our Canonbury house; a drawing by François Dellegret of a total life-support system within a dome house (illustrating the article 'A Home is not a House' by Reyner Banham).

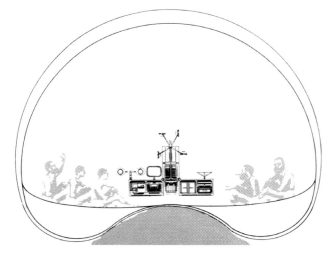

Above: A drawing c. 1840 of Windmill Street, where Farrell/Grimshaw had an office from 1966. Our territory was Nos. 8–10 (centre of picture), where the Middlesex Hospital began in 1745.

Below: Illustration of Cedric Price's plan using railway lines and rolling stock to create a mobile university in Staffordshire devoted to science and technology (The 'Potteries Thinkbelt').

principals going on to careers in their own right: Stirling/Gowan, Foster/Rogers and Farrell/Grimshaw (although Nick and I were to be together for 15 years). Many staff moved from one office to another, and there is a fascinating study to be done on the network of relationships – a sort of family tree linking architects from this area at that time.

It was as much a village of specialized workers as the steelworkers of Sheffield or the lawyers of Lincoln's Inn. We came together for stimulus, access to common services (such as Advance the printer) and a shared liking for the kind of buildings, streets and restaurants of the area, and we were not the only specialist work group in this part of London. Apart from the rag trade and the media companies, another prominent and sprawling neighbour was the Middlesex Hospital. Indeed, the 18th-century terraced house that served as our office had been, more than 200 years earlier, the Middlesex Hospital's first building. Our first full-time secretary, Maggie Jones, left a job at the hospital in 1967 to work for me and has stayed with me ever since, one of her recent tasks being to put this book on computer.

Association in Bedford Square was just to the east, the RIBA to the west, and Ove Arup's large and growing engineering offices a few hundred yards to the north. As a result, many architects had their (at that time, small and new) offices nearby – Norman Foster on Charlotte Street, Richard Rogers behind Marylebone High Street, Cedric Price on Alfred Place, and Denys Lasdun and Stirling & Gowan near Regent's Park. We found ourselves in a 'place' of architects, with the engineers at Ove Arup's providing a serviced focus for many embryonic practices. The growth of this 1960s 'north of Oxford Street' community of architects is interesting to trace. Three embryonic practices established themselves in this location and then divided, with all the separate

The Windmill Street office became for us all a kind of family, which formed part of one specialized community within other, overlapping work communities. The communities of my childhood had consisted of family, residential neighbourhood, school and church. Now my notion of people and family, home and place was evolving and changing – my father died in 1967, the rest of my family was distant, and at the end of 1968, with difficulty and much sadness, Rosemarie and I separated. There were solid, valued, neighbourly relationships here – resulting from propinquity rather than any common work interest. There were the two Greek brothers who set up the corner restaurant, the Greek alterations tailor on the corner and Mr Shiner the ironmonger. This was urban life, metropolitan 'down town' life, quite unlike anything I had experienced before. For a long time afterwards, in fact almost every day, I ate at Tony's and Dino's Greek restaurant, and over 35 years I registered their children being born, growing up and becoming their waiters during college holidays, and then in 2001 the two brothers eventually returned 'home' to Cyprus to retire. Charlotte Street and north Soho has an intertwined, interdependent dynamic that exists because of density and intensity and variety of activity. While this part of London might be described as having its own character, the idea of place needs redefining in such city centres, since its edges and its connections to everything outside itself are a relatively seamless continuum. I began to understand more and more that, although 'place' has a meaning that we all subscribe to, it can be interpreted in many ways; and here it was best defined not by its edges like a walled city or an island, nor by a monocultural activity, nor by managed land ownership, but by a series of focal points. My world at this time had such a focus, namely Charlotte Street, at the heart of an area now known as 'Fitzrovia'. As urban life develops, names are given to mark the evolution of such focal points. In New York, the area south of Houston Street in lower Manhattan gradually became known as SoHo; similarly, in London, many names are invented as local consensus identifies a 'place' within the dense forest of bricks, glass and concrete.

When writing this chapter it occurred to me that, in 1960s London, place had an additional way of being defined that is no longer available today. This was by telephone 'address'. My telephone number pinpointed the particular London village which was my home: for example, in Kensington my number was KEN 6431 and in Canonbury CAN 0963, and this gave one kind of face to the place. The vast increase in numbers, coupled with revolutionary developments in information technology and communications, has created a different spatial context altogether. The relationship between place and telephone numbers is rapidly evaporating because there has been such an extraordinary scale shift. Nowadays people talk not about telephone addresses on the scale of Whitehall or Mayfair, but of global regions like the Pacific Rim, North America and Europe. Thanks to satellites, telephone numbers exist in outer space in a completely new way, and thanks to mobile phones our telephone 'place' is now geographically anywhere – its real home is, well, just each individual's pocket, briefcase or handbag.

Nevertheless, I presume that those people who experienced the very earliest days of the telephone, from the 1920s to the 1940s, lamented what they saw as the subsequent displacing state of affairs in the 1950s and

Left: The Bartlett School of Architecture when Grimshaw and I taught there was housed in an elegant 18th-century building in the Wilkins courtyard of University College London (top), but in the 1970s it moved to an adjacent prefabricated modern building called Wates House (second from top). The third picture from the top shows the completed new Bartlett School.

Left, bottom: The Architectural Association was carved out and converted from a row of fine 18th-century terraced houses in Bedford Square.

SW7	KENsngtn	3531
3dge rd SW11	BATtersea	2994
dwy NW2	GLAdstn	4176
SW3	KNIghtsbge	9440
WC2	GERrard	1094
ins W13	PERivale	9753
le W5	ALPertn	1119
W8	KNIghtsbge	6810
es SW1	KNIghtsbge	9879
inchley rd NW3	HAMpstd	9462
N15	PUTney	3862
Vw rd N8	MOUntvw	3616
V9	COLindale	4415
'eedington rd NW5	GULliv	3343
pl W2	PARk	7998
SW10	FLAxman	9623
s NW10	LADbroke	1376
i W12	SHEphrds Bsh	8535
W6	RENown	5877
17	BALham	3086

In the 1960s telephone numbers identified geographical locations: excerpt from a telephone directory of the time.

Topical architecture in the 1960s: Unité d'Habitation in Marseilles by Le Corbusier (top); Ronan Point tower block in east London (centre), which collapsed after a gas explosion; and James Stirling's library in Cambridge (bottom).

1960s. They had been used to speaking via local operators whose names (as well as their personal family affairs) they knew. In its infancy the telecommunications world was less than half a step away from physical place – you could even go outside your front door and see above your head on poles the very wires that connected you to the faraway person to whom you were speaking. There was a visible physical connection, a tangible world that, as with all technological change, seemed fantastical and avant-garde yet part of an acceptable state of change that society could cope with. Technological changes shifts these constructs of perceived 'reality'; one's sense of place is time-based as well as space-based – the London village-based telephone communities no longer exist.

The energetic heart of this part of my life was the AA, which was (and still is) located in a group of London terraced properties managed by the Bedford estate, showing the inherent flexibility of this Georgian domestic building type. At this period many schools of architecture moved from their fine traditional 'homes' to new-built premises. It seemed an act of moral commitment in the 1960s and 1970s for the Bartlett, for example, to leave its elegant stone-faced home in the William Wilkins neoclassical quadrangle at University College London for an ugly brand-new building two blocks away; for my old graduate school at Penn University to give up its attractive and much-loved home to the fine artists and move into a plain and uninspiring new building; for Edinburgh's architecture school to move out of its lofty classical home to a much inferior modern building; and, much more dramatically, for architecture staff and students in Glasgow to abandon their home in the greatest art and architecture school in the world, designed by Charles Rennie Mackintosh, in favour of an aesthetically sub-standard beast next door. The moves were justified in terms of newness, change, innovation and commitment to 'progress'. But arguably the world's most radical and challenging school of architecture in the past 50 years has stayed put in a row of 230-year-old terraced houses where former maids' and butlers' rooms, grand drawing rooms, dining rooms, hallways and a complex of bedrooms and backstairs utility rooms have all been transformed to sustain a radically challenging educational birthplace for architects. This was, and is, a sense of place to be reckoned with.

The idea of buildings as inherently flexible challenges the modernist preoccupation with 'form follows function', which led to a highly exaggerated reverence for the exaggerated role of 'function'. If it seemed that a library (such as Stirling's in Cambridge) functioned solely around a library supervisor who needed to see the readers, that need became the total driving force behind the whole design. But a library is multilayered. It may be somewhere that people go, say, to enjoy quietness – but Stirling's library underrated quietness: as a result of the big volume designed to facilitate the job of the library supervisor, the place is noisier than a library should be. The belief in 'form follows function' comes from a pseudo-scientific approach that denies the difference between architecture and the design of a product component or a functional machine. It has always seemed obvious to me that form should follow the broadest aspects of human nature rather than function alone.

The AA brought together lively artists, sociologists and stimulating architects (the most conspicuous being Cedric Price and Archigram) and played a central role in another place-defining feature of the 1960s: 'Swinging London'. The spirit of the times was captured in the crossover between architecture, fashion design and photography. The AA architect Mark Fisher became the key designer for Pink Floyd and went on to design sets for the Rolling Stones, and 1960s architecture students such as Janet Bull (now Street-Porter), Tim Street-Porter and Fergus Henderson went on to become well-known players on the fashion, media and restaurant scenes.

The climate of social change in Britain was stimulated by a radical change of government that occurred in late 1964, just as I got back from the USA. Prime Minister Harold Wilson's speech acclaiming the 'white heat of technology' spoke directly to architects, specifically to the high-tech futurists, in a way that no British prime minister has done before or since. Trends in cars, design, pop music and politics all seemed to be bubbling with innovation. This was a culture which gave a freer role to women (the pill had arrived!), which took serious note of its youth, and which marked the beginning of the end of much of Britain's class structure as the postwar meritocracy brigade came of age. John Lennon, David Bailey, Mick Jagger, Peter Cook (the architect), Norman Foster, Alan Bennett, David Hockney and

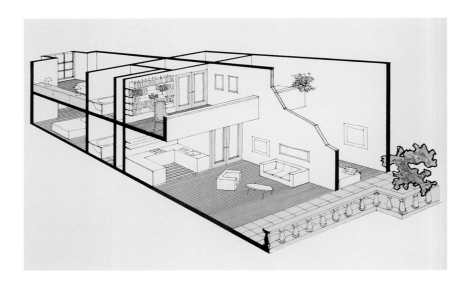

Top row: Among the many houses Farrell/Grimshaw converted into private flats were these at (from left to right) Redcliffe Square, Sussex Gardens and Westbourne Terrace, all in west London.

Above, left and right: Sussex Gardens before and after the houses' interiors were converted into a students' hostel with a service tower at the rear.

Below: The lunar module (left) was the inspiration behind the little service module (centre and right) that I developed for attachment to a range of living spaces – for example, a mobile home, a house in the country with no mains services or a weekend home. The module provided power, water, central heating and all other facilities necessary to make a house habitable. The project was sponsored by the *Sunday Times* to appear in one of its first colour supplements.

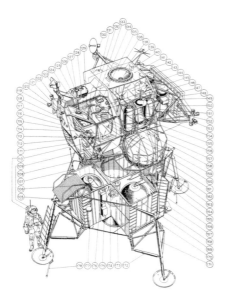

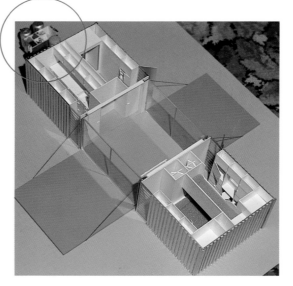

others were all provincial or suburban boys who made good. To my great surprise, I felt immediately at home, having left London for the USA only two or three years earlier feeling quite out of sympathy with what seemed to me then a city founded on unchangeable Victorian attitudes and values.

An AA student, Peter Murray, founded his own magazine, *Clip-Kit*, and published our first project; we were in print – the media acknowledged we existed and we in turn acknowledged the media and its powers. In the 1960s the new colour technology transformed the media. Until then, most photography was black and white, as was television. To me, the printing of the first newspaper colour supplements seemed like the opening of a great door. I had always loved the format of the film *The Wizard of Oz*, which begins in black and white and then transforms to colour; in the same way, I felt that the grey postwar depression had lifted in the two years I had been away and London was a new colourful place.

Bayswater: the students' hostel and other conversions

Farrell/Grimshaw Architects took on work that was very different from that of many of our contemporaries, for whom this was the era of new towns, public housing estates and greenfield universities – all government 'welfare state' projects. We made our living for about ten years from what we would today describe as private-sector urban regeneration, which included converting houses, and eventually whole streets, into flats and mixed uses. The international students' hostel in Sussex Gardens, Bayswater – the brainchild of Nick's Uncle George, a missionary – was very much part of this pattern. The concept was to marry the Church of England's missionary commitment to helping African and other Commonwealth students to the building of low-cost accommodation in London. The initial phase of the project involved the purchase and restoration of six derelict houses on the corner of Westbourne Terrace and Sussex Gardens. Empty since the Second World War, the houses were full of dry rot, and the project was fraught with difficulty from the beginning. Empty derelict houses in an area where now, 40 years later, even the smallest bedsit sells for hundreds of thousands of pounds, was a legacy of the immediate postwar decline in London's fortunes. The houses confirmed

the English Heritage saying that neglect is a great conserver since the basic structure and most of their fine interiors had not been 'modernized' and were therefore mostly intact. But our approach was not merely conservationist, and Buckminster Fuller, when he saw the completed students' hostel, was full of enthusiasm about what we had done, particularly about the service tower and the mobile furniture unit. Like Fuller's dome over New York, our project was characterized by a pragmatic radicalism rather than by the ideological utopianism of Le Corbusier and Gropius.

I began to think more and more at this time about reconciling the two great influences of recent years: Buckminster Fuller and Louis Kahn. When it came to change, permanence and sense of place, at first sight the two architects I most admired were almost at opposite ends of the spectrum. Bucky was drawn to the lightweight and movable and became obsessed by the idea of no-place – famously, he used to ask, 'How much does your building weigh?' – and he described the world as 'spaceship earth'. Conversely, Kahn would seek to find the most permanent and enduring building typologies. He built in brick and designed heavy buildings rooted in the earth. Kahn, looking for the unique occupation of man in space, would ask, 'What is a school? Is a school just a teacher standing under a tree?' And that embrace of ultimate, philosophically driven minimalism was an answer that Bucky Fuller would have recognized. Bucky found normality in change, – 'change is normal' – while Kahn looked for 'the true permanence'. Yet they both ended up nearly at the same place, exploring universal spaces and forms, because they were both fundamentalists and humanists.

Between the two standpoints represented by Fuller and Kahn is the transitory nature of personal life, and indeed of all human experience. It was not long since the mid 1950s. when Crick and Watson in Cambridge had discovered the 'secret of life', bringing together biology and geometry in their research into DNA, to extend to completely new dimensions our understanding of the biological world and our physical constitution. During the 1960s space travel dramatically expanded my generation's grasp of space and man's role in the larger environment. The fundamentals of our lives, we saw, were moving into territories of the ultra-minute and the ultra-enormous, and along with this came insights into the time factor in the evolution of organisms and their ever-shifting nature, and the time factors of the universe and its own vast and changing history. Our collective understanding of transformation and its layered phases gradually went deep down to a few chemical elements, the very fabric that goes into making the concrete, stone and glass of our buildings, as well as to the coded assembly of the atoms that our bodies were ever transforming but on different time scales – as much by chance as design.

My thinking about what is permanent and what changes took on a scale shift at this time. Archigram's fantasies, Buckminster Fuller's radical engineering ideas, Louis Kahn's search for the inner, collectively understood fundamentals, all were to me a collage of architectural influences that had the potential to add up, providing I didn't search for simplistic, idealistic answers. Gradually, it reinforced the death of all certainties relating to political 'isms', religious institutions and artistic and architectural movements. The knowledge that had emerged in the preceding 100 years had seemingly conquered the world; all its nooks and crannies and what we understood could be codified with confidence – but now that all seemed scientifically immature, and we were once again in a vast natural world that went well beyond anyone's immediate vision and understanding.

We each have our own fierce determination, our brief opportunity to reconcile in our lifetime what the short, transitory journey of human life means in relation to permanence. Place reflects the search for a point of rest, and our habitats, the cities and towns, offer substantial scope for expressing this collective anxiety and exploring its dynamic. The permanence of cities and yet the continuous adaptation to which they are subjected fascinated me. At the students' hostel, the act of restoring those fine buildings respected their permanence, yet our conservation approach depended on mobile, lightweight architectural moves; it was a microcosm of many subsequent projects. The buildings themselves were repaired and restored – but with connecting corridors and sleep balconies in double-height rooms. All the additions deliberately preserved the positive qualities of the existing fabric – we were innovatory but also respectful. New bathrooms and

plumbing were installed and housed in a new stand-alone tower at the back, and much of the furniture comprised freestanding mobile units. The spatial potential of the existing honeycomb of cellular rooms was maximized by a new floor of rooftop dormer rooms. Redundant service staircases had new floors at half-landings and the six backyards were united in one double-height, glass-roofed space that linked with the ground and lower-ground communal rooms.

Nick Grimshaw spent almost all his time on the service tower, a very clever and thoughtful piece of work that subsequently attracted much favourable attention. I designed the mobile furniture and the main building, its interiors and all its furniture, but I also had to concentrate a considerable amount of time on the conversion of the houses and running the overall contract, dealing with the big picture. To some extent, this set the pattern for the way we worked for the rest of our time at Farrell/Grimshaw. Nick usually took responsibility for the more self-contained and technically interesting aspects of a job. He had the advantage that we had set up together as the result of his uncle's patronage – and it was a pattern I found hard to shift. It is often said that the first six months of any relationship sets the pattern for its duration; to change people's interactive dynamics is often harder than changing buildings and cities, and I would have to wait a good few years before the disadvantage to me of this interactive imbalance was overcome – but there were nevertheless many advantages in the relationship, and I was determined to use the years well, to discover and learn in the widest way I could.

We were designing in a period of great excitement and invention. It was the brave new London world of PVC and miniskirts, plastic jewellery, pop music and a youth lifestyle that challenged all the stiff British conventions born of decades of conservatism. Underlying the excitement of our first job was an extremely difficult building contract. During my first meeting with the builder, he told me that he was worried about the approvals for the drawings. Did I know whether we had met the means-of-escape requirements? When he asked me if the district surveyor had seen the drawings, I answered, 'What's a district surveyor?' Thinking I must be a junior Farrell, the builder asked me if this was my father's practice, to which I replied that I was a partner and that the

Above: The service tower at Sussex Gardens under construction.

Below: Nick Grimshaw ready for a Beatles fancy-dress party dressed in a Sergeant Pepper outfit.

Above and left: Some of the publicity material we prepared in an attempt to interest a retailer such as Habitat in our mobile furniture unit. The idea was 40 years ahead of its time – similar designs are now being sold at Habitat and elsewhere.

Below left: Carnaby Street, Christmas 1967.

Below: The cover of the first issue of *Clip-Kit* magazine, founded by Peter Murray.

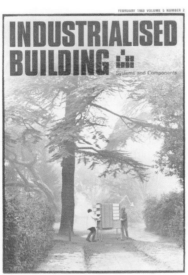

only other partner was a year younger than me. I was now 27 years old and the builder was really alarmed by my youth and lack of experience. I realized how naive I must have sounded, but I persevered and completed the project by sheer application and determination. By the time it was finished – after I had had to sack for incompetence the very contractor who had doubted my credentials – I had learned about, and dealt capably with, a wide variety of contract, construction and consultant coordination issues.

The hostel was built as a private-sector development. Many commentators thought the result, on a fine architectural street in the middle of town, preferable to the new-build greenfield solutions of the state system, and believed that the inherent lack of bureaucracy within the client body had contributed to the successful outcome. By looking at how existing buildings could be reused we kept the costs down, and completed the hostel for less than half the cost and in half the time that the University Grants Committee usually allowed for student hostels. The bedrooms were fitted out for a total of £73 each, with furniture designed by me, and the public-area furniture was built by Nick's cousin, John Grimshaw (who now runs the sustainable transport organization Sustrans). The central feature of each bedroom was a furniture trolley. The trolley wasn't iconic in the way the service tower was, but it was similarly consistent with the idea of the building shell being separated from the new service element within it. I regarded that trolley as innovatory as well as being an accessible and friendly piece of design. Bucky Fuller was much impressed by it and today, 40 years later, there are several reinterpreted versions of it for sale. The idea has at last come of age as a commercially viable lifestyle product.

During construction we experienced small but irritating problems, such as being forced to change the name of the practice from Farrell/Grimshaw Architects to Farrell/Grimshaw Partnership, after it was reported to RIBA that Nick wasn't yet qualified. But this did nothing to spoil our sense of achievement on completion of the scheme in 1968. We had designed and built a hostel that students wanted to live in. We had satisfied the client, and we had launched our reputation for marrying high-tech and lateral thinking with the reuse of existing buildings.

We then began to explore several private-housing conversion projects around Bayswater based on our work on the Sussex Gardens terraces. Characterized by large 19th-century stuccoed houses, Bayswater is one of the classic London neighbourhoods built by Victorian property developers such as the Duke of Westminster's master builder Thomas Cubitt. There are wide boulevards including Westbourne Terrace and fine squares such as Cleveland Square, and the proximity of Hyde Park to the south makes it, in spite of its postwar decline, a fine place to live. Many of the terraced houses are built on an impressive scale: from one house alone on Westbourne Terrace, we quickly and economically created eight ingenious and spacious new flats, exploiting the double-height rooms, basements, light wells, roof voids and galleries, and installing spiral staircases and compact kitchens and bathrooms. Over the next five years we created more than 300 new homes in the area. After the Second World War, the lack of servants to work in large houses fuelled a demand from a new generation of Londoners for smaller dwellings, which in turn brought about a vital shift in mortgage lending regulations. Mortgages had been available for a long time for houses, then eventually for purpose-built flats, but not until the 1960s were they normally available for apartments converted from existing older buildings.

What intrigued me was how the act of transformation, the exploitation of the accidental connections between old and new, created an original new architecture – how could the modernist dictum of 'form follows function' be right if a building built for one purpose could be successfully turned into something radically different? On the planning front, streets built 150 years ago were retained, reinforced and given 150 years' more life – having managed to avoid both comprehensive demolition (in order, it was claimed, to create 'light and air') and car-parking spaces that were then, and for decades to come, mandatory for each new-built dwelling. In contrast with Tecton's fine Hallfield Housing Estate of 1951–59 – flat blocks on nearby Bishop's Bridge Road that had deliberately been placed at a diagonal to the street grain – we were incrementally reinforcing multitudes of well-established terraced houses and streets. And, unlike most of our contemporaries, we were designing private homes for sale in large numbers; we were doing it very quickly and at realistic cost, and were completely immersed in sales brochures and pricing – the whole enterprise.

Several elements of Farrell/Grimshaw's work had their roots in the students' hostel: the more innovative building technology we used later at Park Road and the infill factories; the interest in founding our own co-ownership housing projects; and the ground-breaking urban regeneration Colonnades project in 1970–76. Our approach was to reject the doctrinaire modernist layouts in favour of mixed-use, mixed-building type, pragmatic and often traditional and contextual urban layouts. I enjoyed the challenge of this new kind of urban renewal. It was adaptation, conservation, working with the grain of towns and embracing the private sector in so many ways that were not then fashionable. I viewed many of the public housing schemes of the time almost with contempt. They seemed to me to represent expensive, vainglorious, middle-class concepts of how working-class people should live. The people responsible for these schemes were contributing to a monocultural society – and yet they continued to win all the architectural awards. Refurbishment was not considered important or significant in design circles.

In the dramatic shift in social awareness and public understanding of technological progress that happened in the 1960s, there was much conflict in personal ambitions and people's directions. It was an age of movements and enthusiasms without much resolution. Enthusiasm for space exploration grew alongside the horrors of the nuclear arms race. The peace movement and the 'love society' coexisted with the war in Vietnam, racial conflict and assassinations of civil rights leaders. The colourful and enjoyable application of technology by Archigram and Cedric Price were parallelled by the activities of large architectural practices such as Llewellyn Davies & Weekes, who embarked on a huge programme of soulless concrete hospitals, dubbed 'sick factories', and the planning of a new generation of car-dominated, mechanistic new towns like Milton Keynes. In the midst of these dynamic tensions it was rarely obvious how much technological innovation was appropriate, so Farrell/Grimshaw assessed each case on its merits. Pragmatic conservation and developer's know-how was one important influence, but on the other side

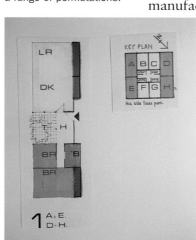

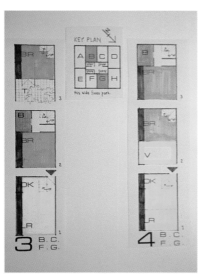

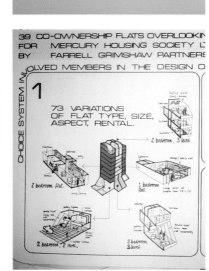

of the intellectual street, and fully embraced by us, was the 'no-where, no-place' of Archigram, in particular Ron Herron's design for a 'Walking City'; another was in the ordinary, everyday world captured in pop art and the 'as found' – finding beauty and stimulus in what we had until then taken for granted. My interest in the idea of the nomad was rekindled. I worked with mobile-home manufacturers, wrote papers on mobile homes for government housing agencies, and designed a plug-in unit to give wheeled service access to remote buildings. With AA students we experimented with inflatables and plastic enclosures, building an inflatable bubble dome in my Canonbury garden that was a forerunner of the ETFE (ethylene tetra-fluoroethylene) that we used much later at the International Centre for Life in Newcastle and the Silvertown Aquarium, and which Nick Grimshaw took further than any-one in his spectacular roof for the millennium Eden Project in Cornwall 40 years later. The beginnings, the roots of both of our careers, were spreading out with boundless youthful energy and fearless enthusiasm – everything was important, all things were possible.

Park Road: a new home, a first new building

By 1968 the government had established the Housing Corporation to promote the con-cept of co-ownership housing societies, whereby groups of individuals could club together and take out 100 per cent mort-gages. From the contacts we had made in the private housing field, we assembled a group of estate agents, surveyors, engineers, designers, teachers and others to form the Mercury Housing Society under the chair-manship of a lawyer, John Scott. I became enthusiastically involved in the whole busi-ness of how the group found the site, secured a 40-year mortgage, built the build-ing, and set about running and managing it. I tried various theoretical experiments such as allowing each member to choose and tailor-make his piece of the building, but in the final scheme the need to keep down costs drove us to make a simple repetitive plan. The chal-lenge of how to maintain choice while enjoying the benefits of mass production has always interested me. In the end, as people's circumstances changed during construction (marriage, children, relocation), it became clear that the real answer lay in maximizing flexibility. As a result, the driving force behind our architectural ideas at that time became flexibility more than individual expression and choice.

Flexibility and low-cost, utilitarian, mass-produced building methods, including a lightweight industrial outside wall, focused us on a simple plan for this, our second large project but our first new building. A building that was designed in plan and construction methods like an office building or a factory turned out to have all the innate flexibility of these building types. The relationship between converting existing build-ings, whatever their complexity, into homes or schools of architecture, for example, and building anew for later adaptation and conversion was not lost on us. We felt that the modernist 'form follows func-tion' mantra had created contorted and fixed housing forms in which exaggeration of functional nuances and excessive differentiation between types of room, orientation to the sun and overstatement of site prob-lems, all combined to make homes which in fact only marginally fulfilled their purpose. This functional expressionism led to homes that were expensive, inflexible, took a long time to build, and in use were more likely to leak and produce alienating complexi-ties of internal circulation.

Our surveyor, Len Baker, found us a site on Park Road, on the edge of Regent's Park, and I immersed myself in agreeing everything from site purchase, gov-ernment loan, planning consents and construction budget. With 40 people now on board at the Mercury Housing Society, we bought the land and began plan-ning what would be a ten-storey tower of 40 flats (which, in January 2002, 32 years after it was complet-ed, was listed by English Heritage as being of Grade II historical importance). It was not a product of top-down paternalistic government housing, nor was it one of developers making a profit from others. It was a genuinely collaborative venture that freed us as architects to explore and express the building as we wanted to. The core of the group went on to develop and build many more co-ownership housing projects, and together we helped others to build more than 1,000 co-owned homes. All in all, it was an illuminating spatial, town-planning, construction and property development experience that kept us going financially. Both Nick and I honed our business and entrepreneurial skills – in contrast to the many architects of our generation who had financed the set-up of their practice by part-time teaching and entering competitions or building state-funded projects. Political fashions then changed and the co-ownership scheme for creating new homes was ended by a Labour government nearly ten years later – and all the lessons learned, the collective teams' know-how and energetic commitment joined the ever-growing rubbish heap of Britain's postwar, stop-go, short-term, party politically motivated housing policies.

I led Park Road up to detailed planning application stage, then Nick developed the cladding and internal detailed planning and building services. It was an extremely cheap building – less than £6.50 per square foot – and the curved corner aluminium cladding and internal finishes were all part of a radical attempt to make basic, utilitarian housing that was also fresh and innovatory compared with the heavy precast-concrete estates being built at the time, such as Patrick Hodgkinson's Brunswick Centre in Bloomsbury.

Although Nick and I separately took overall responsibility for different stages of the Park Road development, there was a great deal of collaboration between us. We invariably worked in the same room, and both of us had a special interest in the outcome because we were both going to live there. Each of us ended up with a penthouse overlooking Regent's Park and the skyline of Westminster for which the repayments were a mere £25 a week. However, neither of us could afford that sum, so we each let half of our apartment to a subtenant. My tenant was a former AA student of mine, John Young, who by then was working for Richard Rogers; during the time John lived at Park Road, Rogers won the competition to design the Pompidou Centre in Paris.

By June 1970 the penthouse at Park Road was ready and we moved in. It was a completely new start for me. I had

Ham & High, July 1970

The press responds to the success of the Park Road housing scheme.

Building Design, August 1970

a new partner, Sue, interesting neighbours, and we had new work in the office. Sue had qualified in painting at art school and brought to my life a view of architecture different from what I had been used to. All the flats at Park Road had white walls, in line with the standard modernist aesthetic. Sue's and my aesthetic became increasingly eclectic and 'non-architectural'. Working in architecture can sometimes promote a rather predictable, cliquey lifestyle and an introverted culture that begins at architecture school and eventually suppresses independence and originality. While the anonymity of the 1970s interiors at Park Road might suit today's concept of good taste and appeal to loft-aspiring retro-modernists, Sue and I were more interested in exploring how popular culture could produce less conformist domestic interiors that were visually unique. It was an exploration that led us to build two permanent homes in the 1980s and 1990s which were richly decorated, highly personal and, I believe, quite original.

Our Park Road penthouse featured patterned carpets, a black floor, off-the-peg furniture, Victorian and art nouveau fabrics, a parrot in a huge cage – I felt I was immersing myself in ordinary life rather than living in an interior where everything was selected to reinforce allegiance to a style club. Furnishing the flat was a liberating experience. In a similar way, when John Scott, the Mercury chairman and lawyer, occupied his flat in Park Road next door to me, he collected antiques and demonstrated a very personal form of placemaking. He moved into what was a modern, office-like block of flats – all white, metal and high-tech – and proceeded to fill his part of it with Victoriana. Scott discovered himself at Park Road. He gave up property development in the mid 1970s and became a world-renowned specialist in Victorian furniture. He later bought two Victorian houses where he made extraordinary interiors from his collections of Guimard, Pugin, Dresser and many others, and went on to influence art and design in the wider neighbourhood of Notting Hill Gate.

My education at Philadelphia in urban planning and the experience of living in Park Road with Sue helped me realize that, although architecture schools throughout the world appeared to provide students with a technical training, in actuality this was not their primary objective. What students really got was a kind of visual literacy training, which taught them a way of seeing. They may have started their course with a love of Victorian, art deco or Indian architecture, or a passion for colour, but they often came out five years later convinced that the world should be grey, white and silver – that modernism was the only way. Everyone had been schooled (or re-educated, as the Chinese would say) into a collective way of seeing. For decades, most architects have 'seen' alike and their houses, for example, are similar, reflecting what they think the world should look like. There has been an imposed, but unacknowledged, visual discipline in the process of teaching architecture. Students were led to believe that studying architecture was about everything other than being told, 'We're going ensure that when you leave here you will have a way of seeing that conforms with most other architecture schools in the world and with how every architecture school has been seeing for the last 50 years.'

Schools of architecture and the differences between them were much on my mind at that time. The neighbouring AA, where we hired student staff, gave lectures and crits and socialized, was in the British tradition of an art school–architectural school, and up the road was the Bartlett, where Professor Richard Llewelyn Davies and John Weeks had driven a very different path – a path that was determinedly academic and scientific. C.P. Snow, author of the contemporary book *The Two Cultures*, would no doubt have enjoyed the spectacle of two such differing and conflicting educational visions for one subject area. One school concerned itself with the aesthetics, the expression of technology, where the search for order, clarity and reason was artfully translated into bright coloured plastics, sensuous metal bolts and connections, and a vision of large-span, clear, open interiors where there was such liberating flexibility that anything could happen. The other school Nick and I learned about at close hand since we became joint unit masters for the years 1969–71.

The reason for our appointment was revealing: the RIBA was seriously worried that students at the Bartlett had become so removed from art and design that the status of the school was threatened. So we two 'artistic' AA types set about teaching the art of architecture to students who had been until then taught that buildings would somehow logically result from the physics of building materials, ergonomics, the application of sociological and psychological principles and, of course, the science of building services.

For me, it all summed up the post-party depression and disorientation that characterized the end of the 1960s. The Wilson government and its 'white heat of technology' had lost its way and would soon give way to another short-lived government under Tory Ted Heath. Pop stars, such youth icons in the mid 1960s, were sinking into drugs or, like Otis Reading and Jimi Hendrix, early deaths; and in the USA liberal and civil rights leaders such as Bobby Kennedy and Martin Luther King were assassinated. The unprincipled opportunist Richard Nixon, whom we thought had been eliminated from national affairs ten years early by John F. Kennedy, now became president of the USA – what a turnaround.

However, there had been an air of stridency and unreality in the 1960s and, if there needed to be a period of reintegration, rebalancing and reflection, then I began to warm to it. The history of art in the 20th century is portrayed as being a straight-line development of the modernist school, but Venturi's book *Complexity and Contradiction* captured the reality. It wasn't a choice between art and science, or between rational order and chaos. Venturi's 'messy vitality', 'both and' (not 'either or'), and particularly 'richness of meaning over clarity of meaning', all seemed so much more attractive now.

In my new apartment I indulged in a modest return to decoration and colour, which I had enjoyed so much as a Newcastle student, and I began again to think about the lessons in conservation and urban planning I had learnt at Pennsylvania. From my tenth-floor viewpoint, I developed a passion for connecting the green spaces of London. I wrote a paper proposing the linking of 'greenways' that became the basis not just of the Royal Parks Study in the 1990s but also of a personal campaign to have walking seen as an intrinsic part of London's urban design. It continued the squares-and-pedestrians studies that I had begun in the USA in the early 1960s, and continues today in pedestrian-based urban-planning projects in different cities around the world.

It was many years later that I learned from Colin Rowe's *Collage City* that much of the planning of the great

Left: The contrasting interiors of some of the apartments in the Park Road development. The one at the top is my flat, and the second from top is Nick Grimshaw's.

Left: A representation of London's estates showing how fields on either side of village stream-beds were laid out to become the great urban estates of the Marylebone and Harley Street area.

Below: My drawing of 1992, based on earlier 1970s ideas to link the royal parks with a continuous green way.

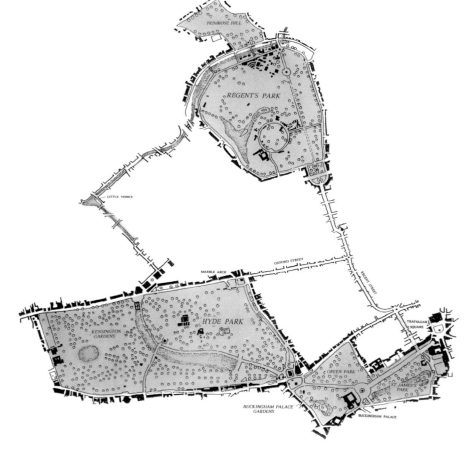

parks and their pedestrian links was based on the pattern of old river beds. Uncovering these layers today makes sense in urban aesthetic terms as well as in the sense that it links history and place. I had dug into London through walking. I used to walk to and from Buchanan's office through Kensington Gardens along the line of the Westbourne River. When we moved to Canonbury, I walked along the New River, to Highbury Fields and through Islington's squares. Later, living in Swiss Cottage, I walked a sublime route to the top of Primrose Hill, down to Regent's Park, along the Broad Walk to Fitzroy Square, Charlotte Street and our office in Windmill Street. And now from Park Road I walked through Regent's Park, along what had been the route of the Tyburn to Marylebone High Street, the old stream bed, to our new offices in Paddington Street. Until the end of the 1970s (when I again started travelling outside Britain), all my holidays had been spent in the Cheviots, Scotland and the Lake District. I was able now, as an increasingly committed urbanist, to expand further the walking experience by envisaging new and extensive walking routes linking the natural and the man-made landscapes of London.

The decorated, eclectic interior of our tenth-floor apartment was where my own architectural identity began to reshape itself, marking my separation from what I saw as straitjacketed tastes focused only on technological issues of architecture as product design. Did technology and science have the answer for architecture? The debate sowed the seeds of difference between me and Nick Grimshaw. Although we were now neighbours as well as work partners, we were living on opposite sides of the tenth floor and each looking out from interiors that, while identical in plan and section, were interpreted rather differently in terms of colour, furniture and interior design.

Far left: Excavations in 1957 under Marylebone Lane revealed the trickle of the River Tyburn.

Left: Marylebone, *c*. 1750, from the site of the present Wigmore Street, showing the Tyburn in the foreground.

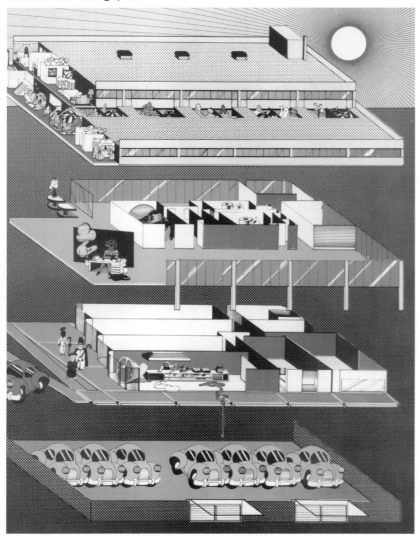

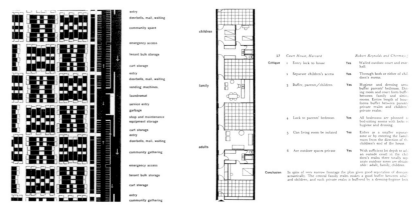

5 Courtyard Housing by Chermayeff and Alex
-ander: Densities up to 50 - 60 people
per acre can be achieved with this lay
-out. The basic layout is simple and cap
-able of a great range of variations.

56 Courtyard Housing by Chermayeff and Alex
-ander : The west has been busy learning
from the east whilst the east is determined to copy the worst western examples!

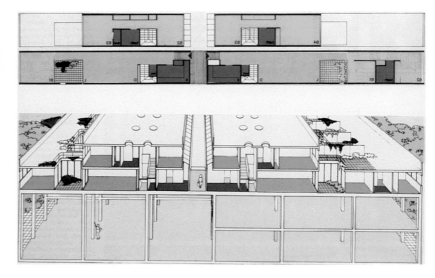

FGP: an established practice

The Colonnades: architecture meets urban design

Through the Mercury Housing Society, the group that built Park Road (see pages 209–12), I organized a bid for a large site in Wimbledon, south-west London. Mercury's bid failed but I approached the winners, Samuel Properties, and they agreed to sell us the unprofitable centre part of the site for flats, for which we developed a metal-clad co-ownership low-rise housing complex. Impressed by the ingenuity and entre-preneurship of Farrell/Grimshaw, Samuel's also put us on their list of architects for a scheme that occupied a complete urban block in Bayswater, stretching from Bishop's Bridge Road to Porchester Square, for which they had been invited to compete by the landowners, the newly created Westminster City Council. The subsequent success of our proposal brought a radical change in the scale of our affairs. The scheme included a shopping centre, 240 flats and houses, offices, an underground car park and a public library. We needed more than 20 staff to design and construct the project, and more substantial offices would be required to accommodate them.

The scheme, eventually called the Colonnades, was first and foremost a piece of urban design, and as such made an interesting contrast with the adjacent Tecton scheme of 20 years earlier on the opposite side of Bayswater Road. Tecton's public housing was deliberately non-contextual, comprising angled slab blocks that sit back from the surrounding

Above left: Cutaway exploded drawing of the plan layers of the Colonnades. From top: patio houses; offices; shopping; car parking.

Top: Courtyard houses – drawings by Chermayeff.

Above: Plan and cross-section of the Colonnades showing the rooftop patio houses.

19th-century terraced streets. Finely designed in themselves, the blocks represent a classic modernist layout that is disconnected from its site. Surrounded by a railed enclosure, the buildings stand in a separate world. As much a place of ideas, even ideology, as it is a 'home', the Tecton scheme was led by the maxim that 'light and air' should be the architect's first priority. In the same way that postmodernism was a reactionary movement, modernism relied to a degree on selective perception – giving too much emphasis to the importance of daylight and the 'overcrowding' of the earlier Victorian terraces to make its case. For there to be harmonious urban and architectural continuity, as I had seen in Kyoto and at the Cordoba mosque, the perceived sins of the fathers needed to be reviewed in a more balanced light. The intolerant narrow certainty of modernism was a reaction against Victorian omnidirectional excess. Postmodernism, an era of greater tolerance and pluralism, had its own inbuilt problems but marked the start of a period in which greater openness was brought to the process of assimilating the work of early times.

Having spent five years converting houses in the area into flats for private sale, I confidently proposed at the competition stage (and ours was the only scheme to do so) that the two-thirds of the Porchester Square terrace that came within the site should be fully retained and made into flats, and that an existing arched opening in the terrace that had once formed the entrance to a mews should be preserved. The next step was to recreate the former street pattern, including the mews, and carry it to its logical conclusion by building the remaining accommodation along the street frontages with ground-floor front doors all around the block.

The Colonnades site in 1970 before construction began; the rear of the retained Porchester Square terrace can be seen in the distance.

There is still a demand today for architecture to be 'innovatory' in the sense that a scientific breakthrough or technological invention is innovatory. I have always argued that it is equally innovatory, or even more so, to go against the grain of fashion and reinstate neglected traditional ideas when they are still alive and appropriate. Interpreted in a broader, non-scientific sense, innovation can be social, artistic and even moral. The trend at that time for demolishing fine buildings and eliminating good streets and neighbourhoods in the name of progress needed to be challenged. Demolition is often in

no one's interest, serving only to bolster the egos of ideologically fixed architects and various ambitious politicians. Jane Jacobs's book *The Death and Life of Great American Cities* (1961) had been embedded in me since my student days at Penn, but Jacobs's views were not yet widely known in the UK. A great deal more demolition would take place and many more bad urban projects would be completed before the real innovation of a creative architecture that included conservation and adaptation of existing buildings was recognized for what it was.

An edition of the London *Evening Standard* in March 1972 described the Colonnades as 'packing them in without the towers' – an observation that anticipated our 1980s work on office buildings such as Embankment Place and Vauxhall Cross, which were groundscrapers rather than towers and firmly urban-design based. Like the two later projects, the tower-less Colonnades was an alternative attempt to achieve high-density buildings in the centre of London. Towers had become badges of credibility for modernist architects and planners, yet at that time they were expensive and badly built as well as housing fewer people and creating worse town-planning layouts than what had gone before.

If the collage of old and new (buildings and street patterns) in the urban-design plan form of the Colonnades was an innovation, so was the vertical layering of the new-build mixed use, with rooftop patio housing above offices, shops and pedestrian arcades, and all of these above an underground car park that set the entire structural grid. Mixed use is a shift away from the sanitized 'zoning' of modernist planning and always makes for complex, less clean and less so-called 'rational' architecture. On reflection, my attempt to organize a visual identity and place based on the cornice line of the retained Porchester Terrace first-floor colonnade may have given the scheme an over-orderly feel that did not fully reflect the mixture of uses and ideas in the project. But two pieces of architectural endeavour particularly engrossed me: the third- and fourth-floor rooftop patio houses above the long-span shopping area on the ground and first floors, and the tight juxtaposition of old and new in the design of the retained terrace of ten houses, which created a challengingly complex section incorporating a great variety of house types.

As mentioned in chapter 2, I was fascinated with court-yard housing and had visited Jørn Utzon's houses and read all of Serge Chermayeff's writings on the subject, so I invented a rooftop courtyard house within the scheme – an urban type I am still interested in today and have used in recent designs at Swiss Cottage. I enjoyed working to a grid plan and developing it in three dimensions, as well as resolving the grid around Victorian houses and street patterns. Grids and flexibility have absorbed me ever since my third year at architecture school, when I designed houses inspired by Mies van der Rohe and Craig Ellwood and became familiar with the urban-planning studies for the city of Philadelphia.

Urban design engages a wider spectrum of political and community interests than architecture does – and for us the Colonnades was a first foray into a public/private partnership. The land was owned by Westminster City Council and the developer, in return for the land and development opportunity, was supposed to build a new public library. In the end, for various political reasons – and to my deep regret – the library was never built. But, by a quirk of fate, in 1979 I returned to the very same site with another project (see page 224).

In the years that followed, it became clear that the evolution of the Colonnades reflected a malaise that persisted in Britain from the 1950s to the 1970s. The malaise was characterized by a deliberate destruction of place and identity for political reasons; it was not just physical and it was not just about streets and buildings. When it comes to valuing the heritage of place, there are some surprising and unexpected differences between the USA and the UK. While American districts, cities and states and the organization of their governance have remained unchanged in most respects, Britain has gone from tinkering to downright abandonment of many traditions that make up our society's collective identity. Our long-established counties have been diced up, scrambled and renamed in the interests of redefining purely political bureaucracies and conveniences. Ancient counties such as Cumberland, Westmorland and Rutland were eliminated. The county of Huntingdonshire was abandoned and then, confusingly and half-heartedly, partially reinvented later in response to public protest. Cumberland and Westmorland became Cumbria; and whole new districts arose with misleading name-making like Avon and

Cleveland. Sale, the small place where I was born 'moved' from Cheshire to Manchester and then to Greater Manchester. The result is that most people are confused about county boundaries and their relevance. Knowledge of where we are is a fundamental part of knowing who we are. The culprit is a kind of radical modernization that makes the past responsible for all our ills – just as children can, if they choose, blame everything on their parents. The changes to the national and regional map of England in the last 30 years were made regardless of meaning or understanding.

I am fascinated by how the USA, that most pragmatic and dynamic of nations, has kept many meaningful, collective-identity traditions while we have not. One is money. I refer not to the pound/euro debate but to the continuous redesign and total reinvention over the years of the shape, colour and graphics of all our coins and banknotes. In contrast with the British currency, the dollar bills that were in existence during my trip to the USA in 1962 are still recognizable and fully workable. What does money recognition stand for if not a commonly understood language of value? The shape and form of life's currencies – political, territorial and financial – create our sense of place. Collectively perceived

THE DAVID WILCOX COLUMN

Packing them in without the towers

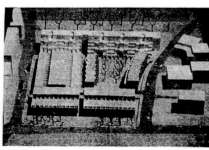

The Porchester Square scheme, with Bishops Bridge Road in foreground.

WORK WILL start next August in Paddington on a scheme which demonstrates how to provide a large number of private homes on scarce land without stacking them up in tower blocks.

Two young architects, only five years in practice, have beaten off larger, long-established firms in a competition to design homes, shops and a library for the Porchester Square site.

Terry Farrell is 32, and Nick Grimshaw 31. The Farrell/Grimshaw partnership has already attracted some attention for the block of aluminium-clad flats beside Regent's Park, which they designed and live in.

Packed

What makes their Porchester Square scheme unusual is the amount they have packed on to the three-acre site, keeping the maximum height down to eight storeys and providing a new garden square, without architectural gimmickry.

Along the two noisiest streets of the square, Porchester Road and Bishops Bridge Road, they have put at ground level a supermarket, shops, offices, a public library and exhibition hall.

On top, served by their own roof-level street, are two-storey patio houses. A block of new flats forms the third side of the square.

Ingeniously, the fourth side is partly made up of Victorian terrace houses which have been "reversed" by building new living rooms and entrances on the backs facing south into the

square. A mews runs down the centre.

"We are really doing just what the Victorian speculative builders did," says Terry Farrell. "Houses around the outside of a square, mews down the middle.

"I don't think anyone has shown that anything much better can be done on a site like this, so we have tried to be practical and economic rather than grandiose."

Before Paddington Council was swallowed by Westminster in 1965, the site was to be a new

civic centre. Westminster still owns the land, and will get a hefty ground rent from the developers, Samuel Properties.

The 237 flats and houses in the £3 million scheme will sell for something betwen £9000 and £25,000, and will house people at over 200 to the acre—a density usually achieved by tower blocks.

The scheme provides a fair profit for the developers because of the commercial content, a large number of new homes, plus important new public buildings.

Evening Standard, 19 March 1972

The concept of low-rise yet high-density housing was at once recognized as a positive urban strategy, counter to what was then the fashion for high-rise buildings.

continuity and identity have to be part of the discourse when debating any change; if they are not, few of our plans will come to fruition.

The land on which the Colonnades was built had been designated as the site of a new town hall for the Borough of Paddington, but when the Greater London Council was set up in the 1960s all the traditional London boroughs were realigned. St Pancras, Marylebone, Paddington and others were gobbled up – some into the Borough of Camden and some into the City of Westminster, which inherited the Colonnades and found the town-hall site surplus to requirements. Marylebone's own wonderful council chambers on the Marylebone Road became almost redundant and the new Westminster Council, large and cumbersome, moved into undemocratically cellular and anonymous offices in Victoria Street. Yes, modernize and improve efficiency – that is always needed – but place and identity are essential to governance. Simplistic 'rationalizations' were part of all aspects of life 30 years ago. Much was lost and a much less coherent world emerged, and actual efficiencies became, as a result, more difficult to achieve.

Survival by design: one office, two diverging viewpoints

The Colonnades – like all urban-design-based projects – was a marathon rather than a sprint. It took seven years of my professional life (later on, Comyn Ching took 15 years, see page 137) and projects of large urban complexity, such as Newcastle's Quayside and Edinburgh's Exchange, are still evolving in their third decade. At the time, the contrast was extreme between this area of activity and the high-tech work on factories that was being done in parallel by Farrell/Grimshaw – the latter projects often took not much more than a year from design to completion, and sometimes even less.

The first big cheque we received after Park Road in 1972 was £25,000 for the Colonnades. Having never been financially secure, we decided we should invest it in property – which, as a consequence of the three-day week and change of government in 1974, completely wrong-footed us. We had not completed the investment by the time the property market collapsed as a result of a change in rental protection for tenants (more futile and short-lived tinkering by politicians in the housing market), and suddenly we found ourselves in debt. We faced a financial crisis but, paradoxically, for the first time we were beginning to receive the recognition we needed to continue our practice, including a special issue on our work in *Architectural Design*. Survival was still uppermost in our thoughts. Today, when architects leave us to set up on their own, I say to them that it's not the first job that matters, it's how you follow it through. While you are busy working on those first jobs, how do you set time aside to think about the next ones? How do you pay for them and how do you staff them? The end of the first five years is the toughest time, as it was for us. By the end of ten years, in 1975, we had established our reputations, but we were still financially shaky and had shrunk from 45 staff to seven: two partners, two associates (John Chatwin and Brian Taggart), two assistants and our secretary, Maggie Jones.

By then, Farrell/Grimshaw had built several factories and warehouses, including Rotork Controls, Bath; Editions Van de Velde, France; Excel Bowl, Reading; the Citroën Warehouse, Runnymede. And in 1976 we had won the commission to design the Herman Miller factory in Bath. All were non-urban explorations of high-tech, lightweight system building that implemented some of the ideas that had excited us in the late 1960s. I personally was particularly fascinated by the work of the architect Ezra Ehrenkrantz and the more abstract concepts of his flexible schools systems. The influence of this fed five years later into urban factories at Wood Green, expressive high-tech at Clifton Nurseries, and the facilities building for Thames Water Authority at Fobney near Reading.

Our bringing together of reuse and new-build – the subject of an essay I and Nick Grimshaw wrote for the *RIBA Journal* in October 1974 entitled 'Survival by Design' – was as innovatory as any other practice's approach at that time. But we did not have the iconic landmark projects of our former rivals. Norman Foster was doing the Willis Faber Building in Ipswich and the Sainsbury Centre in Norwich, and Richard Rogers was building the Pompidou Centre in Paris with Renzo Piano and Peter Rice of Ove Arup. We had outgrown the Windmill Street office and in 1972 had moved to Paddington

Street, where we furnished the studio in Herman Miller Action Office 1. The interior was open-plan with flexible ribbed tubing and hanging-ceiling servicing systems, all in primary colours. Richard Rogers's office was round the corner from us at the Design Research Unit behind Marylebone High Street and we would all meet on occasions to have lunch, compare notes and chat.

Paddington Street was off Marylebone High Street in one of London's most distinctive and clearly focused neighbourhood villages. I mentioned earlier Colin Rowe's book *Collage City*, which includes a map of stream beds as part of Grahame Shane's field analysis of central London; this taught me that Marylebone High Street and Marylebone Lane across to St Christopher's Place were based on the line of the Tyburn river, now culverted somewhere down below. The plan also explained the street grids and squares of the neighbouring estates of the landed aristocratic families of Harley, Howard de Walden, Cavendish and Portman. Benjamin Disraeli had little time for the regular gridded plan of this area that now gives it a fine urban feel. He wrote in *Tancred* in 1847: 'Pancras is like Marylebone, Marylebone is like Paddington; all the streets resemble each other . . . your Gloucester Places, and Baker Streets, and Harley Streets, and Wimpole Streets . . . all of those flat, dull, spiritless streets, resembling each other like a large family of plain children, with Portland Place and Portman Square for their respectable parents.'

Unlike older London's medieval streets, the grid was planned and built at one point in time and, like a good garden, needed to bed down and mature. In my opinion, Marylebone is now a finely arranged part of London with its squares, fine terraced housing and occasional churches, and its overlapping work zones, of which the most renowned is Harley Street. I was intrigued when I first came across Harley Street to see that, although it was a giant hospital district, it consisted of terraces of Georgian and Victorian houses with a few art nouveau domestic-scaled façades on buildings that were all originally conceived as private residences. It provided an object lesson in humane bigness – a total contrast to the vast NHS sick factories being built at the time in system concrete at Hampstead, Northwick Park and other sites around London. The idea of harmonizing areas by disaggregation –

separating out the component parts to make them like a town – appeals strongly to me. Disaggregation of urban giants is a pattern I have followed on subsequent projects. I see it as the difference between corporate culture and collegiate culture, and in 1982 I argued that the BBC should expand its nearby Portland Place headquarters in a collegiate manner as several linked buildings around open public spaces rather than taking a corporate headquarters approach. My proposals for Westminster Hospital and University College Hospital in 1989, as well as for current hospital projects involving St Bartholomew's and the Royal London, reflected my belief in the virtues of integrating large monocultures in diverse mixed-use neighbourhoods, thereby minimizing conflicts of scale and function and creating uniquely interesting urban places. We proposed a collegiate idea for the Middlesex Hospital – in which the overall mass of the building is hidden and only bits are revealed. We called the idea the 'gentle giant', wherein the hospital complex had been harmoniously incorporated into an area of homes, offices, pubs, coffee bars and shops by disaggregating it into its naturally small components.

The Colonnades was my first large-scale urban-designed architectural project; it was followed by Comyn Ching, Byrom Street, Manchester and a scheme for the centre of Aberdeen. They began with issues of context and conservation and revelled in the mixed use and variety of building types. In retrospect, the Colonnades did not explore thoroughly enough the architectural possibilities of this variety, and neither did the overriding new-factory ethos of Farrell/Grimshaw fit in with what I was enthusiastically observing and studying in the urban districts of Marylebone and Paddington, where I lived and worked. But as I explored urban design, timber-frame housing, conservation, variety and individuality more and more in all my projects, a gradual separation was emerging between the two sides of the office.

This was an almost imperceptible process, but by 1976 it was clear to us, our staff and clients that Nick

Above: Industrial FGP buildings in the early to mid 1970s: Herman Miller, Bath (top); Citroën Warehouse, Runnymede (centre); and Rotork Controls, Bath (bottom).

Opposite: Contemporary press articles. The lower one was a landmark for us in that it was the first to define how we differed in our approach to architecture.

Building Design, February 1972

Back in the personality-packed days of the Sixties, in the heyday of the whizzkid when young meteors were discovered, rose and faded with alarming speed and predictability, Nick Grimshaw and Terry Farrell seemed to be the architectural profession's "men most likely to . . ."

And they have. During a period when architectural practices have generally been cutting back or even closing down through lack of work the Farrell Grimshaw Partnership has continued to flourish – expanding its office from two partners and one job to

'Innovative building looks no different'

over 20 assistants and around £5m worth of work on the drawing board.

Recognition started when they had work published in fringe magazines like *Archigram* and *Clip-Kit*; they then received international acclaim for their design for a students' hostel where they plugged a grp bathroom tower into the back of a Georgian terrace

THE MEN MOST LIKELY TO...

Louis Wilkins went to see architects Terry Farrell and Nick Grimshaw: tomorrow's men

perimeter of the building for no extra cost.

"Also, the way that we have built up the units on the Porchester Square site, using the existing facade and getting maximum

built for £227 000 it couldn't be built at all.

"To have put in double glazing at that time would have meant that we would have had to reduce the size of the living area of each flat by about a half.

'We are the young imaginative

provide a much more humanely scaled and liveable environment.

"And it's not just a question of building costs because the difference is minimal.

"Developers come to us

RIBA Journal, May 1976

BUILDINGS AS A RESOURCE

A time of severe recession is a good time to take stock of resources. Our existing buildings should be regarded as a valuable resource to be more fully used. We should design our new buildings so that they add to this resource.

This article expands on a recent lecture by Terence Farrell and Nick Grimshaw of the Farrell Grimshaw Partnership given at the Architectural Association.

TERENCE FARRELL: CONVERSION AND REHABILITATION OF HOUSING

Now is the time to ask if we actually need any new housing in this country. Buildings are a resource which should not be destroyed, even if they are to be replaced by a 'masterpiece'. It requires as much design ingenuity to spatially re-organise existing buildings, adding services and equipment, as it does to design new buildings.

NICK GRIMSHAW: FLEXIBILITY IN INDUSTRIAL BUILDINGS

Today's enclosures must allow for the ebb and flow of new products and processes. They must also encourage a high level of user manipulation of the interior and exterior of the building. We are against custom-built monuments.

RIBAJ May 1976

171

Grimshaw and I were setting off on divergent paths. Earlier on, the public evidence surfaced in our first big lecture in 1974 at the RIBA, part of a series called 'Architects' Approach to Architecture'. The lack of harmony between us made it difficult for us either to organize our slides or to agree on what we wanted to say on the evening – and the lecture was described by commentators as disjointed. But when a year later we were invited by the writer Charles Jencks to give a talk at the AA, we were able to regroup and to rationalize coherently our differences of approach. We followed the AA talk with one at the RIBA, which was published in the *RIBA Journal* under the title 'Buildings as a Resource'. The essence of our thesis was that all buildings change and evolve, and whether you are working on new buildings or converting existing ones, the same issues emerge. Ours was an integrated view that took to task the doctrinaire rigidity of much modernist thinking and treated all buildings as part of a linked pattern of design strategies, but we came at the thesis from quite different entry positions. Contained in this essay were, I believe, all the elements of a postmodern perspective.

Meeting Charles Jencks was one of the most important things that happened to me in the mid 1970s, setting off a train of events that would culminate in the end of my partnership with Nick Grimshaw. At the time there was a mood of uncertainty in the office, fuelled by the collapse of several of our projects, together with the miners' strike, the three-day week and the oil crisis. Much of the optimism of the 1960s and the widespread faith in the modern world of rational scientific and technological progress was evaporating.

The new paradigm: mass housing without modernism

I began to seek to humanize mass production by creating places and homes that were more strongly individual. This was quite different from elevating the industrial product as an aesthetic icon. Since encountering the childhood frustrations of broken bicycle chains and various tyre punctures, I had had mixed feelings about loving technology as an end in itself, even though I saw that, for my elder brother (who liked his Meccano sets), repeatedly taking a bike to bits and rebuilding it was central to his pleasure in the

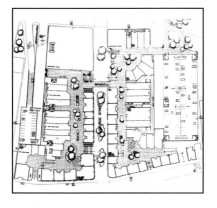

hobby. Not for me the endless joys of the machine for its own sake. At Park Road I became interested in marrying the factory-made with personal choice, although many people around me had difficulties with this idea. Later on, in the housing society projects, I focused more on combining individuality and uniqueness of place with mass production. As the excitement of the 1960s faded a new and more responsible mood began to prevail, caught at Charles Jencks's seminar at the RIBA Hull Conference in 1973, when the architect John Darbourne remarked, 'There is nothing that gets the water off a roof better than tilting it.' There

was applause and much laughter. The use of the 'flat roof', that essential icon of modernism, could no longer be a guaranteed badge of office for the dedicated contemporary architect.

Based on the success of the Mercury Housing Society, which had financed Park Road, I set up another housing society, named after our solicitor's house on Maunsel Square, where we used to meet. Maunsel provided some absorbing work, including masterplanning in Manchester's Byrom Street and a group of infill projects around London. We enjoyed it while it lasted, which was

Conservation projects: Wellbury Boys' Home, Hitchin, 'before' and 'after' (top row); integrating new mixed-use buildings into central Aberdeen (middle row); existing buildings at Comyn Ching (bottom, left and centre); and low-rise, high-density housing association homes at Byrom Street, Manchester (bottom right).

until the new Labour government decided in 1976–77 that the scheme might promote professional self-interest over and above the potential public housing gain.

Many of the housing societies had become very big and were now 'landlords' to a large amount of rented housing – architects, sociologists, lawyers and some highly motivated amateurs had been the pioneers, and the system and its success needed rationalizing. In the space of a few years Maunsel had become responsible for nearly 1,000 tenants and was fast developing into a kind of public housing department. Having been brought up on a council estate, I now seemed to be part-owning and running several, albeit small, public housing projects. We were then instructed by the government and the Housing Corporation to remove all the building professionals from the Maunsel board and to hand over the running of the operation to an independent 'unbiased' professional housing manager who had no potential conflict of interest. This was not at all successful; within two years of the changeover, one of the managers was sacked for gross incompetence and the other was sued for embezzlement. I believe that Maunsel and other housing associations founded at that time, such as the Circle Thirty Three Housing Trust, Toynbee Housing Association and Hyde Park Housing Association, were represented by conscientious and thoughtful professionals who did good work. Realistically, there was a limit to how long we could have continued, but it was an interesting experiment, during which I developed timber-frame housing that had personality and flexibility, and I also learned how to develop, build, own and operate low-cost housing for rental.

The organizational process we invented for construction was as important as the finished product and produced a different and original kind of building. In essence, we persuaded the government agencies to accept one timber-frame contractor for a large number of projects, who then produced the building shell at a predetermined price – it was called a 'serial contract'. The shell would vary from two to four storeys but was always constructed from the same grid and standard panels. Then, quite separately, for each of the infill sites around London, a local contractor was selected to build the foundations and drainage and to complete the cladding and landscaping once the timber frame

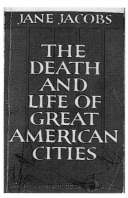

Above: Two books that influenced our urban and conservation projects: Oscar Newman's *Creating Defensible Space* and Jane Jacobs's *The Death and Life of Great American Cities*.

had been erected. All this therefore combined the involvement of local, small-scale builders with a larger contractor's standard core construction. I was determined to combine mass production and benefits of scale with individuality. Some sites had timber-clad houses, others near the airport used brick for sound insulation; some houses were hung with tiles, others combined tiles and timber (see page 224).

In my concern for buildings as a resource and as part of my involvement in developing strategies for public housing that challenged current wisdom, I undertook a study for Westminster City Council of several of their very large estates – which, by 1970, contained a total of more than 1,000 homes between 40 and 60 years old. The study looked at how, instead of being demolished, these homes could, through adaptation and improved services, be replanned and reused to prolong their life by another 60 years. *Creating Defensible Space*, Oscar Newman's book of 1972, gave me some excellent clues about how to create a safer public realm through imaginative and thoughtful urban design and management. The 1,000-dwellings book became a mini-manifesto in which I argued passionately that those proud, well-built housing estates consisted of handsome buildings that we, in the late 20th century, rarely equalled, yet everywhere I was hearing that the case for their demolition was self-evident. The interwar traditional-style brick flats that were purpose-built by the London County Council are among the best housing achievements in London. They frequently remain fresh, liveable and homely. In the large estate near my present home in 2003 there are still good Lutyensesque-style buildings from that period, while the much more recent angled-plan, flat-roofed, postwar buildings are down at heel, despite their much shorter life.

The study was submitted to Westminster City Council's Housing Committee. There were mixed feelings about my recommendations. Some estates were retained, such as those at Ebury Street, but the very fine Portman Buildings were demolished to make way for new housing. It was explained to me at the time by Maunsel's new chairman, Frank West, former chief architect of Westminster, that it was party politics that decided the future of those and so many other public housing estates. In Tory boroughs such as Westminster, the

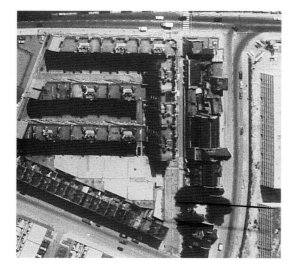

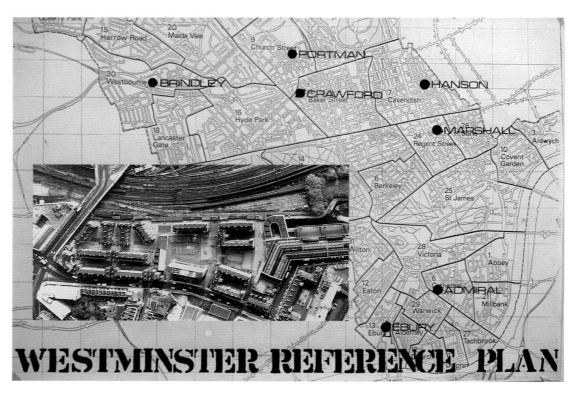

Above and right: The Westminster housing study made proposals for refurbishing 1,000 homes in between-the-war estates across the borough.

Below: The appalling lack of basic internal services and proper planning in these early 20th-century homes is evident from some of the photographs I took for the study.

WESTMINSTER REFERENCE PLAN

Above: Proposals for private gardens and landscaping which civilized the ground levels and created 'defensible space'.

Below: Flexibility and services strategy was the key to all replanning.

Above: The existing outdoor spaces, some bleak, some well loved.

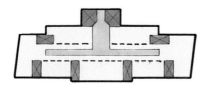

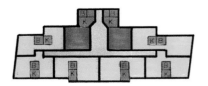

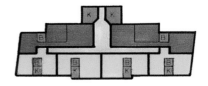

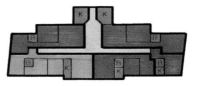

rented-housing tenants who always voted Labour were concentrated in existing Labour wards to keep the total number of elected Labour councillors down. In Labour boroughs, new rented homes were spread out, targeting marginal Tory wards to topple them into the Labour camp. And so the town planning of London and its housing were at the mercy of political machinations – it was like a giant, real-life Monopoly board with what were then only two players. The prize was petty power, and London's future shape was pushed and pulled with no larger vision at all, and with no truly beneficial urban-planning purpose in mind.

In essence, those estates were not made up of obsolete buildings, but were simply neglected places that had gradually been abandoned by younger, more independent people, leaving behind older, less mobile residents. Many housing managers and social workers would, like most architects, have felt that the easiest way to make the problem go away would be to remove those sad remnant

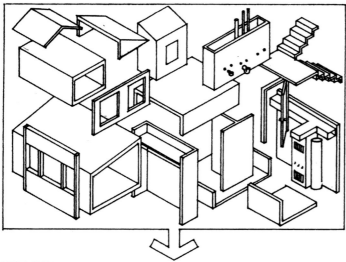

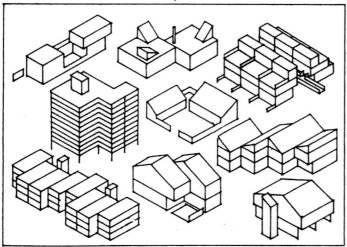

communities, evaporating bricks and mortar as well as the 'problem' people. While working in the private sector, I had restored physical fabric in far worse condition to make fine homes that would sell for high prices. With the same care, imagination, time and money, the physical fabric of public housing could be totally transformed. The same ingredients could put communities back on their feet, but the critical difference from private-sector housing was that public-sector professionals had to work with the residents and acknowledge their needs rather than avoiding them or even denying their existence. In the public sector, a degree of proactive community rehabilitation was required; the very society itself needed conservation policies to parallel the restoration of the buildings its members occupied.

Around 1974, I met the owners of a wonderful triangular block in Seven Dials, Covent Garden. They were a very old firm of ironmongers called Comyn Ching (rather surprisingly, both these Chinese-sounding names were Cornish). Most architects knew them and their extraordinary collection of old buildings. Dickens is said to have partly based his 'rookeries' on this rambling mass, and architects seeking to buy a piece of brassware or door furniture at this time encountered a shopping experience that Dickens might readily have recognized. The buildings on this site had been left to rot because there was simply no future envisaged for them; they were to be demolished as part of an ambitious new road network.

The roads never materialized, and after the fruit and vegetable market moved out of Covent Garden in the 1970s the area saw that decade's most important example of urban renaissance in Britain. It would probably not be an exaggeration to say that what was achieved at Covent Garden spearheaded the most radical shift in British town planning and urban design in the last 50 years of the 20th century – just as the new towns had done in its first 50 years. Continuing the spirit of the new towns all through the 1970s, Milton Keynes, Warrington and Runcorn were being designed and built; the government's Location of Offices Bureau directed white-collar employment out of London, and their Office Development Permit (ODP) scheme effectively tried to bar all new office buildings in London over the modest size of 9,200 square metres

Left: Ezra Ehrenkrantz's work was an inspiration, since it was concerned primarily with the social and economic bonuses of mass production and prefabricated building techniques.

The prefabricated timber
housing schemes for
Maunsel were spread
across many sites in
outer London.

(100,000 square feet). This blinkered denial of private-sector vitality was in stark contrast to the Thatcher years of the 1980s, when the extraordinary demand for London offices showed that the future of London, rather than being endangered by white-collar workers, was, in fact dependent upon them. The deregulation of the Stock Exchange and schemes such as Broadgate, Stockley Park and Canary Wharf had brought hundreds of thousands of occupied new offices, indeed entire new 'towns' of office workers, to London.

The prevailing disregard in the 1970s for urban design – new motorways were still being built through city centres, new towns and expanded towns grew and grew, and in London there was the ban on office building – were set against the miracle of what happened in Covent Garden. In 1965, I had helped Nick Grimshaw to draw up his AA design thesis, which was predicated upon the complete demolition of Covent Garden – yet, ironically, ten years later, I became one of those actively involved in conserving the area.

The vast fruit and vegetable market at Covent Garden had set itself within the urban fabric as a private zone that was so dominatingly monocultural that it smothered all 'normal' urban life. Developed by the 6th Duke of Bedford to connect his country estate and its agricultural produce to the expanding population in London, the glorious 19th-century market buildings and surrounding arcaded piazza comprised a formal architectural set-piece unequalled anywhere in central London. During my work on Covent Garden, I got to know and admire determined conservationists such as Geoff Holland and pioneer developers such as Christina Smith who, over a long period of meetings, lobbyings and protests, successfully prevented wholesale demolition. In addition to Comyn Ching, I designed and converted to flats a large house in Earlham Street for Christina, and converted the Donmar Warehouse opposite into a theatre. The development of the Comyn Ching triangle was a long-term preoccupation for us, and the final buildings on the site were not completed until the late 1980s, 15 or more years after work there had begun.

The buildings and streets – their very physical presence – are what made Covent Garden rise above and survive

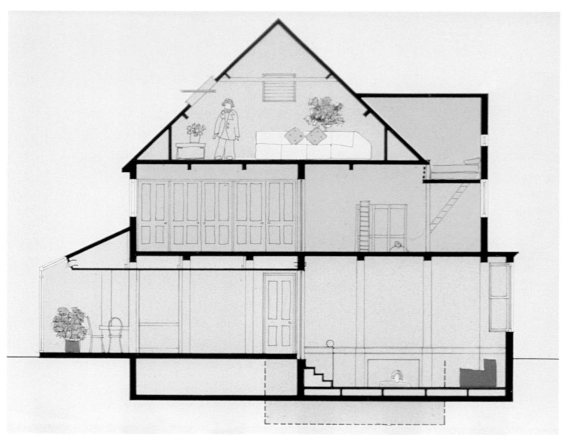

The Royal Free Hospital, one of the huge concrete system hospitals built in 1974.

the great changes in use that have occurred in recent decades. Not only can individual buildings such as Georgian houses be adapted to more modern uses with radically different demands but so can whole districts. The market people moved out and temporary residents, including David Rock's Endell Street architects' community, moved in to colonize and sustain the buildings – and then to pioneer their transformation into offices, shops and restaurants within a heaving tourist district.

The market itself kept its physical character intact so that, together with the adjacent narrow streets, terraced houses, shops, workshops, warehouses and corner pubs, it became a district of well-embedded, bricks-and-mortar-built companions, an indefatigable brigade of united veterans, physical neighbourhoods that have survived and endured in an unlikely way. The other big London market buildings at Smithfield and Spitalfields have undergone comparable transformations, but Covent Garden was the first and the most miraculous. On a recent visit I was struck by how much the 1970s work has its own time-capsuled character; the tiny boutiques, cheese shops, vegetarian specialists, antiques shops and tourist areas look different not simply because of their enduring physical characteristics but because the original personalities involved – the people who ran the 1970s retailing and restaurant businesses and residential pioneers – are still evident today.

I thought often of the great difficulties the campaigners had at Covent Garden and 25 years later, when campaigning for increased awareness of urban design on behalf of the Urban Design Alliance (of which I was founding president), I reflected on how I found myself endlessly explaining that there had been no substantial culture of urbanism in London in the 19th and 20th centuries. I used the royal parks and palaces as examples. They play a vital role in the working of London, highlighting the difference between the City of Westminster and the City of London – or the seat of government and monarchy on one hand and the seat of commerce on the other. These two sectors of London are as contrasting in urban plan as they are in function. Westminster evolved in an extraordinarily suburban, almost rural manner, while the City has more traditional urban roots as a fortified Roman citadel. Typologically, the City is a true European town, planned around dense gridded street patterns, a wall, gated entries and a central high street (Cheapside). Adjacent to this tight form is the expansive open territory of the West End, which is based upon the random placing of four palaces (Buckingham, St James's, Kensington and Westminster) and six royal parks (Kensington Gardens, Hyde Park, Green Park, Buckingham Palace, St James's Park and Regent's Park) within a complex of urban villages. The palaces and parks were built in the West End as anti-urban set-pieces: great country houses surrounded by rural parklands originally intended as hunting grounds. Over the years, the parks have evolved and have become assimilated into the dense 19th-century urban fabric. This shift occurred as London expanded and enveloped the parks, and as monarchical power was replaced by a democratic modern state.

Of the two arenas of power, it is the City of Westminster that now has the true British urban character – while the City of London has become predominantly a much smaller, self-contained commercial centre; in effect, as a specialized trading quarter lacking the diversity and heterogeneity of other urban districts, this Roman town never fully evolved into a true town or the genuine core of London itself. Today, the royal palaces and their parklands are London's centre and London's only public realm, and the traditions of royal countryside parks and rural villages underline what has now become a great metropolis. To understand London, it is essential to see that all its roots, its underlying social attitudes, have been rural rather than urban.

Maida Vale: a new home, a new family, a new view of life

Until 1973, Nick and I had lived side by side on the tenth floor at Park Road. Then I bought a semi-detached 1924 house in Ashworth Road, Maida Vale, which Sue and I moved to – and which became the family home for us and our three children for more than 25 years. Friends told me that I was 'very brave' because the house represented everything most thinking architects had been taught to rebel against. That was one of the reasons why it appealed to me. I was determined to show what could be done with a standard between-the-wars, semi-detached, speculative house whose very ordinariness would make it a place for living, growing and enjoying life without over-intrusive 'architecture'.

The house is part of the Metroland vision derived from the building of the Bakerloo underground line at the very beginning of the 20th century. When the line was built, excavated soil was put in a field in the middle of Maida Vale for 20 years to allow it to settle. In the 20-year gap between the erection of the adjacent mansion blocks, which were built contemporaneously with the tube line, and of the newer houses on the settled excavation land, fashions changed; servants were no longer available, and the compact, easily maintained cottage style evolved. I have always been fascinated by what architects do with houses when they are their own clients because it is a key to the balance between their egos and their humanity. I am also intrigued by unselfconscious architecture without architects, such as the semi-detached builder's house, since it is a touchstone for the vast majority of everyday houses that make up most of our built environment.

At Maida Vale I took another step towards forging my architectural identity. Identity comes just as much from an intense and personal interpretation of the ordinary as from building huge cities or novel architecture. It would not be an exaggeration to say that some entire faceless new towns have a less clear identity than my living room. Was there any clear identity in the standardized greenfield factories and housing schemes created by the advocates of high-tech? There was identity in our students' hostel that came not from the service tower alone but from the combination of the tower, the old buildings and the furniture. I liked the collage, the mixed language, and I decided to do the same with our new house. By 1976, a crash in the property market combined with some unlucky investments meant that I had rapidly to convert the two-storey house into a five-storey block of flats – a test of the house's innate flexibility and my own ingenuity! I uncovered a basement to make our

Revisit 2003
Many projects have been revisited, including Wesley Square in west London, designed in 1976 for a housing association. The photos above and opposite left are general everyday scenes taken in 2003, but the fourth shows a wonderful lunch given for me by the residents more than 25 years after project completion.

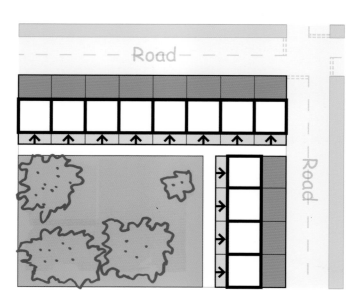
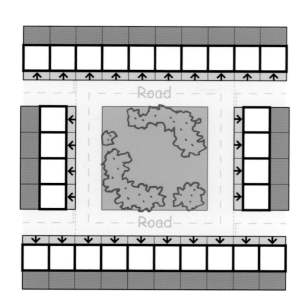

Left: Wesley Square has its own unique plan form in that each residence has front-door access from the central shared space, with 'rear' private gardens facing outwards to surrounding streets.

Right: An 18th-century square form (such as Bedford Square) has limited-size adjoining front and rear private yards to each terraced house and a central garden accessible only to residents.

bedroom and let the whole of the first floor to an American couple, and then I converted the roof space with an added gallery and let that to an AA student. There were now three apartments – three homes – in one small house. From the outside, though, its appearance remained unchanged.

The way the Maida Vale house has developed over the years has been as much for the family as for myself. It is layer upon layer of enjoyment in things that we have bought together. I extended it out into the garden and placed plants and trees on an axis from the front garden right through to the back garden, making a vista 30 metres (100 feet) long. I brought back birdcages from my travels to the Far East, and we bought furniture and designed rugs and tiles, and this eventually became part of our experience of living. The evolution of the house can be explained in many different ways: the

influence of the children (Max, Luke and Milly); the creative interaction between me and my wife; the ups and downs of the architectural profession. All the booms and recessions are writ large within that house.

I still use the drawings for the Maida Vale conversion to demonstrate how, as Leon Battista Alberti said, a house is a small city, changing and accommodating different people in different circumstances. We used to call the house the Tardis – after the police box in the TV series *Dr Who* that contained the whole universe. The Tardis was an acronym for 'Time and Relative Dimension in Space', which said a lot about the psychology of place rather than container as object. I like to think that I altered and converted bits of my home incrementally in a spirit akin to what happened to London itself – reflecting my strong belief that the ad hoc and pragmatic can achieve a particular kind of harmony and beauty.

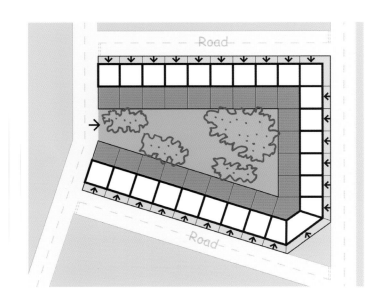

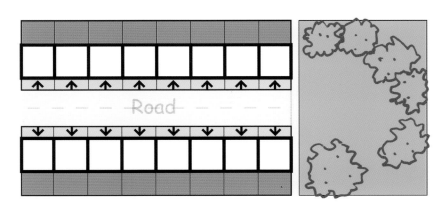

Ending FGP and starting TFP

Rethinking the industrial shed: taking high-tech out to play

In the second half of the 1970s, the state controlled much of the supply of, and demand for, new buildings. The Wilson and Callaghan governments not only initiated more new town growth but also gave incentives to blue-collar industries to move to new towns and attempted to limit urban white-collar workers by rationing new office buildings in London through Office Development Permits. There was also an enormous growth in council-owned housing, both from new-build projects and from the transference of existing private housing to public ownership – 'municipalization', as it was called at the time. Consequently, Farrell/Grimshaw experienced a boom not just in public rented housing but also in industrial buildings, culminating in commissions for entire business and industrial campuses such as Aztec West, near Bristol. At the same time, we won a scheme for BMW in Bracknell, and my former classmate at Penn, Hugh Cannings, chief architect and planner at Warrington, commissioned us to design a factory in the new town.

A gradual realignment of work was occurring between Nick Grimshaw and me. Our 'industrial sheds' were produced mainly by a team led by Nick, with job architects Jeff Scherer and Brian Taggart. My personal interests were expanding laterally into new areas, as I began working with the writer Charles Jencks on his house in Holland Park, west London, and became more involved with interiors, urban planning and large-scale housing projects. I also began to explore different avenues for the regular Farrell/Grimshaw industrial commissions. Compact, urban industrial sites at higher densities and ad hoc adaptations appealed to me more than what had by then become the conventional greenfield factory box. And so, when we were commissioned to build a series of factories at Wood Green, in Haringey, north London, I saw it as a challenging opportunity to rethink the form of the standard high-tech industrial box by incorporating aspects of the new kind of work that my team was exploring.

While much industrial activity is sited in towns and cities, the greenfield factory depends on commuting and car ownership and all their attendant social disconnections. The second half of the 20th century saw a rapid decline in the UK's industrial base and many multi-storey factories and warehouses became redundant. Eventually and increasingly, a large proportion were converted into lofts, studios and offices. Later, in 1984, I began developing an island site in Marylebone that had become vacant after the aircraft-parts manufacturer Palmer Aeroworks closed down; later still, in 2000 I moved my own home there. So buildings that had been incrementally constructed between 1919 and 1930, partly by Wallis Gilbert & Partners, architects of the glorious Hoover Building, as a furniture factory for Bovis the house builders and contractors, became during the war and afterwards an aircraft factory; which I then converted into studios and offices. Then, in 1997–99, most of the buildings were converted once more, this time into loft apartments. What a journey for those robust, flexible buildings – and can we imagine what more transformations they will see in the decades ahead?

Wood Green was a gritty, congested, older urban district containing Bassetts, a large chocolate and sweets manufacturer, gasometers, warehouses, factories and car-repair shops. As part of its support for blue-collar employment, Labour-controlled Haringey Council had obtained several separate sites and our developer client, in a public/private partnership with the council, set about creating a new work district with strategic demolitions, conversions and new infill buildings. I was intrigued by the complex ad hoc site shapes and various neighbouring structures, and the fact that there was, as in most urban models, a site coverage by buildings that was well over 50 per cent. So, instead of making 'pristine' (a favourite Farrell/Grimshaw high-tech word) stand-alone objects, I began to invent workplace courtyards and linked industrial buildings (possibly influenced by Utzon and my own Northampton housing scheme), shaping a neighbourhood united along city streets by a series of solid walls of enclosing brick with, behind them, fully glazed internal courtyards. Instead of the glossy box, the object positive, it was the reverse: the space positive, a series of internal courtyards for deliveries, vehicle manoeuvring, and arrivals and departures. It was these central spaces within a dense, mixed-use

High-tech factory units remained a key part of Farrell/Grimshaw's work: BMW offices, showroom and warehouse at Bracknell, Berkshire (top); Winwick Quay factory units, Warrington (both middle pictures); and Castle Park, Nottingham (bottom).

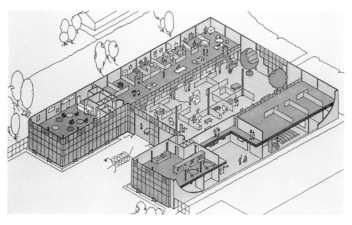

urban grain that were the essence of the scheme. Wrapped around the internal courtyards were high-tech flexible walls that borrowed from what was going on elsewhere at Farrell/Grimshaw. To temper the mechanical effect of these, I introduced 'solid' and 'void' windows within the curtain wall, exposing some gasket-free glazing bars to suggest windows in the mandatory 10 per cent wall area set aside for insulation – a sacrilegious visual pun since it was the only part of the wall that was in fact solid. I am reminded now of Nick's description of a light-hearted mezzanine flooring scheme I had done at that time as 'an immoral use of Dexion'. The difference between Nick's and my religious and moral backgrounds was cleverly perceived by Sutherland Lyall in a critique a few years later in *Building Design* (February 1989). Of our neighbouring Camden Town buildings – my TVam and Nick's Sainsbury store – Lyall wrote:

'On the face of it the two buildings are as unlike as it is possible for two more or less contemporaneous buildings to be. Farrell's was a brilliant tour de force, probably the best example this side of the Atlantic of the early multi-layer-meaning-including-jokes phase of post-modernism before it started taking itself with the utmost seriousness. Ironically it subscribed to part of the hi-tech canon in that the building was designed to last at least the length of the TV.am franchise but not necessarily any longer. Inside it has some fairly exceptional advanced minimalist long-span steelwork courtesy of engineer Peter Brett, without which TV.am would probably have had to look for another site. Refreshingly it poked two fingers up at a number of pompous modern movement set-piece attitudes about visual and stylistic consonances between front and back, outside and inside, about integrity of materials and structures. That sort of thing . . . .

'Sainsbury's on the other hand is a deadly serious building, Calvinist to the lax South American Roman Catholicism of Farrell. At least that is how it would probably seem on first observation. Yet for the hard-line modernists (and one would formerly have placed Grimshaw somewhere among their leading members) there are several seriously niggling worries about the Sainsbury building. They are to do with its scarcely veiled 19th-century engineering structures, what looks like massive structural overkill, and one or two of those problems about front and back, inside and out.'

I had a good job architect, John Petrarca, on the Wood Green project, and we turned the business of designing what could have been earnest utilitarian sheds into buildings full of personality and expressive of place. Around the outside was brickwork – something that would never have been considered in the early Farrell/ Grimshaw high-tech factories – with geometric patterning and stepped windows. We saw this inside-out architecture as resembling a 'geode': protective and hard outside, rich and sparkling inside. I revelled in a series of architectural surprises. For example, the steel prefabricated stairs were not in macho, mechanical primary colours (which had been de rigueur from Archigram and the Pompidou Centre onwards), but pink with small inset rings of cut tubes (leftovers from offcuts of the central circular column), forming a decorative pattern around the central steel column. Petrarca (who was from New York) and I compared the concept of mass production in the USA and Britain, centred on this very detail. At that time, a standardized factory product in the USA was simply that; the size of the country and its huge market created efficiencies and economies of scale that brought prices down but in effect severely limited choice. In 1960s Britain all models of car were idiosyncratically different, and so-called mass production was a craft industry based on a much smaller market than the USA; products were not aimed at the population at large but designed to satisfy the perceived taste and buying power of the middle class. Petrarca chose a 'standard' stair from a British catalogue, but soon found that

no stair was in production and any variation requested was possible. It was a master-and-servant relationship, but with a more aspirational technological aesthetic than any of the American mass-produced products. In this way, the British middle class, including British designers and architects, for decades expressed progression and 'modernity' stylistically but with buildings that were the constructional equivalents of bespoke hand-stitched suits made in Savile Row.

The buildings were let very quickly – the last one to Middlesex University's Art Department, for which we designed and created a sculpture and painting department (with industrial elements forming 'ironic' capitals) in an industrial courtyard unit near Wood Green town centre. The university arts building has since grown in influence to such an extent that a lot of the area had become an arts quarter by the end of the 20th century. I went back to photograph the buildings and found that almost all of them are today delightfully overgrown with ivy (see page 263).

The project that best typified our exploration of lateral thinking around the industrial building type was undertaken for Digital Computers in Reading. This was a somewhat quieter but in some ways an ultimately more subversive project – begun by Farrell/Grimshaw, but finished in my own name. The original building bought by Digital was a dumb developer's shed – the opposite of the chic, high-tech, product-designed box of Foster,

Rogers and Farrell/Grimshaw. Proving that the perhaps over-tightly designed high-tech box was not essential for the creation of a spirited contemporary workspace was a challenge that appealed to me. As at the students' hostel, we made clearly stated, plug-in interventions using, for example, air-conditioning units monumentalized and formalized as circulation foci over staircases to a gallery, and installed above a sealed, climate-controlled showcase displaying computer rooms below. Another add-on was a large off-the-peg conservatory adapted and styled to make a staff cafeteria. We interviewed and got to know the staff during the design process and were rewarded with a standing ovation at the opening party. Initially faceless and 'no-where', the site and building had been transformed into something fun and unique, a real place of work (see pages 219–20).

Before Nick and I went our separate ways, I began the design of a water-treatment works near Reading for the Thames Water Authority (finished two years later in my own name). The location was geographically fixed by the river at Fobney and the existing sewage-treatment works. Operators of public industries were beginning to think about communicating their role in people's lives and explaining what their workplaces were all about, so the brief included a visitors' centre and exhibition area. The Thames Water Building once again eschewed architecture as product design, and we intensified and elaborated the specialized and functionally complex brief rather than reducing it to oversimplified components. A long, low building had been deliberately placed above the water-treatment basements; its purpose was to prevent lift caused by high water-table pressure associated with nearby rivers. We worked to transform what could have been an undignified building by engaging with the potential for symbolism and visual metaphors. We really were, as Deyan Sudjic said in the *Sunday Times Magazine* in January 1983, 'taking high-tech out to play'. The cladding was the pale blue of clear water, with shiny reflective glass bubbles rising up the façade; some black gaskets were removed to reveal bright blue edging of enamelled paintwork. A giant wave surmounted the roofline silhouette, and cascading waves of mirror glass created the impression of rollers big enough for surfing. As a knowing aside, the connecting gasket from wave to wall had to be bigger than anything readily available in the construction industry, so it was made from the ultimate jumbo watery gasket – that is, a standard plastic rainwater pipe split down the centre and bent open into shape.

Inside, the elements of earth, fire and water dominated in symbolic form the entrance hall and visitors' centre – with bright blue foam-seating resembling waves, earth-red bridge and stairs, and five torchère light fittings on columns at the end of the big transverse axis. Although it ventured into new symbolic and visual territory, it was grounded in the technology, materials and know-how of Farrell/Grimshaw, reconnecting me with the excitement of discovery associated with the partnership's early days. Perhaps more importantly, at last I was regaining my contact with the freer artistic creativity of my childhood and student days, which had been characterized by art, colour and joyful, independent creativity.

Temporary buildings and garden centres

By May 1980, when Nick Grimshaw and his team moved out, I had begun to feel that the split was a good thing. The rules of partnership meant that, as I had not instigated the break, it was Nick who had to resign and I could keep the premises in Paddington Street. He changed address but kept his style; I kept the address but over the next few years evolved and changed the style and character of my architecture. Nick and I had been good – at one stage, very good – friends for nearly 20 years and had been in partnership for 15 years. In the partnership we had both been able to establish ourselves and find our feet in the world; our parting was relatively amicable and constructive – and we talked about visiting each other's offices and meeting up for a drink from time to time. But then after we parted, rivalry and press comparisons created a pressure that widened our differences and, sadly, much goodwill and friendship evaporated.

Some people thought that the Farrell/Grimshaw tradition of high-tech would disappear from my work with the end of the partnership, and that I would turn my back on it, but from Thames Water and Wood Green immediately came Clifton Nurseries in Bayswater, with its twin-wall polycarbonate. The Clifton Nurseries buildings in Covent Garden and at Alexandra Palace both pioneered the use of fabric structures in British architecture: I have never lost respect for technology's expressive

EVERY TIME I OPEN A MAGAZINE I SEE A GREENHOUSE.....

LAZLO

potential. Later on, Charing Cross station, although read by many at one level only as an essay in postmodernism, won the European Structural Steel Award for its innovative engineering (all the floors are hung over the existing railway from nine adjustable arches). Similarly, in the 1990s, Seoul airport at Inchon, Kowloon station and Hong Kong's Peak Bowl continued the tradition of high-tech know-how. In those buildings, the complex application of construction technology has been exploited, extending the range of expression rather than becoming a limited architectural style in its own right.

Nothing demonstrated more obviously my faith in high-tech than the series of temporary buildings we did at this time. It was an irony that my interest in context, conservation and the more permanent and traditional characteristics of architecture began to grow during the period when the Farrell/Grimshaw partnership was coming to an end, and in the two or three years that followed I designed and built several lightweight temporary buildings. Every time architects build, they deal with both the particular (of site, context, people, timetable, budget) and the general (standard components, building and other regulations, media interest, and influences on fashion and style). Temporary buildings often have an intensity about them: first ideas reach fruition, cheapness and quickness prevail, and many of the normal rules concerning permissions can be put to one side (the success in the new millennium of the

'temporary' London Eye is an excellent example of this). Essentially, temporary buildings resemble nomadic fairs or exhibition pavilions – they have particularities and generalities all their own. The nomadic parallel was particularly apt in the case of the Clifton Nurseries greenhouse, built in 1980 and re-erected in north Wales in 1984–85. Peter Walker MP opened the first greenhouse as Minister of Agriculture; when, a few years later, he arrived to open the new Prestatyn garden centre in his subsequent job as Secretary of State for Wales, he was very amused to find he was opening the same building again, more than 300 miles from where he had first performed the ceremony. (This was as much a comment on the peripatetic nature of political appointments as on the fate of temporary buildings.)

For many town-dwellers, gardens represent a piece of the countryside, and the urban garden centre has a strong allure as an open marketplace for plants, flowers, garden pots, furniture, trees and hosepipes, connecting the modern town-dweller with his distant agricultural roots by providing everything needed for the land around his own home. My client, Jacob Rothschild, who had recently bought the Clifton Nurseries garden centre around the corner from his house in Maida Vale, wanted to improve and expand the business, and he found for the purpose temporarily vacant sites where buildings were planned but were not to be built for a few years. His brief was that each garden centre should be an urban asset, an instant oasis, where workers and shoppers could find greenery and flowers and anything else they needed to create a more attractive outdoor space of their own. For many of us, allotments, garden sheds and greenhouses are romantic places halfway between urban and rural, between the synthetic man-made world and nature; they are 'in between' places and usually express the very personal and private.

The first location for our instant oasis was coincidentally where the failed library scheme had been planned at the Colonnades in Bayswater (see page 221). I had been disappointed in 1974 when the scheme was halted before completion. Now, on the very same site, the first new building in my own name would be erected with a great fanfare and much attention – from apparent failure came one of the most successful jeux d'esprit I have been involved in (see page 234–37).

Left: This cartoon by Ian Layzell in the *RIBA Journal* (October 1980) typified media interest in my first building in my own name.

Above: Evolution of the Clifton Nurseries scheme in Bayswater. From top, the photographs show a model of the scheme, the building under construction and the completed greenhouse.

Opposite: This series of drawings by Esther Rowley were part of our 'passive solar' winning entry (submitted with Ralph Lebens) for the 'Tomorrow's New World' competition run by the Town & Country Planning Association and the *Guardian* newspaper.

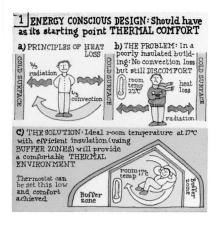

1 ENERGY CONSCIOUS DESIGN: Should have as its starting point THERMAL COMFORT

a) PRINCIPLES OF HEAT LOSS

COLD SURFACE | COLD SURFACE

⅔ radiation
⅓ convection

b) THE PROBLEM: In a poorly insulated building: No convection loss but still DISCOMFORT

room temp 22°C | heat loss | radiation

c) THE SOLUTION: Ideal room temperature at 17°C with efficient insulation (using BUFFER ZONES) will provide a comfortable THERMAL ENVIRONMENT

Thermostat can be set this low and comfort achieved

room 17°C temp | Buffer zone

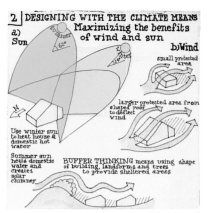

2 DESIGNING WITH THE CLIMATE MEANS Maximizing the benefits of wind and sun

a) Sun

b) Wind

small protected area

larger protected area from shaped roof to deflect wind

Use winter sun to heat house & domestic hot water

Summer sun heats domestic water and creates solar chimney

BUFFER THINKING means using shape of building, landform and trees to provide sheltered areas

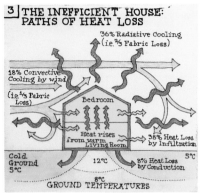

3 THE INEFFICIENT HOUSE: PATHS OF HEAT LOSS

36% Radiative Cooling (i.e. ⅔ Fabric Loss)

18% Convective Cooling by wind (i.e. ⅓ Fabric Loss)

Bedroom

Heat rises from warm Living Room

38% Heat Loss by Infiltration

Cold Ground 5°C | 12°C | 8% Heat Loss by Conduction | 5°C | 8°C

GROUND TEMPERATURES

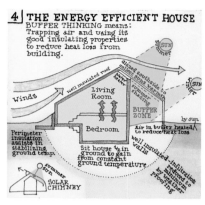

4 THE ENERGY EFFICIENT HOUSE

BUFFER THINKING means: Trapping air and using its good insulating properties to reduce heat loss from building.

Winds | well insulated roof | Living Room | BUFFER ZONE | by sun

Perimeter insulation assists in stabilizing ground temp.

Bedroom

Air in buffer heated to reduce heat loss

Sit house ½ in ground to gain from constant ground temperature

well insulated walls

SOLAR CHIMNEY

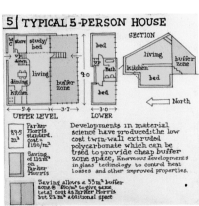

5 TYPICAL 5-PERSON HOUSE

WC | store | study/bed | SECTION | bed
down | living | kitchen | buffer zone | bed
dining | buffer zone | bath | kitchen
kitchen | go to | bed | North

UPPER LEVEL | LOWER

89.5 m² Parker Morris standard cost @ £150/m²

Saving of 112m² on Parker Morris

Developments in material science have produced: the low cost twin-wall extruded polycarbonate which can be used to provide cheap buffer zone space. Enormous developments in glass technology to control heat losses and other improved properties.

Saving allows a 35m² buffer zone - 350m² to give same total cost as Parker Morris but 22m² additional space

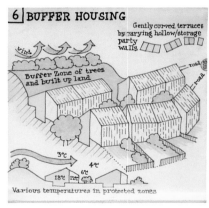

6 BUFFER HOUSING

Gently curved terraces by varying hollow/storage party walls

wind

Buffer Zone of trees and built up land

3°C | 4°C | road

18°C | 12°C | 6°C

Various temperatures in protected zones

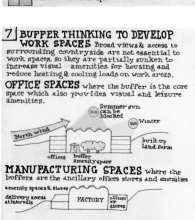

7 BUFFER THINKING TO DEVELOP WORK SPACES Broad views & access to surrounding countryside are not essential to work spaces, so they are partially sunken to increase visual amenities for housing and reduce heating & cooling loads on work areas.

OFFICE SPACES where the buffer is the core space which also provides visual and leisure amenities.

Summer sun can be blocked | Winter

North wind | built up land form

offices | buffer amenity space

MANUFACTURING SPACES where the buffers are the ancillary offices stores and amenities.

amenity spaces & stores

delivery access at intervals | FACTORY | offices & stores

8 BUFFER THINKING TO DEVELOP NEW KINDS OF COMMUNITY SPACES Public capital is used to provide buffer zones between schools, shops and small offices. These would be covered over to produce an arcade and sheltered village squares.

wind

green house florist

Wind buffer zone provided by shops

Covered arcade - portions can be opened up to direct sunlight

South Buffer: Greenhouses, florists, schools, restaurants etc. Portions of South Buffer removed to allow access to air and direct sun.

While working with Charles Jencks on his exuberant house in Holland Park, I had become increasingly conscious of the contrasting obsessions with the anonymity and universality of building systems that were taking hold at Farrell/Grimshaw. It had made me determined to make even these temporary buildings relate to place and context by integrating permanent architectural characteristics of entry and processional route as well as formal symbolism. The greenhouse had a central arcade accessed by its symbolic 'billboard' front entrance that shifted its 'axis' (an unfamiliar word in the Farrell/Grimshaw lexicon) and its cross-section to adjust to overall site movement and ventilation requirements. While this formal touch was lightly done, it was there.

More than anything, the greenhouse was the extension of a form based on the outline shape of a tree, which gave the building a symbolic overall shape and character, and added a new twist and greater expressiveness to the high-tech elements. The undulations of the roof cladding grew partly from the tree outline but also from the stiffening required for the material chosen for the building: twin-wall polycarbonate. Continuing the high-tech tradition of 'cutting-edge innovation' that we had developed at Farrell/Grimshaw, my new practice selected this material and pioneered the first ever use of it in the UK. Its excellent insulation properties suggested that it would have a great future in commercial agriculture. The greenhouse involved some clever fixing details (profiled in a *Design* magazine cover story) and, as a direct result of my work with Ralph Lebens, it used passive solar energy.

I had first met Ralph Lebens in 1979, when he returned from America full of ideas and enthusiasm for solar and passive energy. I agreed that he could work from our office (Nick's departure had left me with surplus space), and he and I formed a passive-solar-energy consultancy. Together we won a competition called 'Tomorrow's New World', which brought together a lot of my interests in the environment and ecology. The results of the competition were announced in *Building Design* in June 1980, in the first week of my independence from Farrell/Grimshaw, with the headline 'Fortune Favours Farrell's Future'. We worked on various European Union initiatives and on studies for the Building Research Station (a government agency), as well as building a solar house in Wales with Oliver Richards, an associate in the practice.

The greenhouse located me in a new architectural place. Magazines and newspapers recognized this fact, and for several years afterwards our new work and its energy and ideas were avidly followed. The office and I were fashionable – creating a double-edged situation in which a lot of people felt they had as much ownership of our work as we did, since they had given us their patronage or (for the time being) their journalistic support. The critical acclaim was gratifying, but I knew it would not last – just as previous fashion had made way in critics' minds for the likes of me, my time would come. The temporary buildings built temporary followers of fashion.

The most exhilarating aspect of the whole endeavour was that the little building was quite beautiful – particularly the curved shapes around the irregular broken ridge and shifted axis. At night, and in sunlight of a certain quality, the twin-wall plastic was a sensational sight, refracting colours and light in extraordinary ways. I take great pleasure from seeing new architectural projects today, 20 years later, such as Hertzog & de Meuron's Laban Dance Centre in Deptford, exploring the same material for its light, semi-transparency and colour refractions.

The first Clifton Nurseries was a matter of creating a silk purse from the sow's ear of an odd corner site in Bayswater – but Jacob Rothschild then asked me to take centre stage with a larger budget and grander expectations all round. The stage itself was intimidating: one end of the piazza in Covent Garden, on the other side of the market buildings from St Paul's church, Inigo Jones's masterpiece. The garden centre would be built on vacant land next to the Opera House, where a large extension was planned. The ever-rotating management of urban land means that buildings are constantly being renewed, repaired and rebuilt; in all towns there are blighted or simply vacant pieces of land awaiting change. Jacob Rothschild saw that, in this case, something good could be made out of what was universally regarded as a problem. Empty land damages the continuity of street life and encourages further decay by becoming a dump for litter and unneighbourly activi-

ties. A garden centre introduced renewal, bringing a bit of the countryside into the town, just as the 6th Duke of Bedford had done two centuries earlier with his fruit and vegetable market.

By then, I was becoming immersed in more formal and traditional architectural ideas, but I was determined to continue exploring the technological innovations possible in temporary buildings. And so, in 1981, with the engineers Peter Rice and John Thornton of Arup, I designed the UK's first Teflon-coated fabric building. To his credit, in spite of large glamorous projects elsewhere, Peter Rice entered fully into the spirit of this little adventure in a classical context, in which a new temple was married to his elegant roof-engineering solution. Axes, alignments and urban references determined the building's precise position, bulk and height. Flowers and plants were part of the formal architecture, and a new public garden landscaped by Clifton Nurseries was laid out as an extension of the building. The building was declared a triumph by many and yet it cost only £100,000. Although it never gave me the same exhilarating sense of self-discovery as my first Clifton Nurseries building in Bayswater did, the Covent Garden building was duly discussed, projected, published and, above all, noticed. It, and therefore my work, had taken its place in the world – it was my work itself, the nature of it, rather than just the physical presence, that had found a place.

Aerial views of Alexandra Palace in north London.

The editorial in *Building Design* of 4 December 1981 by Martin Pawley expressed much of my own thinking about my place in architecture and about the success of this eclectic, mixed-language building. He wrote:

'This small but immodest assembly with its Etruscan columns, painted steel pediment, "living swags" of plants and "seasonal entablature" achieved by the same means, is also the first building in Great Britain to boast a Teflon-coated glass-fibre roof. It is an unbelievable mixture of advanced technology and ancient aesthetics all assimilated by an artist into a comprehensible whole in a manner possible in no other field of human endeavour but architecture.

FESTIVAL EXHIBITION BUILDING 1982

Dingle, Liverpool
for the International Garden Festival 1984

TF with John Chatwin, Steve Ibbotson*, John Langley, Oliver Richards, Gary Young

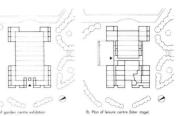

This project was awarded second prize in a national competition organised by the Merseyside Development Corporation. The brief was for a large exhibition building to be converted after the one-year Festival concluded into a public recreation and leisure centre.

The design extends the thinking of the Alexandra Pavilion project; it is a fabric-covered steel-framed structure axially planned, with a large main hall and subsidiary adjacent spaces. The multiple cascading forms at the gable ends house smaller ancillary volumes, as well as reducing the scale of the building at ground level – particularly at the entrance points.

The single skin of PVC fabric would be increased to a double skin for the second stage, and for this a superior fabric with an increased life expectancy such as Teflon-coated glass fibre would be used. The drawings illustrate various colours and designs for the external envelope.

1a Plan of garden centre exhibition 1b Plan of leisure centre (later stage)

2 Axonometric of first stage building envelope

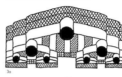
3a

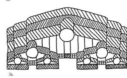
3b

3c

3a,b,c Alternative designs and colour schemes for the external envelope

Top: The building we designed for Clifton Nurseries in Bayswater.

Above: Clifton Nurseries in Covent Garden. The left-hand side is open – to screen a car park not owned by the client.

Top: Our entry for the garden festival building competition in Liverpool – based on Alexandra Palace, but more elaborate and varied.

Above: A night view of the completed Alexandra Palace temporary pavilion designed with Peter Rice and Ian Ritchie.

'The fabric roof alone is a miracle of technological eclecticism, combining Teflon coatings discovered by accident in the DuPont laboratories in Delaware a decade before Fry wrote Fine Building, with woven fibre glass developed in quite a different context 10 years later, and a fixing system derived from racing yacht technology by way of Peter Rice's Shelter-Span tensile fabric system. To this is added the complex of historical references and architectural artifice that converts a monopitch shed into a kind of Greek temple aligned with street axes and background rooflines in a manner that puts to shame the painstaking restoration and refurbishment of the central market building itself. The architecture here is the combination of elements that by themselves are meaningless bits of unrelated technique seldom even found in the same library, let alone in a useful structure. Only a building could do it. Only an architect could make it into a building.'

Above, left and right: Houses in Chigwell, Essex, showing add-ons and other examples of individualization. Both photographs were taken as part of a teaching project, 'Learning from Chigwell', which I undertook at the Architectural Association in 1979–80.

Left: Advertisment for a bungalow, dating from the 1920s.

After completion of the Wood Green estate, I was invited by Haringey Council to submit proposals for a temporary exhibition centre at Alexandra Palace. The Victorian building first opened in 1873 to provide Victorians with a recreation centre within an expansive greater environment. Situated in 196 acres of parkland, with spectacular views over the capital, the palace, joined by a branch line of the Great Northern Railway to Highgate, attracted thousands of people, who arrived by train, carriage or on foot. Sixteen days after its opening the building burnt down as the result of a fire in the dome that could not be extinguished. Less than two years after the destruction of the original building, a new palace opened. Covering 7 acres, it was centred on the Great Hall, which seated 12,000 people in addition to 2,000 seats in the orchestra stalls, beneath the huge Willis organ, which was driven by two steam engines

Some of the photographs I took while designing the Oakwood 18 housing scheme in Warrington. At the time I was fascinated by the bungalow form as an icon of British popular taste.

and vast bellows. In other parts of the palace there were painting and sculpture displays, exhibitions, a museum, lecture hall and library, banqueting rooms, a 3,500-seat concert room (later converted into a roller-skating rink) and a 3,000-seat theatre. The park had a racetrack, trotting ring, cricket ground, ornamental lakes and a permanent funfair. In 1935, the BBC leased the eastern part of the building, from which the world's very first public television transmissions were made in 1936.

Crystal Palace and Alexandra Palace were very different from their counterparts in the royal parks. Set on hills in suburban London, the palaces at one level spoke to the masses as great symbols of human achievement and on another attracted the vulgar and commonplace, inviting a kind of enjoyment quite different from that associated with the gracious activities allowed by the royal family outside their palaces in central London. (The pleasure garden was another London parkland invention – the wonderful gardens at the Tivoli in Copenhagen were inspired by Vauxhall and other London pleasure grounds.) Like Crystal Palace, which had been relocated to south London, Alexandra Palace was a structure where the best of 19th-century industrial building technology in steel and glass was juxtaposed with great parklands. The original idea behind this huge people's palace, as it was called, greatly appealed to me, and reminded me of the all-weather interiors in Blackpool, of the Winter Gardens and the Tower, and of course my thesis project, the Climatron. Glass and metal technology, climate control in a cool, wet country and popular accessibility – what a combination!

After another huge fire, on 10 July 1980, Alexandra Palace was again a burnt-out hulk, a ruin in a rather sad landscape, so a temporary building was needed to house events and exhibitions during the ambitious programme of renewal that was set in train for the once-splendid complex. While considering how to construct the temporary exhibition centre, I remembered having seen a small fabric building for storage use at Heathrow airport with 'Shelterspan' written on it. After a bit of research I found that it had been designed by Peter Rice of Arup and the architect Ian Ritchie. Translated to Alexandra Palace, such a building would need to be much larger than the Heathrow prototype, requiring a steel rather than an aluminium structure. With Peter and

Ian, I proceeded to transform a system into a place-specific building. It was rather like taking a Buckminster Fuller engineering concept and applying it to a specific architectural application, as I had done with my student Climatron thesis. I adapted the building to fit around a tulip tree and I chose to use a two-tone colour – it had only ever been designed in white.

Edwin Lutyens's comment that 'architecture begins where engineering ends' became a tenet for me after the demise of Farrell/Grimshaw. I was more interested in how products were used than in the products themselves. I saw this as another stage in the progress of high-tech, taking it beyond the point it had reached in the late 1970s. When built, Alexandra Palace exhibition centre was for many years the largest fabric building in the UK – and it stood next to the formal architectural gestures of the Victorian palace with, I believe, a degree of happy dialogue. Colour and large-scale lettering and patterns were all possible with this material – using it was, after all, more akin to tailoring than building. It was a real tent, a truly nomadic but inspirational building form.

The temporary building had been due to move to Crystal Palace after completion of the works to restore the main building at Alexandra Palace, but the removal scheme fell through. I had always liked the idea of creating a physical link between this building and one of Britain's greatest ever building achievements: Paxton's Crystal Palace, which was also nomadic – it was moved from Hyde Park to Crystal Palace and, like Alexandra Palace, it was destroyed by fire.

Our involvement at that time in urban renewal through the construction of parks, gardens and temporary buildings came to an end in a competition for a garden festival complex that was intended to rejuvenate parts of Liverpool. The idea was based on successful German precedents, although Glasgow and Gateshead had also pioneered urban renewal through garden festivals – giant versions of the nurseries Jacob Rothschild had set up in London. I later reflected that these festivals were very limited in their success, and Liverpool's garden centre site is today rather a sad spectacle. Our entry, which came second in the competition, carried further the art and pattern-making potential of the high-tech fabric material. Apart from

unsuccessfully competing for a Homebase garden centre – for which our entry was a Venturi-inspired iconic 'home' made of fabric – our work gradually gave way to more permanent, urban projects.

Learning from Chigwell and bungalows

My next venture was to revisit the suburban housing estate – this time at Warrington, in the north-west of England. As part of a national policy in the 1960s and 1970s to get people out of town centres, Warrington, along with neighbouring Runcorn and Skelmersdale, was designated a new town. This development had a devastating effect on the economic and social vitality of neighbouring Liverpool and Manchester, and it is only now, 40 years later, that those cities are getting the kind of concerted attention they should have had then. The naive, simplistic solution of moving people out to new towns actually exacerbated urban problems.

Liverpool and Manchester are effectively two parts of one regional metropolis – historically linked by the great ship canal that made Manchester an inland port. Between the two cities, where the canal crosses the main London to Glasgow railway line west of the M6 motorway, stands Warrington. The town has an industrial past and is characterized by long terraces of houses and a large lively covered market. In Warrington one can witness the extraordinary sight of huge ocean-going ships like great mobile town, gliding between the little houses, streets and parks as though on wheels – the low-lying canal itself is often not a very visible part of the landscape. The ships play little or no part in the life of Warrington; they are on their way from Manchester to the Indian, Atlantic or Pacific oceans, or are coming back again, and it seems that local people pay no more attention to the curiosity than sheep do to a train passing through their field.

Alongside the motorway was Oakwood, a once built-up area of land that had self-seeded and become a nature reserve. When we were appointed to design two large housing schemes there, after having only ever built in urban London, we had an opportunity to learn from new town landscape architects and ecologists about this land, its natural value and how it was changing. Contrary to the visions of the green-belt defenders around London, planned, insightful urbanization can, I learned, benefit and balance the natural landscape. At

Opposite, top: Drawings for the Warrington houses. Top left is Oakwood 13 terraced houses. Top right is Oakwood 18 bungalows showing the variations on one basic plan form, built with standardized components but enabling considerable flexibility.

Opposite, centre: Model studies for Oakwood 13.

Opposite, bottom: Early model studies for Oakwood 18.

Housing schemes in Warrington: Bungalows at Oakwood 18 (top) and the earlier terraced houses at Oakwood 13 (above).

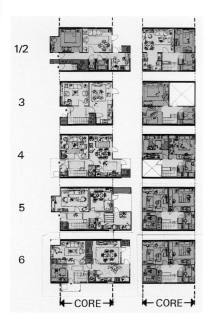

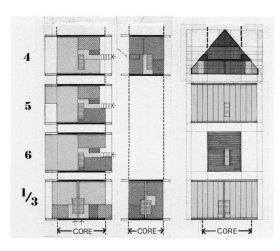

about this time, I had bought a home near Cambridge, where I saw that fenland towns and villages – places that emerged from water as it was transformed into occupied land – can add positive value to the countryside. Characterized by total flatness, the fens of East Anglia are covered in rich black peat that, when drained, is quickly eroded by the wind. The villages of the Cambridgeshire fens, created from reclaimed land, have defended nature and become an ally to ecological stability by reducing wind erosion. There were also lessons in regrowth in the fens that I first learned at Oakwood – of self-seeding and the inexorable stages of natural regeneration.

What absorbed me at Oakwood was how to develop further the concerns with context and popular taste pioneered by the Maunsel Housing Society's timber-frame houses and flats, and to apply them to a large-scale public housing estate. At around the same time, I returned to teach at the AA, where the students and I carried out a study of popular taste and consumers' expectations for rented public housing. I had taken on a joint teaching unit position with Piers Gough and Izzy Metstein in 1979, and my particular group looked at and recorded a suburban mixed-tenure area of east London called Chigwell. I found the real character of Chigwell in the precast-concrete classical urns and gnomes adorning the front of the houses, and in the lean-to add-ons and greenhouses at the back. At the front it was the fashion to pave over the garden for car parking, add coach lamps and a front door with a sunburst design, and individualize the style of the house number and name.

Extrapolating from what we had learned at Chigwell, I was interested in what kind of taste the Oakwood residents would have – how they would express themselves through house 'decoration', garden design, colours, motifs, and so on – and the extent to which they would want to alter and extend the living space in their homes by carrying out attic conversions, for example, or adding conservatories, garden sheds and garages. From my childhood observations of my father's frustrations with home improvements while we were living on an institutionalized housing estate, and from the joys of my own standard suburban private house in Maida Vale, I believed that people wanted to get away from the stigma of state-owned and large-scale managed public housing, and that they had visual tastes far removed from the middle-class views of most architects. Taste in Britain reflects class. As the art critic Brian Sewell once said, 'For the rest of the world it has something to do with our sensory perceptions, but for the British taste means social place.' Having always felt uncomfortable about the prevailing concept in our professional establishment that an architect is chosen as the authority on good taste, I prefer to study Americans such as Robert Venturi, Andy Warhol and Jane Jacobs, who considered that what ordinary people did and what they chose was intensely interesting. Venturi was co-author of a free-spirited book entitled *Learning from Las Vegas*. I called our AA exploration 'Learning from Chigwell' and proceeded to look at the links between Oakwood, Chigwell and the place where I grew up – the Grange Estate in Newcastle.

The timber-frame factory-produced component of Oakwood 13 (the project's first phase) paralleled the steel-frame, asbestos-panel 'prefabs' of Kirkley Close on the Grange Estate. But at Oakwood we saw standardization as the starting point in the architectural scheme. By taking advantage of the extra funds available to overcome existing foundation problems we designed houses that promoted individuality of expression. So, for example, every house had an extra external foundation extending from the ground-floor plan by 2 metres (6 feet 6 inches) at the front and

3 metres (9 feet 9 inches) at the back, to accommodate and encourage later extensions, if needed by the occupants. We also varied decorative details on the houses and made good use of that most British of features, the sunburst design in the glass front door. In a modest tour de force involving myriad pieces of coloured glass and plywood cut-outs, sunburst designs were inserted by architectural students from Manchester Polytechnic into the front-door windows of 120 houses, and every single one was different. During my work at Oakwood, I also designed, with Ralph Lebens, a pilot passive-energy house involving a solar, or 'buffer', greenhouse.

Since becoming familiar with Lytham St Anne's, I had been convinced that in retirement the British built the home type they had always wanted: the bungalow. In recent times, in June 2002, a MORI poll for the Commission for Architecture and the Built Environment (CABE) revealed that this type of home, with its origins in the leisurely colonialist lifestyle of British India, was still the most popular in Britain. For Oakwood 18 (the second phase), I did what I had always wanted to do; unlike Oakwood 13, which was modelled on the terraced and semi-detached houses of Chigwell, Oakwood 18 was modelled on the bungalows typical of seaside retirement towns. With the same consideration for decorative front doors and house extensions, I designed and built an

LEARNING FROM LAS VEGAS
Revised Edition

Robert Venturi   Denise Scott Brown   Steven Izenour

The influential book *Learning from Las Vegas* by Robert Venturi, Denise Scott Brown and Steven Izenour.

Left and opposite: This drawing by Andrew Holmes of Oakwood 13 applies the principles we learnt from Chigwell to the Warrington scheme, incorporating anticipated individualization at the front (left) and back (opposite).

extended neighbourhood of bungalows with dormer windows on the outskirts of Warrington. I went back to the area in 2002, and the photographs I took then show, I believe, friendly and cherished streets of houses. Many owner-occupiers now live there, the freeholds having been bought by the former tenants. A particularly reassuring discovery was that the construction project's working titles of Oakwood 13 and 18 had vanished from everyone's memory – and the houses were now immersed and subsumed into the overall urban fabric and known only by a range of local street names.

Richard MacCormac was building on the next door site to mine in Warrington. When both our projects were finished, I initiated an article in the *Architects' Journal* (September 1978) that allowed us to compare the two projects. I described his most interesting scheme as in the middle-class English tradition of John Ruskin, the architectural equivalent of a Rover motor car; mine, on the other hand, was more like a contemporary Ford with lots of flexibility and clip-on extras. The timber-frame houses I was designing were intended to encourage personal inventiveness by their occupants. I was attempting to design houses with all the characteristics of those in the freer private sector for emerging working-class to lower-middle-class people. I felt that much state housing was patronizing and paternalistic, designed from 'top down' rather than 'bottom up'.

Issues of class, pluralism, individual expression and the need for an architect to understand who he was designing for were becoming increasingly important to me.

The house as a small city; transitions of scale

Unlike Americans in their new land, most British architects, when commissioned to design a home, are faced with adapting and changing an existing building. This is simply because there are so many houses, and buildings generally, in well-settled neighbourhoods that the cost, planning consents and time taken to build new is an option only for the very seriously committed. Many leading British architects live in houses that are centuries old. This was the case with the American Charles Jencks, who approached me in around 1978 to ask if I would collaborate in redesigning an existing London house for him and his wife, Maggie Keswick (by the time the house was finished, they also had two children to accommodate).

The Jencks house, a 19th-century house in Holland Park, has a particularly interesting neighbourhood plan. As in my own home area of Maida Vale, less than 2 miles away, many houses in the Ladbroke Grove/Holland Park area are grouped around shared private gardens. There are several urban areas in London brilliantly based on this plan form. In Regent's Park in the 1820s, John Nash created a singular new residential concept of grand palaces in their parkland – each, in fact,

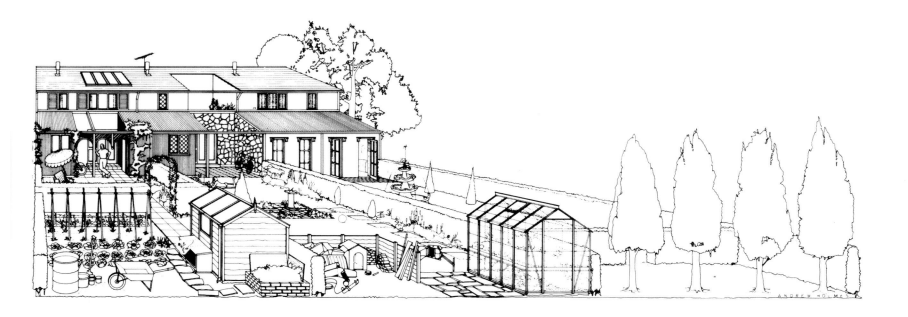

subdivided into terraced houses and flats for rent. This was quite different from John Wood's designs in Bath, where plan forms of crescents and circuses are clearly urban, in that they are based on streets of individual houses each with its own separate, numbered address. In Regent's Park the 'palace' identity predominates; the overall impression is of grand country houses, usually with porticoes, wings and mews – all seemingly part of the recognizable hierarchical composition of the archetypal palace with its wings and ancillary buildings such as stables. But within this concept a great variety of plan forms exists. Sometimes the rows of 'front' doors are hidden at the rear with private grounds at the front. But Ladbroke Grove and Maida Vale have residential street architecture of a type found all over London: the houses have no more than a small yard to the rear, which adjoins beautiful, generous communal gardens; access is normally exclusively from the yards of the terraced houses and flats that ring the gardens. The Jencks house was in such an area, characterized by white and cream stucco houses and terraces, and an abundance of mature trees. Charles and Maggie had big ideas.

It was a unique learning experience for us all – including job architects Simon Hudspith (now at Panter Hudspith), Simon Sturgis, David Quigley, Richard Solomon and Steve Marshall – all of whom went on to set up their own practices. Exterior alterations were quite extensive but only on the side and rear, with the addition of a curved roof over the study and large conservatories opening onto the garden. The interior was extensively restructured, and a circular staircase was installed in the centre, around which the house was symbolically divided into the four seasons. Towards the end of our work on the house, all the furniture and walls were overlaid with Charles's symbolic visions, and gradually I felt ownership of the design slip away. To clarify attribution, Charles and I together wrote a special issue of *Architectural Design* after the completion of the house. It had been an extraordinary but testing exercise, particularly since Charles and Maggie were both clients and collaborators.

Working on the Jencks house inspired me to experiment further with the postmodernism that Charles Jencks was championing in his writings and lectures. It marked the beginning in a change of fortunes and direction – through Jencks I had met Jacob Rothschild, who commissioned me to design the Clifton Nurseries. Over the years I have kept in touch with Charles and collaborated further, particularly on the masterplanning and detailed design of the grass mounds at the National Gallery of Scotland.

I love buildings with complex internal structures, worlds within worlds – and I love exploiting the illusion that the smaller an actual space the more infinite it can seem. This thread runs through my work from the complex three-dimensional layering of some of my student schemes to the students' hostel, my houses at Ashworth Road and Upwood, the Jencks house, the Crafts Council in Waterloo Place, London, and, more recently,

Exterior of the Jencks house in Holland Park, west London before (top) and after it was radically redesigned.

the Dean Gallery in Edinburgh. Much of this reminded me of the collectors' books and collectors' museums I loved in my childhood. At the same time as working on the Jencks house I was helping a friend, John Scott, to convert a pair of houses to make a home for him and his collection of antiques; as it turned out, both the Jencks house and John Scott's house crossed the boundaries between collecting and living.

John had been the chairman of the client body for the cooperative housing scheme at Park Road, but moved to live on the edge of the antiques quarter centred on Portobello Road. Street markets characterize London – I now live next to the bustling market in Church Street, off Edgware Road. Market or town squares in the continental European style do not generally work in Britain, so whole streets are managed on a daily basis to reinvent themselves on key days when a new, vibrant, temporary place emerges. Portobello has increasingly become the focus for the Notting Hill Carnival, during which millions of people converge on otherwise normal, regular London streets to create one of the biggest street fairs in the world. Not for us Londoners the grand Parisian processions on the Champs Elysées: a meandering maze is our stage.

Over the years, John Scott has campaigned to introduce many interventions in his neighbourhood, such as Piers Gough's lavatory and flower-stand on Westbourne Grove and art works all along the main thoroughfare of Notting Hill Gate. It is a wonderful story of scale transitions whereby an individual created his own private domestic world of great intensity. and collected beauties, which then spilt out and spread to the public domain. In John's eyes, the seams between home, street and neighbourhood are blurred; he has enhanced the identity and character of a formerly neglected urban quarter that had little to recommend it. The fascinating thing is that he saw the municipal toilet as the key element and realized that this public necessity, if done with generosity and style, could be enough of an asset to transform a place. Part of Westbourne Grove has since been renamed 'Turquoise Island' after the vibrant colours of the toilets. Urban renewal can occur from the inside out, progressing from the domestic to the public stage, from small detail to large strategy, and be spearheaded by a single passionate individual with or without the backing of the whole community.

To my mind, the archetypal minimalist house is a kind of catatonic architecture expressing a very limited emotional range. I would contrast the minimalist house with the houses of one of the great duets of the 20th century: the architects and designers Charles and Ray Eames. The Eames house in California is extraordinarily diverse and complicated. Great collectors, they loved the richness of life and demonstrated eclecticism in everything they touched. Their world was intense and creative, and recalled to me Keats's lines 'The excellence of all art lies in its intensity' and Shelley's advice to Keats, 'Load

Some complex interior worlds within private houses:

Opposite, left to right: Charles and Ray Eames in their California house; the Jencks house in Holland Park; and John Scott's house in Notting Hill.

Below, left to right: Sir John Soane's house in Lincoln's Inn; the Farrells' hallway in Maida Vale; and the Farrells' dining room/kitchen in Upwood, Cambridgeshire.

every rift with ore'. Charles and Ray Eames put together many different kinds of collection, revelling in the richness and diversity of things, as well as hidden connections. A picture of their cluttered studio shows patterns of order and knowing disorder – but never a total lack of order.

It is the task of the modern urbanist to identify obscure and hidden patterns, to explain the complexity of what's there instead of demolishing or oversimplifying. I look at the apparent chaos of cities, the layered work of history, and I try to understand why a particular city is the way it is, in a process that is akin to psychoanalysing the collective, with the places themselves on the couch.

One way of understanding a city's patterns is to see it as Leon Battista Alberti saw it – as a large house. From this perspective, the traditional city has its living rooms (public spaces), bedrooms (residential streets), dining rooms (restaurants), storage houses and chapels. In *On the Art of Building in Ten Books*, Alberti writes:

'If (as the philosophers maintain) the city is like some large house, and the house is in turn like some small city, cannot the various parts of the house – atria, dining rooms, porticoes, and so on – be considered miniature buildings?'

This question always reminds me of the underlying link between the interior designer and the urban planner – in spite of the scale differences, both can have transferable skills. Probably this is because they deal with voids, the spaces between, while the conventional architectural designer confines himself to the solid, the object. I have seen that many fellow architects both in my office and outside, having been trained as modernists, often struggle to make the connections with urban and interior design. A contemporary of mine at St Cuthbert's school, Frank Duffy, who set up in practice in London about the same time as I did, was a founding partner of DEGW, an international firm of interior-space planners whose specialization has led them to leapfrog architecture and immerse themselves in urban planning – exposing them to the understanding of the common processes involved.

The ultimate experience of the house as a small city is the complete world created in his home by Sir John Soane in Lincoln's Inn, central London. Ancient Rome and Greece, the London of Hogarth and Soane's personal experience of life are captured in a wonderful internal labyrinth that is museum and house all in one. Soane's architecture is physically of a high order. The compositional effects and aesthetic preferences leave little to chance; he was undoubtedly a true artist of the architectural domain. By comparison, his contemporary John Nash was an architectural cavalier and his buildings in themselves are generally of a less reliable quality. Nash's strength lay in his ability to make very great places – a talent that is not often rated as highly as architecture, but I fundamentally believe that it should be. Nash studied Humphry Repton and Capability Brown and adapted what he had learned to an urban model. In reality, his work was truly superb. If one considers that the object is not absolutely all-important, then it is possible to appreciate the great inventiveness of Regent's Park, Regent's Street and Trafalgar Square – powerful places of a different order from the rest of London. In the past, critics have tended to judge Nash's work as being good but not the best, but the collective can have a special kind of good, indeed it can have a greatness all its own, as in Bath or Venice. In architecture, the aesthetic purity of the object is key, but this often neglects the collective magnificence such as that found in John Nash's London, James Craig's Edinburgh New Town and Haussmann's Paris. This kind of art, the art of city-making, has the potential to mean far more to far more people.

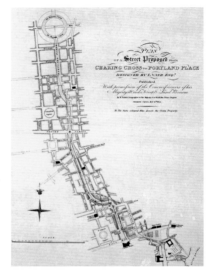

An early scheme for Regent Street by the architect John Nash.

The relationship of scales, the transitions and the continuum from one to another was pictorialized in the 1970s with graphic brilliance in Charles Eames's short film *The Powers of Ten*, in which the individual has his specific personal place, sitting on a beach between the infinitely small world of atoms and molecules and the larger world of planets and the solar system. One of my favourite domestic memories, inspired by Eames, was sitting with my children at the family breakfast table and registering the moment when the night security light would automatically go off. Being controlled by a light sensor, its timing would vary through the year and with the seasons – and so I would say to the children, 'Ah, see the world is going round.' At our dining table in our own small place, our home, we connected with the rotation

John Nash (1752–1835) was engaged by the Prince Regent to plan the layout of the new Regent's Park and its approaches.

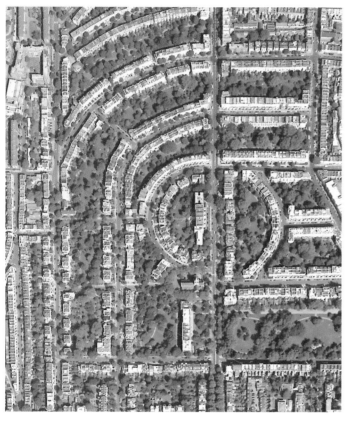

Houses with communal gardens or parklands in the centre of London: Cumberland Terrace, Regent's Park, by John Nash (top left); Ladbroke Grove (centre left and right) and Maida Vale (bottom left, Farrell home circled). See also the drawing of Wesley Square (page 140).

of the earth and with its moon travelling round the sun, a pattern of rotation which affected tides, seasons and the daylight falling on our little light sensor. 'And,' I asked them, 'what can we therefore conclude is the address of our home? We are travellers moving at 30 kilometres per second (108,000 kph), sitting on the third planet from the sun, which is about two-thirds of the way out from the centre of the Milky Way galaxy of about a billion stars, all travelling inexorably outwards from the source of the Big Bang along with a billion other galaxies which all make up our universe. This is where we are right now, this is the place you and I are in.'

End piece

The joy of being released from an increasingly constrained working relationship led to my revisiting both the USA (as a visiting tutor at Penn in 1980–81, and giving lectures in Los Angeles) and the Far East (I stayed in Hong Kong for two months to submit an entry for an architectural competition). The travelling was partly a symbolic gesture – I had been immersed in the Farrell/Grimshaw partnership for more than 15 years and wanted to return to the distant foreign scenes I had not experienced since the early 1960s; I was opening up my horizons again.

After the practice split up, I began at once to redesign the office space at Paddington Street that we had all shared for eight years – primarily because I wanted to get away from a workspace that I saw as expressing too mechanistic a view of the work–life environment. As a result, a central street, a reception hall space and a staff leisure courtyard, all space and place specific, replaced 'techno-bureaulandschaft' with its entropic sense of 'no-place'. New projects were in their embryonic stages at the time. My involvement with TVam began at a lunch at Odin's in January 1981.

At the end of that year, I became interested in the controversy about Peter Palumbo's proposal for a Mies van der Rohe tower at Poultry and Mansion House in the City of London. I met the campaigner Marcus Binney, who ran SAVE Britain's Heritage, and we developed an alternative, conservation-based scheme. As a result of the second Clifton Nurseries greenhouse project, I was invited to reappraise the area around one-quarter of the piazza enclosure that awaited the Royal Opera House plans. With Jacob Rothschild's support and the Opera House's encouragement, we met the directors and board members of the Opera House on several occasions and developed with them a proposal for the land on which the greenhouse stood. I suggested completing the arcading around the piazza, reopening the west front of the Opera House with a door to the piazza and providing a 'layer' of commercial and mixed-use street buildings on the adjacent Floral Street frontage, so that the big bulk of the Opera House would be a good urban neighbour, a semi-submerged gentle giant. All these ideas were 'outside in': derived from the place itself and its powerful existing design forms and character. Much of what I did was incorporated into the brief for the competition, which led to the eventual Opera House redevelopment by Dixon Jones and BDP.

During the 1980s, often voluntarily, I wrote urban briefs through concept-level masterplans that led to the rethinking of many areas of London, including Mansion House, the South Bank, Spitalfields market, Paternoster Square, London Wall, the Thames walkways, and Hammersmith and Richmond town centres. Sometimes my role was to oppose a scheme on behalf of residents or conservation groups, and sometimes it was just to get things moving. The Mansion House, Hammersmith and Covent Garden Opera House schemes were the first of many voluntary independent interventions into the normal flow of urban proceedings that I have embarked on over the years.
It was not my deliberate intention to intervene in the

planning processes in this way. On reflection, there was a convergence of circumstances at the very beginning of the 1980s that made me realize, firstly, that town planning in Britain didn't work and, secondly, that given the way political events were unfolding it was becoming possible to do something about it. The election of Margaret Thatcher in 1979 was the first real political watershed since the advent of the Attlee government of 1945. The Attlee government had set the agenda on the welfare state and town planning (primarily in the 1948 Acts) for the intervening years, and the two went together – town planning was unambiguously conceived as a public-sector activity. The two parallel strands that emerged from this belief was that the state – nationally, regionally and locally – did the planning and the private sector, which was regarded as messy and irresponsibly self-interested, had to be kept in check by what became known as 'development control'.

Development control was not the primary planning tool as long as planning was carried out by a state that had the powers, owned the land, and had the resources to carry out the plans. As things evolved, by the late 1970s we had all realized – as Russia, China and other single-party socialist nations also came to realize – that it couldn't be done that way. This meant that the only real planning left under the old regime was development control, which resulted in two decades and more of non-planning because the issues of who and what were being controlled and, more importantly, who was doing the planning were never properly addressed. Under Mrs Thatcher's governments, the private sector was the only sector doing any planning, some good, some bad; and it did so by confronting development control with independent Development Agencies made up of planning and legal consultants and an array of clever new property developers who operated on a scale not seen since the Victorian era.

For the following 25 to 30 years the pattern of a lot of my work was based on the idea that in Britain nobody plans. But the public realm, our urban places, which belong to us all, cannot be left to let hang, and in my various voluntary schemes from then onwards I intentionally filled a gap. 'Development control' only effectively addresses the landholdings of the private sector, and no one considers the bits in between. All the postwar governments had seen our urban areas as 'problem areas' and, while

Opposite, top left: The Covent Garden piazza as originally designed shows the continuation of the colonnaded façade around all four sides.

The other pictures show our proposals for the Royal Opera House in 1981, which formed a basis for the subsequent competition brief for the eventual redevelopment of the site.

Top right: Proposal for an Opera House extension, including the continuation of the colonnaded façade to give a piazza face and western entrance to the Opera House, and retaining the Floral Hall.

Middle row: Longitudinal sections with a new small auditorium (left) and Bow Street elevation with the retained Floral Hall (right).

Bottom row: Models showing different levels of the proposals.

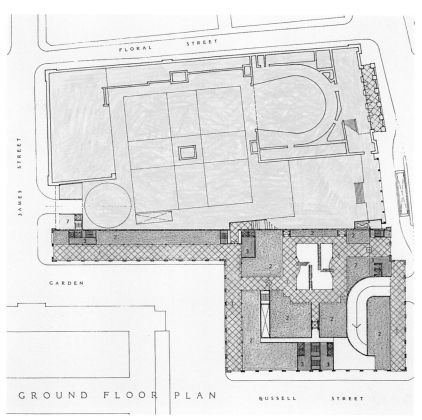

GROUND FLOOR PLAN

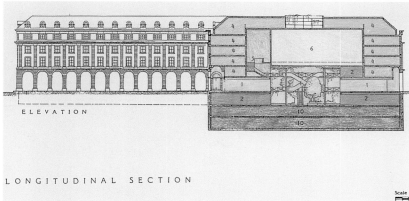

ELEVATION

LONGITUDINAL SECTION

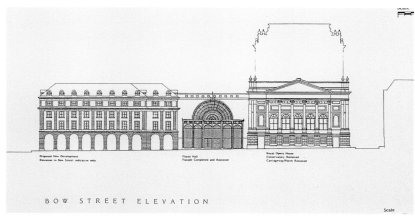

BOW STREET ELEVATION

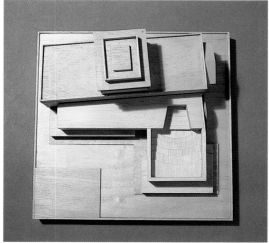

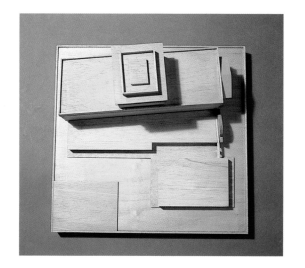

FORECAST FAVOURS FARRELL'S FUTURE

BUILDING DESIGN, June 6, 1980

Lynda Relph-Knight talked to Terry Farrell and Ralph Lebens on tomorrow's community.

YET another award has fallen the way of Terry Farrell, but this time there is a significant difference.

He and passive solar system supremo Ralph Lebens have just been pronounced winners of the Tomorrow's New Community competition, organised by the *Guardian* in conjunction with the Town and Country Planning Association, for two schemes designed along buffer thinking lines and incorporating passive solar heating principles.

The competition entry, which provided designs for community development on two sites in the Wirrall and Milton Keynes, is best described by the illustrations accompanying this article. The basic principle starts with the orientation of the buildings, with solid north facing walls embedded in the soil as a buffer against inclement weather. South facing areas are glazed to make the best of sunny weather. And this theme is continued right through to the use of a particular building. Recreational facilities take advantage of the south-facing areas and, indeed, the development pattern of the entire community follows this pattern.

Passive solar heating design has a lot to do with common sense. It is thinking architecture, using the building itself as a solar collector and as a heat storage and distribution system. The benefits in energy conservation are fairly obvious: to the building user the advantages are best described in terms of comfort.

Buffer thinking, a term coined by Farrell and Lebens, is used to describe this conscious attitude to design because, in their words, "it implies application of awareness and intelligent design skill rather than heavy-handed technology. It is an energy solution which involves the participation of the user individually and collectively."

Trees and earth play an important part as natural insulators and barriers against the cold: masonry and glazing are used to full effect. There is none of the newfangled gadgetry, solar collectors and the like.

The main intention of the competition entry is to get the basic principles understood: "From this point we can build forms which respond to their climate, much as a plant in a dark corner will grow towards the light."

Talking generally about the buffer concept, Farrell and Lebens believe its application could be almost limitless. It is appropriate to all building types, housing, commercial and industrial developments and recreational facilities as the competition entry demonstrates.

Top: This page and opposite: Early press reactions to the first competition win of Terry Farrell & Partners, and early projects.

Bottom: The press took up the contrast of my work with that of Farrell/Grimshaw which unfortunately contributed to driving Nick and me further apart.

Sunday Times, 16 January 1983

THE MAN WHO TOOK HIGH TECH OUT TO PLAY

By Deyan Sudjic, architectural correspondent

In the early Seventies, Terry Farrell was the lesser light of a middle-ranking architectural partnership whose speciality was cool. High Tech buildings like that below left. But two years ago he left his partner Nick Grimshaw (left), turned to a playful, post-modernist style – and became the hottest property in British architecture. His latest building, the studios for TV-AM (due to go on the air next month), has huge glass-fibre boiled eggs on the roof; and the man who commissioned it insists that Farrell is "a genius"

The phone rings; it is architect Terry Farrell, calling his office from Venice: "Look John, what we really need for the roof of this studio is a dozen three-feet-high egg cups, with eggs to match." John Chatwin, Farrell's phlegmatic senior lieutenant takes a deep breath, nods, reaches for a pad and pencil, and calls over the luckless subordinate whose task it will be to explain this latest flash of inspiration to the builders.

Peter Jay and David Frost, prime movers behind TV-AM, the breakfast television station due to open next month, may have fondly imagined that the design of their new studios had finally been settled when Farrell went off for a well-deserved rest in Italy. But the Grand Canal in Venice had suddenly put him in mind of Camden Town and TV-AM. Venice's palaces and churches bristle with statues of princes and saints; so why shouldn't TV-AM, the only television station on the banks of a canal (the not-so-grand Regent's Canal in North London), also have a few equally symbolic decorations – like breakfast eggs?

"There's nothing in the budget for them," Farrell warned Chatwin over the phone, "so we'll have to shop around. See what you can find in the way of cheap plastic urns by the time I get back."

"We bought a whole lot of great big nasty ones from garden centres," remembers Chatwin. "None of them were any good, so we had somebody make up our own designs in glass fibre. The guy who did it was very ➤➤➤

Terry Farrell's astonishing Thame near Reading (above, photograph Richard Bryant) suggests a water symbolism of his TV-AM studios (below, photograph by James Mo clearer: on top of the building wh houses the breakfast television st put these giant breakfast "eggs"

**Architects Journal,
25 June 1980**

**Architectural Review,
September 1980**

**Building,
29 October 1982**

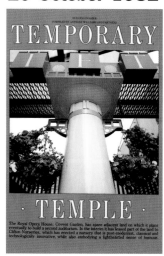

investing heavily in public projects, did not invest in the existing infrastructure of towns and cities but in projects such as new towns and housing estates. The over-steering of the Thatcher years drove the public/private sector balance of investment still further away from the public 'between' places and spaces that are the essence of urban life. In the vacuum, the most creative area of urban design was to make plans where no one else was doing so.

I have chosen to finish this part of the book in 1981, a year or so after I set up in practice solely on my own, and when I felt I had found my own architectural place. I have never felt this sense of identity to be a stylistic one. Rather, it is based on a way of seeing things, working with people I like, building relationships with my own kind of clients or patrons and fulfilling the project opportunities they bring with them, combined with establishing a creative home in terms of studio space, meeting rooms, front door, street and neighbourhood. Place is nurtured in more than physical ways. In the mind, heart and spirit of each of us is an innate need to find ourselves – maturing, changing and ever nomadic as life's personal adventure unfolds, but always rooting down and only growing in the natural and man-made places we find en route.

My particular sense of life as a journey is probably embedded in me from my family origins. The Irish are descended from the nomadic race of Celts and Vikings who lived and travelled on Europe's expansive Atlantic edges, and up until only two or three generations ago they were continuing to travel and spread to North America and Australia. They carried their traditions with them in songs, storytelling and myths so that each arrival point, or 'place', had its own intensified meaning for them. The traditions of the nomad seem to be increasingly relevant to today's world, in which global travel, family restructuring, social mobility and advances in information technology all demand levels of flexibility and continuous adaptability that few earlier ages have had to face. I have travelled socially, intellectually and, like everyone else, through the processes of ageing, where the world of the child is carried through the time-places of childhood, middle age and senior citizenship.

It has been an exhilarating personal journey, a life looking at cities for 40 years and seeing them grow and change. The Newcastle and Manchester of my childhood both exist and yet no longer exist. American cities and Far Eastern cities I saw and studied at a young age gave me an unusual global perspective on the last 40 years of radical urban transformation. I have also been privileged to have revisited so many of them frequently, often as a participant in charge of events as well as a passing visitor.

Constraints in life there are aplenty, but as we are merely existing in a snapshot of time it is these very constraints or contexts that make us what we are, and our places what they are, as each of us explores our temporary visit to the here and now. Cities and towns are brilliant and extraordinary expressions of the human psyche in this search for personal and collective identity. They are statements about who we are, right now – and yet we know the city, the town, the village, the neighbourhood are all part of an accumulation from others in the past that we have added to and that will be adapted and added to by our successors.

TWENTY-FIVE PROJECTS: 1959–81

Furniture study • Urban-planning study • Travel studies • Village planning • The Climatron • Ventilation towers • Courtyard housing • Philadelphia city centre • Doodles and organics • Public squares: USA • Public housing • International students' hostel • Co-ownership flats • Paddington Street offices: 1 • Paddington Street offices: 2 • Industrial buildings • The Colonnades • Low-cost timber-frame housing • Jencks house • Clifton Nurseries: 1 • Clifton Nurseries: 2 • Water-treatment centre • Alexandra Pavilion • Crafts Council Gallery • Urban-infill factories

Text by Jane Tobin

FURNITURE STUDY

Student measured drawings: third year, 1959

In 1958, Terry Farrell had bought a car with some of the insurance money gained from his motorbike accident (see page 40), which gave him the chance to tour the north of England and study its stately homes. With his left leg in plaster, he obtained his tutor's permission to study furniture for his measured-drawing project since he could not climb ladders to measure a building. And so he chose a different chair for each great house, each from a different era. He began with a design from 1590 and went right through to Regency chairs. Each chair was measured in situ, and this was followed by a quarter-full-size watercolour of the side and front. The process was methodical: one drawing was done each day for 14 days. At the end of the day Farrell stretched the paper for the next day's study using a wet process; the paper would be dry by the following morning. In Farrell's words, 'It taught me about the great houses of the north of England, the design and detailing of English furniture and also about decorative and stylistic changes. I thought it was fascinating to study a single object – the chair – and explore the roles of fashion, technology and foreign influence.' In the course of his travels he came across two fine tables, which he also drew and which are shown here.

William and Mary writing cabinet, *c.* 1690.

Jacobean table, *c.* 1620.

Wheelback chair, *c.* 1760.

Glastonbury chair, c. 1620.

Queen Anne chair, c. 1720

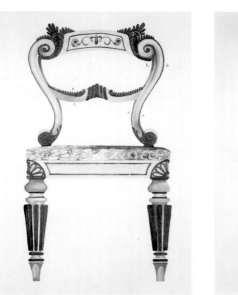

Spindleback chair, c. 1740.

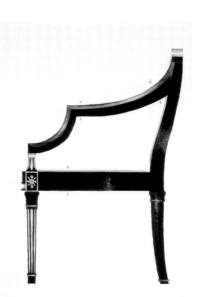

Sheraton chair, c. 1790.

Regency chair, c. 1800.

Late Regency chair, c. 1820.

Furniture studies **167**

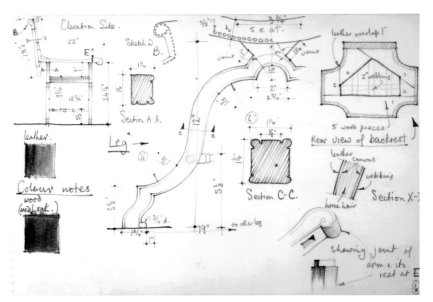

Glastonbury chair, *c.* 1620

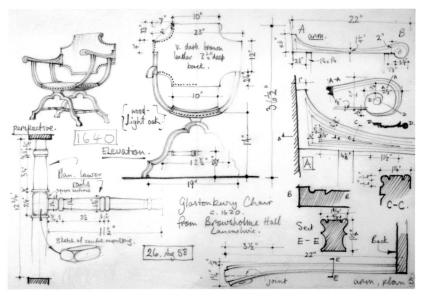

Glastonbury chair, *c.* 1620

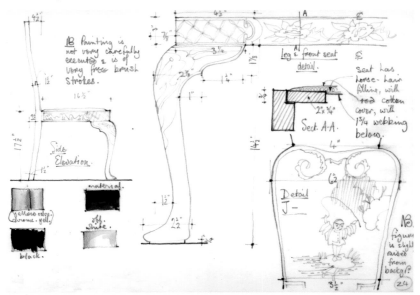

Queen Anne chair, *c.* 1720

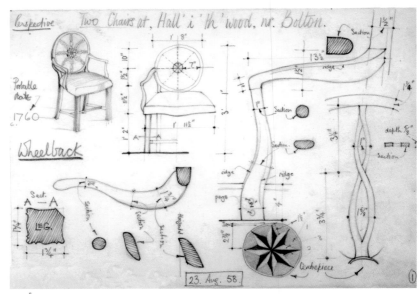

Wheelback chair, *c.* 1760

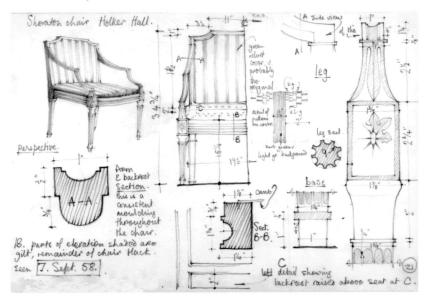

Sheraton chair, *c.* 1790

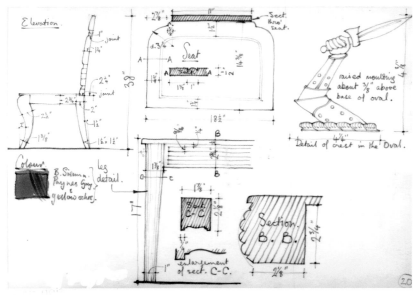

Late Regency chair, *c.* 1820

URBAN-PLANNING STUDY

Student research into the evolution of Lytham, Lancashire: fifth year, 1961.

Below: Estate house types on Henry Street.

Below right: Geological changes on the Fylde coastline.

Right, from top: Early geological evolution of the coastal district (first two drawings); the windmill on the green, Lytham's 'icon'; and the first ancient map of Lytham.

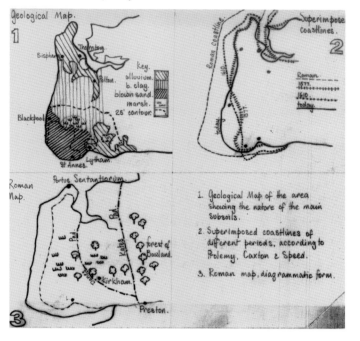

While a fifth-year student, Terry Farrell wrote a dissertation on Lytham St Anne's near Blackpool, where his parents then lived. Unusually for Britain, Lytham was deliberately planned (by the Clifton family) as a piece of urban design. The town plan, which originated mostly in early Victorian times, starts with a pier that intersects with the high street. A market hall follows at a crossroads, which intersects with the gates of the manor house. There is no beach and the seafront is marked by a village green, which is landmarked by a windmill. Even such simple urban plans need time, patience and custodianship to ensure longevity and integration into their context.

A good masterplan, like that of Lytham, is finely drawn and stands as a generic concept, like a DNA of human settlement composed of basic elements such as village green, parish church, railway station, high street, market hall, boat house and many fine streets. Within this basic structure is a building as an iconic element – a 'face' that personifies the place. In Lytham's case, it is the windmill.

The simple principles of Lytham's plan have always been something of a touchstone for Farrell – his parents, various aunts and uncles and his grandfather, as well as he and his brothers lived in various parts of the town, so it has a particular place in his imagination and in his career as an architect and town planner. In Farrell's words, 'I have many clear pictures of streets and houses; sea pebbles patterned in pavements; fine terraced houses and smart houses and bungalows. I have a particular affection for the work of Tom Mellor, a fine local architect who was an exponent of well-crafted, pioneering, modernist yet contextual architecture in the postwar period. The landscape of dunes and grand wide beaches is exhilaratingly open under frequently windy but fresh skies.'

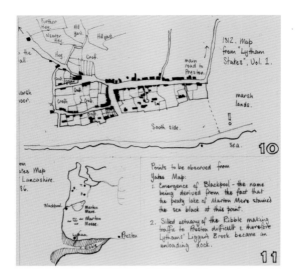

1812. Map from "Lytham States", Vol. 1.

Further Hey · Hill yard · Nearer Hey · Hillyard · Hey · Croft · main road to Preston · South side · sea · marsh lands · marsh moor

10

...tes Map Lancashire. 86.
Blackpool · Marton Mere · Marton Moss · Lytham · Preston

Points to be observed from Yates Map:
1. Emergence of Blackpool — the name being derived from the fact that the peaty lake of Marton Mere stained the sea black at this point.
2. Silted estuary of the Ribble making traffic to Preston difficult & therefore Lytham's Liggard Brook became an unloading dock.

11

lodge or gate-house to Clifton Estate.

13

Customs' House, Henry St. South.

14

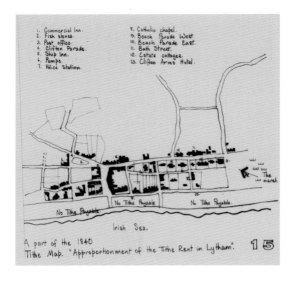

1. Commercial Inn.
2. Fish stones.
3. Post office.
4. Clifton Parade.
5. Ship Inn.
6. Pumps.
7. Police Station.
8. Catholic chapel.
9. Beach Parade West.
10. Beach Parade East.
11. Bath Street.
12. Estate cottages.
13. Clifton Arms Hotel.

No Tithe Payable · No Tithe Payable · The marsh

Irish Sea.

A part of the 1840 Tithe Map. "Apportionment of the Tithe Rent in Lytham".

15

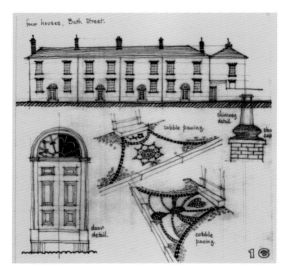

four houses, Bath Street.

chimney detail · stone cap · cobble paving · door detail · cobble paving

16

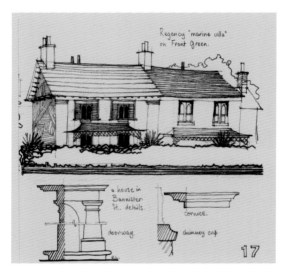

Regency "marine villa" on Front Green.

a house in Bannister St. details. · doorway · cornice · chimney cap

17

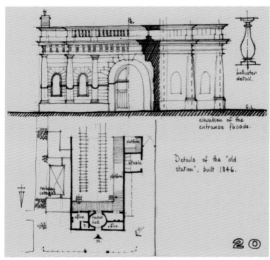

baluster detail.

elevation of the entrance façade.

Details of the "old station", built 1846.

office · booking hall · office · stable · IN

20

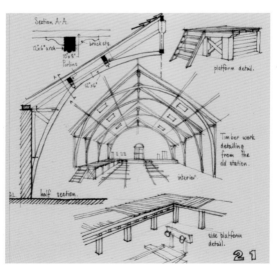

Section A-A.
12x6" arch · brick etc. · 10x8" purlins · 12x6"

platform detail.

Timber work detailling from the old station.

interior

half section.

side platform detail.

21

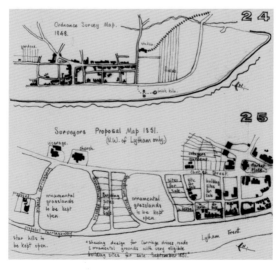

Ordnance Survey Map. 1848.
stables · Irish kiln · fleet

24

gardens

Surveyors Proposal Map 1851. (N.W. of Lytham only).

vicarage · church · cottages gardens · Market Place · ornamental grasslands to be kept open · ornamental grasslands to be kept open · Lytham Front.

star hills to be kept open.

"showing design for carriage drives, roads & ornamental grounds with very eligible building sites for sale. September 1851."

25

26

Mid. Victorian terrace houses.

27

Buildings of the same date with greater "local" influence.

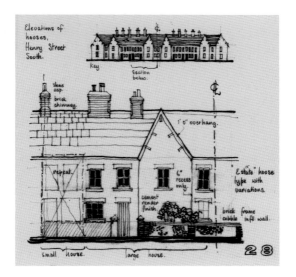

Elevations of houses, Henry Street South.

large house facing the Front Green.

details of an "Estate" house, Westby St.

front elevation.

ground floor   first floor

pinnacle detail.

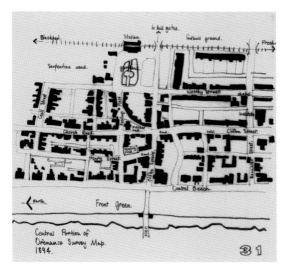

Central Portion of Ordnance Survey Map. 1894.

Views down five streets linking the main inner road "Clifton/Church St." with the Front, showing Front green always visible.

This page and opposite: Reproductions of various pages from the Lytham study. They range in architectural terms from individual local house types to public buildings such as the 1846 railway station; in town-planning terms, from town plans to streetscape to an aerial view (right).

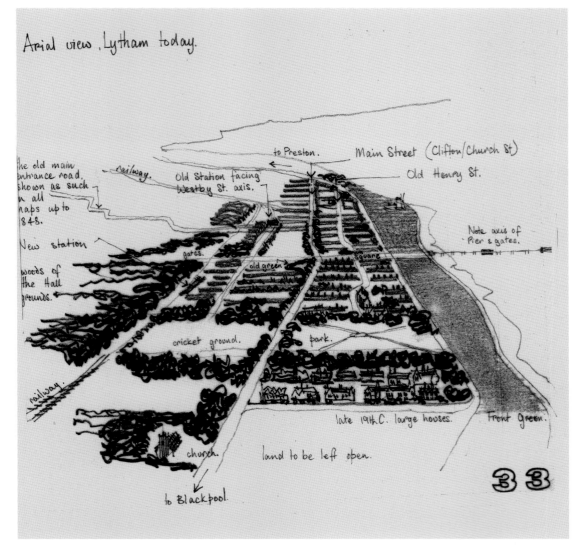

Aerial view, Lytham today.

the old main entrance road, shown as such in all maps up to 1848.

New station

woods of the Hall grounds.

railway.

church.

to Blackpool.

cricket ground.

land to be left open.

to Preston.

railway.

Old Station facing Westby St. axis.

gates.

old green

Main Street (Clifton/Church St)

Old Henry St.

Note axis of Pier & gates.

square.

park.

late 19th C. large houses.

Front green.

TRAVEL STUDIES

Student drawings: Scandinavia, 1959

Combining the money from two prizes, in the summer of 1959 Terry Farrell went to Scandinavia. The resulting watercolours and technical drawings were done during a tour in a bubble car that began in England and took him to Calais and then to Boulogne, and up through Holland and Germany to Denmark. He spent five weeks camping in Denmark, Sweden and Norway, exploring and making paintings and drawings, mainly of modern architecture but also of some traditional buildings. Finally he sailed home from Gothenburg in Sweden to Tilbury, London.

Traditional Interior: Den Gamle Bye, Århus. 5

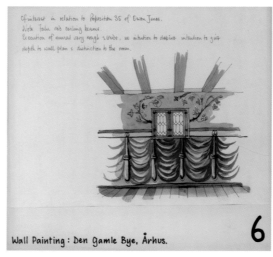

Wall Painting: Den Gamle Bye, Århus. 6

Waiting Room: Crematorium Stockholm. 19

Old Peoples Home: Copenhagen. 21

Flats: Stockholm, Sweden. 25

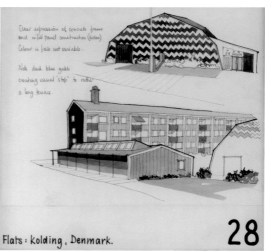

Flats: Kolding, Denmark. 28

Årsta Centre. 35

Bungalow: Copenhagen. 38

Church: Valingby. 39

Opposite: Terry Farrell's studies of colour in architecture included contemporary and traditional buildings.

This page: His technical drawings ranged from interiors to temporary structures to permanent buildings.

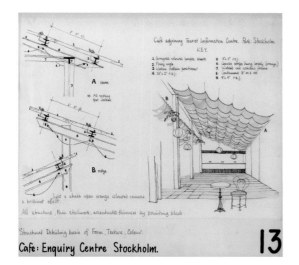

Cafe: Enquiry Centre Stockholm. **13**

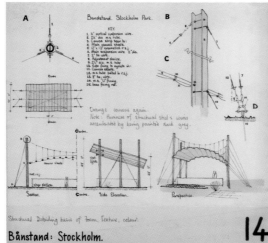

Bånstand: Stockholm. **14**

Park Cafe: Stockholm. **15**

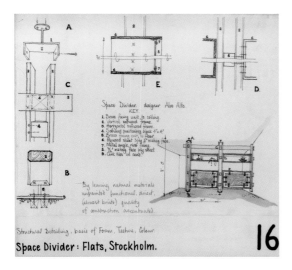

Space Divider: Flats, Stockholm. **16**

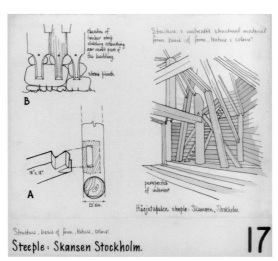

Steeple: Skansen Stockholm. **17**

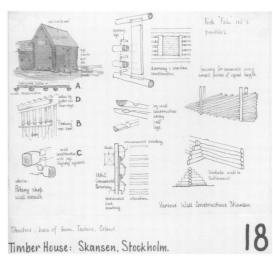

Timber House: Skansen, Stockholm. **18**

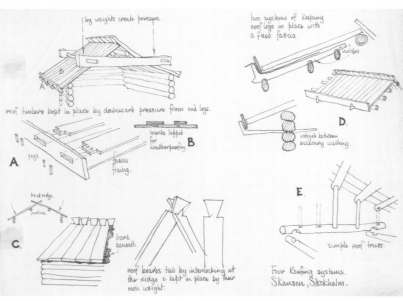

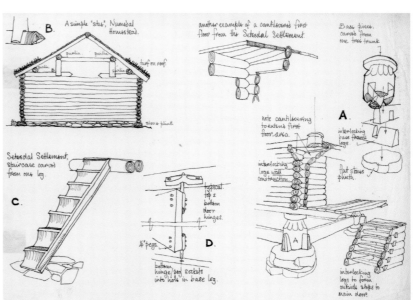

VILLAGE PLANNING
Student project: fourth year, 1960

In a fourth-year project at Newcastle University, Terry Farrell explored the traditional terraced and linear houses of Northumberland villages, many of them mining villages. He focused on what he saw as being an odd mix of high-density terraced L-, Z- and U-shaped housing applied to a rural situation because of the need to crowd miners around the pit. Farrell's response to this context was a Z-shaped unit with a totally self-contained block, with a shop and other facilities within, that could be added to existing villages. Made from in situ concrete, the construction was based on a system of panels that could be removed or added and that could also become voids to make windows and doors. The architectural concept was simple: what guided the project was its urban-design basis. Each Z-shape could be added to in order to make different combinations of enclosures – although the terrace was in itself an object, it had a strong space- or shape-making aspect to it. The project expressed itself as being partly urban system, partly urban tradition and partly space positive.

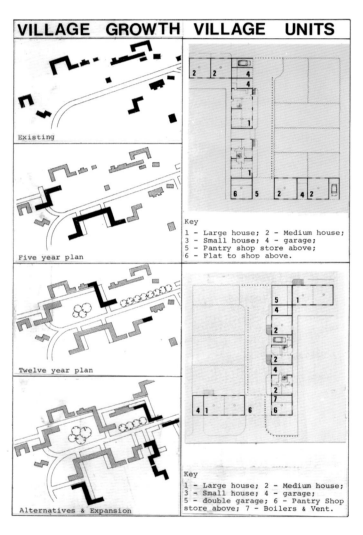

Left and right: Concept drawings showing the growth and flexibility of the generic plan form.

Below: Sketches and plan of existing terraced houses. The sketch on the left shows Tweedies Villas terrace in Ryton, which included Farrell's own stone house.

A "Z" formed neighbourhood unit was adopted as it married naturally with existing buildings and was an ideal unit for expansion, enclosing space and flexibility. Figure 1 shows that space is always enclosed by its arms and when added together (figure 2) or to existing buildings (figure 3). A space organisation develops which is not a static enclosure (found in traditional villages, to obtain military protection) but interlocking flowing spaces achieving an openness suited to today's expansion, transport and military safety.

By placing garages, shops, heating units and terraces at the corners and ends (figure 4) they become flexible hinges where those rooms and services can be "off square" to meet the differing geometric requirements of a layout. The unit then becomes very adaptable to a countryside with varying land forms, trees, existing buildings (figure 5).

The village was considered an organic growing unit and all additions continue with spatial flow that exists. The Five Year Plan is for three housing neighbourhood units with no demolition. The existing church is restored temporarily. Two houses are removed for the Twelve Year Plan to provide the community centre and school. The last plan shows how additions, or removals, at any future date will simply continue the spatial flow – the village has become a living and growing unit.

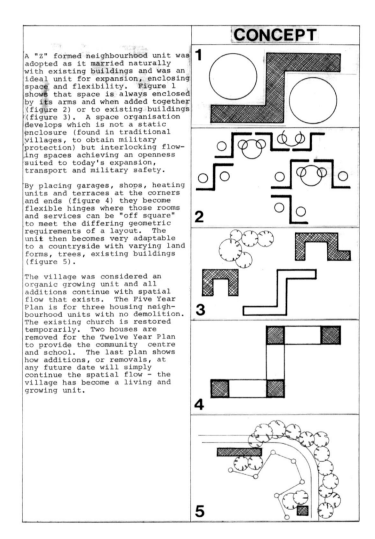

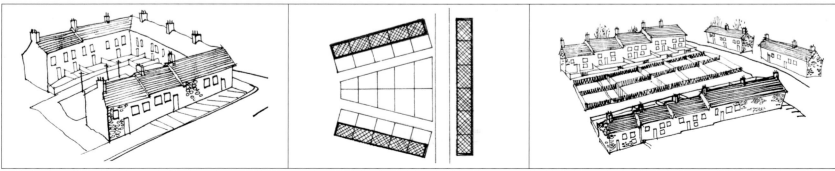

Left: Ink drawings and watercolours on recycled grey card showing a collage of proposals.

Below: 'Unwrapped' elevation drawing of an entire Z-shaped neighbourhood unit.

THE CLIMATRON

Student final-year design thesis: Blackpool, 1961

The Climatron was Farrell's final-year project at Newcastle University School of Architecture. Influenced by the teachings of Buckminster Fuller, the scheme was a high-tech holiday island connected to the base of Blackpool Tower. Rather than being a stand-alone piece of architecture, the Climatron was envisaged as a piece of town planning. It provided a new public square under the tower and was a restoration project in the sense that it revealed and focused on the tower, giving dramatic views of the historic structure from the sea. The link between the new dome and the existing tower was the start of a preoccupation that has continued throughout Farrell's work – as was the railway that linked the dome to the shore: people movement has always been a key concern. Although the Climatron retains the flavour of high-tech on the outside, the internal spaces were compartmentalized into complex areas, as opposed to the oversimplistic high-tech all-purpose interiors

that are, in Charles Jencks's words, 'entropic space'. Activities took place under one roof and focused on beaches and lakes around the edge of the dome and a huge multipurpose dance hall/performance space in the centre. The outside of the Climatron enabled visitors to walk up and down its face, using it like a man-made mountain.

Inspired by the beauty of natural shapes, the Climatron's form grew out of the sinuous shoots, leaves and petals that Farrell had explored in his earlier landscape drawings, and his reading of D'Arcy Thompson's On Growth and Form. Set out at sea and containing an aquarium, its link to nature was further explored by its use of high-tech engineering that references the work of Buckminster Fuller. Unusually for most students, the project featured a business plan, reflecting Farrell's preparation for his life as a pragmatic and realistic practitioner.

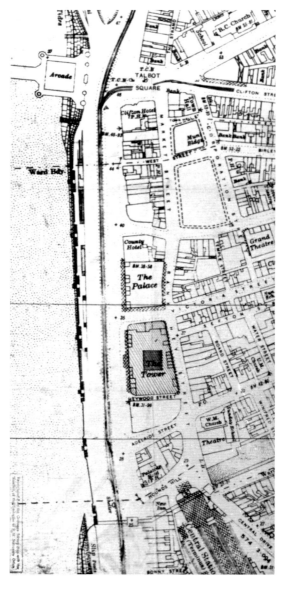

Opposite: Site plans and photographs of existing situation.

Below: View (overlaid on aerial photo) of the Blackpool Tower cleared of surrounding buildings, standing within a new public square with its full height revealed. Between the legs of the tower is a sunken area giving access to a miniature railway that takes visitors along the new pier to the Climatron holiday island out at sea.

Bottom: View of the Blackpool Tower with the existing buildings (see opposite) all removed from its feet, revealing its full shape and height and creating a new public square around its feet.

Below left: Sketch by Farrell based on a Buckminster Fuller drawing showing a suspension structure within a dome.

Below right: Fifth-year geodesic study model by Farrell.

Bottom: Site plan and section. The plan shows the new square at the feet of Blackpool Tower and also the basement-level station for the miniature railway. The section shows that the new pier travels below the promenade level into the basement station. Also shown are sight lines to the newly revealed tower.

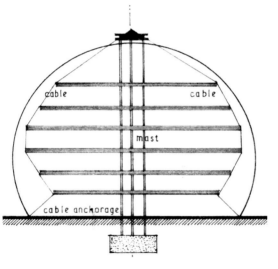

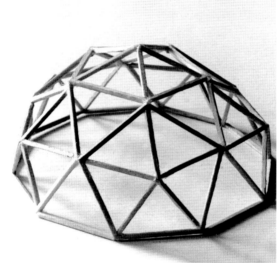

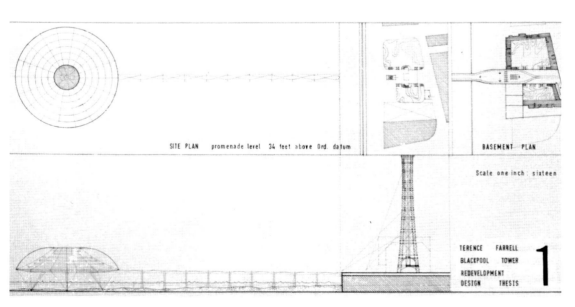

A–E: Farrell fifth-year working details. In 1960 Farrell was proposing neoprene zippered gaskets to seal Antisun double glazing. Tubular steel space-frame elements supported a tensile wire-supported enclosure, which, 10 to 15 years later, high-tech buildings were beginning to make possible.

F–H and J–M: The forces on the wire tensile structure were studied to show variations in geometry when under stress.

I: Wind effect on the dome enclosure.

K and N: The assembled structure showing the combination of compression elements (space-frame struts) and tension elements (cable network).

Opposite, above left: Farrell's drawing based on a tensegrity house by Buckminster Fuller.

Opposite, above centre and right: Two tensegrity study models by Farrell showing discontinuous compression elements all supported by tension elements.

Opposite, below: Assembled structural model of the final design for the Climatron.

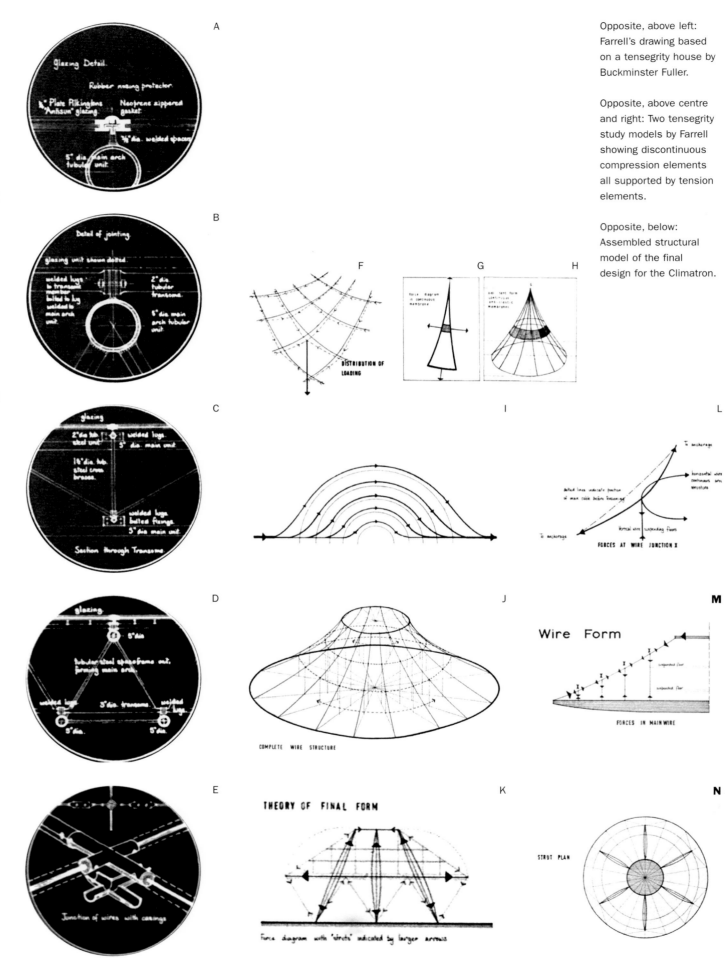

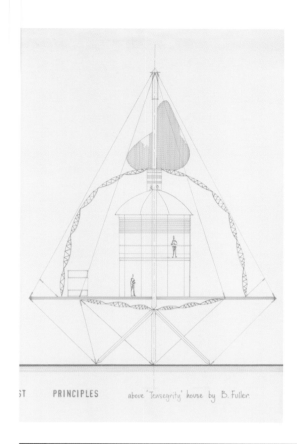

PRINCIPLES above "Tensegrity" house by B. Fuller

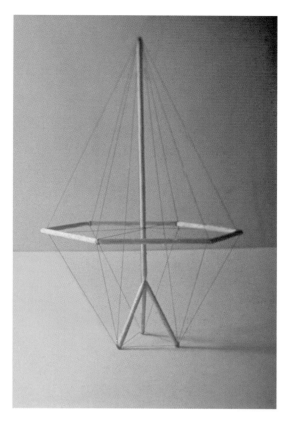

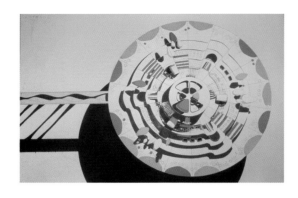

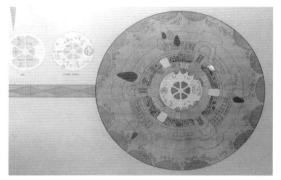

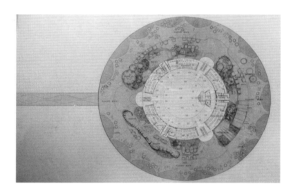

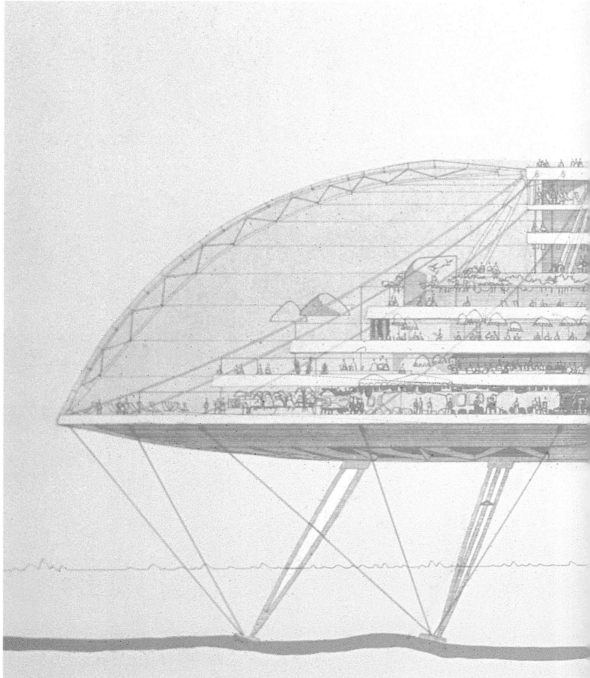

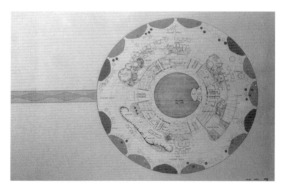

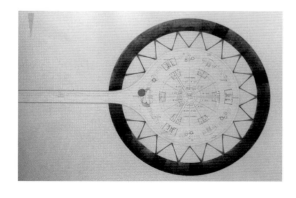

Above, left to right:
Interior perspectives: the
ballroom; the hanging-
gardens terrace; the
tea rooms.

Opposite, left, top to
bottom: All plan levels
from arrivals floor to
roof plan.

Opposite, above right:
Painting of night-time
illuminations in the
tradition of Blackpool's
city-wide illuminations;
in the northern climate,
night lighting of buildings
is a key element in
building design.

Across both pages:
Elevation of Climatron
seen from the land side.

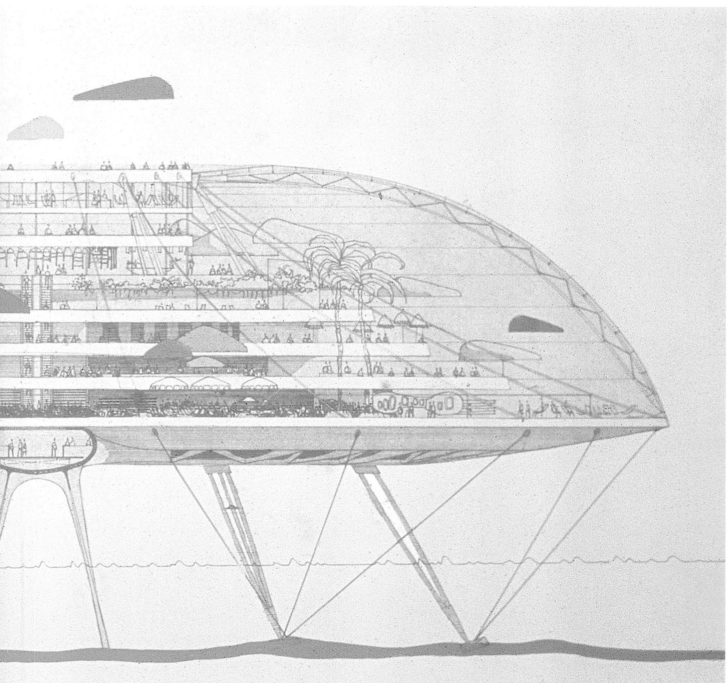

Pages 182–85:
Photographs of the
model of the final
Climatron design.

VENTILATION TOWERS

Blackwall Tunnel, London: 1961–62

The Blackwall Tunnel ventilation towers, designed in 1961–62 by Terry Farrell while he was employed at the London County Council's Department of Architecture, stand on each bank of the River Thames. The job comprised the ventilation buildings for the new Thames tunnel, and offices and workshops for the superintendent supervising the tunnel entrances and selecting the cladding for the tunnel linings. The towers on the south bank of the river now stand within the Millennium Dome.

Each group of towers consists of two distinct elliptical plans that taper upwards and intersect to form a valley before separating into two funnels. The exhaust shaft is 27 metres (90 feet) high, while the inlet shaft is 12 metres (40 feet) high. Below the valley, the towers spread out to enclose four large circular fans and motors.

The buildings' distinctive form derives from their sprayed concrete (gunite) shells supported on stressed cables from a reinforced-concrete slab, over perimeter walls of blue brick and glass. The shell roof is supported from the slab, which contains instruments that measure air pollution. The concrete grillage holding this includes a spiral stair and a crawl-way ducting system that links the electrical installation to the motors from the switch room and transformers, and contains an airlock access to the tunnel below. The shells, coated with bitumen and cement paint to prevent corrosion, represented an early use of gunite as a building material rather than a repair material – chosen because it reduced the need for expensive shuttering.

The towers' curved form was inspired by Oscar Niemeyer's work at Brasília, then appearing for the first time in the architectural press. Farrell compares the romantic structure of the industrial buildings with the machine 'techno aesthetic' subsequently adopted for housing and office buildings in the neighbouring Poplar area of east London – the curved form of the two ventilation towers makes a strong contrast with the nearby Reuters headquarters building by Richard Rogers, the Robin Hood Gardens estate by Alison and Peter Smithson and the Balfron Tower flats by Ernö Goldfinger.

In 2000, the towers were listed of Grade II historical interest. The southern tower will eventually stand within a regeneration scheme by Terry Farrell & Partners that will create a new urban quarter for north Greenwich.

Below: Model of the Terry Farrell & Partners 2003 masterplan proposals for Greenwich peninsula showing the general location of the Millennium Dome, the ventilation towers, and the Isle of Dogs in the background.

Bottom: 2003 Plan of the Blackwall Tunnel and the Greenwich peninsula, with the two ventilation towers ringed in red: (1) northern ventilation tower, (2) southern tower, (3) Richard Rogers & Partners Reuters Building, (4) Millennium Dome by Richard Rogers, (5) North Greenwich Jubilee Line station by Norman Foster and Will Alsop.

Opposite, above: The supervisor's office where new and old Blackwall tunnels meet (left), and Farrell's drawings for the office (centre). The Millennium Dome and the southern tower partly enveloped within its plan form is on the right.

Opposite, below: The northern tower, showing the Goldfinger, Smithson and Rogers buildings.

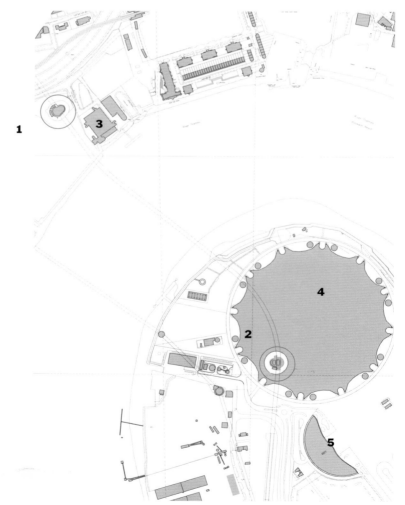

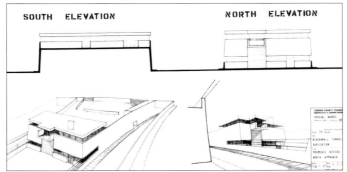

SOUTH ELEVATION   NORTH ELEVATION

Models of a ventilation
building (right and below)
and a model of the four
ventilation towers with
the works arrangement
around them (far right).

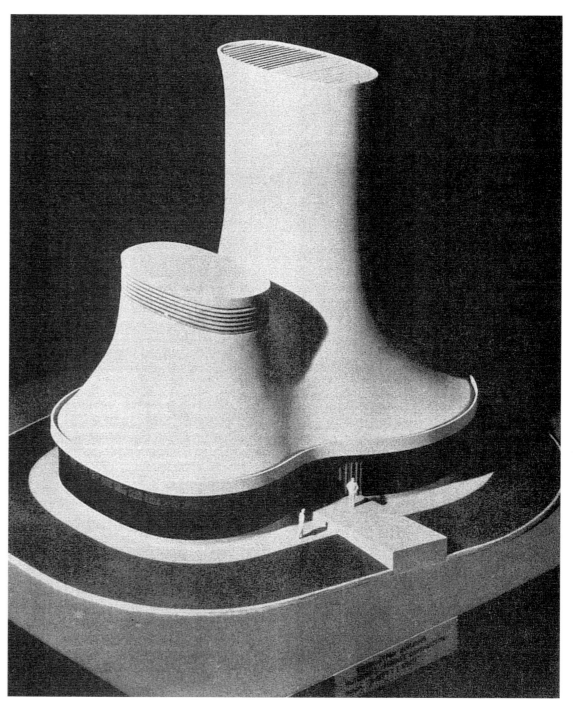

Architects: LCC Architects Department
Project Architect: Terry Farrell
Engineers: Flint & Neill Partnership

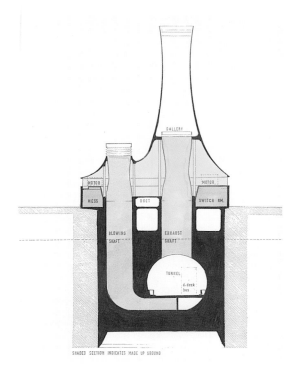

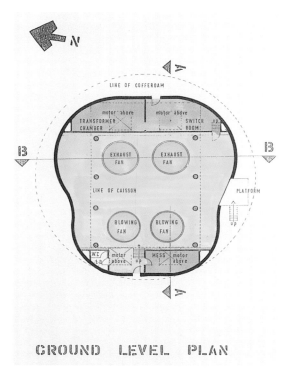

GROUND LEVEL PLAN

Above: Farrell's 1961 drawings of the cross-section and plan of a ventilation tower.

Right, from top: Northern ventilation building at different stages of construction.

Right: Aerial photograph of the Millennium Dome at an early stage of construction, showing the ventilation tower and an outline of the dome with supporting struts laid in the ground.

Below right: Construction photograph of the dome showing the ventilation building before it was part enclosed. Canary Wharf Tower by Cesar Pelli can be seen in the distance.

Far right: External view of the northern ventilation tower in 2000.

Opposite: The Millennium Dome under construction in 1999.

COURTYARD HOUSING

Northampton Hospital: 1962

This project originated as staff housing for a new mental hospital in Northampton. Terry Farrell designed it in 1962, while at Stillman and Eastwick-Field, before he left for America. Farrell's departure meant he was unable to supervise the project on site, but by the time he left he had finished the design and begun the working drawings. The finished building followed these drawings fairly faithfully. In plan, Jørn Utzon's courtyard housing was a strong influence, but in cross-section and roof type the project looked to Arne Jacobsen for inspiration.

The Northampton housing reflected a continuation of Farrell's interest in the village form that integrates with its surroundings rather than being a stand-alone unit, as explored in his fourth-year project at Newcastle (see pages 174–75). Each house was added to the next to create a whole that was accretive, space enclosing and urban. In Farrell's words, 'Patio houses fascinate me because, unlike the detached house, they have an interconnectedness built into them that, through cellular accumulation, eventually makes for a village form. The patio house is embryonic urban design. Within the element itself is the germs of how it adds together to form larger urban-design complexes.' Several modulated types were built at Northampton, which became precedents to some extent for the bungalows that Farrell designed at Farrell/Grimshaw for the Warrington housing in 1979–81 (see pages 226–28). On a recent visit, Farrell saw that the planning of the hospital had changed: instead of the staff living in the houses and the patients living in the hospital block, the houses are now occupied by the patients, and staff are accommodated in mixed-housing units.

Architects: Stillman and Eastwick-Field
Project designer: Terry Farrell

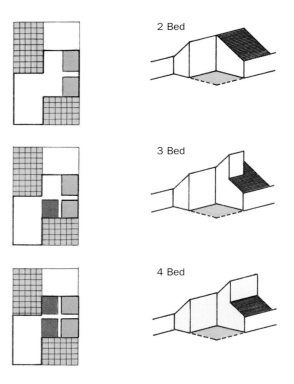

2 Bed

3 Bed

4 Bed

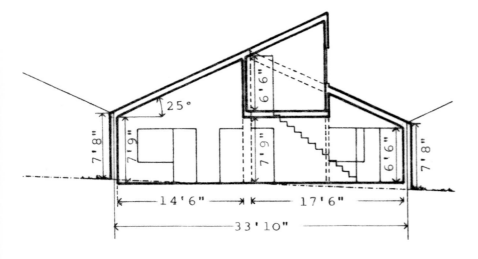

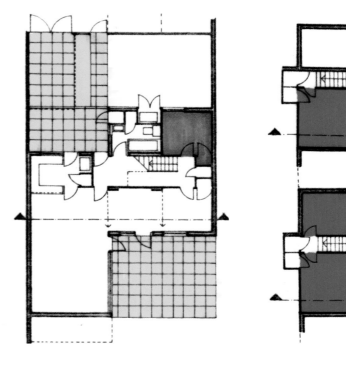

Opposite: Farrell's model at the design stage (top); generic cross-section and typical cross-section (bottom left); permutations of two-, three- and four-bedroomed houses (centre). The basic house plan showing its variations for two, three and four bedrooms is illustrated bottom right.

Revisit 2003

This page: A selection of photographs taken in 2003, when Farrell revisited the project, 40 years after it was completed. Everything appeared to be in good shape but – in a rather pleasing outcome – the houses were occupied by patients rather than nursing staff, as had originally been planned.

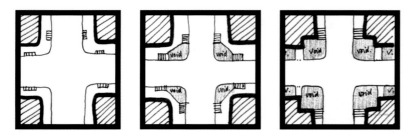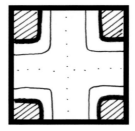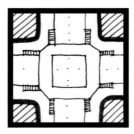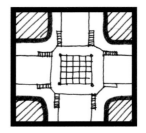

PHILADELPHIA CITY CENTRE

University of Pennsylvania coursework: 1963

Several projects were based on Philadelphia, a city with rich potential for informing the student of urban design. It was also a city in change, with the planning leader available to hold set projects and attend crits, so the city itself was a veritable workshop. The project shown here was for the centre itself, extending westwards from, and including, the city hall building itself. The work used layering techniques to separate elements such as transport and usage type, and extended to include investment levels in both the public realm and private land ownerships – the former looking at the principles of 'capital web' investments utilizing public funds. Also apparent was Farrell's continuing preoccupation with the pedestrian realm and walking itself as a unifying factor in the public realm. Inspired by Louis Kahn's graphic inventions which explained his idea for car movement in Philadelphia, Farrell used a method, with dots representing people, to look at pedestrian movement both at ground and existing sub-ground concourses. Finally Farrell looked at the micro-levels of movement, particularly the pedestrian crossing, and a wide range of alternatives were speculated on for the evolution of a generic intersection.

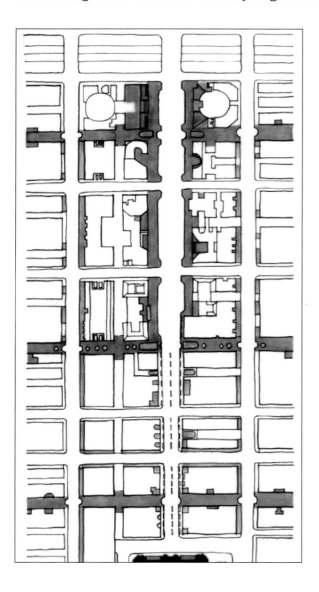

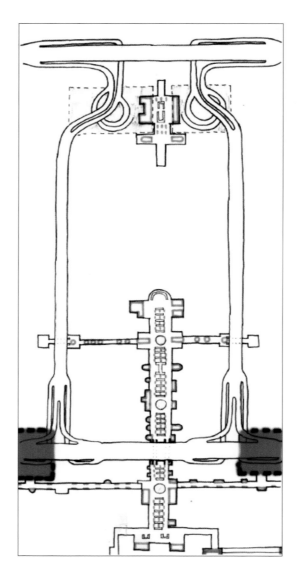

Above: Two of the many studies for the evolution of a pedestrian crossing at an intersection. The three drawings on the left show the gradual change from a basic underpass to four sunken courtyards engaged with the ground and basement of adjoining shops. The three on the right show three stages in a similar evolution of a first-floor bridge crossing.

Left, far left and opposite: Various plan studies for central Philadelphia as part of a project based on ongoing work by the city's planning department under Edmund Bacon.

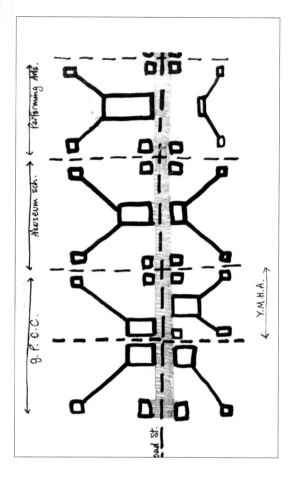

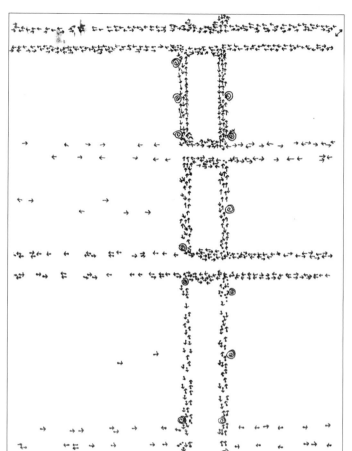

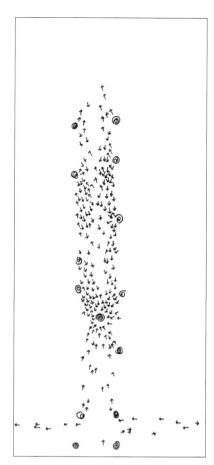

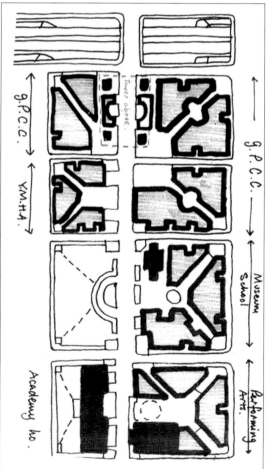

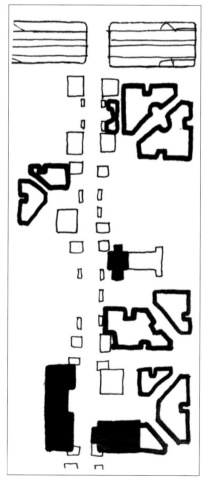

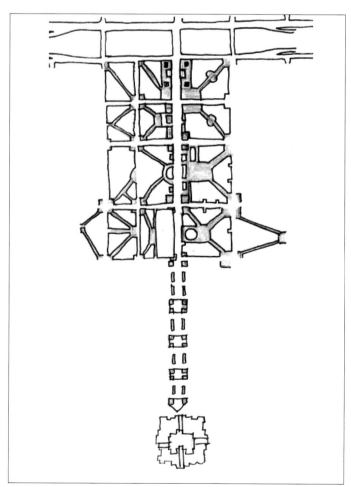

DOODLES AND ORGANICS

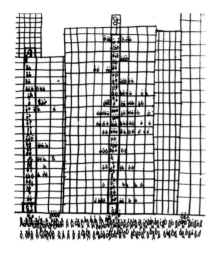
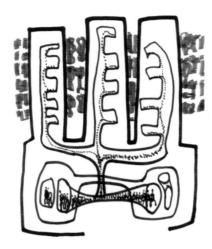
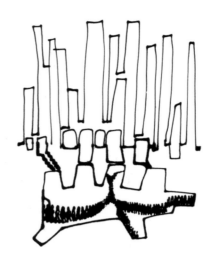

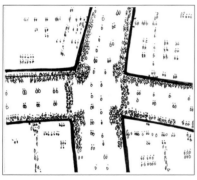

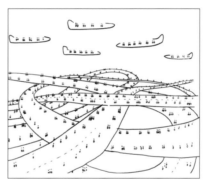

DOODLES
Student sketches and
line drawings: 1962–64

The doodles – an exploration
of the human experience in
space – were attempts to
describe in visual form some
of the thoughts and concerns
that Farrell picked up on from
seminars at Penn about town
planning, architecture and
urbanism. The style was
influenced by the dream-like,
architectural drawings of Paul
Klee, the graphic, cartoonish
quality of Saul Steinberg's
drawings, and the humorous
essays and simple line
drawings of James Thurber.

The doodles explore such
ideas as the container of
space, individuals challenged
by their environment, and
the world of the car and
aeroplane where the individual
becomes less anonymous
within the metal containers
of transport. These are also
what Farrell refers to as
'fantasy' drawings that
question the role of place and
the function of architectural
elements such as walls of
buildings and transport
containers. As Farrell says,
'I was going to lectures on
traffic, traffic engineering and
car movement, which led me
to thinking that the cars are
only containers for the people
in them and the roads are
there for people to cross. My
first explorations were into
pedestrian movement, which
linked with my obsession with
walking and support for the
public realm being about foot
movement. The doodles
express the role of the
pedestrian, the vehicle and
the people they carry, the
choreography of city
movement and the
psychological condition of the
individual and his perception
of these movements.'

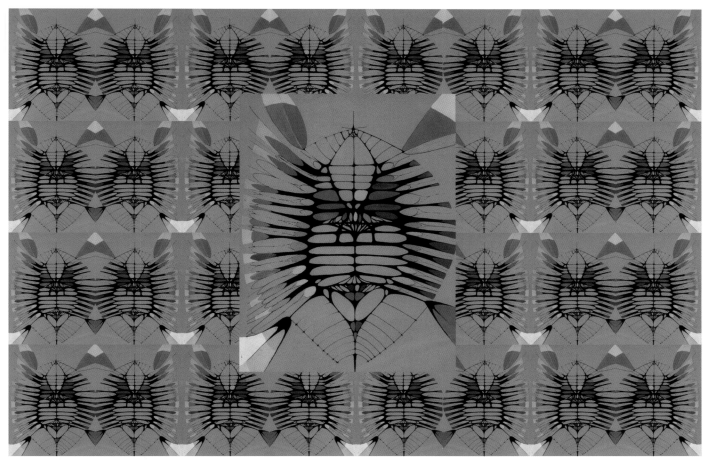

ORGANICS
Student paintings and collages: 1962–64

The organics were a way of exploring a visual world that balanced the intellectual papers, seminars and lectures that Farrell was involved with while studying at Penn. Farrell sees the process of creating them as linked to his preoccupation with making things from different media, from poster colour to watercolour and line drawing to collage. The images were made from cut-outs taken from the colour magazines and newspaper supplements that were starting to circulate at that time. Farrell's technique was to arrange the images as overlays, cover them in a chemical such as acetate or paraffin, and then allow the colours to spread. The process produced what looked like organic shapes – a result that appealed to his preoccupation with the world of nature. The more complex images recall the collages of the artist Kurt Schwitters with their pasted down, stuck-on feel. As Farrell says, 'I came across this technique accidentally as a result of being in a car crash, watching petrol spread across a magazine. When I pulled the magazine open it formed what looked like a Rorschach ink-blot test with a double image that resulted in a slightly different effect on each side. Finally I myself began to make what I called organics, arranging them in repetitive patterns as if they were wallpaper or fabric designs, and I experimented with this quite a bit. The making process was a therapy, working through a visual release.'

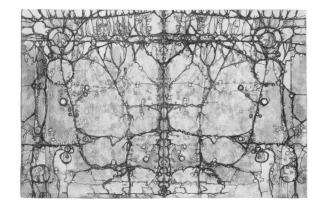

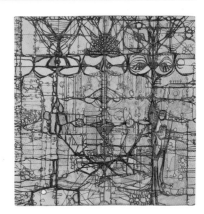

PUBLIC SQUARES: USA

University of Pennsylvania, study project: 1963

This was a travel study in the tradition of the 18th- and 19th-century grand tour when collectors such as Robert Adam and Charles Darwin travelled abroad to collect inspirational ideas and specimens. Farrell chose to study American squares as the space-positive examples of the country's interesting urban inventions. Although much of America was concerned with the future, Farrell found that their concept of the past – expressed through traditional urban design such as squares –

was intriguing. The result of this interest was a comparative study of this type of spatial enclosure, including pedestrian movement, the layout of surrounding buildings and the different scale relations that characterized them. As Farrell says, 'I was particularly fascinated by pedestrian movement. I did little dots on the drawings to show where people were, to show the connecting of movement and how the spaces were actually used. It was a serious study for me that extended over about five months and I really enjoyed drawing it up. It gave me an insight into spaces that has remained with me ever since: how on a grid the square sits so that you can form short cuts across the square; how culs-de-sac interrupt pedestrian flow and create quiet and more private sitting areas, and how experiments with inserting car parks under the squares usually result in serious urban problems.'

Some 20 urban spaces were studied across the USA. Each was recorded on a comparative basis (this page and pages 200–201), by a basic ground-level plan and perspective(s), and then usually two additional drawings showing spatial enclosure pattern and focus points on one drawing, and pedestrian-movement intensity (by dots) on another. Many of the squares were recognizable as European in origin, particularly those in the south where the Spanish influence was more prevalent. Some, however, were from earlier times such as those in Plains Indian and Mountain Indian villages, each so different (shown on this page). Others (not shown) were modern interventions and included multi-level urban shopping malls in Toronto and an out-of-town single-storey mall near Miami, Florida.

1. Chucalisa Village, Memphis, Tennessee

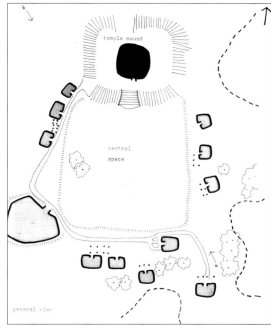

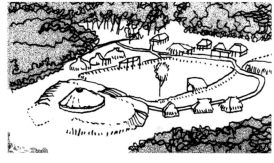

2. Spruce Tree House, Mesa Verde, Colorado

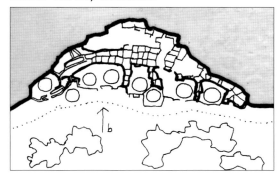

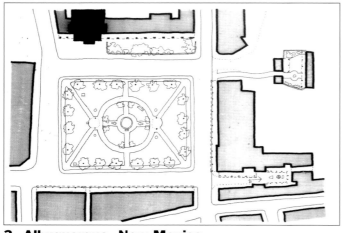

3. Albuquerque, New Mexico

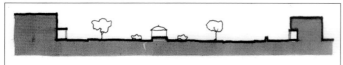

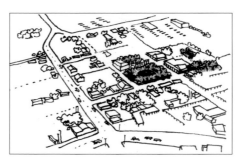

Perspectives

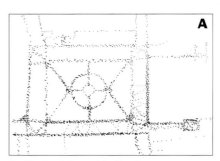

A. Pedestrians B. Enclosures

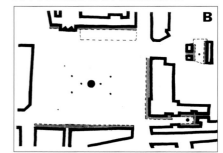

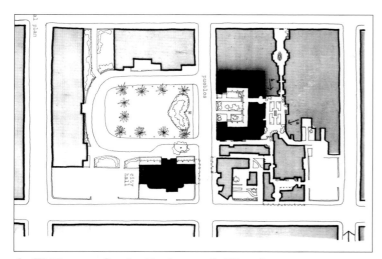

4. El Paseo, Santa Barbara, California

Perspectives

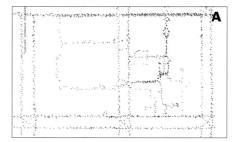

A. Pedestrians B. Enclosures

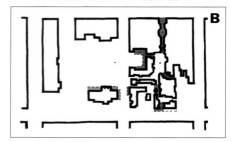

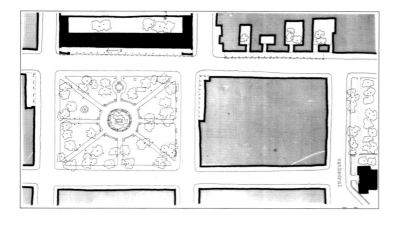

5. Santa Fe, New Mexico

Perspectives

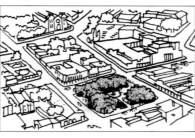

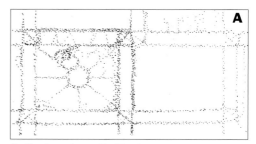

A. Pedestrians B. Enclosures

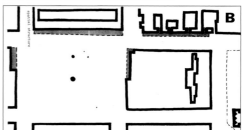

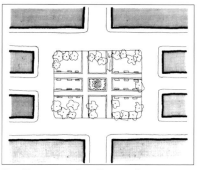

6. Savannah, Georgia

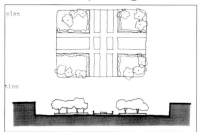

Perspectives

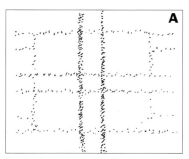

A

A. Pedestrians B. Enclosures

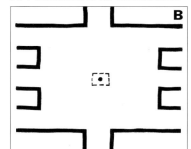

B

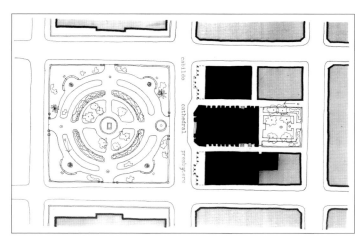

7. Jackson, Louisiana

Perspectives

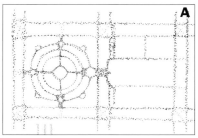

A

A. Pedestrians B. Enclosures

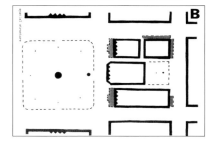

B

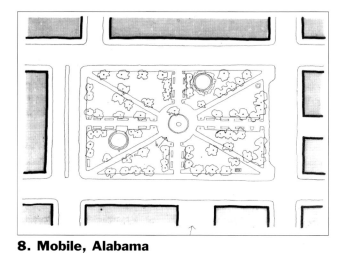

8. Mobile, Alabama

Perspectives

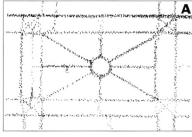

A

A. Pedestrians B. Enclosures

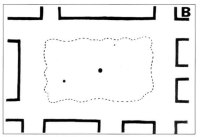

B

This page: After the survey of the squares had been completed, a series of simple, generalized conclusions were made. Drawing A shows the critical design elements of all squares – how they meet the street grid (usually on the corners), diagonal versus orthogonal pedestrian paths and central place focus point(s). B shows a linear space and its more sequential characteristics, and C shows different variations based on the generic plan form in A. Drawings in column D look at the effects of varying heights of focus elements and enclosure elements, and E looks specifically at enclosing walls, their differing heights and tree canopies. Finally, F shows single and clustering focal points.

Opposite: The diagrams show the patterns of basic movement of each of many of the squares studied. From the basic elements and components on page 202, the variety obtained in reality is expressed by each square having its own 'fingerprint' or identifiable visual plan, varied by invention of designers, by pragmatic response to local fixed features, and by growth and change over time. This page shows that each square has its own personality and is its own unique 'place'.

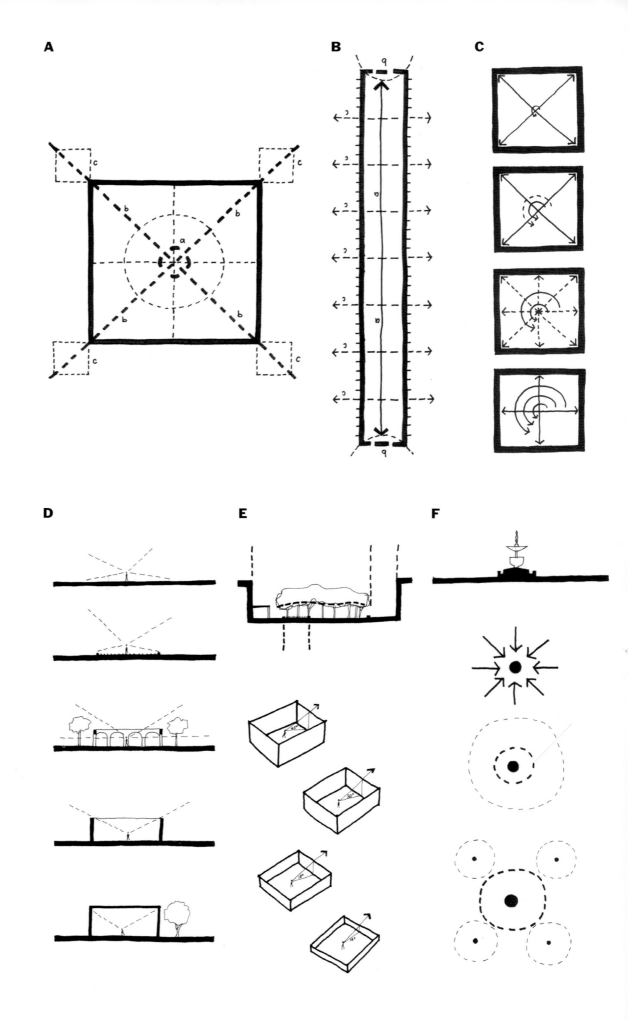

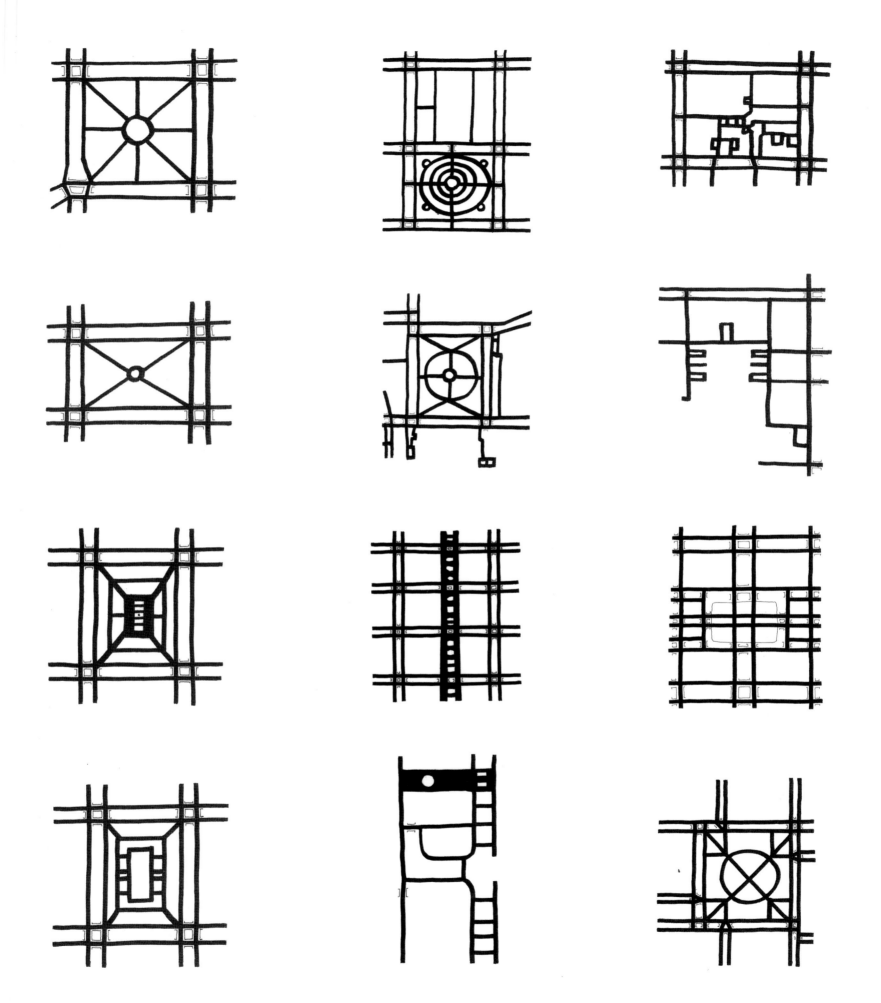

PUBLIC HOUSING

Competition, New York: 1964

This competition entry for public housing and mixed uses was done in the summer of 1964, while Terry Farrell was working at Camden, New Jersey, before returning to England. Like the Northumberland village-housing project, and the experiments with courtyard housing, the competition entry explored the accretive housing type – this time for an area of New York. The project was an experiment to find a high-density housing solution without resorting to high-rise accommodation,

and had elements that would later influence the Colonnades scheme. Farrell looked at alternatives to the 'streets in the air' concept that at the time was being expounded by architects such as the Smithsons. The result was a connecting street that was slightly higher than ground level, which meant that fewer lifts were needed. Other elements to the design included a connecting square and front doors that all faced onto the street. The plan type is characterized by a high degree of flexibility and, in several of the drawings, Farrell delighted in showing all the different permutations that they offered. The squares, street and medium rise gave the scheme a terraced-housing form that suggested rather more than simple high-density housing – an interesting urban-design experiment that, once again, focused on being space positive.

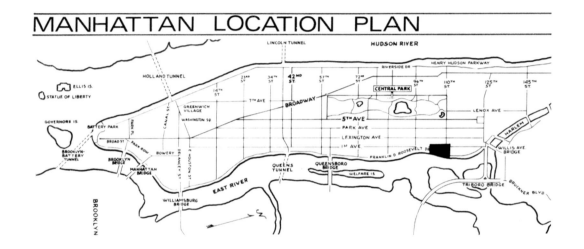

MANHATTAN LOCATION PLAN

Left: Location plan of the competition site in Manhattan.

Below left: Aerial view of the site in a run-down area with adjacent high-rise housing and industries.

AERIAL VIEW OF SITE

Right: Some concept drawings from the report that accompanied the competition submission.

Below right: General site plan at upper-ground level showing the connecting walkway that united the entire scheme. A very high density was achieved yet at a relatively low rise, and with a very large number of dwellings having front-door access to the ground-level street.

SiTE ANALYSIS

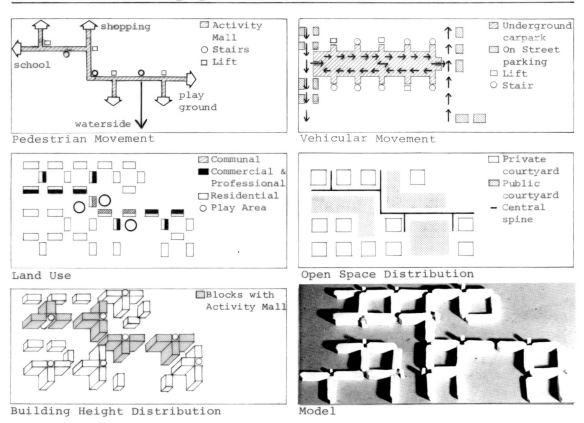

Pedestrian Movement

Vehicular Movement

Land Use

Open Space Distribution

Building Height Distribution

Model

SITE PLAN

0 25 50 100 200 feet

INTERNATIONAL STUDENTS' HOSTEL

Paddington, London W2: 1968

Terry Farrell and Nicholas Grimshaw started their partnership in June 1965 on the strength of a commission to prepare a feasibility study for an international students' hostel – out of their £2,000 fee, a £500 advance allowed them to set up office on the corner of Windmill Street and Charlotte Street. The study escalated into a £250,000 job to convert six 100-year-old listed houses, Nos. 206 to 214 Sussex Gardens and No. 1 Westbourne Terrace, into a residential club for 190 members, 175 of whom were students. Before alteration, the buildings were in poor structural order and very bad decorative condition. The complex nature of the conversion made it imperative to think long and hard about the building's function. Seventy-five per cent of the building elements were existing and costs had to be kept to a minimum (the hostel was non-profit-making). Farrell and Grimshaw realized that the new interventions had to be very clear, even though they would be achieved by a multitude of small adjustments to the existing fabric. An essential part of the brief was to unite the six buildings horizontally and vertically: many of the students to be housed there would have come to England for the first time and would not be fluent in English, so good internal organization was essential.

Farrell felt that the best way to treat the buildings was to accept the nature of the original Victorian spaces. The first priority – a cost issue – was to utilize as much space as possible for flats and study areas. This gave rise to the idea of putting the new bathrooms and laundries on the 'outside' to gain living space 'inside'. Facilities provided included a television room, several lounges, a study/library, workshop/hobbies room, a darkroom, small kitchen and dining room for parties, a main kitchen and dining room, and a games room. Every odd kink produced in carrying out the conversion was made into a sitting area.

The cost and space restraints on furnishing the study bedrooms at Sussex Gardens were overcome by a standard multi-purpose 'trolley' that, together with a bed on wheels, a chair, coffee table and waste-paper basket, formed the furniture for each unit. The trolley measured 195 x 90 x 60 cm (76 x 36 x 24 inches) and was mounted on locking castors with a welded-steel tube frame high enough for the bed to slide under. The wardrobe door was fibreglass fitted with a mirror, wire baskets, a toothmug and towel rails on the outside. A large wire basket was slung below this section. Book shelves slotted into the framework

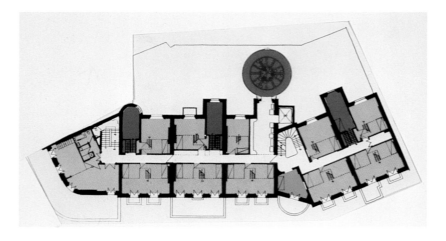

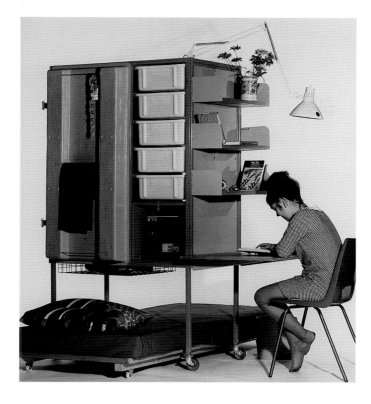

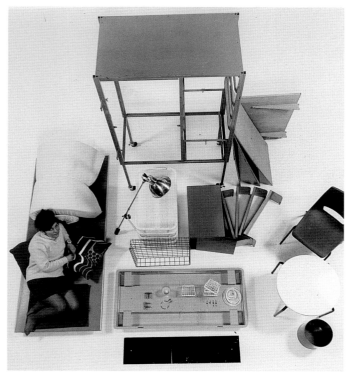

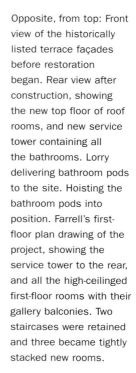

Opposite, from top: Front view of the historically listed terrace façades before restoration began. Rear view after construction, showing the new top floor of roof rooms, and new service tower containing all the bathrooms. Lorry delivering bathroom pods to the site. Hoisting the bathroom pods into position. Farrell's first-floor plan drawing of the project, showing the service tower to the rear, and all the high-ceilinged first-floor rooms with their gallery balconies. Two staircases were retained and three became tightly stacked new rooms.

Above left and above far left: The components of the student's furniture trolley included a bed unit made from a flush door. The trolley cost only £73 (approx.).

Far left: Furniture unit in a double-height room with stairs leading up to a balcony.

Left: Each gallery room on the first floor above the central corridor could accommodate four students. The new staircase rooms, stacked one above the other, can be seen at the rear.

Bottom centre: Furniture trolley unit installed.

Bottom right: Drawing explaining assembled components.

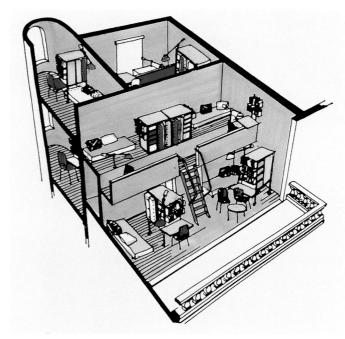

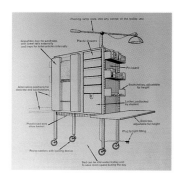

at either end over pin-up boarding, and a pivoting lamp fitted onto the top of the unit. The bed was designed as a hardboard flush 'door' on bearers and castors with a foam mattress. Each trolley unit came in either red, yellow or blue, and there was range of fabric patterns and colours to choose from. The total cost for the furniture package was £73, which was £50 below the officially allocated figure.

The idea of providing a services structure outside the main buildings but centrally placed in relation to them appealed to the clients since it freed up interior space to accommodate more students and obviated the need to insert pipework into the old structure. The bathrooms were arranged to be easily accessible from all floors, even though the floor-to-ceiling heights varied from 2.6 metres (8 feet 6 inches) to 4.2 metres (13 feet 9 inches). The brief for the bathrooms themselves was to provide 'hygienic, washable, waterproof boxes' with efficient and easily maintainable services. Structural limitations were considerable: no loads could be imposed on either the mews wall or the back wall of the hostel buildings, and the use of a crane was impossible since the area where the tower was to stand was totally enclosed by buildings. The 30 bathroom pods were bolted in place on their support beams, while their adjacent ramp units were winched into position and bolted to the respective end portions of the horizontal I-beams. Each pod was made from four quarter-shells that were joined together in the factory so that the pod could be delivered as a complete unit.

The hostel was prototypical of Farrell's concern with the conservation and adaptation of buildings in urban settings. As a low-cost, process-driven building with add-on new technology in the form of the bathroom tower, the hostel perfectly exemplifies his statement in the May 1976 issue of the *RIBA Journal* on 'Buildings as a Resource': 'Now is the time to ask if we actually need any new housing in this country. Buildings are a resource which should not be destroyed, even if they are to be replaced by a "masterpiece". It requires as much design ingenuity to spatially reorganise existing buildings, adding services and equipment, as it does to design new buildings.'

Architects: Farrell/Grimshaw Partnership
Structural engineers: Ove Arup & Partners and
W.H. Smith & Co (Whitechurch) Ltd
Steelwork contractor: W.H. Smith & Co. (Whitechurch) Ltd
Main contractor: A. Bell & Sons (Paddington) Ltd

Right, top and centre:
Studies of room planning
with student's furniture
unit in a variety of rooms.

Right: 1998 drawing – 30
years later Terry Farrell &
Partners reinvented the
student's all-in-one unit.

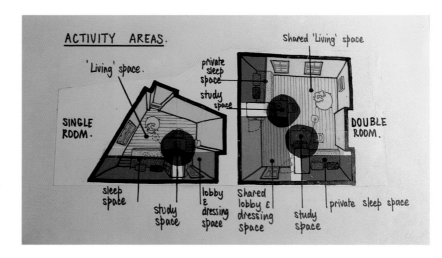

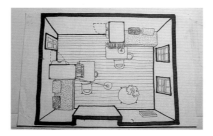

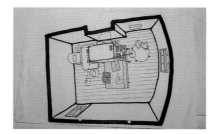
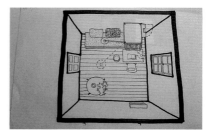

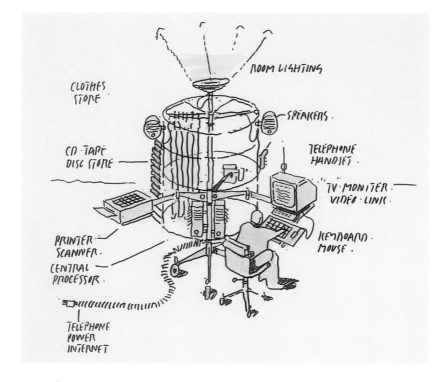

CO-OWNERSHIP FLATS

Park Road, London NW8: 1970

No. 125 Park Road was completed in June 1970 for the Mercury Housing Society – the 40 co-owners who lived in the building while collectively developing it. (The co-owner element of the scheme evolved into Terry Farrell's own Mercury Housing Society, which resulted from his continuing preoccupation with tenant choice, flexibility and self-help housing.) When the block was completed the absence of a developer meant that all the flats could be occupied at cost price on 100 per cent mortgages. The mortgage on the whole block, divided between the 40 flats, resulted in an average price of about £8,500 for each unit – in 1970, about half the estimated market value. When a member wished to move on, the new resident, next in line in a long waiting list, took over the mortgage. The cost of building the block was £228,000 – remarkably low because of the persistence of the architects: apart from obvious economies such as simplifying the façade and repeating floor plans, Farrell/Grimshaw decided against balconies and designed a car park for 34 cars at ground level rather than an underground garage.

Consisting of 18 two-bedroomed flats, 18 one-bedroomed flats and four one-bedroom penthouse flats, plus a caretaker's flat, the plan form developed out of basic ideas about flexibility. The 3,740 square metre (40,680 square foot) building consisted of a central core with multi-access points to a surrounding 'living' zone. This zone, free of structural walls and with continuous perimeter glazing, heating and electrical sockets, allowed maximum flexibility for subdivision. Although at the time of completion the building contained two two-bedroomed and two one-bedroomed flats, the typical floors were designed to be adapted to anything from two large luxury flats to 14 studio flats. Many variations were tried out by the tenants. These included uniting two rooms in the one-bedroomed flats to form one large space divided by screens and furniture, and the construction of additional galleries within the penthouses.

The external cladding also reflected the desire for flexibility. The main aim was to produce a regular grid capable of accepting a wide variation of internal layouts while maintaining good views out of the building with each variation. The system consisted of corrugated anodized aluminium cladding fixed to steel angle frames, with windows positioned in a continuous run without structural mullions. This lightweight system required only minimum structural sizes (in particular columns) and allowed ease of replacement should the requirement arise.

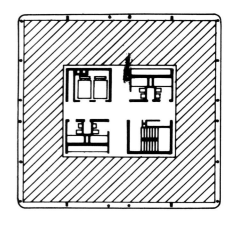

This drawing shows the spatial organization of the central core and the free space around it, designed on the same principle as flexible office space.

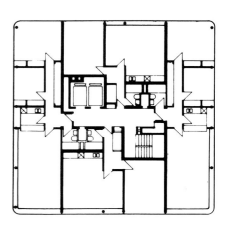

The plan as built had two two-bedroom flats and two one-bedroom flats around the central core. There are three flats with park views on each floor.

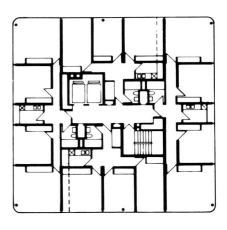

Plan of a possible arrangement comprising 14 bedsits or studio apartments around the central core.

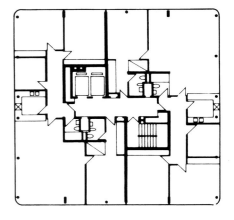

Plan of another possible arrangement, comprising two large four-bedroom family flats around the central core.

This page: An external view from Park Road.

Opposite page:
Left, above and below:
Farrell's very early stage studies of permutations of flat plans and rentals.

Above right: Penthouse floor – of which Farrell occupied the south-west corner and Grimshaw the north-east corner.

Below right: Farrell's original elevation drawing, with version of split-level car parking.

Farrell's own penthouse in the Park Road flats, with its panoramic views over London, led to the development of his ideas about 'greenways' (see page 125), which were seminal to his later campaigns for Buckingham Palace and the royal parks. In 2001, the Park Road building was awarded a Grade II listing by English Heritage.

Architects: Farrell/Grimshaw Partnership
Contractor: H. Fairweather & Co. Ltd
Quantity surveyors: G.A. Hanscomb Partnership
Structural engineers: Anthony Hunt Associates

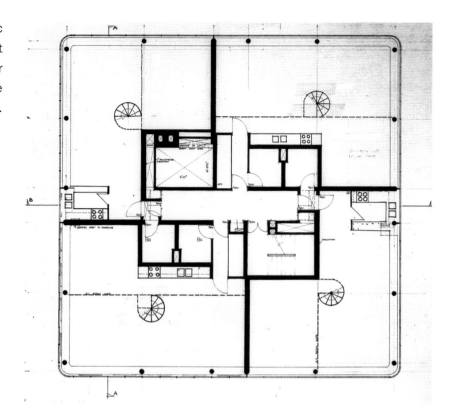

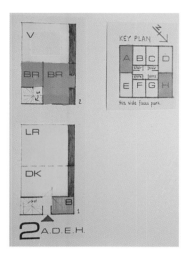 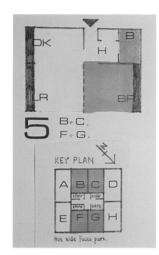

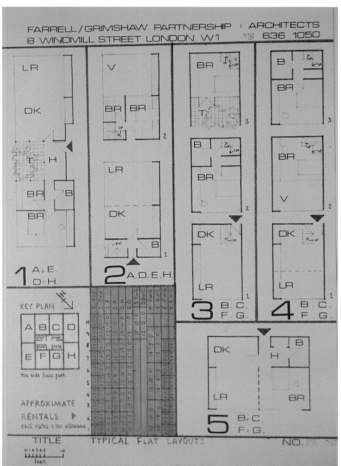

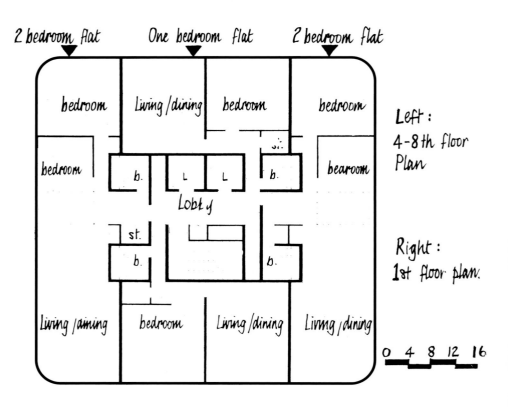

2 bedroom flat   One bedroom flat   2 bedroom flat

bedroom   Living/dining   bedroom   bedroom

bedroom   b.   L   L   st.   b.   bearoom

Lobby

st.   b.   b.

Living/dining   bedroom   Living/dining   Living/dining

Left:
4-8th floor
Plan

Right:
1st floor plan.

0 4 8 12 16

This page:
Left and below left:
Farrell's drawings show
different combinations
of maisonettes at upper
and lower levels and
flats at mid-levels.

Below: Completed mid-
level two-bedroom flat.

Bottom: View from the
entrance area of the
completed block of flats.

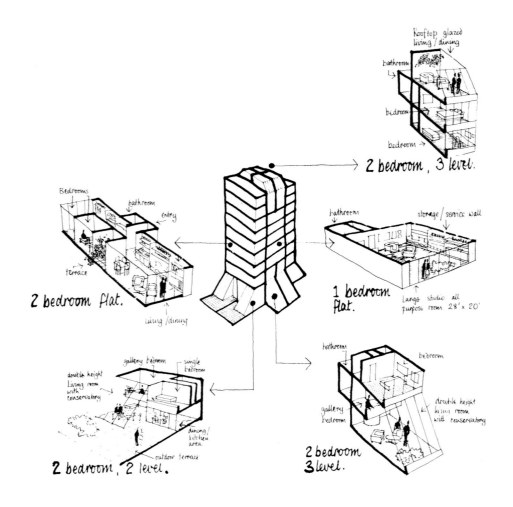

Rooftop glazed
living/dining

bathroom

bedroom

bedroom

2 bedroom, 3 level.

Bedrooms   bathroom   entry

terrace

2 bedroom flat.

living/dining

bathroom   storage/service wall

1 bedroom
flat.

Large studio all
purpose room 28'x 20'

double height
living room
with
conservatory   gallery bedroom   single bedroom

dining/
kitchen
area

outdoor terrace

2 bedroom, 2 level.

bathroom   bedroom

gallery
bedroom   double height
living room
with conservatory

2 bedroom
3 level.

PADDINGTON STREET OFFICES: 1

Farrell/Grimshaw

From its creation in 1965, Farrell/Grimshaw had operated from two floors in an old building off Charlotte Street, north of Soho. Ten people were eventually accommodated there, working in cramped conditions and lacking proper facilities. In 1971, further expansion occurred, which involved taking space in two neighbouring properties, but this also became inadequate and a long search began for new premises.

An office located in the West End was considered important but land costs were prohibitive. The particular requirements necessary for an architects' office suggested that, even if a new commercial office shell were available, the cost of altering the space was likely to be considerable. A late 19th-century building with office use was found in Paddington Street, and a study of the space showed that 36 people could be comfortably accommodated if the interior were substantially demolished and rebuilt.

The 315 square metre (3,400 square foot) offices were laid out over two floors. Although it was felt that a single-floor office was the ideal solution, this was not physically possible: the two partners' offices, a secretary's office, the library and a conference area were located on the first floor, with the architectural staff and another conference area on the ground floor. Various furniture systems, including a custom-made option, were considered. Herman Miller Action Office was eventually selected because of the wide variety of components available and the flexible layout it offered. The practice designed its own adjustable drawing boards, which clipped onto the Action Office panels. Individual yellow pinboards were designed to match the wall lining, and upholstered Eames swivel armchairs were used throughout.

A suspended, overhead trunking system was designed to house telephone and power sources. The system was made up of 'Egatube' components: a lighting tray in the centre with PVC extruded industrial trunking either side. The cables were brought down to each workstation through bright orange plastic tubes that clipped onto the furniture system.

Architects: Farrell/Grimshaw Partnership
Contractor: Farrell/Grimshaw & Andrew Smythe

Top: External view at night showing the ground-floor reception and main meeting room, with the original shopfront at the upper level and the bay windows of Farrell's office (left) and Grimshaw's office (right). Maggie Jones, still today Terry's secretary, had the office and window in the centre.

Centre: Typical office floor space with furniture.

Bottom: Reception area.

PADDINGTON STREET OFFICES: 2

Terry Farrell & Company

After the split with Nicholas Grimshaw, Terry Farrell transformed the high-tech office in Paddington Street into a richer, more metaphorical experience. The new brief was to develop the opportunities for spatial character and visual incident that lay beneath the existing bland surfaces. The sparse use of colour and simplicity of spatial handling were replaced by complex spaces, richer surfaces, illusions and witticisms that reused many of the existing elements. Exposed heating ducts and lighting tracks were part hidden and part revealed in and on marbled columns. The Action Office furniture was reinstated but was integrated with panels, columns and an abundance of exotic plastic flora. The long space was divided into five separate zones: a reception and conference area; staircase and processional corridor; architects' workstations; partners' office incorporating a mezzanine library; and an open-air courtyard. The idea was to replace a faceless, entropic space with somewhere derived from the theme of a central street with varied rooms and a courtyard – what Farrell called 'high-tech thinking with a friendly face'.

Visitors were greeted by a suite of art deco armchairs standing on a complementary carpet and grouped around an art deco-inspired fireplace. The centre of the space led through a sweep of marbled columns surmounted by spherical lamps. The columns culminated, in the infinite distance, in a make-believe archway – an illusion created by the calculated siting of mirrors along the rear and side walls. A playful courtyard recalled an artificial London beach with bright-blue wooden waves, rubber sand, a swinging hammock, lifebelt and beach chairs under a Martini umbrella. Colour and fun replaced an earnest work-only environment.

Architects: Terry Farrell & Company
Contractor: Jim Williams

Top: The central reception area showing seating and reuse of existing filing cabinets as a set-piece.

Above: The central aisle with decorative columns accommodating all the main services.

Axonometric of the new
office layout, showing
rear partners' space.

Partners' meeting room
with the office library in
the gallery above.

INDUSTRIAL BUILDINGS

1971–81

During the 1970s and early 1980s, Farrell/Grimshaw Partnership and Terry Farrell & Partners designed a series of factories and warehouses for a range of clients – some owner-occupiers such as Herman Miller, Rotork Controls and Digital Computers, and some developers who were building units to let, such as those in Nottingham and Wood Green, London.

Top right: Factory for Rotork Controls, Bath, 1973.

Below: Factory units, Queen's Drive, Nottingham, 1980.

Centre right: Winwick Quay, Warrington, 1978.

Bottom right: Distribution centre for BMW, Bracknell, Berkshire, 1978–79.

Herman Miller Furniture Factory, Bath, 1977

On the banks of the River Avon opposite an existing Herman Miller factory was a local authority tip covered in rubbish and overlaid with soft clay and rock. The client required the construction there of a high-quality, low-cost building that offered a high level of future flexibility. The solution was found in a lightweight cladding design, steel-frame construction and fast-track construction contracts. The 5,399 square metre (58,114 square foot) building was designed to reflect the aspirations of the Herman Miller company – famous for its innovations in modern furniture, particularly the manufacture of Eames chairs and its Action Office system. The company philosophy was to foster a sense of ownership and responsibility among its workers – an outlook that was also integral to the thinking of Farrell/Grimshaw. Like other Farrell/Grimshaw buildings, the furniture factory was designed to be easily changed and capable of use for a wide range of industrial processes. The ultimate flexible feature was a movable WC unit, which could be positioned in 16 locations – an idea that refers back to the clip-kit adaptability of the Herman Miller office furniture (the rich and diverse design world of Charles and Ray Eames was a great influence on Terry Farrell).

Client: Herman Miller Ltd
Architects: Farrell/Grimshaw Partnership
Quantity surveyors: Hanscomb Partnership
Services engineers: Ronald Hurst Associates
Structural engineers: Peter Brett Associates
Main contractor: Wiltshier Ltd

Left, far left and below left: Exterior of the Herman Miller Factory, showing the pale cream flexible cladding system.

Below right: Factory interior, showing the service gantry with roof-level access.

Citroën Distribution Centre, Runnymede, Surrey, 1973

The brief comprised a warehouse situated on a barren water-meadow between the Thames and the Staines bypass overlooking historic Runnymede (where the Magna Carta was signed in 1215). The site was originally a paint factory, but a major factor that affected the design was the surrounding land use, which included cottages and weekend retreats. The new warehouse bridged the gap between environmental considerations (that the building should blend into its environment and not dominate the surrounding countryside) and the imperatives of modern industrial architecture.

The main concern was that the warehouse should be low rise – an aim achieved and accentuated by landscaping, planting and the inclusion of a banked grass verge running the length of the building. Environmental concerns were reflected in the plastic-coated olive-green metal cladding, bronze acrylic-coated window frames and the sun-resisting, brown-tinted glass in the office area. Green spa chippings were laid on the roof so that, when viewed from neighbouring high ground, the building blended in with its surroundings.

The warehouse was a single-storey unit containing a clear storage space of 47,011 cubic metres (1,660,180 cubic feet) with an area of around 7,710 square metres (81,730 square feet) and first-floor office space of 930 square metres (10,000 square feet), providing a huge amount of relatively cheap storage space. There were also two residential units to the rear of the building, plus extensive garage facilities with access to the drive and the River Thames. The building was leased by Citroën as its main UK spare-parts depot.

Client: McKay Securities/Citroën Cars
Architects: Farrell/Grimshaw Partnership
Main contractor: Wates Ltd
Engineers: Peter Brett Associates

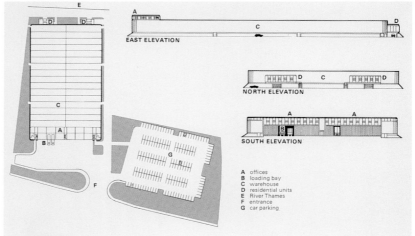

A offices
B loading bay
C warehouse
D residential units
E River Thames
F entrance
G car parking

Top: Citroën warehouse in Runnymede.

Centre: Plans and elevations.

Bottom: View to the River Thames showing the two fully glazed residential units.

Digital Computer Centre for Digital Equipment Co.,
Reading, 1980

In June 1979 Terry Farrell was commissioned to carry out a feasibility study for the use of a speculatively built industrial shed on which Digital Equipment Co. had taken out a long lease. Digital wished to use part of the building to provide immediate short-term accommodation for groups of software workers.

The feasibility study demonstrated how full use could be made of the volume and natural light in the building to create a better environment and increase the amount of flexible floor space. An open-plan solution was proposed on two levels, with enclosed cellular spaces underneath an open mezzanine. Long internal views were opened up, and controlled views into the outside world were proposed through conservatories to be placed across roller-shutter doors, and into an internal courtyard to be cut through the roof of the shed in the deepest part of the plan.

Terry Farrell & Partners gave the three interconnected parts of the building order and identity. The budget was very limited, and a large part of it had to be spent on services and the computer room, the most important and expensive part of the project. The decision was taken to insert a long, thin mezzanine inside, and structurally independent from, the existing building shell. It was on this mezzanine, which hovered over the computer room, that Terry Farrell decided to lavish what little extra was available in the budget to be spent on identity and placemaking. The decision was taken to support the heating system from the balustrade of the mezzanine, in prime view, and to detail it as a pair of camshafts. It was painted a lilac blue, establishing the building's colour scheme, with the enclosing walls painted in various shades of harmonious grey. Pairs of heating units were hung from the roof, with the fresh-air ducts and flues cutting through the roof. Either side of the heater assemblies were vertical connectors to the horizontal balustrade ducts. These formed processional archways to the mezzanine, penetrated by the stairs and bridge. The ductwork was used to define areas of circulation on both levels, giving the building a strong industrial identity, while allowing its working parts to change without detriment to its overall character.

The adapted building inverted the traditional concern for the external skin of industrial architecture, which had been a key concern of Farrell/Grimshaw. A very ordinary speculative shell existed, appropriate for the client's needs, so Farrell focused on providing a series of independent objects within the shell that could be built with minimum interruption to the existing building, at the least cost and greatest speed.

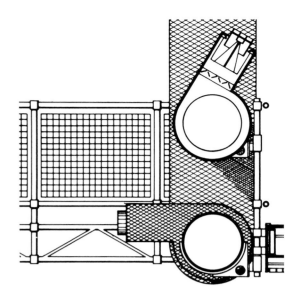

Top: Detail drawings of the overhead gantry and air-conditioning system.

Centre: The main stairs with air-conditioning units arranged in such a way as to make a gateway.

Bottom: A standardized add-on conservatory unit was installed as the social centre.

Client:
Digital Equipment Co. Ltd, UK Region
Architects: Terry Farrell & Partners
Consulting engineers: Ronald Hurst
Associates
Quantity surveyors: Michael F. Edwards
and Associates
Specialist consultants: Peter Brett
Associates, consulting engineers
Main contractor: George Kemp, Stroud
and Co. Ltd

Above: General view
inside the converted
factory shed showing the
air-conditioning above a
computer room.

Below: Air-conditioning
ductwork.

THE COLONNADES

Porchester Square, London W2: 1974–76

The Colonnades project, a comprehensive redevelopment for Samuel Properties Ltd, consisted of 243 houses, flats and maisonettes, a supermarket, eight shops, offices, a pub and an underground car park. In 1969 Westminster City Council invited a shortlist of developers and their architects to submit sketch proposals for the site, originally intended as the new Paddington Town Hall and Civic Centre. The brief was to create a high-density redevelopment of principally residential accommodation, with limited shopping and commercial use. It also included a new library commissioned by the City of Westminster – but this never materialized; instead, Clifton Nurseries used the space to commission a temporary garden centre (see pages 234–37). The aim was to create maximum possible open space at the same time as giving the scheme a powerful identity that would regenerate interest and investment in the area, which at that time was declining.

The site lay between the fine early Victorian houses of Westbourne and Gloucester terraces to the east and the speculative developments of Westbourne Grove and Queensway to the west. Its position reinforced the need for a strong solution to create a new centre of interest in the area. The site's north side was bounded by a row of Victorian houses that, although not listed, were worthy of retention. The site also had an undistinguished group of Victorian houses to the east, which were to be demolished. To the west was a bomb site, which was being used as a temporary car park. A mews running north–south was entered through an arch in the Victorian terrace from Porchester Square, and the line of the mews was retained in the new scheme. It was decided to keep Nos. 36 to 46 Porchester Square and to demolish the rest of the frontage, completing the line of the square with a new building similar in bulk and character to its predecessors. The new block in Porchester Terrace North was staggered to follow the line of the street and limited in height to reflect the scale of the adjoining properties. On the west and south were the busy streets of Porchester Road and Bishop's Bridge Road. The former already had shopping facilities, so the commercial content of the scheme was located on this frontage.

To make use of the large flat roofs covering the library and commercial areas, a new house type was developed in the form of a series of narrow patio houses entered from landscaped walkways. The buildings on the two sides of the site were intentionally kept low to prevent overshadowing of the flats, and to allow maximum sun and light into the residents' square. This formed the focal point of the development and incorporated the mature trees and planting retained from the rear gardens of Porchester Terrace North.

Previous page: Views of the completed project.

Right: Farrell's collage at the competition stage, showing the Tecton estate to the right. The overall aim was to integrate the redevelopment into the grain, height and massing of the surrounding area.

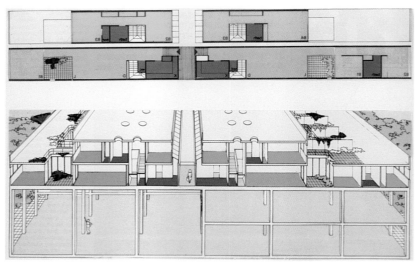

Above: Plan and sectional perspective of residential units above the shops and offices.

Right: Part plan of the existing buildings showing new rear additions.

Below left: Original view down the mews terrace before work began.

Below right: Section through the existing buildings showing new rear additions.

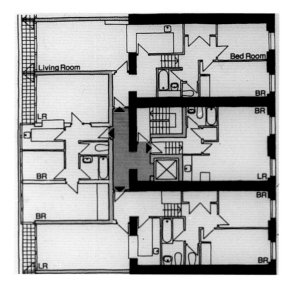

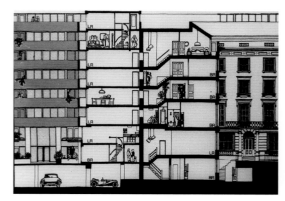

The 11 Victorian terraced properties – originally elegant, single-family houses – had been adapted for use as small hotels, bedsits and flatlets. In order to achieve the high density of large units while retaining the bulk of the houses, it was decided to demolish the conglomeration of rear additions and build a new extension framed with reinforced concrete to the rear. The existing houses were linked at ground level to the rest of the scheme by an indoor pedestrian street that formed a bridge over the mews to connect with the main entrance in the adjacent eight-storey block. Along the length of the pedestrian street, two double-height conservatory areas gave access to and views over the residents' square.

During the initial design stages it became obvious that a multi-level separation of use would be the only way to obtain the accommodation required within the confines of the site. The three basic uses – parking, commercial and residential – were horizontally layered. The shopfronts were set back from the perimeter of the building to provide protected space for the public, and a glazed arcade between shops served as a waterproof shopping precinct that retained contact with the street.

A reinforced-concrete frame based on a 7,300 square metre (78,550 square foot) grid was infilled with external cladding elements appropriate to the function of the space enclosed. The supermarket and pub were infilled with dark brown tiles on blockwork, while the offices and restaurant had a glazed curtain-wall enclosure; the colonnades were expressed with brown tile infill panels, and the mews houses were finished in the same brick with tile infill.

The design of the patio houses offered maximum seclusion within the scope of a high-density urban redevelopment. The internal patio provided a private external space and allowed the development of the deep plan forms. Access to the patio houses is via the eight-storey-block entrance hall or an entrance hall adjacent to the offices.

The Colonnades scheme showed the importance of knitting together urban design with the conservation of buildings by retaining the scale of the original terraces and the mews. The existing site levels were strictly adhered to, entirely avoiding steps and stairs in the open, and the general urban scale and character of the area were maintained.

Client: Samuel Properties Ltd
Architects: Farrell/Grimshaw Partnership
Local authority: Westminster City Council
Structural engineers: C.J. Pell Frischman & Partners
Quantity surveyors: Monk & Dunstone Associates
Mechanical and electrical services: Wates (Services) Ltd
Contractors: Wates Ltd

Right and below left: The new building element facing Porchester Square.

Below right: View of the completed development from a balcony on the earlier Tecton flats, on the opposite side of Bishop's Bridge Road.

LOW-COST TIMBER-FRAME HOUSING

1974–81

Seven small schemes for the Maunsel Housing Society

In 1974 the Maunsel Housing Society commissioned Farrell/Grimshaw to build a series of small infill housing schemes that lent themselves to a common approach. The structure and basic spatial organization were systematized, and the Department of the Environment relaxed its rules against serial tendering to allow a single timber-frame contractor to erect all the timber shells. The cost advantages of using local contractors were combined with the best use of appropriate mass-production methods (see the drawing at the top of page 225). The sites were spread out around London's perimeter, from Luton to Romford to Croydon. Each was semi-urban and relatively nondescript in its surroundings.

The commission was to design, concurrently, seven housing schemes comprising more than 200 houses, although several of the individual schemes were for fewer than ten dwellings. Dwelling types were family houses with gardens, or family maisonettes over a lower-ground-floor storey planned as a separate flat, so that each dwelling had access to its own garden and a front door to the street. A narrow party wall width of 3.6 metres (12 feet) was chosen to give maximum potential for individual street frontages, and the simple repetitive plan form that was developed proved very adaptable to the different site constraints and family uses – in the manner of the Victorian terraced house.

The design concept was to give each infill site its own character and context, with the result that it had a distinct 'face', easily identifiable by occupiers and visitors. The aim was to provide simpler management and greater tenant identification with and control over individual homes. For this reason, shared open spaces were kept to a minimum, and internal common parts such as lifts, stairs and corridors were completely eliminated. Much time was spent negotiating with the local authorities and postal service to have the address of each dwelling numbered as a continuation of the adjoining street rather than as part of an impersonal 'block' with a name.

Architects: Farrell/Grimshaw Partnership
Quantity surveyors: Monk & Dunstone Associates
Structural engineers: Peter Brett Associates

Top: Red tile hanging and timber cladding at Luton; two floors of flats above ground- and first-floor maisonettes with gardens.

Centre left: Rear of the above.

Centre right: Blue tile cladding at Luton; one storey of flats above two-storey maisonettes with patios.

Bottom left: 'Face' balcony at Romford.

Three floors of flats, the bottom two with terraces or gardens.

Bottom right: The Grove, Isleworth. Two-storey maisonettes above two-storey maisonettes.

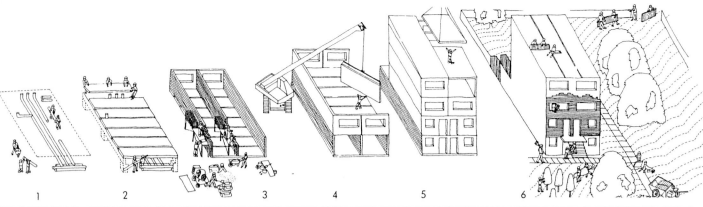

Maunsel housing, showing the construction sequence: 1/2/3 and 6 by a local contractor; 4/5 by a serial prefabricated-timber subcontractor.

1   2   3   4   5   6

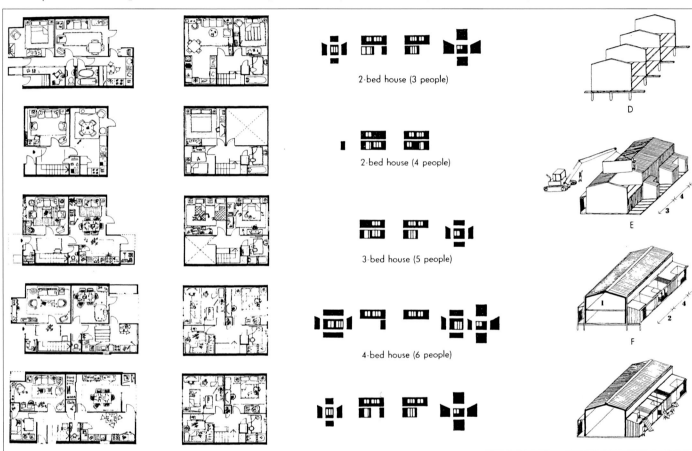

2-bed house (3 people)

2-bed house (4 people)

3-bed house (5 people)

4-bed house (6 people)

D

E

F

Oakwood 13, Warrington New Town, showing varied plan types (left); panel variations to achieve these plan types (centre); and the sequence of construction (right, from top).

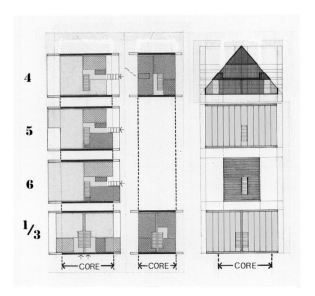

4

5

6

1/3

←CORE→   ←CORE→   ←CORE→

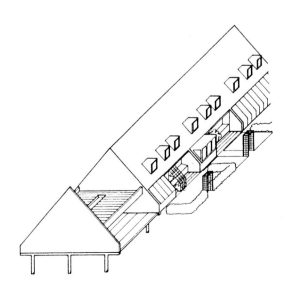

Oakwood 18, Warrington New Town, showing the plans and standardized section with four house types (left) and the assembled 'bungalow' house form (right).

200 houses for Warrington New Town

The project showed that it was possible to design well with a wide range of appropriate materials, including vertically hung tiles, lapped vertical timber boarding, horizontal tongue-and-groove boarding and brickwork (the latter was used at Hounslow to reduce noise from aircraft landing at Heathrow). The commission in 1978 by Warrington New Town Development Corporation to undertake the design of two large adjacent housing sites in Oakwood (Oakwood 13 and 18) went to Farrell/Grimshaw and was completed by Terry Farrell; it provided the opportunity to explore further the concept of standardization in construction and individuality of context and personal expression.

A key theme of the project was the assumed aspirations of future residents (how they would use their homes to express their lifestyle) and the amount and form of choice they would be offered. The design approach was also based on the location, overall plan, organization and management of Warrington New Town itself. These two concepts had been confused in the past by architects determined to build the truly flexible house, who had invested limited resources in mechanistic solutions at the expense of an initial range of choice, day-to-day adaptability and the opportunity for ingenious do-it-yourself schemes.

The site access lanes ran north–south, giving good orientation and terminating at the retained woodland edge in a row of bollards, and continued as footpaths to an adjacent park. A lane consisted of no more than 35 houses, each with its own front garden and front gate. Standardized timber-frame techniques were used to economize on construction time and cost; but, rather than the simple repetitive plans of the Maunsel schemes, a concept was developed of the 'universal core' (the main service, circulation and living spaces of the house). This core was common to all house types, whose variation in size and character was achieved by adding extensions in defined zones at the front and rear of each house, so that – both physically and by the adoption of traditionally decorative suburban elements of trellis, porch and patio – tenants were encouraged to extend, adapt and decorate their houses through add-ons such as bay windows, front porches and ad hoc extensions to meet individual needs.

While this approach is common to both Oakwood 13 and 18, there is some difference in interpretation between the two schemes. Oakwood 13 is based on the terraced-house model: a simple two-storey structure with three bedrooms on the top floor. The four-person house has an addition at the rear to increase kitchen and dining space; the five-person house has an addition at the front; and the six-person house has a side entry that allows the addition of a fourth bedroom at ground level. Oakwood 18 comprises bungalows with roof or loft

Opposite: Oakwood 13:
Front elevation of
perimeter terraces
(top); front entrances of
flats and maisonettes
(centre); grouped houses
for old people (bottom).

This page: Oakwood 18:
The housing seen from
the perimeter footpath;
low-rise bungalows were
adopted throughout (left);
factory- prefabricated
timber-frame construction
showing the components
of one house (below
left); typical views down
Oakwood 18 lanes
(below right).

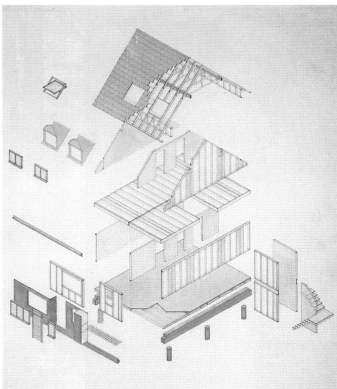

Next page:
These photographs of
Oakwood 18 (above left
and right) and Oakwood
13 (below) were taken
when Farrell revisited the
estates 20 years after
they were completed.
Particularly amusing is
Oakwood 13 with its new
front walls and bunting
to celebrate the Queen's
Golden Jubilee in 2002.

Revisit 2002: with residents' own brick garden walls, trellis and planting

rooms, developed to produce a non-deterministic house plan. The essential task was the creation of a framework for individual adaptation rather than an idealized architectural 'house' form. As Farrell later explained, 'Designing homes which take into account personal taste and individual needs for self-expression places the architect in the role of a scriptwriter rather than an actor on stage.'

Client: Warrington New Town Development Corporation
Architects: Terry Farrell & Partners
Quantity surveyors, landscape architects, structural and civil engineering services: WNTDC
Mechanical and electrical consultants: Ronald Hurst Associates

JENCKS HOUSE

Holland Park, London: 1978–81

Charles Jencks, Maggie Keswick and Terry Farrell worked together on the conversion of the Jencks family home in Holland Park, west London. The house evolved over many years, but the initial phase of renovation, shown here, was largely designed by Farrell, who was responsible for the shell; Jencks did the follow-on decorative work. Despite his architectural background, Jencks was unable to produce the shell himself and approached Farrell specifically to get it done – but he nevertheless had strong desires to personalize it after Farrell's work was over.

Farrell devised a complex and ambitious contractual approach whereby a main contractor produced serial tenders and had a host of smaller subcontractors who were directed on a day-to-day basis. It was not the most economical way to proceed but it was the most flexible, and it drew heavily on the contractual know-how of fast-track programming that Farrell had developed in his earlier work on industrial buildings.

Adding to London terraced housing to extend the spatial volume of a property or to introduce modern amenities was the basis of many of Farrell's early projects, and the Jencks house fitted into that tradition. Much of Farrell's conversion work has begun with reassessing the standard house type's disregard of aspects. The students' hostel in Paddington (see pages 206–208) involved the addition of a service tower to free existing staircases for bedrooms and to add on new service elements. At the Colonnades (see pages 221–23), the existing rooms of the terraced houses looked out over the newly created square, so an extension was added to the rear, butting onto an old back wall to make the houses three rooms deep from front to back and allowing the living rooms to look out onto a newly created private garden on the south side. Farrell's own London home, begun in 1974, became known as 'the Tardis' because the three-bedroom semi-detached house was eventually made into a five-storey multi-roomed house by exploiting the subterranean and rooftop spaces. The aim was that all these houses should embody personal interventions over time; they became complete worlds of their own – Soanian expressions of complexity quite different from the universal, introverted quality of conventionally modernist space. In the Jencks house, the shell was therefore designed as a series of set-pieces, resolved

Right: A model of the study annexe. The roof and stairwell structures, worked out with the engineer David French, show the interaction of symbolism with constructive logic. Five 'London columns' were abstracted and used to order the side elevation (top). In the ceiling plan (centre and bottom), the sun's rays radiate from the central stairwell, known as the 'sunwell' .

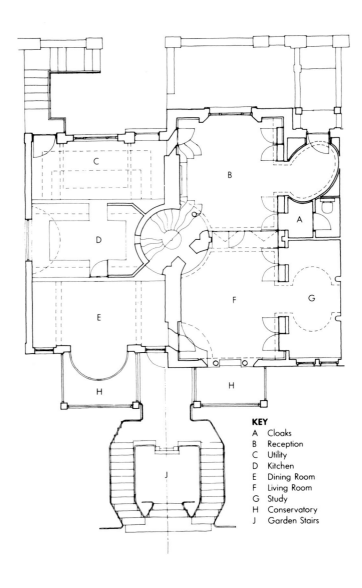

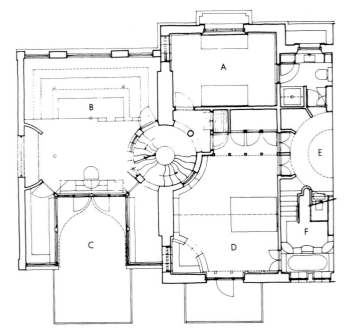

KEY

A Cloaks
B Reception
C Utility
D Kitchen
E Dining Room
F Living Room
G Study
H Conservatory
J Garden Stairs

KEY

A Guest Bedroom
B Study
C Terace
D Master Bedroom
E Dressing
F Bathroom

Above left:
Ground-floor plan.

Above right:
First-floor plan.

Below left:
First floor showing
annexe roof structure.

Below right:
Second-floor plan.

First Floor Plan

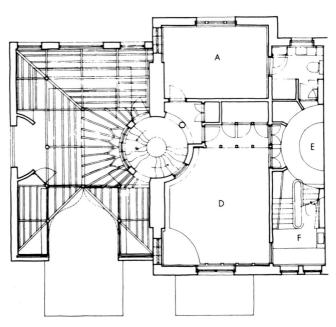

Second Floor Plan

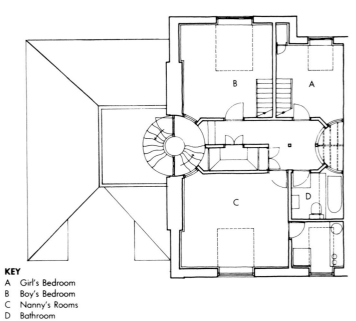

KEY

A Girl's Bedroom
B Boy's Bedroom
C Nanny's Rooms
D Bathroom

to a certain point of concept and detail, onto which was layered the personal decorative work of the owners, which in itself had its own existence and story to tell.

Farrell's main intervention in the Jencks house was a 'four seasons' theme. At that time, he was collaborating with Ralph Lebens on various passive-solar-energy schemes, and an idea arose that the conservatories in the Jencks house could be used as heat traps in winter. This solar idea led to the house's symbolic theme. The centrality of the stair and its circular form soon established itself as a solar motif, or a symbol for the sun. All the symbolism in the house evolved from this single idea. The 'moonwell' design developed later. Having focused the circulation in the centre of the house, Farrell had been concerned that there were windows on three sides only; there was one quite dark area of the plan resulting from a party wall with the adjoining property. The insertion of a light well became possible during construction. It was designed to be semicircular in form with a mirror on the party wall to reflect the light that came down the light shaft. At the same time, the moonwell was a pale reflection of the central staircase, which benefited from direct sunlight. The moonwell extended the dynamics of the spatial complexity into an area of the house that until that point had been spatially static. These two circulation routes became the hub of the house in terms of lighting, spatial organization and movement. They reflected a key theme of Farrell's work: that circulation is a structure and form in its own right, and its celebration is the essence of the architectural solution.

Clients: Charles Jencks and Maggie Keswick
Architects: Terry Farrell & Partners
Interiors and furniture: Charles Jencks
Garden design: Maggie Keswick
Jacuzzi design: Piers Gough
Winter and spring fireplaces: Michael Graves
Structural engineer: David French
Main building contractors: Hodgson Brothers, David Kitchener
Specialist carpenter: Jack Culbert
Roof work and painting: Eddie and Barnie O'Brien

Top: The rear garden elevation before the start of construction work.

Centre and bottom: Internal views during construction.

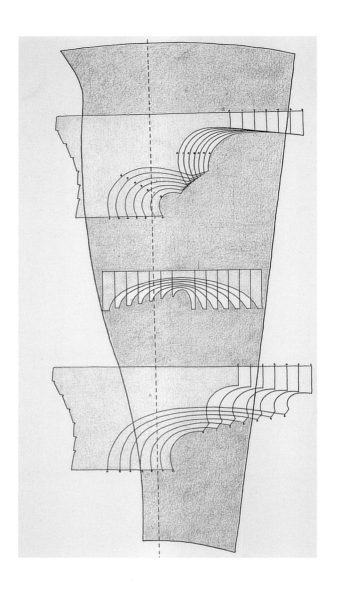

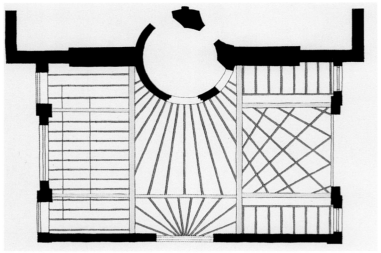

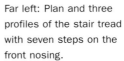

Far left: Plan and three profiles of the stair tread with seven steps on the front nosing.

Left: Reflective ceiling plans show the 'sun rays' in the the stairwell intersected by other geometries, underlining the space below.

Far left: View of the stairwell face, the 'Jencksiana' layered construction, 'rays of the sun', 'clouds' and 'bookcase-skyscraper': a mixed metaphor.

Left: The sun and light orders, made from Runtal radiators and sconces, frame the dining area and garden view. Overhead the diagonal structure of the sun's rays spreads from the sunwell.

Right: The west elevation, worked up jointly by Jencks and Farrell, shows the tall chimney orders, two 'London columns' setting the theme of duality that organizes this façade. The curved 'Hildebrantian motif' of the roof will be complemented by sculptural elements. The sun and face images organize the centre of the façade, which is further emphasized by a dropped ornamental band.

Right: The two-storey moonwell, opposite the sunwell, shows the 'seasons' theme, which runs through the house, reflecting crescent moons in the mirrors.

Far right: The sunwell brings light not only to the basement but also to adjoining rooms; spatial interpenetration is mixed with cut-through vistas.

CLIFTON NURSERIES: 1

Greenhouse, Garden Centre and Shop, Bayswater, London: 1979–80

Clifton Nurseries in Bayswater was the first of two urban design/ architectural schemes built by Terry Farrell as part of an effort to revitalize vacant city sites earmarked for future development. The client was Jacob Rothschild, who drew inspiration from the idea that, if NCP car parks could take over prominent derelict sites on short leases, he could do the same with a chain of nurseries that would provide both a retail outlet and an environmental improvement for the community. Designed as a highly energy-efficient structure, the Clifton Nurseries greenhouse was used to demonstrate to local authorities that temporarily derelict sites can be used for something more exciting than bland car parks.

The project grew out of an earlier link with the adjoining Colonnades development – Farrell had originally been commissioned to design a new library to complete the Colonnades scheme but this proposal had fallen through (see page 221). In this context, the nursery building is integrated into its urban-design setting as a local landmark. The cross-section is projected beyond the ends of the building onto huge yellow cut-outs that match the tiles of the Colonnades on the hoardings that fence in the site. Integral to the brief from Clifton Nurseries was the belief that the building should be more than just the usual cheap wood and glass lean-to; it should be something that represented more clearly the visual pleasure provided by plants and gardens, and it should be very much of the 20th century, as emblematic of its day as the great Victorian greenhouses were of theirs.

An investigation into existing off-the-peg systems quickly revealed the need to start from scratch. The building's final design evolved from several concerns relating to this and other projects in Farrell's office. The axially organized undulating form was derived from the combination of the extruded plan and the use of large sheet materials recently made available for certain types of agricultural greenhouse. Double-walled polycarbonate sheet for cladding was used for the first time in Britain on this building, and was considered appropriate since it combined high impact resistance with high thermal insulation and excellent light transmission, as well as being relatively cheap.

The structure to which the cladding was fixed comprised a demountable steel frame with a double-curved profile that both gracefully alluded to traditional garden conservatories and, with its undulations, gave strength and stiffness to the long lengths of narrow

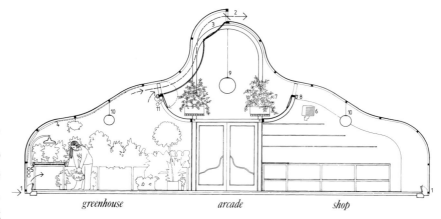

greenhouse   arcade   shop

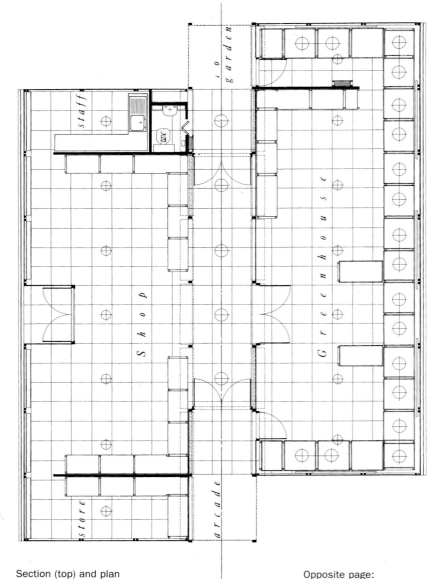

Section (top) and plan (above). The building in plan consists of a central arcade through which customers pass to enter the nursery proper. The shop is on the north side and the greenhouse on the south.

Opposite page:
Above: Axonometric of the nursery building.

Below (left to right): An early model; construction stage showing the steel frame; *Guardian* article by Steven Games.

polycarbonate sheets without sagging. An M-shaped flexible sealing gasket in a polyurethane elastomer and a specially-made PVC fixing button with a screw running down its centre ensured that large thermal movements and bending stresses could be accommodated without causing damage.

The concept behind the building owes much to Buffer Thinking, Farrell's competition-winning scheme designed with Ralph Lebens for an energy-efficient community of the future, which made use of simple conservatories, banks of earth and belts of trees to control the sun and wind. At Clifton Nurseries, environmental control to counteract large heat gains in summer and heat losses in winter was achieved by a combination of devices. Winter heat losses were controlled by the insulation of the polycarbonate; summer heat gain was controlled by blinds on the south elevations and by a self-ventilating and heat-regulating system based on the principles of a solar chimney. A series of floor-level and roof-level vents, and a suspended quilt under the southern roof of the arcade, drew air naturally through the building and accelerated the ventilation by natural convection of the greenhouse, with the primary outlets formed by a vertical shift in the section alignment along the ridge. The shift in plan form along the central axis accommodated two entrances in different parts of the building, and the solid gable-shaped cut-outs in the perimeter fence extended these axes beyond the building to the site boundaries.

Client: Clifton Nurseries
Architects: Terry Farrell & Partners
Structural engineers: Peter Brett Associates
Energy consultants: Ralph Lebens Associates
Contractors: Direct labour, architectural students and client

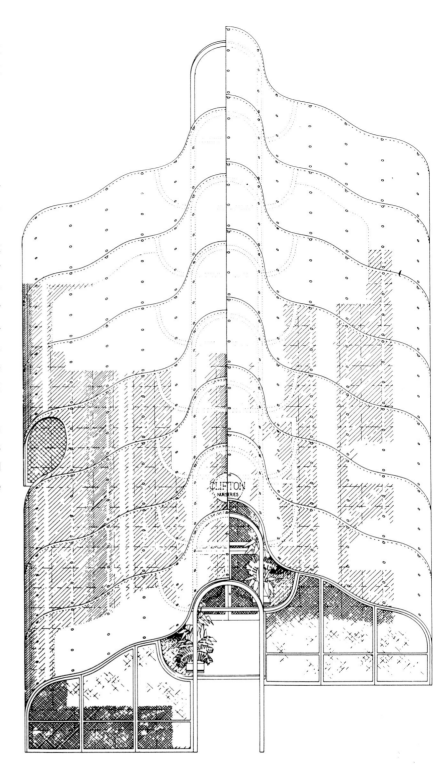

(i)

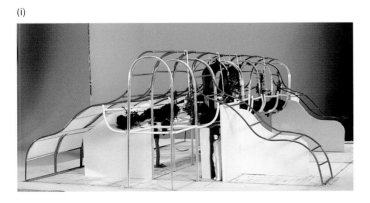

(ii)

(iii)

Right: Exterior of the entrance side. Columned internal illumination and the refraction of light on the webs separating the double walls of the polycarbonate sheet give the building a shimmering night-time presence.

Right: Exterior view from the garden-centre side.

Far right: Interior of the central arcade.

Left: Interior of the greenhouse.

Left and far left: Details of the external cladding with oversized gaskets and fixing buttons connecting the twin-wall polycarbonate to the steel frame.

CLIFTON NURSERIES: 2

Garden Shop and Public Park, Covent Garden, London: 1980-81

The garden shop in Covent Garden was the second temporary building designed for Clifton Nurseries on a short-lease site in London – in this case, a site owned by the Royal Opera House. At that time, before a second auditorium was built for the Opera House, the land was vacant and badly in need of regeneration. The architectural response was to combine a formal solution that took its cue from the surrounding streets and buildings with the expressive qualities of new technology, particularly when applied to lightweight demountable structures.

Given the location of the building – terminating a major street near the market buildings – and the formality of the nearby street patterns, it was decided to align the building centrally on the axis of King Street. The available land did not extend symmetrically about this axis, but permission was obtained for the façade to be extended along a narrow strip on the other side of the axis as a half screen, which completed the symmetry and hid the car-parking land behind. The problem of how to create a façade and a building of appropriate scale and appearance for this historic context was resolved by adapting a classical portico, based on the precedent of the numerous porticoes of the nearby market buildings and of Inigo Jones's St Paul's church, and extending it in a 'temple' form to become the underlying image of the design.

The interpretation of this classical form in the architectural detail of the new building was relaxed and light-hearted. The adoption of classical details went hand in hand with the introduction of modern technology, combined with a certain irreverence for their sources. The portico façade was a framework split along its central axis, each side containing planting and lighting displays that changed with the seasons. Indoor plants and flowers from the shop were incorporated into the glazed window-half of the portico, and outdoor plants were arranged in the open framework side. The open columns allowed for plants to grow inside, and all the columns had living plant swags. In this way, the business side of the shop – marketing plants and flowers – was reflected in live form and classical stone decorations (which, in turn, derived their forms from seasonal plant foliage). On the long façade a rusticated glass and timber wall, representing the heavy stone side-walls of a temple, occupied three of the four garden bays. A largely glazed, non-rusticated shopfront turned the corner below the pediment and occupied the fourth entrance bay in the manner of a temple stoa. The roof of the building was fabricated from Teflon-coated glass fibre, the first instance of use of this material in Britain.

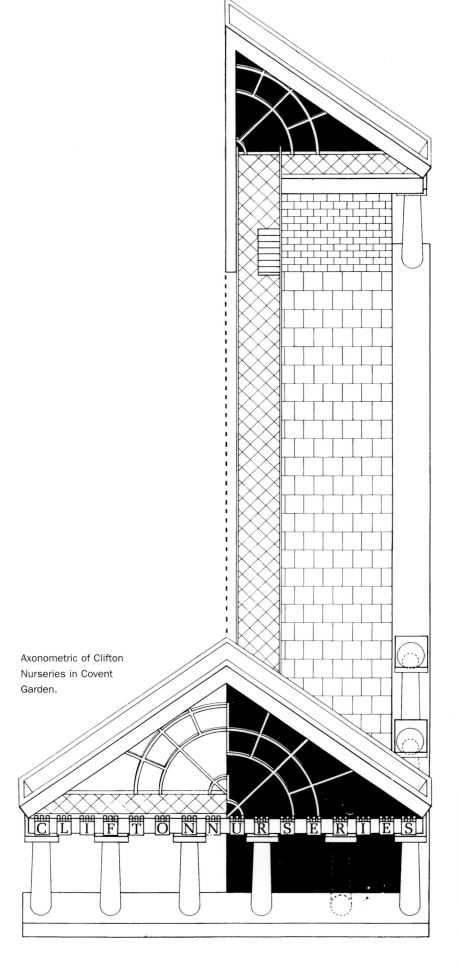

Axonometric of Clifton Nurseries in Covent Garden.

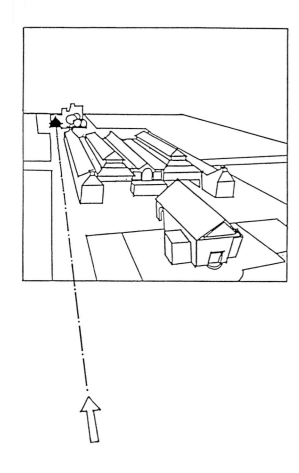

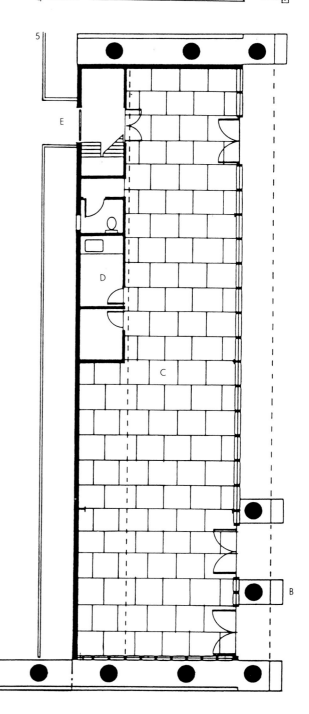

Above left: Although not occupying the full site needed, by means of a false half trompe l'oeil the building sits squarely on the axis of King Street, in an area unusually (for London) full of set-pieces of formal town planning.

Above: An aerial view of Covent Garden piazza; the site is at the bottom right-hand corner.

Right: Cross-section (above) and plan (below).

Left: Site plan showing Inigo Jones's St Paul's church (A), market hall buildings (B), and the new Clifton Nurseries garden shop (C).

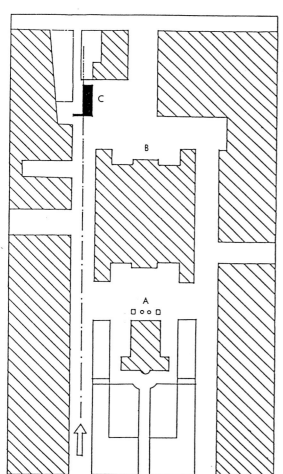

Client: Clifton Nurseries (Covent Garden)
Architects: Terry Farrell & Partners
Consulting engineers: Ove Arup & Partners (Lightweight Structures Group)
Landscape architects: Clifton Nurseries (Holdings) Ltd
Specialist consultants: Peter Rice, Ove Arup & Partners, and Ove Arup and Partners (Lightweight Structures Group)
Main contractor: Wiltshier (London) Ltd

Left: Front portico on the axis of King Street, with the false 'half-screen' on the left-hand side.

Opposite page:
Above, left to right: Detail of the trompe l'oeil screen; view down King Street; night view.

Below: Exterior view of the Clifton Nurseries building from inside the restored piazza buildings.

WATER-TREATMENT CENTRE

Reading, Berkshire: 1979–82

This building was constructed as part of a new operations centre overseeing sewage treatment and water supply for the Thames Water Authority, one of the largest water authorities in the world. Apart from the underground tanks and water-treatment plant (part of a separate civil engineering contract), facilities were required in the building for workers maintaining other installations in the area; these included laboratories, stores, cafeterias, workshops, offices and a computer room. A centrally placed visitors' centre was also included.

Resembling a catamaran, the building straddles a vast treatment tank set into the ground and containing several million gallons of water. Weight and stability are provided by the above-ground building since the underground elements are made unstable by the rising and falling water-table caused by the proximity of the River Kennet. Earth mounded for 1 metre (39 inches) up the wall externally to the top of the underground water tank reduces the visible height of the building and prevents damage to the cladding from operational vehicles.

Externally the building is clad in light blue glass, which provides a low-maintenance skin reflecting the colour of the sky. This blue colour and the cascading curved form of the central block allude to water. The cladding grid responds to the requirements of different areas of the building. A rectangular grid covers the single-storey windowless stores, which need large openings for deliveries. A smaller square grid encloses the two-storey accommodation, which requires many small openings. The low cost of the rectangular grid compared with the 'average' cost of the square grid produced a net saving which was used to pay for the higher cost of curved grids. Louvres on the southern end-walls exclude solar gain.

Internally, the planning reflects the two separate uses by visitors and workers. Visitors approach along the central axial entry, through the main doors and into the ground-floor exhibition area, where the seating and the main door-handles echo the Thames Water Authority's symbol of rising and falling waves. A central stair leads up to the full-width vaulted mezzanine gallery, the ends of which are, respectively, the platform for viewing the works and the spiral staircase leading to the cavernous machinery hall in the underground structure. The staff entrances are directly below the gallery ends on each side of the building. Contrasting with the sky and water allusions of the external colours, the internal colours are earthlike, warmer and more varied.

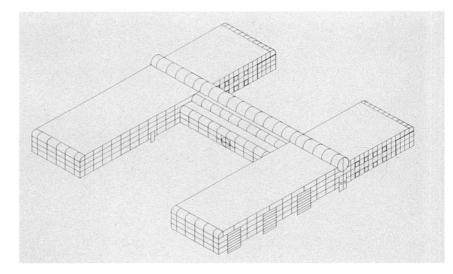

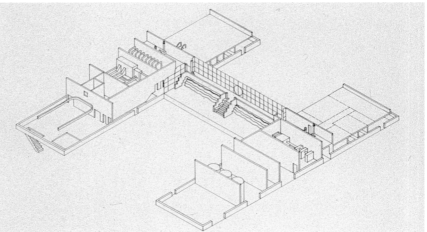

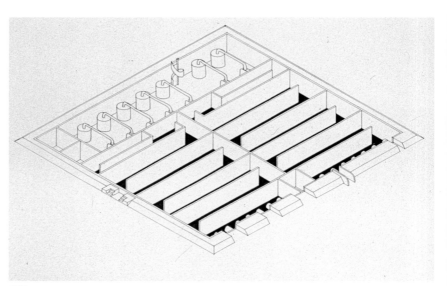

Client: Thames Water Authority, Southern Division
Architects: Terry Farrell & Partners
Quantity surveyors: Michael F. Edwards and Associates
Services/electrical and mechanical engineers: Ronald Hurst
Structural engineers: Peter Brett Associates
Main contractors: Goodall Barnard Ltd, Boulton & Paul

Above: The completed building.

Right: Concept diagrams.

Below: The completed building looking towards the entrance area.

Opposite: Axonometric drawings of the building envelope (top); internal ground- and first-floor accommodation (centre); and underground water-treatment tanks (bottom).

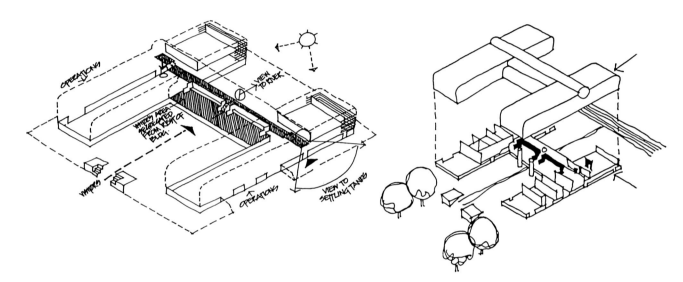

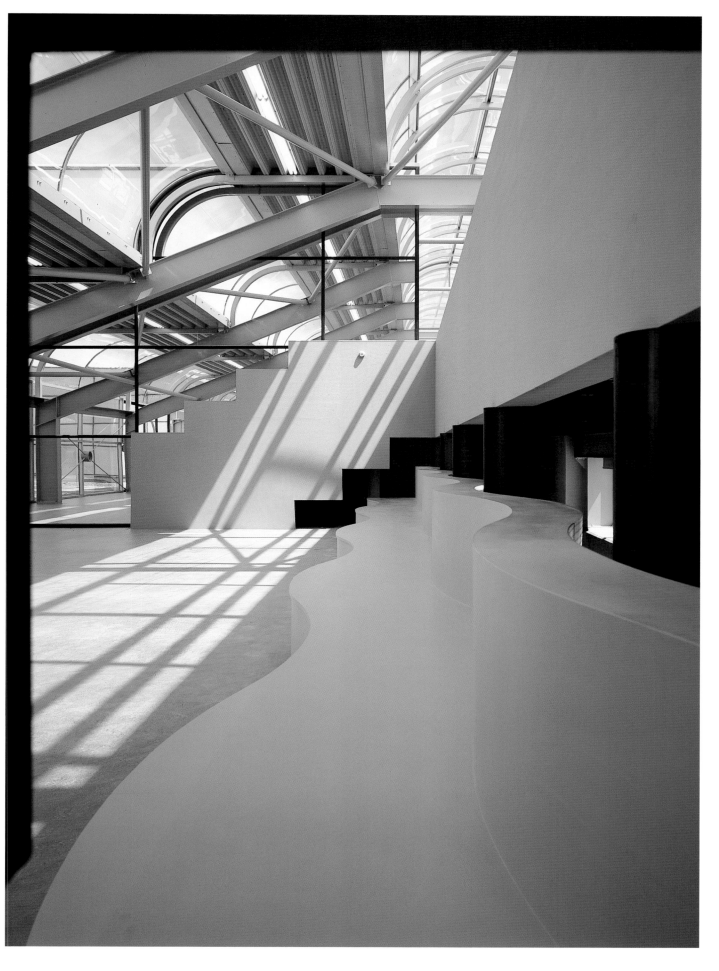

Left: Visitors' centre and exhibition space. Thematically the interior expresses the elements: water (blue-wave seating), earth (terracotta stairs and bridge), and fire (neon torchères) – see opposite page, below right.

Opposite page:
Above: Looking towards the entrance at night.

Below, left and right: Internal exhibition area and upper-level gallery.

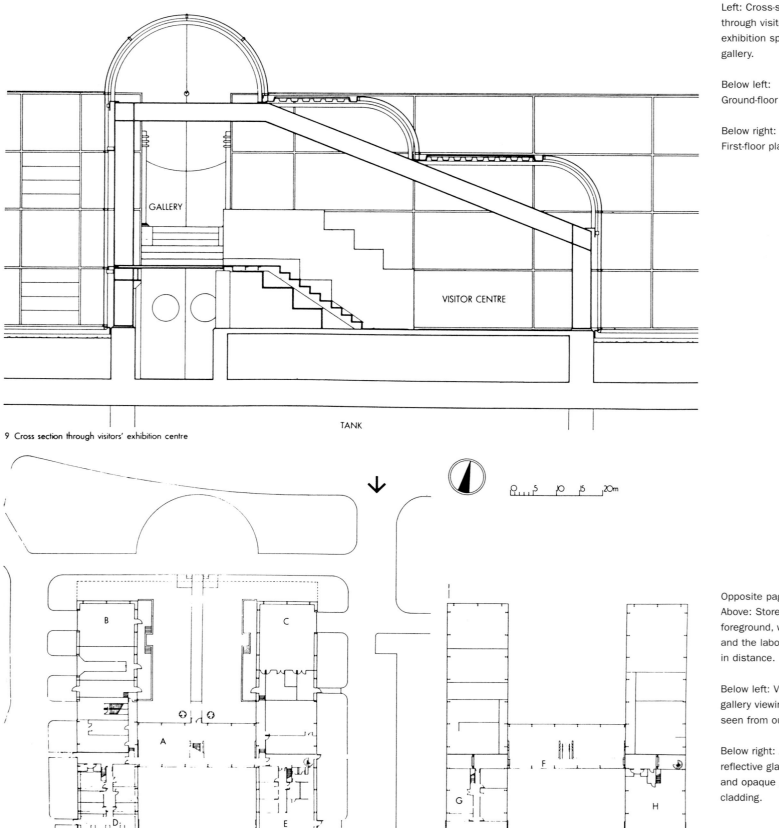

Left: Cross-section through visitors' exhibition space and gallery.

Below left: Ground-floor plan.

Below right: First-floor plan.

GALLERY

VISITOR CENTRE

TANK

9 Cross section through visitors' exhibition centre

0 5 10 15 20m

B

C

A

D

E

F

G

H

Opposite page:
Above: Stores wing in the foreground, with offices and the laboratory wing in distance.

Below left: Visitors' gallery viewing-window seen from outside.

Below right: Junction of reflective glass walls and opaque glass 'solid' cladding.

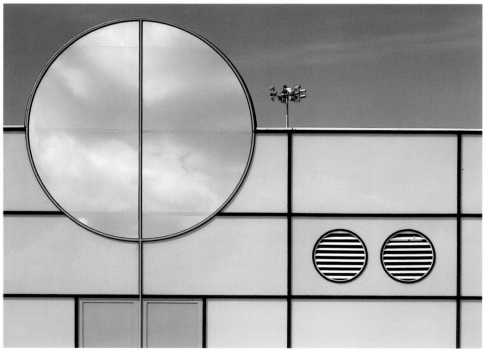

ALEXANDRA PAVILION

Haringey, London: 1980–81

When the Victorian Alexandra Palace in north London was gutted by fire in 1980, the local authority owners decided to house exhibitions, concerts, sports events and conferences in a temporary structure until the original building was reconstructed. The commission was won in competition in 1980.

The completed pavilion was a radically adapted version of the standard Shelterspan system – an enclosing membrane of PVC-coated terylene woven fabric panels supported on a rigid structure of aluminium portal frames. The technique of fixing the fabric derived from sail technology and consisted of a luff groove set on the structural member into which is slotted a bolt rope attached to the edge of the fabric panel. The fabric panels were tailored to double-curved patterns using welded schemes. The stable, double-curved form of the panels prevented wear and tear through flapping in the wind, while at the same time creating the attractive scalloped appearance.

The large 36 metre (118 foot) span required for this pavilion had to be achieved by substituting steel for the standard Shelterspan aluminium portal frames. The steel portals were clad on the upper and lower flanges with standard aluminium fabric-retention grooves fixed with chromium-plated bolts and plastic separating membranes. External purlins and diagonal rod bracing provided longitudinal stability. With an uninterrupted clear space of 3,620 square metres (39,000 square feet), the building, when completed, was the largest double-skinned fabric structure in Europe.

The characteristic cascading appearance of the building derived from the internal organization, which consisted of a large clear-spanned hall bounded by side aisles of ancillary spaces such as stores, kitchens, lavatory facilities, first-aid rooms, bars and snack bars. At the entrance end the building's extruded section was extended along one side of its central axis only, to avoid an existing mature tulip tree and to provide a formal termination to the linear form.

The internal environmental conditions were regulated by the thermal insulation of the double fabric skin, by fan-assisted natural ventilation and by gas warm-air heating ducted into the main space through a functional 'cornice' around the perimeter of the enclosure. The pavilion was designed to be demountable and had the facility to be easily unbolted and re-erected on another site.

Aerial views of Alexandra Palace.

Liverpool garden centre design. A competition entry based on the Alexandra Pavilion, this took the design a stage further in terms of size, complexity and graphic decorative effects upon the fabric itself.

1 Alternative designs and colour schemes for the external envelope.

2 Axonometric of the first-stage building envelope.

3 Plan of the garden centre exhibition.

4 Plan of a leisure centre (later stage).

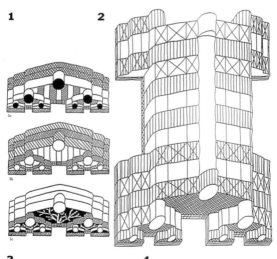

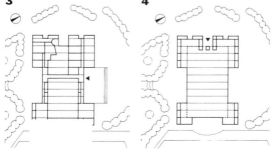

The form of the building related closely to the first Clifton Nurseries building (see pages 234–37), which also explored the formal resolution of an engineering structure in which a long length of 'soft' material was fitted into a steel framework, like rolls of fabric along curved ladders. The internal uplighters in the pavilion transformed the building into an enormous lampshade at night, giving it a dramatic luminous solidity.

Architects: Terry Farrell & Partners
Designed in conjunction with Peter Rice and Ian Ritchie, who developed the Shelterspan system, and Dr Peter Smith of the London Borough of Haringey.
Clients: Henry Boot Ltd., and the London Borough of Haringey.

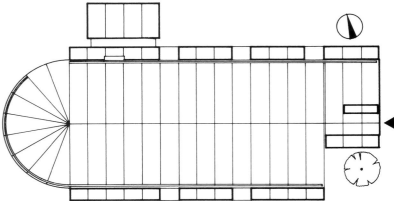

Top: Completed building.

Centre: Overall plan, showing the notch in the plan to retain the existing tulip tree.

Bottom: Interior view, showing the graphics superimposed on fabric discs hanging from the roof, and the perimeter heating duct.

Right and below left:
Night-time views of the
pavilion.

Below right: The rounded
'apse' end.

Opposite page:
Above: Entrance area
with fabric graphics and
the retained tulip tree.

Below left: Interior during
a surfing show.

Below right: Entrance
area of the completed
building.

CRAFTS COUNCIL GALLERY

Offices, Art Gallery & Information Centre
Waterloo Place, London: 1980–81

Having acquired the lease of the basement, ground and mezzanine of the building next to their existing premises in central London, the Crafts Council wanted a new gallery space capable of subdivision into three separate areas as well as provision for a slide index, information and coffee area, and office, storage, workshop and conference facilities. The new building had a ground-floor level 0.6 metre (2 feet) above the existing gallery, but since the mezzanine areas of both premises were on the same level as the new entrance door and reception area, it was possible to make a new entry ramp (providing easy wheelchair access around the entire ground floor). The ramp generated the building's main architectural strategy – the central circulation axis from entrance to stair was crossed by a cranked minor axis running through the two major gallery spaces. The entrance axis orientated visitors on the gallery floor and directed them through the reception and sales area to the staircase up to the mezzanine and information centre.

The detailed architectural problem was to create an internal identity for the building at the same time as finding a visual language that reconciled the different characteristics of the two historically listed Victorian interiors, as well as providing a neutral background for the display of objects in the gallery spaces. The more idiosyncratic of the original mouldings and decorations were replaced by new, larger-scale mouldings. Blank white wall spaces were created where possible above a common skirting line that formed a plinth to the counter, book shelf and other elements in the lower-floor areas. Recessed tracks for spotlights were incorporated into additions to the existing ceiling modelling. Subtle patterning in the new timber flooring worked with the modified ceilings to define sub-spaces within the two single-storey galleries. The taller space of the original gallery had its suspended ceiling removed to reveal a splendid and ornate strap-moulded plaster ceiling, and the new gallery lighting was suspended below on two trussed lighting gantries. New fibrous plaster columns flanked the principal axes; a storage unit, reception desk and book shelves defined the reception and sales area, and the geometry of the linoleum flooring was designed to respond to the various activities along its length.

At mezzanine level, the removal of part of the wall dividing the two mezzanines allowed the introduction of a set of slide-display cases to create views back down into the gallery below. A long-profiled coffee bar and specially commissioned bar stools were designed by Fred Baier.

This page: The existing building before construction and alteration work began.

Opposite, top left:
A Nolli plan of the Crafts Council and its surroundings, showing the various clubs and great interior spaces of the area, including the Athenaeum (1), Reform (2), RAC (3) and Travellers clubs (4) – and our proposals in the 1990s for Lloyds Bank (5) as well as the Crafts Council (6) on Waterloo Place.

Opposite, top right:
Reference alcove on the first floor, with reused slide-index cabinets.

Opposite, bottom right:
Reception areas and the front door.

Opposite, bottom left:
Axonometric of the three ground-floor galleries.

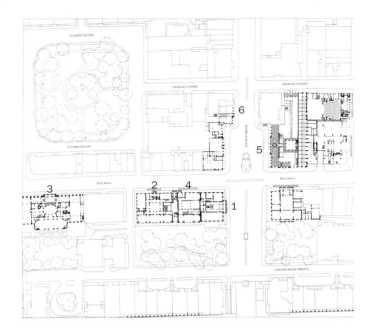

Architects: Terry Farrell & Partners
Client: Crafts Council

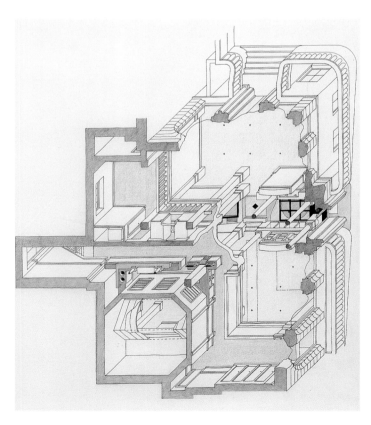

The toop end of the new ramp with the existing staircase to the mezzanine beyond.

Opposite page:
Above: The reception area, with desk, book shelves/display cabinet and fibrous plaster columns.

Below (left to right): Gallery Number One, Mezzanine coffee bar and Gallery Number Three.

COFFEE
SLIDE INDEX
INFORMATION

LAVATORIES DOWNSTAIRS

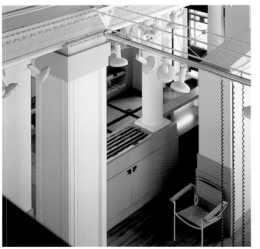

URBAN-INFILL FACTORIES

Wood Green, London: 1979–81

The commission for six factory units at Wood Green in north London was won in a developer's limited competition. A strategy for combining renovation and piecemeal redevelopment was adapted by the Borough of Haringey, and the most run-down and least reusable existing properties were cleared to create six sites. These were developed by Samuel Properties as a single scheme of speculative industrial units, each ranging in size from 400 to 2,000 square metres (4,300 to 21,520 square feet), with considerable flexibility for subdivision into different factory sizes.

A common solution was developed and adapted for each site whereby, whatever the plan profile, each building was built up to its site boundaries around partially enclosed courts. One of the characteristics of urban planning is that the design of open space becomes as critical as the design of the buildings themselves; at Wood Green, each courtyard was a tightly designed formal arrangement based on the turning circles and unloading positions of large vehicles, the car parking for staff and visitors, and the access and entry points for all vehicles and pedestrians.

The external walls at the boundaries of each site were constructed in banded brickwork to enclose and protect. The walls facing onto the courtyards were constructed of a proprietary wall system with reflective glazing sealed in neoprene. The wide range of functions behind the factories' glass walls were partly hidden by the reflectivity of the glass, and the use of this material in an enclosing ribbon wall made the inside of each courtyard a sparkling, visually intensive area compared with the soft-coloured evenness of the outside brick walls – analogous in concept to a geode. To comply with thermal insulation regulations, the courtyard walls have insulation in the form of set-pieces of four square black opaque 'windows' – a contradictory image reinforced by stripping the neoprene gaskets away around the black zones to reveal shiny aluminium window 'frames'. The courtyard glazing turns the corner at mid-span with silicon butt joints, and it steps back and up around the corner to the roof, articulating the distinction between courtyard glazing and exterior brickwork, while visually stitching the two together; it also provides visual contact between the mezzanine offices and the street.

Goods access is through a pair of double-height doors centrally positioned below the offices, which extend at mezzanine level around

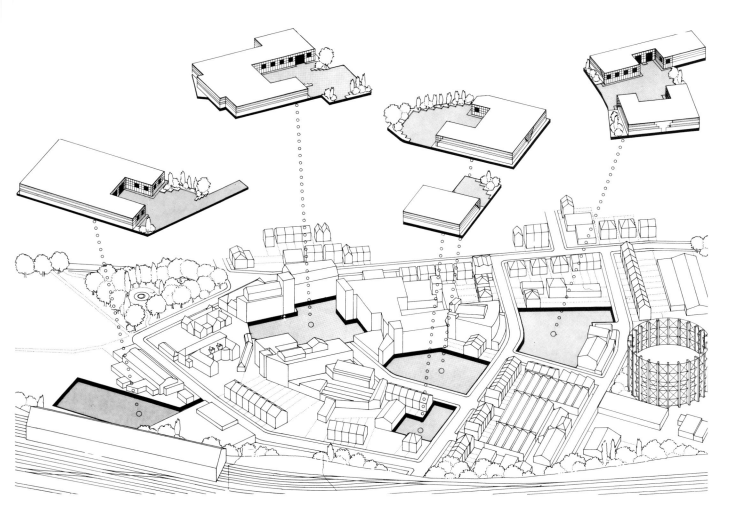

Opposite page:
Top and centre: What the sites looked like before construction work began.

Bottom: Aerial view after completion of the work, showing the factories with their distinctive courtyard areas set in the industrial area of Wood Green.

Axonometric of six courtyard factory units on different sites but in the same neighbourhood.

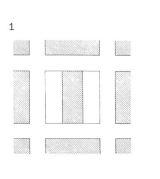

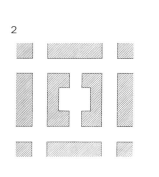

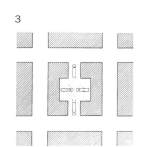

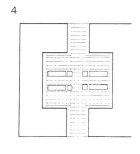

1 Isolated building with no response to context.
2 Courtyard becomes the form determinant.
3 Vehicle-movement geometry establishes configuration.
4 Four factories serviced from one courtyard.

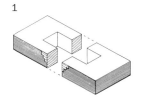

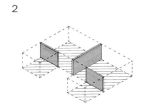

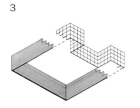

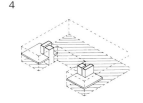

1 Two buildings.
2 Internal subdivision into two units.
3 Two wall types.
4 Two cores.

the glazed courtyard walls. The location of stairs and toilets is fixed, but their careful location between the office and industrial zones allows for flexible use. All the elements in the curtain walling are interchangeable and arranged within a square grid – a geometry repeated on freestanding elements such as gates, barriers and signs.

The buildings were easily let – the last one to Middlesex University's Art Department. Revisiting the site today, it is remarkable to see how the area has been revitalized, with the university's arts building having grown in influence to such as extent that the whole neighbourhood has become an arts quarter.

Architects: Terry Farrell & Partners
Client: Samuel Properties Ltd. with London Borough of Haringey
Services engineers: Ronald Hurst Associates/Barndale Building Services
Quantity surveyors: Monk, Dunstone, Mahon & Scears
Main contractors: Farrow Construction Ltd
Steelwork subcontractors: Dyer (Structural Steelwork) Ltd

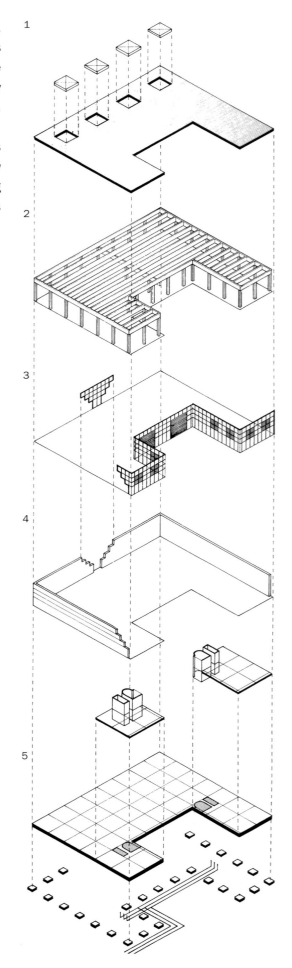

1 Roof covering and rooflights.
2 Steel frame structure.
3 Internal flexible glass cladding to courtyard.
4 Exterior perimeter brick wall and service/ access cores.
5 Concrete foundations and floor slab.

Left: Two factory entry doors flanked by office and administration wings.

Below left: Mirror-glass wall with black glass insets, louvre panels and steel vehicle barriers.

Opposite page:
Three views of perimeter walls: perimeter banded brick wall interrupted by upper-level windows and ground-floor doors (above); perimeter wall meets courtyard opening (below left); gates, glazing and brickwork junction (below right).

This page:
Two views of internal courtyard glazing walls: factory delivery door flanked by two 'solid' windows of insulation panels (above); further views of courtyard glazing (below left and right).

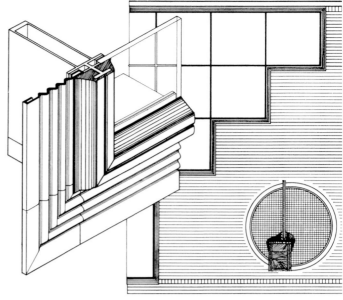

Above left: 'Ironic'
high-tech column of vent
grills and cable trays –
the interiors Farrell &
Partners designed for
Middlesex University's
Art department.

Left: Typical internal
staircase – adapted
from an off-the-peg stair,
with inset rings from
central tubular column
'cast-offs'.

Above: Specially
developed neoprene
gaskets for brickwork/
glass junctions and for
timber door insets.

Revisit 2003: overgrown with ivy

The buildings as they were photographed in 2003, covered in ivy. They are well liked and well looked after, and the whole area has become a lively arts quarter.

The projects chapter ends with a revisit to a scheme designed 25 years ago. A suitable symbolic metaphor – 25 years of ivy and other changes have grown and been layered onto all these buildings and projects.

AFTERWORDS

Interviews and comments edited by Nico Jackson

Conclusion: Reappraising Farrell by Kester Rattenbury

Interviews and comments

edited by Nico Jackson

Introduction

When Terry Farrell told me he was writing the story of his early life and career, I suggested that he might include in the book interviews with those who could throw light on how he was seen by his contemporaries during this period.

The last interview in a series of eight took place in January 2003, with Farrell's former teacher at the University of Pennsylvania, Denise Scott Brown. We sat in the open and airy Venturi Scott Brown Associates' studio in snow-covered Philadelphia and traced the VSBA influences in Farrell's work, some visible and some invisible. Back home, a train journey to Newcastle took me to Harry Faulkner-Brown, who taught Farrell at Newcastle University. The fact that he still lives there stands in contrast with the adventurous travels earlier in his career that so impressed and influenced his pupil.

The other conversations took place in London, still the centre of gravity for England's architectural world. Charles Jencks recalled working with Farrell on his Holland Park house, where we sat looking out over an unusually verdant London garden. A short journey north found me at the home of critic and teacher Robert Maxwell in Hampstead. Peter Murray was responsible for one of the first publications of Farrell's work with Nicholas Grimshaw in the magazine *Clip-Kit*. Today he continues to publish and communicate the work of leading architects and developers from the Wordsearch studio in Clerkenwell. Architects Tom Jestico and Ron Siddell both began their careers in the office of Farrell/Grimshaw, and went on to set up their own practices, Jestico + Whiles and Siddell Gibson, from where – when time permitted – they were happy to reminisce about their introduction to professional life.

This book is all about places; from the villages and towns in north-east England, where Farrell grew up, to the new and exciting cities of New York, Philadelphia and Hong Kong. He has explained in his own words his

reaction to these places and their influence upon his work, as well as his childhood experiences of placemaking. But it is also a book about Farrell's place in the evolving history of contemporary British architecture. As a postscript to these interviews, Kester Rattenbury reflects on his unique career and the critics' often vociferous response to his work. Ever resistant to stylistic labels, Farrell has nevertheless been pushed reluctantly into pigeonholes, a new one every decade or so. When the Farrell/Grimshaw Partnership split up, the general assumption was that Grimshaw was leaving for a rigorous pursuit of high-tech and that Farrell was staying behind to wrap himself in the indulgences of symbolic postmodernism. The reality is, of course, far more complex. Farrell's recollections, and the interviews with his teachers and contemporaries, throw a new light on one of Britain's best-known architects. They reveal how much of the spirit of that early partnership, including a lateral approach to project briefs and an insistence on flexible solutions and innovation, was kept alive by the ambitious, creative architect after his partner left.

Maurice McPartlan

After the interviews had been completed, a letter from Farrell's schoolteacher Maurice McPartlan came to light. Since McPartlan is no longer alive to interview, the letter seemed an appropriate document to include in this section. With typical modesty, McPartlan turns the tables and claims that the privilege of the teacher/ student relationship was all his: 'I feel that to my advantage was the fact that to a student who is talented and keen on the arts especially, their first specialist teacher in that subject is privileged, like the first real girl friend, never really to be forgotten.'

Dear Terry
It was a wonderful surprise to hear from you and to receive your Progress Report. I was aware at our last meeting that I was obviously missing out on something – i.e. your architectural activities up to then, and now I see why.

I really do congratulate you on your very great achievements and I trust that they will continue and prosper.

Your comments on the fly leaf are much appreciated even though I feel that to my advantage was the fact that, to a student who is talented and keen on the arts especially, their first specialist teacher in that subject is privileged, like the first real girl friend, never really to be forgotten.

I must remind you also that I found it always to be a two-way thing – the good student did much for the tutor.

Funnily enough, I rather took for granted your impressive, imaginative work at school and at college, (I remember well the Blackpool Scheme), but what impressed me most at that time was your housing venture. I think in Ryton – which both my wife and I thought showed a practicality that the other talented students didn't have.

Anyway, it's all very marvellous and we are very glad for you and your wife and family and as I have said, long may you continue to prosper.

I have now retired from education (last September) and am concentrating on achieving my life long ambition to do an honest painting or two. On my return

to education I suffered greatly from frustration as I became more and more embroiled in administration and the politics of Further and Higher Education. Pragmatism was ever the watchword and I am temperamentally unable to be pragmatic.

Anyway, that is all behind me and I am now up to my neck in painting. You have no idea how glorious it is to waken up in the morning and know that you can get on with the painting you left the night before. The effect on my work has been quite amazing, I am actually improving and can feel and see it. So much so that though I have been exhibiting with the Pastel Society and the R.I. on and off for ten years or so, I am leaving all that for a year or so and then I will give them a real go. At that stage I shall write and tell you – as a potential client/patron of course. The phrase will be that no good architect's office should be without a McPartlan or two.

Kindest regards, sincerely
Maurice

26 March 1985
35 Preston Road
North Shields
Tyne & Wear NE29 0ND

Harry Faulkner-Brown

The second teacher to have a particularly strong influence on Farrell was Harry Faulkner-Brown, his fifth-year tutor at Newcastle. Both McPartlan and Faulkner-Brown were strong leaders and inspirational teachers and, most importantly for Farrell, facilitators of his ambitious ideas. Faulkner-Brown's experience of practising in Canada and the USA was unusual in the university faculty, and not just because he had worked abroad. He had been involved in significant commercial projects, unlike his contemporaries, who had built very little. He showed students what was possible, filling them with enthusiasm and taking them to see buildings around the country. On learning of Farrell's interest in Buckminster Fuller, Faulkner-Brown introduced him to engineers to help him with his thesis, the Climatron – a high-tech holiday island connected to the base of Blackpool Tower.

The way architecture was taught at Durham University's King's College, which later became part of the University of Newcastle, was rather beaux arts. We had a very good professor called Edwards, who I liked very much, and who had worked in Lutyens's office. He was impressive, but on the whole the department revolved around teaching exercises in small developments. Everything was really quite traditional – the modern movement was only really starting to get going by the time I was teaching Terry. However, my experience of working in North America brought something new to the department, and it seemed to be of particular interest to Terry.

I had taken time out of architectural training during the war and on my return got a job with Howard Robertson and also lecturing at the AA. From there I went to work in Southsea, but I soon felt restricted by the work I was doing. Although there had been extensive bomb damage, the country was in a recession and all the work was limited specification. So, the idea came to follow my wife Maxine's family out to Toronto.

I worked for Mathers and Haldenby, a large practice involved in major projects. Mathers was the leading architect in Canada and I was given the job of resident architect on site for the building of the new headquarters for the Bank of Nova Scotia, in downtown

Toronto. Here I witnessed the use of more materials than I'd ever imagined, and I watched how the materials were being used and how they were installed. My knowledge of construction improved week by week and we ended up staying 12 years – nine years longer than we'd originally intended. I learned more in this short stay than I would have in a lifetime of practice in Newcastle.

When I returned to Newcastle the differences were even more glaring than I'd imagined. Toronto was booming but the UK was still in a desperate state. The faculty at Newcastle were the archetypal architects in bow ties doing small house extensions, but to be fair they really hadn't had the opportunities I'd had. I began practising on my own at home, and got a break with a small library in Newcastle, which gained an RIBA bronze medal and which was recently listed. But equally importantly, I began teaching the fifth year at the university.

It soon became apparent that my knowledge of building was quite different to that of my teaching colleagues. So I started giving lectures in building construction based on my experience – which was multi-storey buildings and mainly steel or reinforced-concrete structures. My lectures were on big buildings. I was able to talk about air-conditioning and double-glazing – concepts I'd never even heard of before my time in Canada, and this immediately attracted the students' attention.

I also distinctly remember introducing them to the world of Buckminster Fuller and his tensegrity structures, and Terry was particularly enamoured with this. Interestingly, two years after Terry graduated, I was on the RIBA gold medal jury and Fuller's name came up. Only two of us had heard of him – myself and Norman Foster. The others didn't know anything at all about him, that's how new he was to this country.

I used to set the students lots of sketch design exercises and I tried to get them to look at the wider context of their work. I realized to my horror that these students hadn't been looking at any buildings, not even at the buildings around them in Northumberland. I felt

desperate to remedy this and organized a trip to London to show them what the business of building was really like – how these structures were made to stand up, and what was involved in the design and construction of a building. I knew the contractor Higgs & Hill from my time building in Jamaica, and I took the students to Millbank Tower, which was a Higgs and Hill building nearing completion, and to the contractor's offices. We also went to the Barbican, and to Sandersons. I think it opened their eyes, and made them look beyond Newcastle.

I also remember they were set a measured drawing exercise. Terry had broken his leg and was unable to walk around a building, so chose to draw a Regency-style chair from a country house interior. I was very impressed by this, both because of the initiative he had shown, and the technique displayed in the resulting drawing.

When it came to choosing the subject for his final-year thesis, Terry decided that he would like to design something that would appeal to the people of Blackpool. He had been a barman there during the vacations and knew how the town operated behind the scenes. I had shown the students lots of slides about domes. I was very enthusiastic about leisure buildings, and he and I used to talk about the possibilities of building dome structures. In the end he came up with the Climatron. Not only did he construct a dome, to accommodate the unpredictable climate of Blackpool, but he also raised it on legs and put it in the sea! I worked very closely with Terry on his thesis, and we had a good lecturer in structural mechanics called Dennis Cooper, who had come up with an ingenious scheme for my circular library. Dennis and Terry and I talked about the structure of the Climatron at length. It was an excellent exercise in cooperation.

I recognized from the beginning that Terry was an exceptional student, the brightest in his year. He was intuitive and logical. He also had very good technique and artistic skills – and he was ambitious. I asked him to come and work with me after he graduated, but he was dead set on making it in London.

I've enjoyed watching Terry's successful career over the years, and we have kept in touch. He has always been full of creative ideas and brilliant solutions to each client's brief and their building's location. That's what determines his buildings' form. I remember he told me he got the concept for the egg-cups on the TVam building when he was on holiday in Venice, and he immediately phoned the client, Peter Jay, with this brilliant idea. He had been presented with a boiled egg in an egg cup at breakfast and he thought it was a perfect symbol. It's the sort of crazy thing that he does, but he can bring it off.

Denise Scott Brown

When Farrell arrived at the Graduate School of Fine Arts at the University of Pennsylvania, where he studied from 1962 to 1964, he was faced with a teacher of awesome notoriety, Louis Kahn. Farrell admired his design discipline and his constant question to his students: 'What does your building want to be?' But, unlike many of his contemporaries, Farrell's ideas differed from that of the guru, and he never became a Kahn groupie. Of more obvious influence on his work in urban design was another of his teachers there, Denise Scott Brown, partner and wife of Robert Venturi. Scott Brown and Venturi met in 1960 and set up Venturi Scott Brown and Associates in 1967. Through Scott Brown, Farrell met Venturi, who at that time was writing his seminal book Complexity and Contradictions in Architecture. *Both VSBA and Terry Farrell's work rejects categorization, embraces diversity and celebrates the ordinary. Here Scott Brown reflects on how her class informed Farrell's later work.*

Every year I was responsible for the introductory studio for the civic-design students and for a 'new city' studio for civic designers and planners. On the first day of the semester I'd look at these 16 people, and all I'd be sure of was that by its end I'd know them very well, sharing hopes and building camaraderie and passion. At first there was a big disappointment for the students; they thought they would be getting Louis Kahn, and they got me. I guess they thought, 'Who's

she? We're older than she is.' I responded by taking them to the first Kahn studio, during which Lou would sometimes demolish his students rather unkindly. And those civic-design students would think, 'We can wait a little while before we get into that.' That was how things started. They were a motley bunch from many different countries. I had to weld them into a group. Among them was this kid from England.

Farrell came from the same school of architecture as the Smithsons. My intellectual history includes the new brutalism and the England of the 1950s in which it developed. Growing up in South Africa I had always been aware that the dominant culture there was English. But the landscape around me didn't look like Surrey – and, though I lived in that landscape, I didn't read about it in books. That was an ongoing conflict and challenge for me. Then I discovered that in England, at that time, the equivalent conflict/challenge was about class. There was the life of the streets of London, then there was how middle-class architects thought people should live in the new towns; the way Londoners really lived and the way the planners were making them live. And here in my studio was this northerner from a working-class background but educated within an English middle-class architectural culture, who came to the United States and found himself in the midst of a social and civil rights revolution. It hit him more powerfully perhaps than the other students because it made explicit the conflict of cultures and classes he'd experienced at home. His eyes were opened by the social scientists and social planners at Penn. In classes on urban economics and sociology, I think particularly one by Chester Rapkin, he began to recognize his own situation and to understand that you could apply a class-based analysis to many things, to urbanism, to architecture, and to his life. This social-planning perspective is one he would never have found in an architectural school in England or elsewhere in America, and one that few of his classmates in architecture at Penn paid attention to.

As an architect with a foot in both camps, one of my roles was to help would-be urban designers like Terry learn from the social planners, to step into this scary, fascinating 'other' world that could make them better designers – but to see the ongoing revolution as an architect, not as a social scientist. The planners were anti-architecture; I felt young architects could, without help from me, come to believe there was no role for them professionally in the changes going on.

At Penn, the urban-design students were not given the opportunity to study with Bob Venturi because Holmes Perkins [head of the school] thought Bob's work and ideas had little to do with cities. He was wrong, but I got around the problem by inviting Bob back to the studio after we'd been on dates, and my students met him that way. He'd give crits in the studio simply because I asked him to, and many of the students were grateful for that.

The civic design (later urban design) programme was conducted jointly by Penn's urban-planning and architecture departments. Terry was first taught by me in the planning department. When he moved to architecture, I remember, he was a rebel. One studio was given by Holmes Perkins and another by Lou Kahn. Holmes Perkins's chosen project was interesting in the light of what happened later. It was to introduce arts and culture along Philadelphia's South Broad Street, to convert it into an avenue of the arts. And, of course, the name avenue of the arts has been taken up in the last decade, and there's now a large new regional performing arts centre [originally awarded to VSBA but subsequently designed by Rafael Viñoly] on Broad Street. What Terry did with that project was in line with what we said 30 years later – 'this is old Main Street, don't lose its character. And you don't have to build an outrageously expensive building to get something wonderful.' Anyway, Terry – who was by now immersed in social planning and the ideas of people like Paul Davidoff – advocated letting Broad Street merely be part of the surrounding lower-income neighbourhoods. He was probably wrong, but at the other extreme is something much too exaggeratedly monumental. Somewhere in between, Philadelphia could have had a wonderful, lively, multicultural main street, with a veneer of arts avenue applied to it where appropriate. Terry was much nearer to that than to what has resulted. I remember that studio profoundly.

Terry's reaction to Louis Kahn was fascinating. People in Kahn's studio jostled each other to get close to him, to be admired by him and have their future careers helped by him. In their designs they used Lou's

vocabulary. Terry didn't do that, and I fought Lou too when I took his studio. Yet Lou looked sceptically at the designs that followed his lead and contrasted them with Terry's. He told me he thought Terry's design was potentially more interesting. He had a kind of respect for Terry. In contrast, Holmes Perkins thought Terry was not a talented architect because of his refusal to build an avenue of the arts. He felt he wasn't going to be an architect. But Terry started to design and build before any of the others – as soon as he got back to England. I thought he was very bright and very able and talented, so I wasn't surprised.

You can more or less see when each of Kahn's former students took their studio with him by observing the point of departure of their own work. It corresponds to where Kahn was at that time. In Terry's case, his points of departure (and his continuing passion for urban planning) seem to derive from Penn's planning programme and my studios in the early 1960s. I taught that, although architects say form follows function, in urbanism – and to a large extent architecture – form is determined by forces within the economy and society. Look at a Zulu village and a transportation plan of London. You can see the first is a subsistence economy without trade and trade routes, and the second has to do with exchange and communication worldwide. You can perceive these conditions in the plans and respond to them in the design  of buildings. Although Terry's studio with me predated our research in Las Vegas, I was deeply involved then with studies in popular culture and roadside architecture in Philadelphia. I was trying, as well, to link the Smithsons' 'active socioplastics', in London, to social planning as it was evolving in the United States. Terry saw this and he read *Learning from Las Vegas*, but his reactions to it were mediated by the nature of his practice and its base in England. The divergences between our work can perhaps be traced to our different locations and subsequent histories.

Terry, as a student, made the most of being in America. There were English people who scorned it all. They could live in Philadelphia, they averred, only because the English Speaking Union and cricket on Fairmount Park were available. By contrast, people like Terry bought an old car and went travelling, entering into the spirit of what they saw and learning from it. Ironically, the ones who couldn't stand it stayed, and the ones who entered into the spirit went home.

Terry worked hard and took much from his time in America. This was to his advantage when he returned to England as one of the few young architects who, through his training, had experienced quite profoundly the swirling political, social and artistic worlds of America in the 1960s.

Ron Sidell

Ron Siddell joined the Farrell/Grimshaw Partnership in 1968. His university friend and future partner, Paul Gibson, was already working there. The Siddell Gibson Partnership was formed in 1973. Siddell's overriding memory of working for FGP is the ability Farrell had to resolve practical issues. He was 'skilful at manipulating the building, getting more out of less' and always found the right words when meeting clients. 'He was entrepreneurial right across the board; one of the first of a generation of architects to work as a skilled designer and demonstrate commercial value through design.'

When I joined Farrell/Grimshaw, the offices were in Windmill Street, and I was asked to work on their first project, the international students' hostel. Paul was working on the Park Road flats. I remember thinking that they [Farrell and Grimshaw] had a personal and business partnership that was first class. It was

complementary, the whole was greater than the sum of the parts, and there was a great feeling of camaraderie. Nick's focus was engineering and innovation. Terry's interests were more expansive, covering a wider range of issues. His work was more contextual and perhaps the more entrepreneurial of the two.

Terry's signature is a difficult one to determine. It embraces a broad vocabulary and behind it all is a sense of making things, of really building. He was always good at resolving practical issues. I remember he would sit in meetings, drawing out charts or timetables in order to resolve issues with contractors. He was skilful at manipulating the building – getting more out of less – and he had an acute commercial awareness. He was always good at working with the clients. Watching him work like that made me realize that architects really ought to have that gumption. Commercially, at that time, architects were a pretty poor bunch. Terry had great creativity, but at the same time he knew how to speak the client's language.

Terry always had an eye for the bigger picture, which was beyond the threshold of the buildings themselves. He understood three-dimensional planning and had a good skill at visualizing, in the same way perhaps as an artist. He was, and is, a master at reinventing buildings and always enjoyed working with clients who were stuck with a problematic site.

I never understood what drove the partnership apart. I thought it was highly balanced and complementary, but I suppose inevitably there were stylistic differences. I didn't think that either would be more or less successful than the other, I just assumed they'd plot their own courses, which of course they have done. The buildings they are both designing now I like to think are what they would have done together, had they stayed partners.

I enjoyed my time at Farrell/Grimshaw and we've had four or five reunions since the early 1970s. Terry was always a hugely generous patron of young architects – almost paternalistic. I hope he's proud of that. He was entrepreneurial right across the board; one of the first of a generation of architects to work as a skilled designer and show commercial value through design.

Tom Jestico

The members of another well-known partnership, Tom Jestico and John Whiles, worked for the Farrell/ Grimshaw Partnership in the early years. Jestico + Whiles was formed in 1979, and Jestico also met his wife Vivien Fowler at the practice. 'There was no such thing as freezing the design with Terry. The project monopolized us and we were expected to give it our all.'

I joined the Farrell/Grimshaw Partnership after working at YRM. I'd seen the students' hostel in magazines, and a friend suggested I apply to work there. I had lunch with Nick and Terry at the new kebab house near their office in Windmill Street, and I clearly remember the circular menus which they had designed for the restaurant, and which kept falling off the table! We agreed that I would resign from YRM and come and work for FGP, but on the day I left I had a call from Nick (or Terry?) explaining that there wasn't enough work in the office and that they couldn't honour the agreement.

So I went to work for Castlepark Dean and Hook for 18 months, after which the Farrell/Grimshaw door reopened; in 1973 I joined the team working on the Colonnades for Samuel Properties. I remember Terry using felt-tip pen to produce conceptual sketches in 2D and 3D, concentrating on reducing the space standards to a minimum. He was unusually skilled at squeezing everything in. The layering of a mixed-use development was innovative in itself, and the patio housing on top of the commercial and retail elements was totally new. The client was exceptionally tough, but there was one character, Michael Burman, who was keen to push the design side of the project and that helped. When the costs escalated, it always fell to me to call the finance director with the news, and he was rather less accommodating. But despite the increased cost the client always got more architecture for their money.

There was no such thing as freezing the design with Terry. The project monopolized us and we were expected to give it our all. He was also commercially astute, and I guess that's why FGP got the job despite the partners' youth and lack of experience. Both Terry and Nick were opportunistic and quite happy to cold-call clients. Terry was probably more pushy and persistent than Nick.

When the Colonnades project was finished in 1976, I spent about a year shuffling papers and waiting for work. I remember a meeting with the partners and associates (of which I was one) where Terry and Nick announced that we had a £30,000 overdraft. On what could have been a depressing, solemn occasion we got very drunk and swore that we would stick together like the Knights of the Round Table. There was a great spirit of camaraderie, but sadly the business had to come first and our drunken promises came to nothing. Two weeks later I was made redundant.

I arrived at work to find a white envelope on my desk. Terry's response when I marched into his office and demanded an explanation has stayed with me ever since, and I've probably used it once or twice myself. He said, 'That's just typical of you. I knew you of all people would react like this. Can't you see you're being given a creative opportunity?' Which of course I was, but it didn't seem like it at the time.

I learned a lot from my time with Terry. It was a practice in which you very much worked for one partner, and, much as I would have liked to work with Nick too, I never did. They had the ingredients for a perfect collaborative partnership, with Nick's technical innovation, Terry's skills as an urban designer and his commercial instinct. But they just didn't feed off each other.

Terry's wife, Sue, was an influence on the practice. She was always running counter to prevalent architectural fashion, introducing sofas with Mae West lips, and kitsch elements everywhere. She and Terry had very eclectic taste, and it was reflected in their flat at Park Road, where I spent many happy evenings with several bottles of wine, and their parrot.

Charles Jencks

The architect and writer Charles Jencks has been both client and critic of Farrell's work. He coined the term postmodernism and was a great influence on Farrell throughout the 1970s. He commissioned him to work on the house in which he still lives, in Holland Park, and introduced him to Jacob Rothschild, the owner of Clifton Nurseries. 'The fact that he is eclectic is a position in itself, and he sees that as a kind of critique of the purism and rigidity of the British architects who doggedly refuse to move ahead or anywhere at all.'

I remember inviting Terry and Nick Grimshaw to speak at the AA in the early 1970s, when I was teaching there. It was possible to guess where they were diverging. Nick was focusing on high-tech, advocating the flexibility and modest cost of his buildings and their industrial components, which, he boasted, could even be brought in by hand. He contrasted this with Foster's and Rogers's use of heavier, less flexible elements. Terry, however, was committed to the client and to rehabilitation of a pragmatic kind — making one thing work for another thing, the double-functioning element, the shrewdness of the bricoleur.

Although he was not a postmodernist at that time, his work married the past to the present and incorporated a future technology. While he used advanced technology, he did not make a fetish of it; a position described as 'expedient tech'. The way he used the past urban fabric as a resource was ingenious, and when it came to collaborating on our house he was creative in figuring out how you could shoe-horn activities into the basement, the roof or an old stairway, where no one else would have thought there was room. He did that with his own house in Ashworth Road too. He is a canny rehabilitator and social realist, something that relates him, philosophically, to the work of Jane Jacobs and Robert Venturi. So, in a way, you could say that he was an incipient postmodernist.

In 1978 Maggie Keswick and I bought a 19th-century house in Holland Park and for five months worked with an architect, Michael Fisher, to carry out our designs. His office, however, was too small to handle the job, so after this we went to Terry and he said he would be delighted to work with us. At the beginning, we would have a three-way design session — a real collaboration. I also invited a group of artists and architects to work on it with us — Eduardo Paolozzi and Allen Jones, among others, and the designers Michael Graves, Piers Gough, Jeremy Dixon and Rem Koolhaas. It was a time when the latter three were underemployed. The idea was to create synergetic collaboration out of a common symbolic programme. I would give the architects and artists an iconographic and functional programme

and tell them that they did not have to carry it out in detail, but should see it as a challenge for their design, ornament and expression — the freer and more artistic aspects of their work. This, I hoped, would become a symbolic architecture rather than the 'signolic' architecture of Robert Venturi, the 'shed' with signs stuck all over it. *The Thematic House* was a polemic against such signolic architecture, a dissociated approach that, in the late 1970s and early 1980s, was threatening to overwhelm postmodernism

Terry provided the back-up, the nuts and bolts, continuity, and also some of the design and technological expertise. I knew that I would enjoy working with him when I saw some of his early housing and heard him talking about 'housing as a resource'. The postmodern tradition at that time was that you should not tear down a piece of existing urbanism, you transform it — an idea of his as well. I thought we would complement each other because I assumed that he and Grimshaw would bring a technical expertise, that they were more of a team than they turned out to be. Perhaps this house came between them? If so, it is a pity, because I have always respected and liked Nick and Lavinia. But I imagine the problems were also ideological. Nick had something of an engineering ethos that sees the will to form as a corrupting influence and the will to style as wrong-headed. He probably did not have much truck with symbolism either, so I can imagine that *The Thematic House* was anathema to him. But I think that, in addition to style and ideology, there was a third reason why the pair split, and that was the inevitable problem of two strong, individual designers sharing a single stable. You find this with Bernini and Borromini, or Foster and Rogers.

Architectural Design became a centre for the dissemination of British postmodernism, which was more or less hated by the old guard. We had meetings in our London home with Jeremy Dixon, John Outram, Piers Gough and Terry. There were others on the edge like Leon Krier, who influenced Terry a great deal in terms of urbanism and architecture. Leon draws like an angel, and thinks about the city in a radical way through his drawings. This led to a seductive form of architecture and urbanism. Michael Graves, Krier, Venturi and others forged the postmodern classical style, and the formation of Graves was then taken up by Terry in this country. In that sense, and given his training in the States, you could say that Terry was at this time an American postmodernist.

Terry is good at being influenced and influencing. One of his strengths is to organize consent, to participate with all sorts of different people. That is his social skill as an urbanist. While most other architects are inwardly focused and cannot see how social resources can be brought together and empowered, he is a natural synergizer. Furthermore, he has a gift of bringing out other people's creativity, whether it is artistic, financial, social or conceptual. In his urbanist schemes, such as Charing Cross, he talks to a wide range of people and gets their cooperation and expertise. He's an entrepreneur, a doer, but his creativity is not manipulative. He puts people together and makes them work, and that's a great quality to have, especially among British architects. That makes his urbanism, like the Jane Jacobs ideal of a mixed economy, a hybrid and complex structure of diversity. The city, after all, is a synergetic conjunction of difference. I think it is fair to say Terry does not wrestle with architecture as a formal language, nor attempt to be a form-giver. He is happy as a pluralist to follow changing conventions of classicism or abstraction. He was a postmodernist for seven years, a classicist for two years, and today he's switched to an 'International Modern – Not – Minimalism'. In that sense, he follows the temperature of the times rather than turning up the heat.

Terry's genius is social organization and making the city work. I suppose the fact that he is eclectic is a position in itself, and he sees that as a kind of critique of the purism and the rigidity of architects who doggedly refuse to move ahead. He is not ideological, except when it comes to urbanism, and there I would say lies his greatest commitment. Perhaps one should compare him with John Nash, also an eclectic and an urbanist who changed London. It is the big picture of cities that interests him and Richard Rogers, and if the powers that be could exploit these

two together the city would be a much more convivial and richly linked environment than it is today.

Robert Maxwell

In his essay 'A Creative Dialogue: Contemporary British Architecture and the Urban Environment' from the catalogue for the New Urban Environments exhibition in 1998, critic and architect Robert Maxwell referred to Terry Farrell's 'highly personal blend of technological and semiological aspects'. He described the work featured in the exhibition as 'a solid sequence of high-tech designing from Farrell through Foster and Future Systems, to Grimshaw and, after a gap, to Hopkins and finally Rogers. In this sequence, Farrell is something of an exception: he started out as a partner with Grimshaw, but has diverted somewhat by way of an interest in symbolic form and city context. He can, however, summon up the high-tech look whenever he thinks it appropriate. The others all espouse the hands-on approach that asks the question "How does it work?" before the question "How does it look?"'

The way I saw Nick and Terry in the 1970s was a bit like the jazz partnership of Ken Collyer and Chris Barber. Collyer was intuitional, more in line with the New Orleans school; Barber was more organized and liked his music arranged. He was more influenced by the Chicago school. There's a degree of freedom in Terry's work, and he's shown that he can do high-tech, but not to the exclusion of all else. Nick has always been more referential, even Ruskinian, in his attitude towards high-tech and the use of industrial components.

James Stirling, who like Farrell could do high-tech but never designed a completely high-tech building, expanded the possibilities of placing British architects. Terry is in that expanded envelope and has a good chance of expanding it further. He's not as constrained as some of his contemporaries.

Terry's postmodern work is better than most other postmodern architecture, which really tends to be rather superficial. I don't regard the relevant issue as being a choice of style, of postmodernism versus high-tech. The important issue is the creation of new ideas and quality. Let's have a mixture.

Terry has always considered architecture from several angles. He is concerned about function, but not to the extent of adopting the dogma of form following function. His buildings are all pretty formal, but varied. He can be surprising and good in unexpected ways. High-tech, in contrast, can be very canonic. Secondly, he has an appreciation of the scale of the city and the interrelation of the buildings within it. He's always been good with structural plans. Finally, he puts buildings and spaces together so they share the ground.

Terry has always liked the big gesture, but he also looks at art and at the other surrounding buildings. Cities are heterogeneous. They should never be designed by one architect, but should express different periods and styles and events, like a living museum. Terry embraces that. He knows how to expand the envelope of thinking and still exercise taste and quality. Others are afraid and want to be more prescriptive, to produce designs that will guarantee a critical 'yes'.

Peter Murray

Peter Murray worked on several architectural publications during and after the Farrell/Grimshaw years. He published the students' hostel in Clip-Kit *and a selection of the practice's work in* Architectural Design *in 1973. Farrell introduced Murray to his future wife, Jane Wood, following the Folkestone conference, IDEA, in 1967. 'There's no doubt that Charles Jencks was the biggest thing that happened to Terry [in the 1970s], and I wonder whether he might have gone down a slightly different route without him . . . . Terry has one of the best analytical minds in terms of the planning and organization of buildings and the building process.'*

Clip-Kit, as the name suggests, was named after the plastic clips which held together the six monthly instalments of our student magazine. I launched it with Geoffrey Smyth, a fellow student at the AA, who later went to work for Farrell/Grimshaw and was the project architect on the Paddington Street office along with Vivien Fowler, who is now married to Tom Jestico. Our mentor was Cedric Price. He gave us lots of his time, providing we'd made an appointment. If you didn't have an appointment he wouldn't see you on principle.

Clip-Kit was a students' attempt at an Archigram-style magazine. Peter Cook and Warren Chalk were my tutors in the fifth year at the AA, and despite being totally in awe of Archigram's ideas we rather arrogantly thought there were some things we could do better. Archigram was very much about imagery and little to do with how things worked, we thought. We aimed to publish ways in which this new world might actually be built, and we included everything from inflatables and car-manufacturing components through to technology borrowed from NASA. Cedric was a contributor, as were Michael Webb of Archigram and Reyner Banham.

One of the buildings we published was Nick and Terry's students' hostel. We were particularly interested in the bathroom pods and the flexible furniture units – the whole Eamesian idea of off-the-shelf components, plastic trays and made-up frames that was current at the time. The pods were an extension of work by Arthur Quarmby at ICI, who'd produced a capsule bathroom in the mid 1960s, moulded out of two pieces of Perspex. But that was just for exhibition purposes, and the hostel was the first time it had been done properly.

Terry introduced me to my wife at around the time of the Folkestone conference, IDEA, in 1967. IDEA was a seminal event. It was put together by Peter Cook and the Archigram team, and brought together a range of architects and designers in Europe who were interested in the world of mega structures, where whole linear cities could run from Edinburgh to Milan. Again Cedric was a major figure in this.

Nova magazine, which was the trendy woman's magazine of the day, was going to do a big feature on contemporary architecture, and part of that was on IDEA. One of their journalists, Jane Wood, had been to interview Terry about his work, and he said that if she wanted to know about the student scene she should speak to Peter Murray. Terry rang me in my flat in St John's Wood and asked me to come over and meet this journalist, so I dashed over. The piece never appeared, but it led to me taking over as *Nova*'s design and architecture correspondent for a year or so, instead of doing my thesis, and ultimately to marrying Jane.

When I moved to *Architectural Design* under the editorship of Monica Pigeon, we published the Park Road tower. It was a total disaster because we had the order of the text muddled up (in those days we pasted text down by hand) and Monica insisted that we stuck an addendum in every copy to cover it up. It was at a time when the finances of the magazine had taken a dive (despite a 15,000 circulation) and we'd had to move to an offset-litho printer instead of the more expensive letterpress. On top of that, the recycled paper we used was poor quality and soaked up the ink.

My interest was moving away from architectural style, and more towards recycling, environmental issues and urban change. These were clearly issues that needed to be addressed nationally, during a time of increased oil prices. People like Gerry Foley at the AA were looking at wind power, solar power and other environmental solutions, which were regarded as very wacky at the time.

I saw Terry and Nick as a successful partnership, both speaking the same architectural language. I interviewed the two of them for *Building Design* in 1972. The piece was headlined 'The men most likely to . . .' In it Terry complained of architects thinking that 'innovation has to be a visual thing'. And much of the piece was taken up with a discussion of how the compact core of the Park Road flats allowed an extra 4 feet on the perimeter for no extra cost.

Farrell/Grimshaw at the time were moving towards prefabrication and high-tech architecture, for which the Rotork Controls factory in Bath really set the tone: a panelled, flexible, prefabricated product more than a building. What disappointed me was that in subsequent buildings, like Herman Miller and Warrington, the same principles were being used but the buildings were being entirely redesigned. There was a real requirement at that stage for high quality prefabricated buildings and I didn't see them doing this.

As soon as Terry started working with Charles Jencks he became more vociferously postmodern. I think Clifton Nurseries marked a big shift in approach. There's no doubt that Jencks was the biggest thing that happened to Terry at that time, and I wonder whether Terry might have gone down a slightly different route without him.

The way in which Terry Farrell & Partners is changing today suggests that Terry is searching again for an architecture with which he is comfortable. He has one of the best analytical minds in terms of the planning and organization of buildings and the building process. TVam had a very articulate plan, and the end result could have been in a whole range of styles or appearances. The fact that it's got knobs on is not relevant to the fundamental aspect of its planning. As Terry said to me in 1972, 'Innovative building looks no different from ordinary building.'

Martin Pawley

We conclude with an extract rather than an interview. Martin Pawley has known Terry Farrell since the start of the architect's career. When he was editor of World Architecture, *he commissioned 'Lightweight Classic: Terry Farrell's Covent Garden nursery building' for the World Masterpiece series (published in 1993). The following is an extract from Pawley's introduction. Pawley dubbed the nursery 'The Barcelona Pavilion of post-Modernism' and was absolutely right when he predicted that it 'will be remembered long after it is demolished'.*

The Covent Garden Clifton Nurseries building has fascinated me ever since I first went inside it at the Press opening in December 1981. I think the reason is that, just as some human beings achieve greatness in proportion to the astonishing number of contradictions they can embody, so can a piece of architecture attain greatness in the same way. And in this building is a bundle of contradictions without parallel. At the lowest level it is a temporary building on a glamorous site that is already five years past its sell by date. Beyond that it is a cheap building that was designed for a wealthy and fastidious client. Then it is a Classical design drawn up by an architect who knew (at that time) nothing about classicism, and a building erected in a place where not only does every vista end in a Classical façade, but in the Classical façades of historically important buildings. Beyond that it is a design in the shape of a Tuscan Temple that was erected where there is really only room for half of one. Furthermore it is a Tuscan Temple made out of steel, glass and Teflon-coated glassfibre fixed in place with technology borrowed from racing yachts: a step toward the concept of a high-tech classicism that has been talked about by architects for a decade, but so far only really been exploited by this one architect in this one building. Terry Farrell has no difficulty coming to terms with the axial planning principles of ancient Rome while masking a car park. He can achieve the effect of Doric colonnade and entablature by means of ticky-tacky, glassfibre, skeletal steel bars, acrylic capitals and a frieze of living plants. He is the only architect who could ever have conceived of it.

From the beginning this little building with its jumble of elements was touched by a kind of omnivorous, untrammelled genius. Everything about it, from its client's original idea, to its architect's wild and ingenious design, to its innovative light-structures engineering by the late Peter Rice, to its first tenant's verdant display of energy and enterprise, all of it was pure magic. And when you analyse that magic, most of it consists in making something out of nothing, which was the once and future genius of Terry Farrell – as visible in the conception of the giant Alban Gate, built in thin air over London Wall, as it was 10 years earlier on that tiny site in Covent Garden. Notwithstanding such spectacular later commissions, and perverse as it may sound, Clifton Nurseries Covent Garden will be remembered long after it is demolished. In 1981, with some trepidation, I dubbed it 'The Barcelona Pavilion of post-Modernism'. Today I would not even be surprised if, like that illustrious predecessor, it did not go down once only to rise again in replica.

Martin Pawley, December 1992

Conclusion: Reappraising Farrell

by Kester Rattenbury

The first edition of *Clip-Kit* must be something of a collector's item. Inside a very hip cover is a collection of A4 photocopies: pods and vehicles; a fold-out Sant'Elia manifesto; a fold-out poster for an Archigram 'thing' at Folkestone – and right at the back, but right in style, the service capsule tower which launched Farrell/ Grimshaw Partnership to fame

Among the multitude of labels that have been variously and spiritedly applied to the resolutely pigeonhole-resistant Terry Farrell, I don't imagine many people have dubbed him a quintessential product of the 1960s and 1970s. Yet going through the early work – up to and beyond his split with Nicholas Grimshaw – opens a long-needed reinterpretation of Farrell's hotly debated career, with its wildly swinging and often bemused critical reception.

For a while, especially in the 1980s and 1990s, Farrell's career was portrayed as a series of baffling, almost treacherous recantations: high-tech turned postmodernist; community and conservation hero turned developers' promoter. In the late 1990s, we thought he had changed again: international big-scale commercial architect turned sensitive urbanist; postmodernist turned abstract expressionist. Every time it happened we were puzzled – and, largely, wrong. Looking at Farrell's career from the other end of the telescope suggests that this view (partly a product of the tiny, self-referential world of architectural criticism) – misses the point completely. Farrell has been many things, yet in many ways he has been the most consistent of all his generation.

The 1960s in Britain could have gone a number of ways – and, in fact, they did just that. Against the background of uniform state modernism, architectural ideas were exploding into extraordinary technical and production advances, into new thought and forms and movements. At its best, the boom in technology fused with radical free thought: an explosion which took many channels and which continues to dominate British architecture 40 years on. Its great experimenters, Archigram and Cedric Price, remained Britain's most influential radical architectural thinkers. Its crown princes, Foster and Rogers, led a whole new movement into the high-tech architecture which came to dominate the British contemporary mainstream.

But the creative boom of the 1960s and 1970s was followed almost immediately by psychological collapse. Hit from all sides by the oil crisis, the economic recession and the failure of public housing projects,

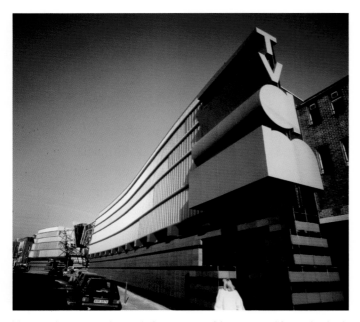

the architectural world's sense of heroic self-imploded. The idea of a modernist mainstream – already under challenge – collapsed. Architecture split into diverse, guerrilla factions, expanding from, or reacting against, uniform modernism. The state mainstream softened into the contextual, stratified modernism of the last massive low-rise housing and civic schemes, before running out of civic funds and into the wall of privatization and disaffection. In reaction or diversion, supporters of contextual modernism, neoclassicism, community architecture, new-fogeyism, eco-architecture, neovernacular, romantic pragmatism, conservation and postmodernism sprang to arms, hiding out in the hills, forming factions and fighting bitterly among themselves.

Farrell's path through this era – both advertised and unadvertised – is instructive. At first, Farrell/Grimshaw were a leading part of the mainstream of young radical thought. The Sussex Gardens student housing with its pod-bathroom tower in Paddington, and the Park Road co-ownership flats overlooking Regent's Park (1970), an aluminium-clad flexible-plan tower, were leading innovative projects of their time: probably the first true clip-on-pod servicing and the first true 'core' building respectively. And there were many other classic funk-age projects: Rotork Controls, flexible housing, fun-factory systems. When Farrell and Grimshaw painfully split, it was deemed to be a simple style issue, with Grimshaw digging in to high-tech – a definition which has never really been called into question – and Farrell moving out into symbolic postmodernism.

Farrell's direction was at first a popular hit. Heretically (but in line with the spirit of the time), he reclad the Herman Miller perfect office system, which he used to share with Grimshaw, with ziggurats, columns and a 'beach'. His entertaining postmodernist TVam with its egg-cup finials and neon keystone was well received, and set up Camden Town as the battleground for the new style wars – Grimshaw's high-tech Sainsbury's and housing was built just down the canal. As architects re-evaluated their relationship with the public – following the Prince of Wales's attack on them at the RIBA's 150th anniversary – Farrell seemed to have judged it just right. Best of all were his Clifton Nurseries projects, which seemed an ideal overlap of user-friendliness with pop-on, pop-age construction. The *RIBA Journal* called it 'technical thinking with a friendly face' (October 1980). Steven Games said, 'Terry Farrell has invented a new kind of building

and the architectural world is enthralled' (*Guardian*, 23 August). It signalled, briefly, that architecture could mend the schism of popular taste and architectural experimentation in loved-by-all temporary structures.

The redevelopment of the Comyn Ching triangle in Covent Garden in 1976 was a different sort of revolution and attracted a different sort of fan. Farrell

1981–83
Left: Television centre for TVam, London. Part radical refurbishment, partly collaged new elements that created a memorable on- and off-screen visual identity, and part regeneration of a run-down area of Camden Town, north London.

1978–85
Above: Comyn Ching, London. An island block in Covent Garden with a courtyard in the centre; new corner towers were combined with converted historic terraces in a mixed-use development.

has always been a strong advocate of the reuse of existing buildings for new purposes. Comyn Ching was ground-breaking – a residential and mixed-use scheme, militating for a balanced development which converted and retained as many existing buildings as possible, supported the existing community activity – and built only as much new development as would make the project commercially viable. It countered the idea of untrammelled, exploitative, as-much-as-you-can-get-away-with commercial development, which was just getting into its stride.

Comyn Ching made Farrell the hero of the community and conservation movements. He became the great alternative architect – designing the community-based alternative to the Mansion House scheme, retaining many of the listed buildings and demonstrating that community-based developments with reuse of existing buildings could be commercially and architecturally viable. These alternative proposals were a role for which he was ideally suited, because of his way of thinking laterally round a project. But, for Farrell, they were specific projects with specific, individual conditions. So, when the big 1980s office blocks were built, his fans were shocked beyond measure. In the UK in particular, early postmodernism had seemed a way to bridge the divide between popular and architectural taste – a language available to both sides, and particularly proper to the community project. Here it was seen to be a weapon which Farrell had handed to the developers – for them to use against the sensitive nascent relationship between architect and community project.

In fact, Farrell was unusual in having never been against developers. In early interviews, both Farrell and Grimshaw are quoted on this matter, seeing developers as potentially positive in a way that was not really to become architecturally acceptable until the late 1990s. Moreover, Farrell did only three big office buildings in this era – while other darlings of the architectural left built massive, largely unpublicized commercial developments. This was perhaps the point. It was the ethics of luxuriating in big-spend commerce for which we deemed him beyond the pale.

If Farrell was seen as a traitor, his treachery was to factions to which he had never signed up – in faction fights which he indeed deliberately eschewed. Every

project had different needs, offered different possibilities and required its own particular strategy; no available approach was ruled out. Looking at the earlier work, and the earlier interviews, this becomes clear. Farrell has always taken a broad, responsive approach to specific conditions – in style, approach and ethos – and he has always said as much. His strong liking for style (a weakness, Colin Amery once called it) has confused us critics into thinking he means the same thing by it as we do. Those engaged in the puzzled reappraisal of Farrell which has been tentatively going on in the first years of the new century – partly in response to the mass of his major new buildings which have a contemporary expressionist style (and which would, one cannot help thinking, be getting a great deal more publicity if they were by unknown architects) – have something to learn from his early work.

Returning to his early work – and his early claims about his work, both with and without Grimshaw – is salutary.

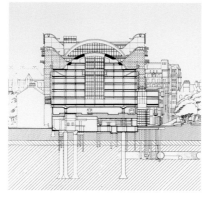

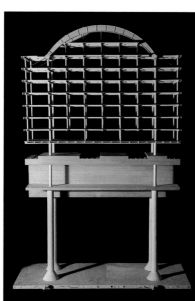

1987–90

Above and right: Embankment Place/ Charing Cross station, London. A new building set within an urban-regeneration project. Like the Climatron, this is an heroic-scaled suspension structure (see model above). The building has become a well-known Thameside landmark, particularly when illuminated at night.

For one thing, all the issues that later took commentators by surprise were there right from the start. Notable is his urbanism, which he studied in detail as a graduate student in Pennsylvania and in Japan, and during his work as architect–planner in Camden, New Jersey, in the 1960s – and which has figured in appropriate projects ever since. Farrell's early projects are extraordinarily catholic – far more so than accepted history allows. From the start, they feature cutting-edge technology alongside conservation, reuse and sometimes intricate, sometimes simple urban proposals. They include work for a range of clients – often new types of client – from the collaborative to the commercial, and from the most ephemeral groupings (protest groups) to the most institutional (big, secretive government departments). And, by Farrell's own lights, that is just the way it should be. Then there is – right from the word go – an extraordinary range of architectural styles and architectural thinking. In the early interviews, both Farrell and Grimshaw assert as being central to their ethos the maxim 'light on our feet and keep flexible'. Their approach was intended to be broad church, unrestrictive, inclusive – each approach specific to its conditions.

Looking at this body of work from the other end of the time tunnel gives you a much clearer idea of why Farrell does not fit the categories into which we writers have resolutely tried to put on him. At this early period, the massive range of architectural movements in which

Farrell's work would sometimes appear – high-tech, new-tech, postmodernist, community, façadism, commercial, urbanism, expressionism – had not split into factions; and presumably, for Farrell, they never would. That this was not recognized was the start of the misapprehension, which persisted not least because his extraordinarily diverse range of work is so unevenly known – and some parts are much more media-friendly (not necessarily the same as better) than others.

Farrell/Grimshaw's first project – Sussex Gardens – is a case in point. This was the conversion of a row of six run-down Victorian houses into a Church hostel for 200 overseas students. To maximize space, staircases, services and corridors were entirely stripped out, with mezzanine shared dormitories in the grand front rooms, apsidal single rooms in the former stairwells of the Victorian spaces, and so on. To provide flexibility in the varied spaces there was no fitted furniture. Each student had a furniture trolley and loose components – bed on wheels, chair, table, rolling storage unit and desk – another classic funk-rm proage, free-foject. The new stairs and bathrooms were grouped in the new, external service pod tower – a central mast with a spiral of prefabricated bathroom pods wrapped around it.

Inevitably, the service tower got all the publicity. Indeed, *Clip-Kit* magazine published the capsule tower exclusively. This was 1968: Sussex Gardens was an inside-out building – eight years before the Pompidou Centre and 18 before Lloyds. It was the first built example of the hot new ideas of prefabrication, variability and mass production creating new living forms, of which larger speculations filled the pages of *Clip-Kit*. The integration of space, services and the free-plan furniture was essential – but much less immediately eye-catching on the news front. It was Grimshaw who had got the job, as an unqualified architect, and is often given all the credit for the tower, but the project was a joint one. The

Left: MI6 headquarters, Vauxhall Cross, London; part of a larger-scale masterplan and new river walk. 'Placemaking' here on the neglected post-industrial south bank was the first priority, but 'facemaking' ensured an unforgettable iconic identity for a building that has become more familiar – thanks to international controversies as well as James Bond movies – than any other building Terry Farrell has designed.

1989–95
Above: Conference centre and masterplan, Edinburgh. Part urban renewal of the site of an old railway goods yard and part new public building whose entrance pavilion has a distinctive fabric canopy.

1991–98

Above and right: Hong Kong. Several projects were completed in Hong Kong in the 1990s, including the harbour-level tunnel ventilation building (above, foreground); the Peak Tower (above, hilltop background), a hilltop visitor attraction accessible by funicular railway; the new British Consulate and British Council headquarters, and a vast new urban district in Kowloon based on and around a new railway station (right: compare this cross-section with student 'Doodle' top right, p196).

1996–99

Below: The Dean Gallery, Edinburgh. A layered adaptation that delights in transformation and spatial interplay, like Terry Farrell's houses and the earlier Sussex Gardens conversion.

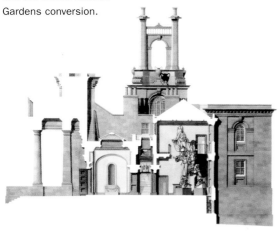

simplification of this complex project to its big headline component could well have been the start of a misplacement of Farrell.

FGP continued to produce a flood of projects which fitted the high-tech headline — Rotork Controls in 1973 with its principles of expansion, flexibility and just-in-time construction, for example, or the Island Record recording studio in a van. Yet, alongside this theme, diverging from it in all directions — and at first undifferentiated by an architectural press that had not yet slid into the 1980s style and ethics wars — there was a much broader and more diverse stream of work.

Notably unknown among the very early work is the quietly massive Colonnades at Porchester Square (1971) — Farrell's project, and one which occupied most of his time as one of the largest projects in the office. This is far from FGP's headline work. It is shown in the architectural press of the time as a late modern integrated civic and housing scheme. And, indeed, its raised plaza and its elegant proportions seem to place it in the clear tradition of complex, late-modern urban housing projects: modulating space, access, facilities and privacy within a modest if substantial urban format. The scheme is also complex (including an integrated refurbishment of existing Victorian houses on a tight site) compositionally, stylistically and in its urban form. Nor was it alone in exploring those areas.

Other housing schemes moved in still different directions. Some were timber-framed 'systems' with a range of

different 'local' claddings which themselves seem to place the buildings in different architectural genres. Some are plain and elegant, soft modern schemes, clad with tiles or bricks. The add–on 'face' balconies place others in the postmodernist pen. Some look like Ed Cullinan. Some exhibit sensitive modern regionalism with a touch of early Venturi. One version (illustrated by Andrew Holmes)

shows half-timber and stone cladding — somewhere between Suburban Sets, Segal and the dead-normal. None of this fits the various pigeon-holes into which Farrell's early work was put, but it is very much of its time and part of a consistent flexibility of approach. The lateral thought is always manifest. Sounding like Cedric Price, Farrell is quoted saying of architects: 'When asked to design an airport, he should be in a position that what's really needed is a better taxi rank at the American embassy.' It is a way of approaching design which dominates the descriptions of the early work.

There is a notable consistency of innovation. Apart from a good crop of firsts (first capsule building; first real core building; first pop-on building construction), almost every project demonstrated the application of new thinking to new technology. FGP, and Farrell particularly, were years, sometimes decades, ahead of the game. Farrell identified building-energy-conservation issues as being hugely significant in 1973. He was always proactive in promoting the reuse of buildings. He suggested that developers were frequently better than local authorities in the 1960s – 30 years before most architects came to agree. He emerged – briefly – as a figurehead for the growing conservation movement. He saw big office buildings as opportunities for conducting experiments in style in the 1980s, when that approach was generally regarded as being beyond the pale. He was big in China a good decade before Koolhaas – though in a different way. He suggested using redundant offices for housing in 1976 – 30 years before the lofts boom.

You could say that Farrell is something of a chameleon: he takes up and projects his background conditions in his own idiosyncratic way. This is a form of strong, individual thought. Sometimes he has anticipated things which proved to be unpopular. If his eclectic passage through his times was seen as treacherous, this was surely at least in part because he produced ground-breaking projects in many divergent areas which, for everyone else, were to be bitterly hostile territories for decades. Farrell didn't play by team rules – and, again, he anticipated an era where such factionalism would begin to disappear. To see him as turncoat missed the point. Despite massive buildings and powerful styles, a part of his strategy remains rooted in the light-footed, lateral experimental thought and lack of repetitive rules from which FGP originally sprang.

When FGP was dissolved it was sometimes said that Grimshaw would be the one to watch. In fact, Grimshaw's career has been more predictable than would have seemed possible. It is Farrell who has provided the architectural writers with their 'interesting times' – often to the extent that we hardly knew what to write at all. Farrell's career has been extraordinarily

inclusive, and it is extremely helpful to see it in context. The elements of the 1960s and 1970s as we think of them now – low energy, loose fit, clip on, tune in, drop out – were meant to add up to an architecture which could embrace everything. In fact – and symbolically in Farrell's case – it did embrace everything: high-tech, postmodernism, cute vernacular, spec development, conservation, symbolism, urban planning, expressionism. It embraced far more than most architectural critics liked dealing with all at once, and which we saw as changes of direction rather than as continuing experimentation on many fronts.

Farrell has never fitted the critical framework. 'You have to stick your neck out and hope it works,' he once told the *Ham and High* newspaper. Inevitably, people don't always like the results. There is a wonderful interview with Farrell in the 1970s in a special feature on systems building. Farrell carefully explains why systems, though often useful in themselves, are not always the answer,

1997–2002
Above: Airport transportation hub, Inchon, Korea. A vast, huge-span, steel-and-glass organic structure that forms a focus and identity for the entire airport, but with the planning complexity of an urban centre.

1998–2002
Left: The Deep, Hull. Farrell's interest in habitats is realized in the design of an aquarium – in this case, set within an overall urban renewal masterplan. It was to be followed by two more: one in Seattle and one, a lottery-funded, urban-regeneration project, in London.

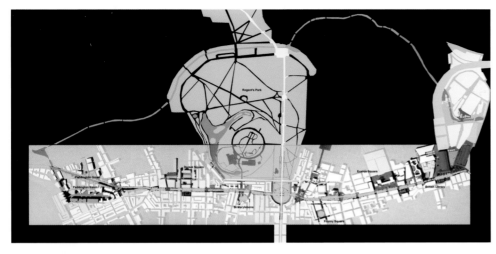

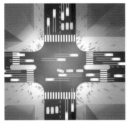

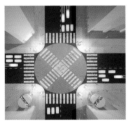

2002

Above: Euston Road, London. An urban-design initiative that rethinks the relationship between cars and pedestrians (compare pedestrian crossing studies with student drawing, p. 194 top).

2003

In London (right) and Newcastle (far right) For 30 years Farrell has promoted major new pedestrian routes that enhance the identity and form of underlying city structures.

and why it is absolutely wrong to call him a systems architect. He points out that, of course, the media tends to simplify things – eventually to a single headline or catchphrase. At a far more recent lecture at the Soane Museum, he quoted Hugo Young's critique of media coverage: 'The truth is too complicated.'

This book looks at the early work, but it does so through the framework of what Farrell has done since, and thereby offers a reappraisal of the later work, uncovering a consistency in its experimental, broad-ranging approach. It assumes the reader's knowledge of his later work – not just the postmodernist era but, significantly, the later projects such as The Deep, which has still not yet been fully assimilated by the critics. It offers a backdrop against which the later work – outside the scope of this book – can be reconsidered.

Farrell remains broader than the narrow definitions to which we still try to adhere. What is probably most underrated and underdiscussed about his later work is the serious, broad-ranging, urban-planning and infra-structural approach which he pioneers – much of which, of course, remains outside the media's narrow, building- and style-focused spyglass. For me, proposals such as unlocking the gates on the axis of Greenwich Park in south London or studying the pedestrian use of Euston Road should be far more important projects than the buildings.

In a letter about my first draft of this introduction, Farrell worried that I was accusing him of 'dabbling', which was certainly not the intention – the opposite, in fact. He went on to say:

'And so my first contribution has been in pioneering and advocating change. Far from dabbling, I've been intensely interested in change – from reappraising the monarchy and how it is expressed in palaces and parks to conservation, building reuse, popular taste and inclusive taste, i.e. their taste, not architects' alone, energy and, above all, the return to urbanism and placemaking. I haven't dabbled, wandering merely curiously, I've really influenced the situation and state of architecture. By work, lectures, writing and being active beyond the profession on English Heritage, Royal Parks, establishing UDAL and now working with the GLA. The face of London was changed by radical and alternative plans which really influenced what then happened from Smithfields to Hammersmith, South Bank, Paternoster, Hungerford Bridge, London Bridge station, the South Bank walkway, Royal Parks and Palaces, Paddington (all the area around), and so on. Kester, I was not wandering and dabbling; I've made a real difference by influencing. And then postmodernism – well, the change in modern architecture would never have happened without the flushing out effect of postmodernism which I always saw as a mood, a rethinking and not a style (as only narrow observers could ever see it – looking from their

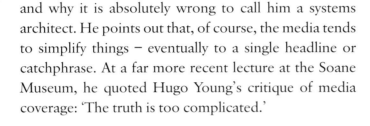

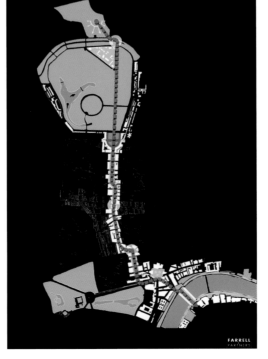

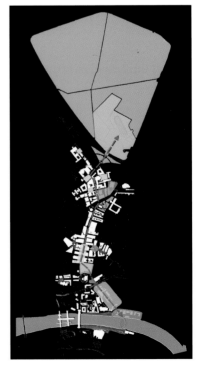

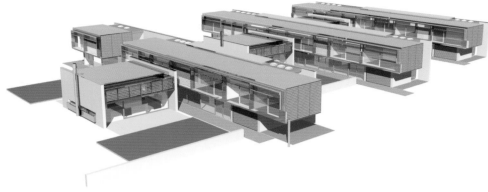

pigeon-holing self-appointed roles). Art, individuality, engagement with tastes outside the 'club', colour, pattern, visual indulgence, all did not exist in UK architecture before 1980. Stirling Wilford, myself and a minor contribution from a few helped change all that for good – from the awful mechanical mass-production welfare nanny-state, where supply-driven government, architects, critics thought of architecture as not engaged with so many broad issues.

'I have always tended to move on to find new areas to influence and change – but what my last steps were, were integrated and taken on with me. I firmly believe my career has been cumulative. I would like you to come and see the pictures of The Deep, Inchon, and see how the project in Manchester encompasses all the influences you could see as disjointed, patchy resting places. They do connect together and I believe that is the "revolution" or innovation in my work.'

Farrell still divides critics (sometimes the same critic), who find, say, the two Clifton Nurseries with their billboard tree and their innovative construction and funny symbolism increasingly compelling and clever – but still can't take, say, Alban Gate. Or the critics who find the lectures wonderful, the strategies and breadth of thought impressive – and the buildings wildly divergent in terms not just of strategy but also of status. Farrell's strong, catholic, stylistic inclusiveness; his ever-evolving, deeply founded tastes may always dominate the critics' frame of reference – and prevent us from noticing what he's doing elsewhere.

From this end of the telescope, the early work is indeed the key to a better, broader interpretation of Farrell,

into which and against which the buildings can be seen and tested more clearly. There is, for instance, still a more overt comparison with the metabolists to be made, in their parallel moves from early radicalism to mass commercial success, and their fusion of small-scale urban grain with megastructures.

Farrell's flexibility and broad range, his interest in change, his lack of systematization, his eclecticism, his

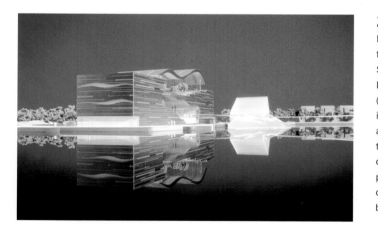

lateral thinking are clearly continued from the Farrell/Grimshaw days. And these are the framework within which all the work – not just the buildings or the stylism – will have to be seen and assessed. That will probably happen at a later date, when the large-scale historical shifts can be seen in the buildings as well as in the fractional adjustments of how people use and regard them. To say that he is still changing is not to accuse him of dabbling or dilettantism; it is simply to say that he is far from being stuck in a groove; that – like it or not – he is (as he often has been) probably still ahead of the game.

2000–2003

Above: Courtyard Housing, Petersham, Surrey. 'Space positive' figure–ground reversal of the basic house type is the key to this plan form, which continues to interest Farrell, from the Northampton Housing (p.192) to the Colonnades rooftop patio houses (p.222).

2002–2008

Left: National Aquarium for the Royal Zoological Society, London. Europe's largest aquarium (continuing Farrell's interest in habitats and aquariums; see student thesis p.180-81), part of an urban-regeneration project in Newham, one of London's poorest boroughs.

Page references in *italics* refer to illustrations

PICTURE CREDITS

All images courtesy of Terry Farrell and Partners unless specified below.
Abbreviations:
b = bottom, c = centre, l = left, r = right, t = top

8 tl, cl, bl: © DCT Syndication / D.C. Thomson & Co. Ltd, tr, cr, br: Trafford Local Studies Centre; 13 photos Manchester Archives and Local Studies, Central Library, Manchester; 14 photos: Manchester Archives and Local Studies, Central Library, Manchester; 15 t & br: Manchester Archives and Local Studies, Central Library, Manchester; 16 tr: Simmons Aerofilms Ltd, cr: Manchester Archives and Local Studies, Central Library, Manchester; 18 br: www.graeme-peacock.com; 22 t & c: RIBA Library Drawings Collection, b: © Disney Enterprises, Inc.; 23 tr: www.graeme-peacock.com; br: © The Estate of A.Wainwright. Reproduced by permission of Frances Lincoln Ltd.; 25 tr: Simmons Aerofilms Ltd, bl: Architectural Press; bc: The Illustrated London News; 26 t: Newcastle Upon Tyne City Libraries and Arts Local Studies Section, c: Laing Art Gallery (Tyne and Wear Museums), b: Oriel Press; 29 t & bl: by kind permission of the McPartlan family; 30 t: Philipson & Son Ltd, c & b: Percy Parr; 31 c & r: Newcastle Upon Tyne Libraries and Arts, Local Studies Section; 33 photos: Robert Haley; 36 t: Colin Cuthbert, cr: University of Newcastle Upon Tyne; 37 t & c: The Caravan Club; 44 t & bl: The Hancock Museum, tr: Chrysalis Books Group / B.T. Batsford, br: Studio Editions; 45 from left to right: Bolton Borough Council, The Samlesbury Hall Trust, The Lytham Heritage Group, Holker Hall and Lakeland Motor Museum, The Parker Family; 48 l: Simmons Aerofilms Ltd, t & br: www.graeme-peacock.com; 49 b: © 2004 Lucia Eames dba Eames Office (www.eamesoffice.com); 52 t & c: Leisure Parcs Ltd; 53 bl: Simmons Aerofilms Ltd; 55 t: Ryder HKS, c: Science Museum/Science & Society Picture Library, b: Durham Mining Museum (© John Ryan Collection) ; 56 t & cl: Newcastle Upon Tyne Libraries and Arts Local Studies Section, bl: Percy Parr; 57 c & b: Newcastle Upon Tyne Libraries and Arts Local Studies Section; 58 c: www.graeme-peacock.com, b: Permission of Robert Colls and Bill Lancaster; 59 t: BBC Photo Library, c: © TfL (source: London's Transport Museum), b: Ken Garland; 60 top two: Simmons Aerofilms Ltd, b: 'The Sphere'; 61 t: © Peter Cook, c: Jim Byrne / QA Photos, b: Simmons Aerofilms Ltd; 62 t: Marion Jones; 63 photos: Simmons Aerofilms Ltd; 64 photos: Simmons Aerofilms Ltd; 65 photos: Simmons Aerofilms Ltd; 67 photos: © Andrew Putler; 70 t: Maxtone-Graham Collection, c: Bridgeman Art Library, bc: Kenzo Tange, br: University of Tokyo, School of Engineering; 74 Philadelphia City Planning Commission; 76 tr: Jo Farrell; 78 tl : The Architectural Archives of the University of Pennsylvania; 82 tr: HMSO / Crown Copyright; 83 tl: HMSO / Crown Copyright, b: Architectural Record; 89 tr: Lee Copeland, br: Cameron & Co; 94 t & c: Courtesy The Frank Lloyd Wright Archives, Scottsdale, AZ, b: Maki and Associates; 97 br: Airphoto International; 102 Department of Environmental Development, Manchester City Council; 105 t & bl: Simmons Aerofilms Ltd; 107 t & b: Courtesy of Colin Buchanan and Partners, c: HMSO / Crown Copyright; 110 second from t: Simmons Aerofilms Ltd, second from b: Stephen Conlin, b: Di Hope and Kathy Kerr; 112 t: © Peter Cook Archigram 1964, second from t: RIBA Library photograph collection, b: Reyner Banham; 113 b: Cedric Price / Canadian Architectural Association; 114 b: Architectural Association Photo Library (© Paul Dawson); 115 t & b: RIBA Library Photograph Collection; 116 bl: The Flight Collection; 119 bl: Hulton Archive; 124 photos: Tim Street-Porter; 125 t: Grahame Shane, b row: Historical Publications Ltd; 130 t: Richard Bryant, c: Jo Reid & John Peck, b: Tim Street-Porter; 133 t: U.S. Department of Housing and Urban Development, b: Vintage Books; 137 photos: Jo Reid & John Peck; 138 tl: Hulton Archive, c row, c & r: Tim Soar, bl: © TfL (source: London's Transport Museum); 140 t row: ©Andrew Putler; 141 tl: ©Andrew Putler, tr: Phillipa Collie-Cousins; 144 l: David Read, r: James Mortimer; 14 tl: Ian Layzelle, br: Jo Reid & John Peck; 148 Simmons Aerofilms Ltd; 149 photos: John Reid & Jo Peck; 152 ©Andrew Putler; 154 tr: The MIT Press; 156 cr: Richard Bryant, bl: © 2004 Lucia Eames dba Eames Office (www.eames office.com), bc: Richard Bryant, br: Richard Cheatle; 157 bl: Sir John Soane's Museum (photo: Martin Charles), bc & r: Tim Soar; 158 b: RIBA Library Photograph Collection; 159 cl, bl & r: Simmons Aerofilms Ltd; 186 t: © Andrew Putler; 187 tl: © Andrew Putler, tr: Simmons Aerofilms Ltd, b: © Peter Cook; 190 tl: PA News Photo Library, tr: © Peter Cook, b: Jim Byrne / QA Photos Ltd; 191 © Marcus Fairs; 193 © Andrew Putler; 207 photos: Geoffrey Smyth; 210 Tessa Traegar; 212 tr: Tim Street-Porter, br: Tessa Traegar; 213 t: James Mortimer, c & b: David Read; 214 photos: James Mortimer; 215 b: James Mortimer; 216 t: Tim Street-Porter; 217 photos: Richard Bryant; 218 photos: Jo Reid & John Peck; 219 photos: Jo Reid & John Peck; 220–221 photos: Jo Reid & John Peck; 223–224 photos: Jo Reid & John Peck; 226–227 photos: Graham Challifour; 228 photos: ©Andrew Putler; 232 photos: Satish Patel; 233 t & bl: Richard Bryant, br: Satish Patel; 236–237 photos: Jo Reid & John Peck; 240 Jo Reid & John Peck; 241 photos: Graham Challifour; 243–245 photos: Richard Bryant; 247 photos: Richard Bryant; 248 second from t: Simmons Aerofilms Ltd; 249 t & b: Jo Reid & John Peck; 250 t & bl: Jo Reid & John Peck, br: Graham Challifour; 251 t & br: P. Shanahan, bl: Satish Patel; 253–254 photos: Richard Bryant; 255 t, bl & c: Richard Bryant, br: Graham Challifour; 256 b: Jo Reid & John Peck; 259–262 photos: Jo Reid & John Peck; 263 photos: ©Andrew Putler; 269 by kind permission of the McPartlan Family; 278 photos: Richard Bryant; 279 r: Nigel Young; 280 l: Nigel Young, r: Keith Hunter; 281 tl: Colin Wade, bl: Tim Soar; 282 t: Kim Jaen Youn, b: Richard Bryant; 284 tl: Richard Bryant / Arcaid.co.uk